CONGRESS

CONGRESS

Peter Woll

Brandeis University

LITTLE, BROWN AND COMPANY
BOSTON · TORONTO

Library of Congress Cataloging in Publication Data

Woll, Peter, 1933–
  Congress.

  Includes index.
  1. United States. Congress.   I. Title.
  JK1061.W86   1985   328.73   84-28936
  ISBN 0–316–95156–0

LIBRARY OF CONGRESS CATALOG CARD NO. 84–28936

ISBN 0-316-95156-0

9 8 7 6 5 4 3 2 1

MV

PUBLISHED SIMULTANEOUSLY IN CANADA
BY LITTLE, BROWN & COMPANY (CANADA) LIMITED

PRINTED IN THE UNITED STATES OF AMERICA

ACKNOWLEDGMENTS

Text excerpts from "The Education of David Stockman" by William Greider in *The Atlantic Monthly*, December 1981. Reprinted by permission of the author.

Text excerpts from *O Congress* by Donald Riegle. Copyright © 1972 by Donald W. Riegle, Jr. Reprinted by permission of Doubleday & Company, Inc.

(continued on page 453)

For my brother,
John

Preface

Designed to give students not only the nuts and bolts of Congress but also the flavor of Capitol Hill politics and congressional campaigning, this introductory text covers the wide spectrum of topics that are normally taught in courses on Congress. At the same time, the book can profitably be used in the many courses that touch upon various facets of the role of Congress in the political system.

After presenting a brief overview of Congress, the book proceeds to an analysis of the role of Congress in the broader constitutional system. Discussion centers on the constitutional provisions that have formally shaped many of the characteristics of Congress, including bicameralism, size, apportionment, qualifications of members and voters, terms of office, and internal organization and procedures. The Founding Fathers speak for themselves in Chapter 1 as they debate Congress and determine its representative role and position in the system of separation of powers and checks and balances.

An account of the evolving Congress in Chapter 2 completes the background information that is important to an understanding of contemporary legislative politics. As the text turns to an examination of the internal world of Capitol Hill, Chapter 3 focuses on the all-important topic of committees. These feudal baronies, so described by Woodrow Wilson as long ago as the late nineteenth century, presided over by their lords and masters, continue to dominate Congress even in the face of repeated efforts at "reform" and reorganization designed to constrict their numbers and limit, however slightly, their independence.

Committees are powerful, but other internal influences are also important. The common view of congressional parties is that they are notoriously weak; however, they are often surprisingly strong. Chapter

4 examines the ebb and flow of party discipline, and the ways in which party leaders work in their continual attempts to bring members into line.

Congress is also viewed as an institution that is primarily responsive to demands from the outside, particularly those of constituents. Examined in Part III is the nature of the electoral connection, beginning in Chapter 5 with the setting of congressional elections, and proceeding in Chapter 6 to the lively topic of campaigning for Congress.

In Part IV the role of Congress is analyzed as the keystone of the Washington political establishment. The rhetoric of Washington politics, accepting the constitutional separation of powers, implies constant conflict between the legislature and executive. The reality described in Chapter 7, however, is that Congress has woven close ties to the bureaucracy, creating political "iron triangles" that link committees, agencies, and clientele groups in collusive power networks.

Congressional support of the bureaucracy often frustrates White House efforts to control the executive branch. Chapter 8 points out that the president understandably views Congress with suspicion, if not alarm. The imperial presidency has not completely faded, but has been tightly reined by contemporary Congresses' jealously guarding their legislative prerogatives.

While Congress, the bureaucracy, and the president jockey for power in a political arena that often frustrates the goals of each branch, Washington lobbyists ply their trade on Capitol Hill at the same time as they try to influence the downtown executive establishment and the White House. Chapter 9 points out that lobbyists are no strangers to the Washington political scene in which incestuous power relationships often exist. Former members of Congress and staffers frequently catch "Potomac fever" and stay in Washington to peddle their influence.

Chapter 10, the final chapter, ties the text together by relating congressional politics to public policy. Applying the theoretical framework of Theodore Lowi and others, discussion focuses on the ways in which contrasting arenas of public policy shape how Congress deals with them.

I would like to thank William Ethridge, who guided the book in its early stage; Don Palm, who saw it to completion; and John Covell, who made penetrating last-minute suggestions. All provided invaluable assistance that improved the book at many points. Thanks are also owed to all those who helped with the book's production. Writing the book would not have been possible without Capitol Hill experience, which for me has been greatly enhanced by the help of Rochelle Jones. Bill Goodwin's aid and insights are also greatly appreciated. Finally, special thanks yet again go to Barbara Nagy, my transcribing and typing infrastructure over the years, whose dedication and skill made the book a joy to write.

Contents

CONGRESS

Introduction: An Overview of Congress

Atop land once known as Jenkins Heights, eighty-eight feet above the Potomac River and, appropriately, the highest point in the seat of government, is the majestic home of the United States Congress. From the west front the expansive view down the mall to the Potomac takes in the seemingly endless gray granite buildings of the executive branch, although the White House, at the far end of Pennsylvania Avenue, is tucked behind the Treasury Building and out of sight. Pierre Charles L'Enfant's grand plan for the city provided, along with broad avenues and expansive spaces, for a triangular design that would link the homes of the three branches of government. With Pennsylvania Avenue as the base, connecting the Capitol with the White House, the Supreme Court would be placed midway between the two to the north. The plan was left partially completed because of insufficient funds, which forced the Supreme Court into a tiny chamber in the basement of the Capitol. It later moved into the old Senate chamber until 1935, when it finally occupied a new Supreme Court building directly east of the Capitol.

The chambers and rooms of the Capitol and adjacent office buildings have witnessed the political drama of American government. There Kentuckian Henry Clay presided over the House wearing a brace of pistols, Daniel Webster's oratory echoed throughout the Senate chamber, Thaddeus Stevens and the radical Republicans impeached Andrew Johnson but failed by one vote to convict him in the Senate for high crimes and misdemeanors. Patrician Henry Cabot Lodge, Sr., defeated Woodrow Wilson's League of Nations, and New Jersey Congressman Peter Rodino led a House Judiciary Committee to impeach President Nixon for attempting to cover up the Watergate break-in.

Politics is a combative contact sport that is played particularly well in the legislative arena. Sometimes — rarely, it is fortunate — the combatants become violent. Mississippi Senator Henry Foote drew a pistol, luckily deflected, on Missouri Senator Thomas Benton as he was charging Foote, who had made a particularly vitriolic and personal attack on him during a debate over slavery. Massachusetts Senator Charles Sumner was not so lucky when, during another slavery debate, he made derogatory remarks about the uncle of South Carolina Representative Preston Brooks, who was observing the proceedings from the gallery. Brooks rushed into the Senate chamber and beat Sumner unconscious with his heavy cane, preventing him from resuming his Senate duties for three years. On yet another occasion violence involved the press, when in 1890 a *Louisville Times* reporter shot a former representative in an argument over stories the *Times* had printed involving the congressman in scandal. Fortunately, with the exception of these incidents, Capitol Hill politics does not lead to physical violence, although tempers are often raised to the boiling point.

STUDYING CONGRESS

Congress can be viewed on many levels and studied from varied perspectives. The average citizen relates to Congress through his or her representative or senator, but usually knows little about the institution itself beyond its job, which is making laws that affect the interests of everyone. The public, encouraged by press accounts of scandal, waste, and inefficiency on Capitol Hill, holds Congress as an *institution* in low esteem. But, as political scientist Richard Fenno points out, people respect and admire *their* congressperson, who often finds it electorally profitable to run against the institution.[1]

Although legislators, the media, and more than a few political scientists portray a less than favorable image of Congress, the reality is quite different. The framers of the Constitution designed Congress to be a representative body in which the sovereignty of the people would reside. It was to be politically responsive and deliberative, not efficient. Some of its powers were to be shared with the president

[1] Richard F. Fenno, Jr., "If, As Ralph Nader Says, Congress Is 'The Broken Branch,' How Come We Love Our Congressmen So Much?" In Peter Woll, ed., *American Government: Readings and Cases*, 8th ed. (Boston: Little, Brown, 1984), pp. 477–485.

under a system of checks and balances that would guarantee limited government.

The Constitution links Congress and the president, but at the same time gives each branch independent powers and political constituencies. Neither branch depends on the other for its existence, but congressional legislation requires a presidential signature before becoming law, and the president cannot enact his programs without congressional approval.

In the political arena they constructed and under the rules they devised, the founding fathers intended for Congress and the president to struggle for ascendancy. And so they have. The balance of power between the two branches was relatively equal in the early days of the Republic, with a slight tilt toward the executive. The balance continued roughly equal until Congress became ascendant at the end of the Civil War and held that position until the administration of Theodore Roosevelt.[2] The twentieth century witnessed the rise of the imperial presidency, which increasingly overshadowed Congress in both foreign and domestic affairs. Congress acquiesced in its own demise by delegating broad authority to the executive branch to make policy. Congress attempted to correct the imbalance of power on several occasions by increasing its staff to balance executive expertise, and by attempting to strengthen leadership powers and reduce committee fragmentation. The "resurgent" Congress of the 1970s and 1980s, reacting to the imperial presidencies of Lyndon B. Johnson and particularly Richard M. Nixon, which had unilaterally spawned Vietnam, Watergate, and, during the Nixon years, open defiance of Congress in many domestic policy spheres, increasingly challenged the president. Efforts were undertaken to streamline congressional procedures, boost staff, expand use of the legislative veto over executive actions, and withdraw presidential authority unilaterally to make war and to impound funds appropriated by Congress.

From a constitutional perspective, Congress acts as an institutional check upon the president. It exercises the primary law-making authority of government. It represents popular interests in the House, and the states' interests in the Senate.

Congress, as a collective body, has an important institutional role to play in our system of constitutional democracy, but as an institu-

---

[2] James L. Sundquist, *The Decline and Resurgence of Congress* (Washington, D.C.: Brookings Institution, 1981), traces presidential-congressional power cycles.

tion it is perhaps less than the sum of its parts. Generalizations about Congress as a whole can be misleading, because Congress, particularly in the twentieth century, has rarely acted for more than short periods as a unified body. Congress is the most individualistic legislature in the world, reflecting in its organization and procedures the pluralism of the broader political system.

Politics more than constitutional prescriptions shape Congress. Particularly vital are members' incentives, which political scientist Richard Fenno identifies as reelection, power and influence on Capitol Hill, and "good public policy." [3] Congressional scholar David Mayhew argues that Congress has organized itself for the purpose of securing the reelection of its members.[4] Members must be free to tailor their reelection campaigns to fit the distinctive requirements of their districts and states. They want to be able to claim credit for benefits flowing to their districts from the federal government, and to be free to take positions that will appeal to their electorates. They want to advertise themselves as much as possible to make their names familiar throughout their districts.

Committee fragmentation and diversity, as well as weak congressional parties, serve the members' electoral goals. Chairmen of committees and subcommittees dealing with such areas as Defense, Energy and Natural Resources, the Merchant Marine, Public Works, and Agriculture use their posts to channel benefits to their districts. Weak political parties enhance the power of committees and their chairmen, who understandably oppose moves to strengthen party discipline.

Also served by the fragmentation of Congress is the members' goal of achieving internal power. Committees are independent fiefdoms, their chairmen the barons of Capitol Hill. The more committees there are to chair, the more power is dispersed. Committee chairmen have a vested interest in maintaining the status quo, and over the years have successfully thwarted efforts by congressional "reformers" to reduce the number of committees to make the congressional decision-making process less chaotic.

An overview of Congress must take into account both the external and the internal politics of Capitol Hill. The Constitution makes the

[3] Richard F. Fenno, Jr., *Congressmen in Committees* (Boston: Little, Brown, 1972).
[4] David R. Mayhew, *Congress: The Electoral Connection* (New Haven: Yale University Press, 1924).

president a partner in the legislative process, and the demands of the White House are always important in shaping what goes on in Congress. Presidential measures are often at the top of the legislative agenda, put there by congressional party leaders who recognize the constitutional role of the president in initiating legislation. Although presidential proposals do not always fare well on Capitol Hill, those on which the White House takes a strong stand have a better than average chance of passage.

Congress must also deal with a bureaucracy of its own creation. The many departments and agencies of government are political powers in their own right. Congress has given the president the formal power to control their budgets and their legislative recommendations to Capitol Hill, both of which must be channeled through the Office of Management and Budget, which is part of the Executive Office of the President. Committee chairmen, however, and, often more important, their staffs, have informal channels of communication to the agencies, which in turn can make their wishes known to key legislators. The expert advice and political support of the bureaucracy is often essential to the development and passage of legislation.

Completing the external political environment of Congress are constituent and pressure groups. That members of Congress do what their constituents want is common knowledge, but a vast oversimplification of a highly complex relationship. Each congressional district contains approximately 500,000 people, and the statewide constituencies of senators are much larger and more diverse. What constituents want is usually not clear. Many are not aware of issues before Congress, many do not know the name of their member of Congress, and the politically knowledgeable and active who remain usually do not agree on what action, if any, should be taken by their representative. Members of Congress pay strict attention to their constituencies, but their efforts more often than not are directed at developing an effective and highly personal home style to ingratiate themselves with voters.[5] Effective home styles are often devoid of issue content as members concentrate upon projecting personal images. Constituencies with dominant or important economic interests expect their representatives to vote accordingly, but beyond that they are free to pursue their Washington careers as they choose.

[5] Richard F. Fenno, Jr., *Home Style* (Boston: Little, Brown, 1978).

Interest groups have always focused upon Congress to gain passage of favorable legislation. Labor, corporate, farm, professional, religious, and ideological groups all seek to influence Capitol Hill. More than 3,000 political action committees have been organized to raise money for candidates and causes. Although their direct contributions are limited, they can spend an unlimited amount indirectly to influence political campaigns. Although Common Cause, itself a pressure group, charges that PAC money exerts far too much influence on Congress, interest groups are a healthy and vital part of the political process. They express the legitimate demands of important sectors of society. They help Congress govern with a political sensitivity that it otherwise would not have. Political pluralism checks their power, for groups often balance each other by taking opposing sides. In some policy spheres, however, particularly those involving government subsidies to narrow interests, group power can be dominant as it forges "iron triangles" of power among congressional subcommittees, agencies, and special interests.

Congress is not simply a body that reflects outside pressures. Its complex inner world of committees, parties, special caucuses, state delegations, and staff shape congressional politics as significantly as do external forces. Committee chairmen and their aides fight to protect their turfs, the jurisdictions of their committees over certain spheres of legislation. Turf battles can stall or even prevent the legislative process from working. Aggressive committee chairmen and staffs are political entrepreneurs who constantly search for new legislative ideas to work with and develop, in part to advance their reputations for power and influence within Congress. Legislation may reflect member and staff goals for internal influence as much as it does external pressures.

Once committees have reported legislation and it has been brought to the floor through regular parliamentary procedures, Congress as a whole must act. In deciding how they will vote, members take their cue from their fellow congressmen, especially those on the committees that develop the legislation and in their state delegations, and also respond to pressures from party leaders, the views of their staffs, and external demands from the White House, interest groups, and constituents. On balance, internal rather than external influences dictate voting behavior.

The contrasting politics of different policy spheres often determines the way in which Congress works. The relative importance of committees, parties, staffs, the president, the bureaucracy, interest groups, and constituents all affect the congressional decision-making process. Broad, macropolitical issues, such as tax policy, activate wide-ranging political forces, requiring the tax-writing committees to forge broad political compromises. By contrast, subsidy policies generally involve relatively narrow interests that combine with congressional committees to make decisions. Committees have more independence and power in the micropolitical world of subsidy or distributive politics than they do in areas such as taxation, which involves many interests. Distinctive features also characterize the congressional process in foreign and defense policy making. The president, for example, is more deeply involved in these than in other policy spheres. The Foreign Affairs and Policy committees have traditionally seen their role as being the president's congressional advocates, although the reassertive Congress of the 1970s and 1980s required the committees also to take into account increasing congressional demands for control of foreign policy. In the defense sphere, the Department of Defense has been dominant, reflecting in procurement policy a military-industrial complex that, closely tied to congressional committees, usually has its way on Capitol Hill. Once again, the resurgent Congress of the post-Vietnam era has made defense policy a matter of more general debate than in the past.

JUDGING CONGRESS

Congress is a mirror image of our political system. Its organization, procedure, politics, and decisions reflect the pluralistic political forces on Capitol Hill. It can be no more nor less responsible than these forces dictate.

Applying constitutional and political norms, Congress, far from being the corrupt and inefficient institution it is often pictured to be, has fulfilled its responsibilities very well.

From a *constitutional* perspective, Congress is supposed to check the president, represent popular and group interests, and be the primary law-making body for the nation. Historically, Congress has performed these roles. Even the most powerful presidents, after a honeymoon with Congress, have found their influence diminished by the separation-of-powers and checks-and-balances system that pits the legislature against the executive in political battle. Congress has delegated substantial authority to the executive to govern, a shift that began in the administration of Franklin D. Roosevelt in 1933. The ability of Congress to check executive initiative was not diminished, however. Formally legislative standards guided executive action, procedural requirements were written into laws delegating authority, often provisions were made for a legislative veto by one or both branches of Congress or a designated committee, and the continuing authorization and appropriations process was used to impose congressional intent. Committee and subcommittee chairmen on Capitol Hill have also never hesitated informally to communicate their wishes to bureaucrats whose agencies are under their jurisdiction, a procedure that has been used under the most "imperial" presidencies.

These methods of congressional control over the executive are, however, piecemeal. From 1933 to 1972 Congress as a whole abdicated much of its responsibility for making foreign and domestic policy.[6] James Sundquist writes,

> The posture of the Congress during this long period of presidential aggrandizement was . . . much more than one of simple acquiescence to the presidential initiative, as represented in such innovations as Roosevelt's Legislative Clearance Process or Nixon's Domestic Council. Perhaps even more significant in reflecting the congressional attitude was the long series of affirmative steps the legislature took, on its own initiative, to assign to the president specific tasks for the planning and initiating of legislative policy — tasks that in earlier times the Congress might have considered to be more appropriately handled within the legislative branch itself.[7]

It was with the assent of Congress that the president became "Chief Legislator." Beneath the surface congressional committees and administrative agencies worked out the details of policy implementation, but the president set the legislative agenda on major issues.[8]

That the president is unified and Congress is not is both a constitutional and a political reality. Congress has been able to check the president most effectively when it has been unified by party discipline, as in the post-Civil War period and particularly at the end of the nineteenth century and the beginning of the twentieth. Changing

---

[6] James L. Sundquist, *Decline and Resurgence of Congress*, pp. 143–154.
[7] Sundquist, *Decline and Resurgence of Congress*, p. 143.
[8] A valuable study of agenda setting is John W. Kingdon, *Agendas, Alternatives, and Public Policies* (Boston: Little, Brown, 1984).

political forces within and outside of Congress, however, brought about decentralization of power on Capitol Hill and ascendancy of committees after 1910. Congress has remained a fragmented body ever since, although sporadic attempts have been made to unify it to make it a more effective challenger to the president. The resurgent Congress of the 1970s and 1980s, however, continues its piecemeal exercise of its constitutional responsibilities in checking the president. Efforts have been made to reduce the number of committees and integrate decision-making procedures, but the number of subcommittees continues to expand. New budget committees, established under the Budget and Impoundment Control Act of 1974, oversee a budgeting process that before was completely under the control of the authorization and appropriations committees. The power of the budget committee depends mainly on the ability of Congress to marshal majorities in favor of reining in the power that individual committees customarily have had to determine government expenditures and revenues.

Congress not only has the constitutional responsibility of checking the president, but also of representing the interests of the people in local and state constituencies. The independent electoral constituencies of the House and the Senate were an important part of the checks-and-balances system itself, providing Congress with its own base of political support separate from the president's. At the same time as the electoral system buttresses the independence of Congress as a whole, electoral pluralism supports the autonomy of congressmen. Members serve and represent their constituencies as they choose, knowing that on election day they will be judged as individuals, not for their party loyalty or support of the president. A decentralized Congress will continue to best serve the diverse electoral needs of the members.

The constitutional structure and the pluralistic political context of Congress help to explain why as an *institution* it so often fails to display the leadership that congressional critics seem fervently to desire. The electoral system, writes political scientist Gary Jacobson, produces a Congress of "great individual *responsiveness*, equally great collective *irresponsibility*." [9] He concludes, "As long as members are not held individually responsible for Congress's performance as an

[9] Gary C. Jacobson, *The Politics of Congressional Elections* (Boston: Little, Brown, 1983), p. 189.

10 Introduction

institution, a crucial form of representation is missing. Responsiveness is insufficient without responsibility. Political parties are the only instruments we have managed to develop for imposing collective responsibility on legislators." [10] Disciplined political parties are, however, antithetical to both our constitutional system of separation of powers and checks and balances, and the pluralism that characterizes our political process. We will examine in the following chapters the ways in which the Constitution and politics shape Congress and its role in the political system.

[10] Jacobson, *Politics of Congressional Elections*, p. 190.

PART
I

The Setting of Congress

CHAPTER ONE

Role of Congress in the Constitutional System

Congress is the first branch of government, the keystone of the Washington political establishment. The 535 members of Congress and their aides, numbering more than 14,000, play the game of politics with skill and finesse as they seek to dominate national politics. The Constitution has pitted Congress against the president with the separation-of-powers and checks-and-balances system that provides different constituencies and allocates contrasting powers to the legislative and executive branches. Members of Congress soon learn, if they do not already know, that the sovereignty of the people resides in their hands, for they are the representatives of the people and the lawgivers for the nation. Although the president has important legislative responsibilities and can check Congress by using the veto, the primary legislative authority remains in congressional hands.

Congress has changed dramatically from the institution envisioned by the founding fathers. Much of congressional organization, procedures, norms, rituals, and incentives have been dictated by history and politics more than by the Constitution. The constitutional framework still stands, however, to provide the setting within which Congress functions. That framework has been filled in on numerous occasions by Supreme Court decisions interpreting the powers and responsibilities of Congress.

CONGRESS IN THE CONSTITUTION

Congress has many distinguishing constitutional features, most of which are the result of political compromises won only after hard-fought battles among delegates to the Constitutional Convention. No principles engraved in stone were there to guide the delegates, who drew their conclusions not from abstract political theories but from experience in governing the colonies and the states. In a broader sense, the Anglo-American political tradition was used as an important reference point in constructing the new government.

Origins of Congress

As the colonies moved toward independence and federation, they met in the First and Second Continental Congresses to take joint action against Great Britain. The Declaration of Independence was an act of the Second Continental Congress. The states were equally represented in the Continental Congresses as they were in the Congress created by the Articles of Confederation, adopted in 1777. Congress was the sole organ of the national government before the Constitution was ratified.

The Congress of the Constitution was profoundly different from its predecessor both in structure and in powers. As the Constitutional Convention opened, the Randolph or Virginia plan proposed a bicameral legislature, the first branch to be elected by the people and the members of the second branch to be elected by the first. Edmund Randolph also proposed a national executive and a national judiciary.

Although the Continental Congresses and the Congress under the Articles of Confederation were unicameral, the Anglo-American political tradition was one of bicameral legislatures. Bicameralism allowed representation of different interests in the separate branches of the legislature, and bicameralism arose because of the political necessity of providing different representation. The greatest legislature of all, the British Parliament, was of course a bicameral body consisting of the House of Commons and the House of Lords. The purpose of British bicameralism was to provide for separate representation of two of the three estates of the Realm — the Barons or Lords and the "Commons," who were the freemen of England. British bicameralism has been traced to the middle of the fourteenth century. At that time it was the king who summoned Parliament to advise him on important matters of state, and the House of Lords and the House of Commons sat in separate buildings, the Lords in the Parliament chamber of the king's palace, and the Commons in a chamber at Westminster Abbey.

Bicameralism in the early governments of the American colonies and states was not designed to secure representation of different estates of the realm, but to create checks and balances within the legislative body that would prevent it from taking hasty and ill-conceived action impelled by the will of a passionate majority. By the time the early state governments were being formed, the principle of bicameralism was firmly established. Of the thirteen original state constitutions, only those of Georgia, Pennsylvania, and Vermont provided for a unicameral legislature. Generally the bicameral legislatures consisted of two branches separately elected by the people.

Congressional characteristics other than bicameralism had important precedents in the first state constitutions, many of which were in turn based upon practices in the governments of the colonies. Without exception, the legislatures were considered to be the most important parts of the state governments, and although the separation of powers among executive, legislative, and judicial branches was adopted by all the new state governments, their major powers resided in the legislative bodies. The power of the state legislatures was so great that Thomas Jefferson warned of potential legislative despotism. In his *Notes on Virginia* he observed that under the new Virginia constitution all the powers of government, legislative, executive, and judiciary, "result to the legislative body. The concentrating of these in the same hands is precisely the definition of despotic government. It will be no alleviation that these powers will be exercised by a plurality of hands, not by a single one. One hundred and seventy-three despots would surely be as oppressive as one ... an elective despotism was not the government we fought for...." [1] Echoing Jefferson's views, James Madison later was to warn in *The Federalist* of the inherent superiority of the legislative body over the executive and judicial branches.[2]

As the delegates met in Philadelphia in the hot summer of 1787, most had little doubt that the new Congress would be at once both bicameral and powerful. Bicameralism, however, was not unanimously espoused as the Convention opened, nor was there agreement on the extent of the powers of the new Congress.

Bicameralism came into being after the Great Compromise, worked

---

[1] Thomas Jefferson, "Notes on Virginia," in Adrienne Koch and William Peden, eds., *Selected Writings of Thomas Jefferson* (New York: Random House [Modern Library], 1944), p. 237.

[2] See *Federalist* 48.

out by the delegates after months of negotiation, which took the middle ground between the Randolph (Virginia) and Paterson (New Jersey) plans representing the interests of the large and small states, respectively. Edmund Randolph proposed a bicameral legislature, but William Paterson of New Jersey argued for retaining the unicameral Congress of the Articles of Confederation, in which large and small states would be equally represented. It was not the bicameralism of the Randolph plan that Paterson and the delegates from the small states objected to, but Randolph's proposal that the number of delegates allotted to each state in the first branch would depend on the number of free inhabitants of the states. Paterson told the Convention that there was "no more reason that a great individual state contributing much, should have more votes than a small one contributing little, than that a rich individual citizen should have more votes than an indigent one." [3] New Jersey, said Paterson, will never confederate under the Virginia plan because she "would be swallowed up," and he would "rather submit to a monarch, to a despot, than to such a fate." [4]

The intractable position of the small states backing representation by state units rather than by population threatened to stalemate the Convention. Bicameralism, however, provided a way for the large and small states to reach agreement. The Great Compromise gave to the small states representation equal to that of the large states in the Senate. The House became the representative of the people, each state being given one vote in the House for every 30,000 inhabitants. For the purposes of representation the population of the slave states was augmented by counting three-fifths of their slaves as part of their inhabitants. The result was that five free voters in a slave state were equal to seven free voters in a nonslave state.

The Three-Fifths Compromise was by any measure a remarkable one. Why did the free states agree to it? Essentially it was agreed upon in return for the constitutional provision that direct taxes would be apportioned among the several states by the same formula as that for representation in the House. Direct taxes were seen as the principal revenue-raising method that would be used by the government; therefore, because the states were required to pay their direct taxes in proportion to their inhabitants, counting three-fifths of the slaves

[3] Max Farrand, ed., *The Records of the Federal Constitutional Convention of 1787*, 4 vols. (New Haven: Yale University Press, 1911, 1937), vol. I, 178. Hereafter cited as Farrand, *Records*.
[4] Farrand, *Records*, vol. I, p. 179.

as part of the populations of the slave states, the free states would receive less burdensome taxation in return for their reduced representation in the House. Rufus King, a delegate from Massachusetts to the Convention, remarked in a speech to the Senate in 1819 that the "inequality in the apportionment of representatives was not misunderstood at the adoption of the Constitution; but as no one anticipated the fact that the whole of the revenue of the United States would be derived from indirect taxes . . . , but it was believed that a part of the contribution to the common treasury would be apportioned among the states by the rule for the apportionment of representatives — the states in which slavery is prohibited ultimately, though with reluctance, acquiesced in the proportionate number of representatives. . . . The concession was, at the time, believed to be a great one, and has proved to have been the greatest which was made to secure the adoption of the Constitution. . . . The departure from this principle [of equality of rights] in the disproportionate power and influence allotted to the slave states, was a necessary sacrifice to the establishment of the Constitution." [5]

The Great Compromise was adopted on July 16, 1787, by a vote of five states to four, with the majority being formed by Connecticut, Delaware, New Jersey, Virginia, and North Carolina.[6] At the time the Great Compromise was voted the Convention was on the verge of dissolution. The character of the bicameral Congress, giving the smaller states a voice equal to that of the larger states in the Senate, saved the day and guaranteed the support of the smaller states for the new national Constitution. It is significant that the Great Compromise affected the structure of Congress, and indirectly its powers, and not the role of the executive or the judiciary. The primary importance of the legislature was recognized by all the delegates, who agreed that the major powers of the new national government would reside in the Congress.

Characteristics of Congress

The Great Compromise settled the major characteristics of the bicameral Congress and produced the needed fundamental agreement

---

[5] Cited in Charles Warren, *The Making of the Constitution* (Cambridge: Harvard University Press, 1947), p. 292. (First published in 1928.)
[6] Georgia, Maryland, South Carolina, and Pennsylvania voted no. Massachusetts was divided, and New York was absent.

among delegates from the large and small states, especially Virginia
and New Jersey, on the form the government was to take.[7] In addition to equality of state representation in the Senate, Convention
compromises determined the suffrage in the House and the Senate,
the size of Congress, terms of office, qualifications of voters and members, members' eligibility and pay, and internal congressional organization and procedures.

ELECTION OF THE HOUSE. The nationalists at the Convention were
in agreement from the start that the "first branch of government," or
the House, should be elected directly by the people. The Randolph
plan provided: "That the members of the first branch of the national
legislature ought to be elected by the people of the several states."
The Randolph resolution was debated on May 31, and supported by
distinguished delegates from various states. George Mason of Virginia

[7] The absence of the New York delegates when the final vote on the Great Compromise was taken is an interesting story. Alexander Hamilton, Robert Yates, and
John Lansing at various times had represented the state in the Convention proceedings until July. Hamilton left the Convention early because of his persistent
disagreement with the other two New York delegates, only to return after they
finally left on July 10. On July 2, an initial Convention vote was taken on the
Great Compromise, New York being represented by Yates, who voted in the
affirmative. The vote was 5–5, however, and so the plan was not adopted, but a
committee was appointed to break the deadlock. The Great Compromise would
have been defeated had the full Georgia delegation been in attendance. One
of the Georgia delegates opposed to equality of representation in the Senate
had gone to New York, and even the remaining Georgia delegates divided on
the issue. Moreover, another opponent to equality of representation from
Maryland arrived late, and the Maryland vote was cast by its delegate in
attendance in favor of the Great Compromise. The tardiness of the Maryland
delegate presented a split in the state's vote, which then would have been
neutral.
    On July 10, 1787, less than a week before the Great Compromise was
adopted, the two New York delegates in attendance — Robert Yates and John
Lansing — left the Convention, never to return. Hamilton, who had been absent when the Great Compromise was adopted, then returned to represent
New York. Had the three New York delegates been present when the vote on
the Great Compromise was finally taken, the position of New York could not
have been unequivocally predicted. Yates would have voted in favor, possibly persuading Lansing to adopt his point of view. On June 11, Hamilton had voted
against equality of representation for the states in the Senate. At various times
throughout the Convention, both before and after the Great Compromise was
adopted, Hamilton expressed his opposition to equality of representation in
the Senate. Hamilton was a great nationalist, however, and in the end he
might have voted in favor of the Compromise in order to prevent dissolution
of the Convention.

stressed his belief that the House "was to be the grand depository of the democratic principle of the government. It was, so to speak, to be our House of Commons — it ought to know and sympathize with every part of the community; and ought therefore to be taken not only from the different parts of the whole Republic, but also from different districts from the larger members of it, which had in several instances, particularly in Virginia, different interests and views arising from differences of produce, of habit, etc." [8] Mason admitted that in many respects the state governments had been too democratic, but feared that the convention would "incautiously run into the opposite extreme. We ought to attend to the rights of every class of the people." [9]

Support for the popular election of the House was also voiced by Pennsylvania delegate James Wilson, who argued that popular suffrage for the House would provide an important base of support for the new national government. "No government could long subsist without the confidence of the people." [10] The state legislatures, said Wilson, should not be the electors of Congress, because all "interference between the general and local governments should be obviated as much as possible. On examination it would be found that the opposition of states to federal measures had proceeded much more from the officers of the states, than from the people at large." [11]

James Madison considered the popular election of one branch of the national legislature to be essential "to every plan of free government." [12] He feared that the new national government might become too far removed from the people. He pointed out that "if the first branch of the general legislature should be elected by the state legislatures, the second branch elected by the first — the executive by the second together with the first; and other appointments again made for subordinate purposes by the executive, the people would be lost sight of altogether; and the necessary sympathy between them and their rulers and officers too little felt." [13] Madison, like the other nationalists supporting popular suffrage for the House, recognized that at the same time it was important to filter the voice of the peo-

[8] Farrand, *Records*, vol. I, pp. 48–49.
[9] Farrand, *Records*, vol. I, p. 49.
[10] Farrand, *Records*, vol. I, p. 49.
[11] Farrand, *Records*, vol. I, p. 49.
[12] Farrand, *Records*, vol. I, p. 49.
[13] Farrand, *Records*, vol. I, p. 50.

ple in government by providing for indirect election of the Senate and the president.

The nationalists clearly did not support the popular election of the House because they were uncompromising democrats, but because of their belief that popular suffrage would expand the base of political support for the national government. At the same time, direct election by the people of the House would help to reduce competition between the national government and the states, and prevent state legislatures from completely dominating the new federal government.

The proponents of states' rights at the Convention recognized the political significance of popular suffrage as a device for buttressing national power over the states, and for that reason they opposed direct popular election of the House. Their arguments against popular election, however, were couched as the dangers of democracy, not the perils of national power. Elbridge Gerry of Massachusetts told the delegates, "The evils we experience flow from the excess of democracy. The people do not want virtue; but are the dupes of pretended patriots. In Massachusetts it has been fully confirmed by experience that they are daily misled into the most baneful measures and opinions by the false reports circulated by designing men, and which no one on the spot can refute." [14] Election by the people, concluded Gerry, was a dangerous practice. Moreover, he found that "the state legislatures drawn immediately from the people did not always possess their confidence." [15]

Roger Sherman of Connecticut was even blunter than Gerry in opposing popular suffrage. "The people," he said, "should have as little to do as may be about the government. They want information and are constantly liable to be misled." [16]

When the question was called on the resolution providing for direct popular election of the House, it passed with six states in favor, two against, and two divided.[17]

ELECTION OF THE SENATE. As the Convention moved to consider the election of the Senate, agreement was general that the "second

---

[14] Farrand, *Records*, vol. I, p. 48.
[15] Farrand, *Records*, vol. I, p. 50.
[16] Farrand, *Records*, vol. I, p. 48.
[17] In favor: Massachusetts, New York, Pennsylvania, Virginia, North Carolina, and Georgia. Against: New Jersey, South Carolina. Divided: Connecticut, Delaware.

branch" should be indirectly chosen. The advocates of states' rights moved immediately to make the Senate a federal institution by having its members chosen directly by the state legislatures. The Randolph plan would not have gone that far, proposing that the Senate be chosen by the House from persons nominated by the state legislatures. Although powerful nationalists and Convention leaders such as James Madison, Rufus King, and James Wilson proposed popular election for the Senate, their views represented a distinct minority of the delegates. Madison recognized that popular election of the Senate would strengthen the national government, a major reason he and others proposed popular suffrage for the Senate. Moreover, responding to advocates of election of the Senate by the House, James Wilson pointed out that under such a system the Senate would not be as independent of the first branch as it would be if it were popularly elected. All the delegates recognized that a principal role for the Senate was to check ill-considered House action responsive to the whims of popular majorities. A Senate dependent upon the House for its election would not have as great an incentive to check the first branch as it would with an independent base of political support.

The Convention deadlocked on May 31 over election of the Senate, but on June 7 the matter again surfaced and the proponents of states' rights renewed their struggle to make the Senate a bastion of state power through the electoral process. Equal representation of the states in the Senate, the most important federal aspect of the body, was not yet before the Convention. Nor did the delegates originally consider the Senate to be important because it would represent the states, but because it would be a smaller and more deliberative body that would act as a check upon the House. The Randolph plan, for example, presented as the Convention opened, did not allude in any way to the desirability of establishing a Senate controlled by the states, but provided for selection of the upper body by the House.

When Thomas Jefferson returned from France he called upon George Washington, who explained the role of the Senate to him during a breakfast conversation. "Why," asked Washington, "did you pour that coffee into your saucer?" "To cool it," said Jefferson. "Even so," replied Washington, "we pour legislation into the senatorial saucer to cool it." [18]

[18] Farrand, *Records*, vol. III, p. 359.

Washington's view of the role of the Senate was accepted by Randolph, who called for a second branch to be much smaller than the House of Representatives, "so small as to be exempt from the passionate proceedings to which numerous assemblies are liable." Randolph told the delegates that the general object of the Senate was "to provide a cure for the evils under which the United States labored," and "in tracing these evils to their origin every man had found it in the turbulence and follies of democracy [and] some check therefore was to be sought for against this tendency of our governments and . . . a good Senate seemed most likely to answer the purpose." [19]

As the delegates debated the method of election to the Senate there was general agreement that the "second branch" should be a smaller body with longer terms of office that would enable it to act as a check upon the first branch or House of Representatives. But there was not a consensus upon the method of election of the Senate. Many of the strong nationalists, such as Madison and Wilson, clearly saw that selection of members of the Senate by state legislatures would help the states to short-circuit the exercise of national power. Madison wanted the election of the Senate to be directly by the people for the same reason that he advocated direct popular suffrage for the House. It would expand the base of political support for the national government and help it to act independently of the states. Commenting upon the proposal for selection of the Senate by state legislatures, James Wilson stressed that he wanted to keep the states "from devouring the national government." [20]

The Convention finally settled, almost by default, upon selection of the Senate by state legislatures. Virginia delegate George Mason reflected the views of most advocates of state election of the first branch when he declared that "whatever power may be necessary for the national government, a certain portion must necessarily be left in the states. It is impossible for one power to pervade the extreme parts of the United States so as to carry equal justice to them. The state legislatures also ought to have some means of defending themselves against encroachments of the national government. In every other department [of the government] we have studiously endeavored

---

[19] The preceding quotations from Randolph are in Farrand, *Records*, vol. I, p. 51.
[20] Farrand, *Records*, vol. I, p. 153.

to provide for its self-defense. Shall we leave the states alone un-provided with a means for this purpose? And what better means can we provide than the giving them some share in or rather to make them a constituent part of, the national establishment." [21]

On June 7, 1787, the motion to have the Senate chosen by the state legislatures was adopted on a state vote of 10–0.

SIZE OF CONGRESS. Although the Convention arrived at consensus that the House of Representatives would be larger than the Senate, some agreement had to be reached on the size of the House. The size of the Senate was settled when it was decided that each state would have two senators.

The Three-Fifths Compromise, which determined the basis for representation in the House, reflected the divergent intcrests of the northern and southern states. It was the potential clash between the North and the South that forced the delegates to fix the formula for representation in the Constitution, which would prevent a majority of Congress on either the northern or southern side to change the criteria for representation to benefit its own cause.

Having determined how the inhabitants of the states were to be counted for representation, the delegates faced the question of how to take into account future changes in the populations of the current states, and in the new states that everyone recognized would inevita-bly become part of an expanding Union. Edmund Randolph pro-posed the plan that was finally adopted by the Convention, requiring Congress to provide for an enumeration to be made every ten years of the inhabitants of the states, and to apportion representation ac-cordingly. The constitutional provision for the decennial census pre-vented interests entrenched in Congress from failing to act to pre-vent the malapportionment of the House. The census and subsequent reapportionment requirements removed an important potential source of friction among the states from the political arena.

The actual size of the House is up to Congress itself, with the constitutional stipulation that there shall not be more than one representative for every 30,000 state inhabitants. Rough estimates of the populations of the states at the time the Constitution was framed led the delegates to stipulate that sixty-five representatives would be

[21] Farrand, *Records*, vol. I, pp. 155–156.

allotted to the states. The representation from each state was set forth in Article 1.

As the nation has grown and state populations have shifted, numerous changes have been made in the size and apportionment of the House. Although the provisions of the Constitution establishing the formula for representation and the reapportionment requirement were fairly specific, they left many questions unanswered. Under the constitutional formula the first House had sixty-five members, but clearly as the population of the nation grew it could not so remain.

SIZE AND APPORTIONMENT. Not only did the framers leave the question of size of the House unanswered, but they did not address themselves to apportionment of representatives within the states. The states themselves could not be malapportioned under the Constitution, but there was no constitutional requirement for the equal apportionment of electoral districts within states should the states decide to choose their representatives from local districts rather than at large.

The first Congress attempted to amend the constitutional-apportionment formula to provide one representative for every 30,000 inhabitants of a state until the House membership reached one hundred, "after which the proportion shall be so regulated by Congress that there shall be not less than one hundred representatives, nor less than one representative for every 40,000 persons, until the number of representatives shall amount to two hundred, after which the proportion shall not be less than 200 representatives nor more than one representative for every 50,000 persons." [22] The failure of this amendment to pass left it up to Congress to determine its size and method of apportionment in the future. Congress struggled with the question and devised various methods allocating representatives to the states by rounded numbers of inhabitants, 30,000 under the first Apportionment Act of 1792, vetoed by President Washington on the grounds that eight of the fifteen states then members of the Union would receive more than their fair share of representation in the House. [23]

[22] *Guide to U.S. Elections* (Washington, D.C.: Congressional Quarterly, 1975), p. 525.
[23] Under the law, members were distributed to the states on the basis of one representative for 30,000 inhabitants, but an additional member was given to each state whose population, after being divided by 30,000, exceeded 15,000.

Congress failed to override Washington's veto, and made a second attempt to settle the apportionment controversy by passing a new law apportioning representatives for every 33,000 inhabitants of a state, the remainder being discarded after a state's population was divided under the formula. The size of the House was set at 105.

The new method of apportionment discarding remainders was devised by Thomas Jefferson and was in effect until 1840.

Although Jefferson's method of apportionment resulted in inequalities among the states, the emphasis at the time was upon the importance of keeping electoral districts relatively equal. A similar implication in the Constitution itself required equal apportionment among the states and implied that at that time the ideal congressional district would contain 30,000 inhabitants.

Although the debates of the Constitutional Convention implied a "one person-one vote" rule for selection of representatives, the question of equality of populations in congressional districts was soon lost sight of as Congress and the states struggled over the broader issue of House size and mathematical formulas for determining the number of representatives from each state. In 1842 Congress did enact legislation requiring representatives to be "elected by districts composed of contiguous territory equal in number to the representatives to which said states may be entitled, no one district electing more than one representative." [24] But the 1842 law did not establish a one person-one vote rule.

The question of House size and apportionment among the states plagued many Congresses throughout the nineteenth century. State political leaders often complained of congressional unfairness in apportionment formulas. It was not until 1911 that Congress fixed its membership at 435. And it was not until 1964 that the growing controversy over unequal apportionment of congressional districts within the states was settled, not by Congress but by the Supreme Court.[25]

QUALIFICATIONS OF VOTERS. When the Constitution was being drafted the qualifications of voters for state legislatures varied widely from one state to another. The delegates recognized that any attempt to create a uniform national standard of suffrage for the House would

[24] *Guide to U.S. Elections*, p. 526.
[25] See Chapter 3 for further discussion of congressional apportionment.

be viewed with suspicion and indignation by the states. The Committee of Detail, which the Convention had appointed to draft the Constitution on the basis of agreements that had been reached among the delegates, proposed that the electors for the House of Representatives "shall be the same, from time to time, as those of the electors in the several states, of the most numerous branch of their own legislatures."

Because all the states except Pennsylvania, Georgia, and New Hampshire required ownership of property to vote, the proposal of the Committee of Detail would continue the states' relatively severe restrictions upon the franchise. For the most part, women could not vote, and only one out of five adult white males owned sufficient property to qualify for the vote.

The restrictions the states had placed upon suffrage, however, were considered inadequate by some of the delegates. Gouverneur Morris of Pennsylvania, the most frequent speaker on the floor of the Convention, proposed going beyond the restrictions on suffrage of some of the states by limiting the suffrage to freeholders. "Give the votes to people who have no property," said Morris, "and they will sell them to the rich who will be able to buy them. We should not confine our attention to the present moment. The time is not distant when this country will abound with mechanics and manufacturers who will receive their bread from their employers. Will such men be the secure and faithful guardians of liberty? Will they be the impregnable barrier against aristocracy?" [26] Morris was careful to distinguish freemen from freeholders, who owned property and who therefore in his view were qualified to vote. Connecticut delegate Oliver Ellsworth replied to Morris that if Congress were given the authority to "alter the qualifications [for voters], they may disqualify three-fourths or any greater proportion from being electors. This would go far in favor of aristocracy. We are safe as it is, because the states have staked their liberties on the qualifications as they now stand." [27]

Though Morris, and other nationalists such as James Madison, argued strongly for limiting suffrage to freeholders — a freehold being a stake in land and not intangible property — the Convention adopted the recommendation of its Committee of Detail without

[26] Farrand, *Records*, vol. I, p. 202.
[27] Farrand, *Records*, vol. I, p. 207.

dissent. The voting qualifications in the states stood as the suffrage requirements for the House of Representatives.

QUALIFICATIONS OF MEMBERS. Age, citizenship, and residency requirements for members of Congress were passed by the Convention after extensive debate. The delegates cared about the quality of their future legislators, and sought to establish at least minimal requirements that would be necessary to achieve the degree of quality they wanted in the House and the Senate. The minimum age for senators was set at thirty, and representatives had to be at least twenty-five years of age. The final constitutional provisions required seven years of citizenship to be elected to the House and nine years of citizenship for senators. Finally, both representatives and senators were required to be inhabitants of the states they represented when elected.

The delegates seriously considered imposing property qualifications for members of the Congress. Such qualifications applied in all the states but New York. The Committee of Detail was instructed to report a property qualification that could be either a landholding (freeholder) or another form of tangible property. South Carolina delegate Charles Pinckney went so far as to propose property qualifications not only for Congress, but also for the president and federal judges. Pinckney stressed that he was "opposed to the establishment of undue aristocratic influence in the Constitution but he thought it essential that the members of the legislature, the executive, and the judges should be possessed of competent property to make them independent and respectable. It was prudent when such great powers were to be trusted to connect the tie of property with that of reputation in securing a faithful administration." [28]

Pinckney's motion was resoundingly rejected. Some delegates wanted to leave the matter of qualifications for members of Congress in the hands of the state legislatures. Others proposed leaving the matter up to Congress. The debate over property qualifications was stalemated, reflecting a division of the delegates on the issue.

Article I, Section 5 of the Constitution seemed to leave the matter of general qualifications for members of Congress up to each branch: "Each House shall be the judge of the election, returns, and qualifications of its own members." Although this provision would appear to give Congress the authority to impose property or any other quali-

[28] Farrand, *Records*, vol. I, p. 248.

fications upon membership, careful reading of the Convention debates clearly indicates that it was not the intent of the framers to grant discretion to the legislature to expand the qualifications for membership beyond those already stated in the Constitution. The Convention rejected, for example, proposals that would have allowed Congress to impose property qualifications for membership. James Madison expressed the views of a majority of the delegates when, responding to a proposal to allow Congress to fix its qualifications, he said it would vest "an improper and dangerous power in the legislature. The qualifications of electors and elected were fundamental articles in a republican government and ought to be fixed by the Constitution. If the legislature could regulate those of either, it can by degrees subvert the Constitution." [29] The intent of the final provision in the Constitution regarding qualifications of members allows Congress only to judge whether or not elected representatives or senators meet the constitutional standards of citizenship, age, and residency.

TERMS OF OFFICE. There was no disagreement at the Convention that the House would serve for a shorter term than the Senate. The "First Branch" had to be kept close to the people, and frequent popular elections were seen as the way to achieve the necessary dependence upon the people. The popular assemblies in the colonies had annual elections and sessions that the colonists strongly supported to check the colonial governors. "Our people are accustomed to annual elections," said Roger Sherman of Connecticut. He argued that if the members of the House had a longer term, "and remain at the seat of government, they may forget their constituents, and perhaps imbibe the interest of the state in which they reside, or there may be danger of catching the esprit de corps." [30]

Other delegates proposed a two- or three-year term for the House, and the Convention, accepting Alexander Hamilton's view that there "is a medium in everything," [31] finally decided upon the two-year term.

The Convention decision on the term of office for senators was, like that for the House, based upon practices in the states. Among

[29] Farrand, *Records*, vol. I, pp. 249–250.
[30] Farrand, *Records*, vol. I, p. 365.
[31] Farrand, *Records*, vol. I, p. 366.

the states, it was customary for the terms of senators to be longer than those for members of the popular branches. In addition to longer terms of office, in New York, Virginia, and Delaware a system of rotation prevailed in their senates. The delegates decided with a minimum of debate upon the six-year term for the Senate, one third to be elected biennially.

The longer term of office for the Senate was particularly important to Madison, Hamilton, and other nationalists who saw in the upper body an important bastion against the popular majorities they thought would dominate the House. The Senate's deliberative function would best be served by the longer term that would enable senators to approach their legislative subjects with some detachment from popular demands. Moreover, the extended term would give continuity and expertise to the second branch that would be an important complement to a House that the framers thought would be highly political and even unstable, subject to the whims of the electorate. James Madison comments that in order to judge the form to be given to the Senate, it will be proper to take a view of the ends to be served by it. "These [are] first to protect the people against their rulers; secondly, to protect the people against the transient impressions into which they themselves might be led." [32]

During the debate on the terms of office for the Senate, Alexander Hamilton added his voice to that of Madison, telling the delegates that he concurred with Madison "in thinking we [are] now to decide forever the fate of republican government; and that if we [do] not give to that form due stability and wisdom, it [will] be disgraced and lost among ourselves, disgraced and lost to mankind forever." [33] Echoing Madison's view that the differences in the distribution of property were a major cause of political instability against which the propertied classes should protect themselves, he pointed out that the character of the House rendered it the guardian "of the poorer order of citizens," [34] against which the Senate should act as a check.

In the end, both Madison and Hamilton, and most of the delegates who agreed with them on the role of the Senate, were satisfied that the six-year term of office would help the "second branch" to perform its proper role in the constitutional system of checks and balances.

[32] Farrand, *Records*, vol. I, p. 421.
[33] Farrand, *Records*, vol. I, p. 424.
[34] Farrand, *Records*, vol. I, p. 424.

COMPENSATION OF MEMBERS. The issue of how members of Congress were to be compensated was, as were most of the issues of the Convention, debated as the appropriate balance between national and state power. Simply stated, the issue was whether the pay of members should be determined by the states or by the national government. The nationalists were understandably unhappy with the plan of the Articles of Confederation, under which members of the national Congress were paid by their states, giving state governments potentially important leverage over their congressional representatives. Randolph's original plan provided for "liberal stipends" for members of Congress, but did not stipulate who was to pay them. Randolph, however, strongly opposed giving the states control over compensation of members. "If the state legislatures pay the members," stated Randolph, "they will control the members, and compel them to pursue state measures." [35] Madison agreed with his fellow Virginian, declaring, "Our national government must operate for the good of the whole, and the people must have a general interest in its support; but if you make its legislators subject to and at the mercy of the state governments, you ruin the fabric." [36]

Alexander Hamilton perhaps best expressed the consensus of the nationalists on the issue of who should pay members of Congress. "It has been often asserted," said Hamilton, "that the interests of the general and of the state legislatures are precisely the same. This cannot be true. The views of the governed are often materially different from those who govern. The science of policy is the knowledge of human nature. A state government will ever be the rival power of the general government. It is therefore highly improper that the state legislatures should be the paymasters of the members of the national government. All political bodies love power, and it will often be improperly attained." [37] Because Hamilton believed that "he who pays is the master," [38] he strongly opposed state control over the compensation of members of Congress.

The views of Hamilton, Madison, and Randolph eventually prevailed on the issue of who was to pay the national legislators, but only after extensive debate and strong opposition from many delegates who proposed that compensation of the national legislature be

35 Farrand, *Records*, vol. I, p. 377.
36 Farrand, *Records*, vol. I, p. 378.
37 Farrand, *Records*, vol. I, pp. 378–379.
38 Farrand, *Records*, vol. I, p. 378.

in the hands of the states. A motion to have the states pay representatives was defeated four states to five, and a corresponding motion that would have given the states control over compensation of senators was defeated five states to six. The state delegations to the convention finally voted 9–2 to pay members of Congress out of the national treasury.

Finally, although Madison declared that "it is indecent that the legislature should put their hands in the public purse to convey it into their own," [39] the Convention finally decided to give Congress the authority to determine the pay of its members.

ELIGIBILITY OF MEMBERS FOR OFFICE. The Constitution prohibits members of Congress during their terms of office from accepting or holding any other civil office under the authority of the United States. Although the Articles of Confederation had barred members of Congress from holding additional offices for which they received benefits, money, or emoluments of any kind, it was the practice of the Confederation Congress to appoint its members to diplomatic and other nonpaying posts. Moreover, the members of many of the state legislatures held other offices within their states.

The delegates saw a distinct danger in allowing members of Congress to occupy additional offices in the federal government. It was even proposed, unsuccessfully, that legislators be prevented from holding federal offices for a time after they had served in Congress. The delegates readily agreed, however, that legislators should not hold other civil offices at the same time as they were members of Congress. The majority of state delegations accepted Madison's position that if legislators were not excluded from holding other offices "there may be danger of creating offices or augmenting the stipends of those already created, in order to gratify some members [of Congress]." [40]

Although the proposal to exclude legislators from holding other civil offices was the major eligibility issue before the Convention, Edmund Randolph had proposed in his original plan that members of Congress be ineligible for reelection. Randolph's recommendation was based upon the practice of rotation in office established in many state constitutions, which limited the amount of time legislators could serve. The Articles of Confederation had limited state delegates

---

[39] Farrand, *Records*, vol. I, p. 378.
[40] Farrand, *Records*, vol. I, p. 380.

to three years in any six-year period. Randolph's recommendation for rotation in office was never taken up by the Convention, which accepted without debate or dissent a motion to eliminate the proposal from the Randolph plan.

INTERNAL ORGANIZATION AND PROCEDURES. The few constitutional provisions on regulation of Congress were based mostly on state and English precedent and were agreed to without important debate.

First, the provision that "Each House shall be the judge of the elections, returns, and qualifications of its own members..." was the same as that found in the constitutions of eight states. The clause did not give Congress the authority to determine on its own the qualifications of members, but only to judge whether or not members met the age, citizenship, and residency requirements of the Constitution.

Second, the Constitution unanimously adopted the provision that "Each House may determine the rules of its proceedings, punish its members for disorderly behavior, and, with the concurrence of two-thirds, expel a member." The two-thirds requirement was adopted overwhelmingly after Madison observed that "the right of expulsion (Article VI, Section 6) was too important to be exercised by the bare majority of a quorum; and in emerging of faction might be dangerously abused." [41] The Convention was apparently not swayed by Gouverneur Morris's remarks that the expulsion power "may be safely trusted to a majority. To require more may produce abuses on the side of the minority. A few men from factious motives may keep in a member who ought to be expelled." [42]

Third, Congress must keep an official record of its proceedings: "Each House shall keep a journal, and from time to time publish the same...." Excepted from this requirement are such parts of the proceedings of Congress "as may in their judgment require secrecy." Madison had at first proposed that only the Senate be allowed to keep its proceedings secret when in its judgment it was acting in a nonlegislative capacity. For example, the Senate had important responsibilities in foreign affairs that were not directly legislative. James Wilson expressed the objections of many delegates to allowing the Senate or the House to conceal their proceedings, stating that the

41 Farrand, *Records*, vol. II, p. 254.
42 Farrand, *Records*, vol. I, p. 54.

"people have a right to know what their agents are doing or have done, and it should not be in the option of the legislature to conceal their proceedings." [43] George Mason agreed, declaring that the provision for secrecy "would give a just alarm to the people, to make a conclave of their legislature." [44]

The *Journal* proceedings were required to include the yea and nay votes of the legislature.[45] There was no unanimous consent, however, that the yea and nay votes should be part of the record. Connecticut delegate Roger Sherman wanted to exclude the yeas and nays from the record, arguing that "they never have done any good, and have done much mischief. They are not proper as the reasons governing the voter never appear along with them." [46] Massachusetts delegate Nathaniel Gorham also opposed recording the yea and nay votes, commenting that the practice in Massachusetts resulted "in stuffing the journals with them [the votes] on frivolous occasions," and "misleading the people who never know the reasons determining the votes." [47] The scattered opposition to recording yea and nay votes had no effect upon the Convention, which adopted the provision without formal opposition by any of the state delegations.

The *Journal* required to be kept by the Constitution should not be confused with the *Congressional Record*. The *Journal* records congressional bills, resolutions, and votes. The *Record* goes far beyond the *Journal* in recording what is said, and a large amount of extraneous matter, including birthday congratulations for constituents, poems, newspaper articles, and other material members think would appeal to their constituents. In accordance with the Constitution the *Journal* has been kept from the first Congress. Not until 1855, however, did Congress employ reporters at public expense to keep a record of its debates, and only in 1865 were congressional proceedings and debates systematically published in a form analogous to the contemporary *Congressional Record*. From 1865 to 1873 the

[43] Farrand, *Records*, vol. I, p. 260.
[44] Farrand, *Records*, vol. I, p. 260.
[45] Article I, Sect. 5 of the Constitution provides: "Each House shall keep a journal of its proceedings, and from time to time publish the same, excepting such parts as may in their judgment require secrecy; and the yeas and nays of the members of either House on any question shall, at the desire of one-fifth of those present, be entered on the journal." Article I, Sect. 7 requires the recording of yea and nay votes on motions to override presidential vetoes.
[46] Farrand, *Records*, vol. II, p. 255.
[47] Farrand, *Records*, vol. II, p. 255.

record was called *The Congressional Globe*. The *Congressional Record* began publication at the end of 1873.

Fourth, the Constitution states that "Neither House, during the session of Congress, shall, without the consent of the other, adjourn for more than three days, nor to any other place than that in which the two Houses shall be sitting." [48] The adjournment provision was based on state constitutions, which generally were careful to give the power of adjournment to their legislatures to make them independent of the executive. Colonial legislatures had frequently been subject to dissolution by royal governors. In the unlikely event that the two branches of Congress could not agree upon a time of adjournment, the Constitution did provide that the president "may adjourn them to such time as he shall think proper." [49] The delegates did not, however, foresee any threat to legislative independence in giving the president the potential power of dissolution, because it really could not be exercised without congressional acquiescence. Knowing the possibility of executive intervention, it seemed highly unlikely that Congress would fail to agree upon a time of adjournment. At no time in history has the presidential power of dissolution been used.

James Madison commented to the Virginia ratifying convention that concern for the public interest required agreement between the two Houses for the adjournment of either one.[50] On the subject of possible presidential dissolution because of the failure of Congress to agree on a time of adjournment, Edmund Randolph observed that "if the President was honest, he will do what is right. If dishonest, the representatives of the people will have power of impeaching him." [51] Finally, and most important, the Constitution provides for the Speaker of House, to be elected by the body, and for the vice-president to be the president of the Senate and to have a vote if necessary to break a tie.

EXPLAINING CONGRESS

Two of the principal architects of the Constitution, James Madison and Alexander Hamilton, eloquently and elaborately explained the role of Congress under the new Constitution in *The Federalist*. Ad-

48 Article I, Sect. 5 (4).
49 Article II, Sect. 3.
50 Farrand, *Records*, vol. II, p. 312.
51 Farrand, *Records*, vol. II, p. 312.

dressed principally to the New York State ratifying convention and more broadly to the New York electorate, the series of articles that composed *The Federalist* appeared in New York City newspapers under the pseudonym Publius. Most were written by Hamilton, but Madison was called upon by the brilliant New Yorker to join in articulating the purposes of the Constitution. The distinguished New York lawyer John Jay, who was to become the first chief justice of the Supreme Court, joined Hamilton and Madison but was unable to write more than five of the eighty-five papers because of illness.

Although Hamilton and Madison at various times during the Convention argued for a different course of action than the one taken, in general their views in *The Federalist*, which supported the final result, corresponded remarkably well with the opinions they had expressed at the Convention. Both men clearly would have liked to see a Senate either elected by the House or directly by the people rather than controlled by the states, but they recognized, as did other nationalist delegates from the large states, that the federal character of the Senate was a necessary political compromise.

Checks and Balances

The Federalist, repeating the arguments of Madison and Hamilton at the Convention, stressed the bicameral legislature as an important mechanism for checking ill-considered popular action by the House of Representatives. The House "is so constituted as to support in the members an habitual recollection of their dependence on the people," [52] a dependence that was considered to be necessary but important to control by having a Senate with the power to check the popular assembly. James Madison stressed in *Federalist* 62 that a Senate is necessary because of "the propensity of all single and numerous assemblies to yield to the impulse of sudden and violent passions, and to be seduced by factious leaders into intemperate and pernicious resolutions."

Representation of Interests

Bicameralism was explained not only by the need to establish checks and balances within Congress, but also because separate legislative bodies were required to represent popular and group (state) interests.

[52] *Federalist* 57.

Moreover, the objects of legislation of the two bodies would differ, the Senate being called upon to deal with matters such as foreign affairs that required more deliberation and detachment from popular constituencies than would be possible in the popular branch, which, because of its attachment to the people and short term of office, would not be able to deal with the higher matters of state with reasoned detachment. The Senate would add continuity and expertise to the legislative process that could not be achieved by the House acting alone.

DELEGATE AND TRUSTEE. The discourse of *The Federalist* distinguished by implication between the representative roles of delegate and trustee. Representatives acting as delegates simply follow the will of the people, accede to their demands, and translate their views into legislation. But as trustees, legislators are acting in a fiduciary capacity, and base decisions on their best judgments of the national interest and the interests of their constituents. The trustee certainly takes into account constituent demands, but does not blindly follow them. The framers and the authors of *The Federalist* recognized the importance of balancing the delegate and trustee responsibilities in the national legislature. In some cases, stated Madison in *Federalist* 63, there is paradoxically the lack of "a due responsibility in the government to the people, arising from that frequency of elections which in other cases produces this responsibility." Madison explained the paradox by pointing out the two general classes of legislative jurisdiction, one pertaining to immediate local interests that were best served by the legislators acting as delegates of the people, and the other consisting of broad national problems the solution of which depended on a "succession of well-chosen and well-connected measures which have a gradual and perhaps unobserved operation." [53] In the latter category, legislators should act as trustees, which they can do only in a body such as the Senate, which is not directly elected by the people, and which serves a far longer term than do members of the House.

Explaining the importance of bicameralism to the people of New York and their ratifying convention was not as difficult for the authors of *The Federalist*, for there was little disagreement within the states on the importance of the principle. It is interesting that even though the small states were delighted with the federal character of the Senate, in which they received representation vastly out of proportion

[53] Federalist 63.

to their size, the larger states such as New York could not help but look with suspicion upon the result of the Great Compromise that had in the final analysis made the Constitution possible. Hamilton and Madison, representatives of the large states of New York and Virginia, respectively, and strong nationalists, were not at all happy with the equal representation of the states in the Senate. Throughout *The Federalist* their discussion of the Senate avoided praise for its federal character but rather stressed its importance as a deliberative body that would act as a check upon the House.

Powers of National Legislature

As Hamilton and Madison turned from the issue of bicameralism to explain other aspects of Congress they focused primarily upon the powers of the national legislature. They did not hesitate to stress in the strongest words that Congress would have the authority to act directly upon the people in broad areas of national policy enumerated and *implied* in Article I. Alexander Hamilton declared unequivocally in *Federalist* 33 that Congress would have all the necessary means required to execute its enumerated powers. But, asked Hamilton, "Who is to judge of the *necessity* and *propriety* of the laws to be passed for executing the powers of the Union?" The judge, responded Hamilton, must be the national government itself. Congress "must judge in the first instance, of the proper exercise of its power, and its constituents [must judge the propriety of congressional action] in the last. If the federal government should overpass the just balance of its authority and make tyrannical use of its powers, the people, whose creature it is, must appeal to the standard they have formed, and take such measures to redress the injury done to the Constitution as the exigency may suggest and prudence justify." Later, in *Federalist* 78, Hamilton was to declare it was the authority of the Supreme Court to exercise judicial review over congressional legislation and declare laws repugnant to the Constitution null and void.

IMPLIED POWERS. Madison, too, did not hesitate to suggest that Congress would have sweeping powers under the necessary and proper clause. But the legislature would be constrained by the system of checks and balances that had been created to ensure continuation of the separation of powers among the three branches of the government. Moreover, Madison pointed out as Hamilton had done that ultimately the people would have the power to check acts of usurpation by their representatives whom they directly control in the House and over whom they could exercise indirect influence through state legislatures in the Senate.

Reviewing *The Federalist* suggests that Congress was explained as the most important and powerful branch of the national government, the repository of the trust of the people and of the states. There was no attempt to diminish the important role of Congress that was foreseen by the framers of the Constitution. Hamilton did go beyond the Constitution in proclaiming the authority of the Supreme Court to overturn acts of Congress, but the point was not stressed. Far more important in controlling legislative action was to be the separation-of-powers and checks-and-balances system described by Madison in *Federalist* 47, 48, and 51.

Control over Congress

Both at the Convention and in *The Federalist*, Madison and Hamilton expressed the widely held views of the framers that Congress would be both powerful but subject to direct (House) or indirect (Senate) control. An important aspect of such control was the simple fact that the legislators themselves would be chosen from as well as by the people. They would be "citizen-legislators," leaving their private pursuits to come to the seat of government for relatively short periods to represent their constituents and advance the national interest. Neither the framers nor those who ratified the Constitution conceived of a Congress composed of relatively permanent members pursuing political power as a career. Politics was, of course, important in eighteenth-century America, but national politics was overshadowed by state politics. In the early years of Congress, more than a few members of the Senate, finding the six-year term to be overly burdensome, resigned to return to what they considered to be the more fruitful and interesting arena of state politics. There was no permanent seat of government until 1800, travel was difficult, and above all, the endless opportunities in what would now be called the private sector were a powerful magnet drawing persons away from political careers. Rotation in office had formally been established in many state constitutions. At the national level, members of Congress rotated without being required to do so simply because they considered their congressional responsibilities to be more of a duty than an opportunity to enhance their personal lives and careers.

CHAPTER TWO

Evolution of Congress

The modern Congress represents over 194 years of history. During that time the size and powers of Congress had increased enormously. Its internal organization and procedures had been drastically altered. Its relationships with the president and the Supreme Court had been shaped and reshaped by constantly shifting political forces. An entirely new branch of the government — the bureaucracy — had developed, altering the role of Congress in the political system. An expanding electorate, and the rise of mass media to keep it attuned to newsworthy events on Capitol Hill, had, many congressmen felt, made them far more dependent upon the people than the framers had envisioned. Capitol Hill itself had become the symbol of the seat of government, one that had become permanent in 1800 when the Capitol moved to Washington. Just as the seat of government became permanent, too, in the minds of the electorate, had government itself become an ever-present force dictating major aspects of their lives.

EVOLUTION OF THE HOUSE

The members of the House who take their oath of office in the 1980s sit in a Congress that was not foreseen by the framers of the Constitution. Not only Congress but its role in the broader political system had fundamentally shifted. Congress was no longer the most powerful branch of the government, but in many ways had become subordinate to the president, the bureaucracy, and the Supreme Court. At the same time, over the 194 years of congressional history Congress had gradually been recognized by the Supreme Court to have virtually unchecked potential authority under Article I and the necessary-and-proper clause. The last real battle over the extent of congressional au-

thority had been fought during the New Deal, when the Supreme
Court, under the conservative direction of Chief Justice Charles
Evans Hughes, had limited the scope of congressional authority, particularly under the commerce clause, and declared many major pieces
of New Deal legislation unconstitutional. By 1937, however, the New
Deal Court acquiesced in the broad exercise of congressional powers,
particularly in the economic sphere. The New Deal marked the end
of serious challenges to the formal constitutional authority of Congress under Article I. Congressional power thereafter depended upon
politics far more than on constitutional law, although the Court did
continue to hand down significant decisions defining both presidential and congressional power.

The internal as well as the external world of Congress had completely changed from its origins to the 1980s. The size of both the
House and the Senate had multiplied, and Capitol Hill had become
dominated by hundreds of specialized committees that were virtual
fiefdoms. The committees were the little legislatures of Congress,
and in the minds of many presidents, administrators, and lobbyists
who had to deal with Congress, the real power of the legislature resided in its committees.

Although the modern Congress differs sharply in many respects
from its predecessors in the nineteenth century, many aspects of
Congress in the 1980s find their origins directly in congressional history dating to the 1790s.

Organization and Procedure

The first House that convened in New York in April 1789 adopted
an organization and procedures that became the seeds of future
House practices. Under the Constitution a Speaker was chosen by
the body as a whole, and it was his responsibility to put questions
to the House, decide points of order, announce results of votes, and
himself vote when formal ballots were taken. Informal committees
were appointed by the Speaker to deal ad hoc with specialized legislative matters.

Generally during its early years the House operated as a committee of the whole, which in parliamentary language means that it resolved itself into a committee to discuss informally matters before it.
Because the formal membership of the House was set at sixty-five
(only fifty-nine representatives were elected to the first Congress),

it was feasible for the body to act as a committee of the whole, although the general lack of decorum and of control upon the time of individual speakers often made the procedure cumbersome and time-consuming.

The early informality of House proceedings soon led to adoption of more formal rules. The Speaker was given power to name the chairman of the committee of the whole, and the Congresses in the 1790s and early 1800s increasingly relied upon standing or permanent committees to deal with legislation. Standing, unlike ad hoc, committees, had permanency from one Congress to another. By 1809 ten standing committees had been created, including the committees on Interstate and Foreign Commerce (1795), Ways and Means (created as a select committee in 1795 and made permanent in 1802), and Public Lands (1805).

Emergence of Congressional Parties

In the early decades of the new republic, Congress was the focal point of politics, and as political parties were formed they coalesced around their membership in Congress. After 1800 the Federalist and Republican caucuses of the House and Senate nominated the presidential and vice-presidential candidates of their parties. The practice continued until an expanded electorate and the rise of the Jacksonian Democrats forced expansion of the congressional base of national party politics. In 1831 and 1832, respectively, the Republicans and Jacksonian Democrats held national conventions to choose their candidates. The broadening in the country's politics brought an entirely new dimension to party politics, causing a split between congressional and presidential parties that has continued to this day.

The Speaker

The rise of congressional parties immediately made the Speaker's office partisan. The party that controlled the House determined who was to be Speaker. Partisan Speakers then as now used the powers of their office to advance party programs.

EARLY YEARS. Speakers, however, were not at first the legislative leaders of the House that they were to become. The cohesiveness of

the national parties was reflected in executive control over the legislative process, and skillful presidents and administration spokesmen
led members of their own parties in Congress. While he was secretary
of the Treasury during Washington's administration, Alexander Hamilton was able to sway Federalist members of Congress to a degree
that has not been known since. Commenting upon Hamilton's political skills as secretary of the Treasury, Thomas Jefferson remarked,
"The whole action of the legislature was now under the direction of
the Treasury." [1] As president, Jefferson continued the tradition of
executive control over the House, using his own secretary of the
Treasury, who had been leader of the House Republicans, to guide
his administration's measures through the legislature. Jefferson was
able to choose the House floor leader, and named the chairman of
the Ways and Means Committee.

STRONG SPEAKERS. It was not until the relatively weak presidential administration of James Madison that began in 1809, and the strong
speakership of Kentucky representative Henry Clay beginning in 1811,
that White House control over the House came to an abrupt end.
Clay was a brilliant and successful lawyer who had studied under the
same law professor in Richmond who had taught Thomas Jefferson
and John Marshall. He was a particularly adept legislative strategist
who mapped his plans around the dinner table with like-minded
colleagues at a boarding house on New Jersey Avenue in the District
of Columbia. Although both Madison and Clay were Republicans,
their party ties did not bind them as Clay successfully sought to establish his own independent reputation for power on Capitol Hill.
Clay turned the Republican Caucus of the House into an instrument
of power for his own purposes, rather than using it as a vehicle for
cooperation with the White House. He used the Speaker's power over
parliamentary procedure to dominate the House, establishing an important precedent that was used later by powerful Speakers.

Clay's model of the speakership was used by his successors, sometimes to advance the party programs of the White House, but more
often to exert independent power within and outside of the House.
By the end of the nineteenth century the powers of the Speaker had
become so excessive and grasping that members of the House, bent

[1] Edward S. Corwin, *The President: Office and Powers*, 4th ed. (New York: New
York University Press, 1957), pp. 17–18.

on pursuing their own political careers and quests for power, moved in the direction of curbing the Speaker.

CHALLENGE TO THE STRONG SPEAKERSHIP. The immediate impetus for change in the powers of the Speaker came after a succession of particularly strong Speakers in the late nineteenth and early twentieth centuries. Kentucky Democrat John G. Carlisle, who was Speaker from 1883 to 1889, turned the House into an extension of his own personality and policies. He was a master of parliamentary procedure, writing the script for House proceedings, often refusing to recognize those opposing him. He used the Speaker's power over appointment of committees to cast them in his own image. The lack of a cohesive House majority in opposition to the Speaker allowed Carlisle maximum opportunity to manipulate the body.

The successor to Carlisle's speakership was an equally powerful leader, Maine Republican Thomas B. Reed, commonly referred to as "Czar" Reed. Reed's parliamentary rulings were as arbitrary as those of Carlisle, but unlike his predecessor he did not attempt to base his power upon procedural manipulations that favored minority interests but chose to forge a majority that could control the House. He eliminated many of the obstructionist tactics that Carlisle had introduced. Under Reed the Rules Committee became an important adjunct of the Speaker's power. Since 1858 the Speaker had chaired the committee, which in the 1890s was given the power to stop House filibustering, vastly increasing the committee's power to prevent obstructionist tactics by the minority from controlling the House.

THE REVOLT OF 1910. The power of the Speaker peaked under Illinois Republican Joseph G. Cannon, who was also referred to as "Czar." Cannon became Speaker in 1903 and continued in the post until 1911. The arbitrary and authoritarian manner in which he ruled the House, however, resulted in Republicans and Democrats joining forces to liberalize the rules in 1910 to reduce significantly the Speaker's power. After the 1910 revolt, the Speaker was prohibited from appointing or serving on the Rules Committee, and even more significantly, his power to appoint House committees was taken away. Formerly all committees were to be appointed by the full House, which meant in effect that Democratic and Republican committees on committees would have the power to select which members of their parties would serve on the various committees. The 1910 revolt, eliminating the Speaker's power to appoint committees, also reduced his parliamentary discretion to use the power of recognition to manipulate the House. No longer did sponsors of legislation have to be recognized by the Speaker in order to have their bills considered. The Speaker, however, in effect still retained significant power, because in order to bypass the requirement of recognition to have the House take up legislation there had to be unanimous consent of the members present and constituting a quorum.

DECENTRALIZATION OF POWER. After 1910, power in the House began to disperse to party leaders and committee chairmen. The Speaker could still be a dominating force, but only if he was politically astute and able to persuade powerful members that it was in their interest to join forces with him. Powerful House speakers have always been politically adept, but before liberalization of House rules in 1910, they had greater formal powers than they possessed subsequently.

As the House evolved after 1910, it gradually moved toward decentralizing power, characterized by the growing power of committee chairmen. The seniority rule, a twentieth-century phenomenon, under which the most senior committee members of the majority party had the first claim upon the chairmanship of a committee, came to replace the Speaker's power to appoint chairmen. At first, the seniority rule was considered an important part of the liberal reforms of House rules in the early part of the century.

EBB AND FLOW OF POWER. After the 1910 rules changes there was a fluctuating of House politics and personalities that was reflected in changing patterns of decentralization and centralization. Strong Speakers alternated with weak ones. Attempts to centralize House power under party leaders, including the Speaker, were periodically made primarily to buttress Congress itself as a collective body against the growing power of the president. Strong Speakers, such as Ohio Republican Nicholas Longworth (1925–1931) and Texas Democrat Sam Rayburn (1940–1947, 1949–1953, 1955–1961) continued to increase the prestige and power of the speakership. Both men organized small coteries of members to help them dominate their own congressional party and the House as well. Neither Longworth nor Rayburn was able to exert the kind of power that had been exercised by "Czars" Reed and Cannon. The lessening of the Speaker's powers, growing fragmentation of the House into fiefdoms of committees, and disintegration of congressional parties helped to mitigate the influence of all twentieth-century Speakers.

The Speakers who succeeded Rayburn, Massachusetts Democrat John W. McCormack (1962–1971), Oklahoma Democrat Carl Albert (1971–1977), and Massachusetts Democrat Thomas P. ("Tip") O'Neill, Jr. were unable to exert the strong leadership characteristic of Rayburn. The change was due in part to the styles of the individuals, and to the changing politics of the House as well. McCormack and Albert were essentially consensus Speakers who did not have the persuasiveness of Rayburn and were unable to develop and rely upon a cohesive group of party leaders within the body to direct it.

STRENGTHENING THE SPEAKER. Major changes occurred in the politics of the House before Tip O'Neill ascended to the leadership in 1977. In some respects the politics of the House had come full circle since 1910, when both parties found it in their interest to curb the Speaker's authority. The more liberal Democratic members of the House in the late 1960s began to see in a weak speakership the loss of a potentially important countervailing force to powerful conservative committee chairmen who had systematically excluded them from vital arenas of legislation and power in the House. Conservatives, usually southerners, controlled such key committees as Rules and Ways and Means, whose Democratic members constituted a committee on committees that appointed all Democrats to House committees, such as Appropriations, Interstate and Foreign Commerce, Administration, and Public Works.

As the 1970s approached liberals grew in numerical strength within the Democratic Party of the House until they formed a majority. Nevertheless they continued to be excluded from power. Finally, in the 93rd and the 94th Congresses (1973–1976), the Democratic Caucus, now dominated by the more liberal and moderate elements of the party, voted to make significant changes in party organization and procedures. Several modifications affected the role of the Speaker, who was given the power to select the Democratic members of the Rules Committee, a change made to prevent the obstructionist tactics that had so often been practiced by that committee in the past under its conservative southern chairmen. Moreover, the Democrats changed their committee on committees from the members of the Ways and Means Committee to the Steering and Policy Committee, chaired by the Speaker, who also had the authority to appoint many of its members. The Speaker in the mid-1970s was viewed by a majority of House Democrats as an instrument of liberal reform, not as a bastion of conservative obstructionism and authoritarianism, which was the way members of both parties saw the Speaker in the late nineteenth century and the early twentieth.

As Tip O'Neill took the Speaker's gavel in 1977, he confronted a House that had undergone almost revolutionary changes in the preceding four years. The political turmoil of Vietnam, and more important, Watergate, was reflected in increasing House turnover. A majority of the 95th Congress (1977–1978) had been elected in the preceding six years. The power of incumbency continued, but seniority no longer gave the body the conservative cast so characteristic of the institution in the past. The Speaker found, however, even with new powers, that the prevailing mood of the House supported the continued decentralization of power in committees and subcommittees. O'Neill had to deal with more than 150 committees and subcommittees, whose chairmen considered themselves to be at least equal in importance to the Speaker himself. Moreover, the Speaker had to deal with new caucus groups, such as the Black Caucus, as well as the resurgent caucus of his own party, whose chairman and members might or might not agree with the course of action desired by the Speaker. Ironically, the increase in the Speaker's powers during the 1970s reflected only a short-term interest in buttressing the speakership, mainly to ensure in the long run more equal distribution of decentralized power throughout the body.

Other Leadership Organizations

Although the Constitution creates the office of Speaker, it leaves to the House itself power over all other aspects of its organization.

PARTY LEADERS. The emergence of political parties resulted in a leadership organization developed to serve party interests. Majority and minority leaders, whips, caucuses, committees on committees, and finally steering and policy committees were established at various times in the history of Congress to provide party leadership. The first majority leader was appointed in 1899. The position of minority leader was established in 1883. Though various members of the congressional parties served informally as whips to help members coordinate their activities along party lines, it was not until the twentieth century that formal whip organizations developed in both parties.

PARTY CAUCUSES. Consisting of meetings of the full membership of the parties in the House, caucuses were used for organizational purposes since parties appeared in the late 1790s. During certain historical periods party caucuses were highly effective as instruments of legislative strategy, party discipline, and at the height of their power they even chose party nominees for the presidency. In 1909 the Democrats adopted a rule under which a two-thirds vote of their caucus would bind party members on floor votes. The rule was used during the term of President Woodrow Wilson and during the first term of Franklin D. Roosevelt, but fell into disuse as an instrument of party discipline. The Republican Caucus, called the Conference, has intermittently been an important body discussing legislative strategy and proposals to help coordinate party efforts in the legislative process.

Both parties have created steering committees to help the leadership in scheduling legislation and in party strategy. The Republican Steering Committee was first appointed in 1919, continuing in existence until 1949 when it became the Policy Committee. The Democratic Steering Committee was established in 1933, and has now become the Steering and Policy Committee, which not only involves itself in strategy but also appoints Democratic committee members. The policy committees of both parties were created out of the Legislative Reorganization Act of 1946, which recommended their creation to foster party discipline on both sides of Capitol Hill. The policy committees, however, have never been effective instruments of party leadership in Congress.

EVOLUTION OF THE SENATE

The constitutional origins of the Senate suggest how profoundly different and more exalted its role in the legislative process was to be than that of the House of Representatives. The Senate was to represent the sovereignty of the states, and the House reflected the sovereignty of the people. The distrust of direct popular government, however, led the framers to give the Senate a uniqueness that has shaped it throughout history.

Unique Character

The Senate was to be the expert, deliberative, rational body that would check hasty and ill-conceived House actions. The six-year Senate term coupled with indirect election guaranteed the body a capacity for both expertise and detachment from temporary popular demands. The Senate was to be directly involved in making foreign policy, approving executive and judicial appointments, and determining ultimately whether or not a House impeachment of a civil officer, including the president, would result in a conviction. The House shared in some of these responsibilities, but there was no doubt that the Senate was to be the predominant body.

PRESTIGE. The prestige of the Senate made it more attractive than the House for a political career. "On entering the House of Representatives at Washington," remarked Tocqueville in the 1830s, "one is struck by the vulgar demeanor of that great assembly. Often there is not a distinguished man in the whole number. Its members are almost all obscure individuals, whose names bring no associations to mind. They are mostly village lawyers, men in trade, or persons belonging to the lower classes of society. In a country in which education is very general, it is said that the representatives of the people do not always know how to write correctly." [2]

By contrast, continued Tocqueville, "At a few yards' distance is the door of the Senate, which contains within a small space a large proportion of the celebrated men of America. Scarcely an individual is to be seen in it who has not had an active and illustrious career: The Senate is composed of eloquent advocates, distinguished generals, wise magistrates, and statesmen of note, whose arguments could do honor to the most remarkable parliamentary debates of Europe." [3]

Although Tocqueville attributed the differences he perceived in the qualities of the members of the House and the Senate to the contrasting modes of election of the two bodies, at the time he wrote, with little doubt the Senate was perceived to be the more important body by those seeking national political office. From the beginning the Senate was a collegial body of the elite.

[2] Alexis de Tocqueville, *Democracy in America*, vol. I (New York: Vintage, 1954), p. 211.
[3] De Tocqueville, *Democracy in America*, vol. I, pp. 211–212.

Organization and Procedure

In many ways the Senate has always been a club, characterized by informality, courtesy, and respect for the importance of the institution. The Senate soon became a collegial body, composed of a fellowship of the elect. The original conception of the Senate was that its members would represent sovereign states. Even as the concept of state sovereignty receded, senators considered themselves to be sovereign members of the legislature, a posture that has continued to the present.

EARLY YEARS. The early Senate, in keeping with its clubby atmosphere, adopted few rules. In the 1980s, the Senate manual consisted of 756 pages of fine print governing everything from its parliamentary procedure to the maintenance of the physical facilities and grounds of the Capitol. By contrast, the rules of the first Senate encompassed only one page. The early rules were principally designed to maintain Senate decorum and informality. Members were not permitted to interrupt each other, to speak twice in any one debate on the same day without permission of the body, and when "a member shall be called to order, he shall sit down until the President shall have determined whether he is in order or not." [4] Members were to give their yeas and nays when called for by one-fifth of the members present, and, in accordance with the Constitution, a journal was to be kept of Senate proceedings. Senate attendance was taken seriously, for no member "shall absent himself from the service of the Senate without leave of the Senate first obtained." [5]

The Senate met secretly until 1795, when it voted to open its legislative sessions. Even after 1795, however, executive sessions were held when treaties and presidential nominations were under consideration. Treaties were considered openly for the first time in 1888, and it was not until 1929 that the Senate voted for open consideration of nominations. Secret sessions continued to be held by the Senate, but only intermittently to consider classified information and sensitive matters of national security.

COMMITTEE SYSTEM. The Senate committee system originally, as in the House, consisted of ad hoc panels elected by the body. Between

[4] *Guide to Congress* (Washington, D.C.: Congressional Quarterly, 1976), p. 72.
[5] *Guide to Congress*, p. 72.

1789 and 1816 only four standing committees were created. The time-consuming chore of choosing ad hoc panels, however, numbering 100 in the 1815–1816 session, led the Senate to expand its standing committees by creating eleven panels in 1816, including Foreign Relations, Finance, Commerce and Manufactures, Military Affairs, and Judiciary.

The standing committees of the senate were first appointed by the body, but in 1823 committee members were chosen by the president pro tempore, who was selected by the Senate. For a short time, between 1825 and 1827, the vice president, who presided over the Senate under the Constitution, appointed committee members, but the political use of the appointment power by the then presiding officer, Vice President John C. Calhoun, caused the Senate once again to assume control over committee appointments before the end of Calhoun's term.

INDIVIDUALISM. During the first half of the nineteenth century the Senate was usually dominated by illustrious, powerful, and politically skillful members who were able to exert influence on the body as a whole, bypassing committee jurisdictions. Senators such as Martin Van Buren, Andrew Jackson, William Henry Harrison, and John Tyler, who served in the Senate between 1809 and 1829, and who were later to become presidents, did not have to rely upon committee chairmanships as springboards for their power. Significantly, Daniel Webster described the Senate of 1830 as a body "of equals, of men of individual honor and personal character, and of absolute independence." [6] No person or committee was the master of the Senate.

GROWING COMMITTEE IMPORTANCE. Senate committees, however, and more particularly their chairmen, gradually became predominant in the proceedings of the upper body. By 1850 advancement within Senate committees was made on the basis of seniority. Although parties had developed sufficient discipline within the chamber to determine the membership of the different committees, party leaders could not make the most important decisions on those who were to be selected as committee chairmen. The expansion of committees and their power, combined with the seniority rule, made committee chairmen a force in their own right that could defy the wishes of

[6] George H. Haynes, *The Senate of the United States: Its History and Practice*, vol. I (Boston: Houghton Mifflin, 1938), p. vii.

members of their own party and the broader membership of the Senate as well.

After the Civil War, Senate committees continued to expand in number and power. Woodrow Wilson wrote in 1884 that the Senate "has those same radical defects of organization which weakened the House. Its functions also, like those of the House, are segregated in the prerogatives of numerous Standing Committees. In this regard Congress is all of a piece. There is in the Senate no more opportunity than exists in the House for gaining such recognized party leadership as should be likely to enlarge a man by giving him a sense of power, and to study and sober him by filling him with a grave sense of responsibility." [7] Senate proceedings, concluded Wilson, "bear most of the characteristic features of committee rule." [8]

By 1913, the Senate had seventy-four standing committees. Committee chairmanships were found useful in the Senate as in the House because the committees employed clerical aides, the precursors of modern staffers. Because of the clerical support that accompanied committee chairmanships, chairmen and rising committee members made every effort to retain committees long after they had lost usefulness to the Senate as a whole. The committee on Revolutionary Claims, for example, was not abolished until 1921.

The history of Senate committees has witnessed various efforts at "reform," which essentially always mirrors underlying efforts to redistribute power. In 1921, for example, the Republican Senate majority insisted on "reforming" the committee system to increase Republican memberships on important panels. Periodically attempts were made to reduce the number of standing committees and consolidate their jurisdictions. The Reorganization Act of 1946 was a major attempt to cut back the number of committees in both the Senate and the House, which succeeded temporarily but which eventually was subverted by a vast and seemingly endless increase in the number of subcommittees on both sides of Capitol Hill.

Emergence of Parties

Parties have played various roles at different times in Senate history. As parties formed at the turn of the nineteenth century, their power

[7] Woodrow Wilson, *Congressional Government* (New York: Meridian, 1956), p. 146.
[8] Wilson, *Congressional Government*, p. 146.

as a collective force within the Senate ebbed and flowed in response
to politics within and outside of the body. As the Republican and
Federalist parties came into being in the 1790s, Virginia Senator
John Taylor wrote: "The existence of two parties in Congress is
apparent. The fact is disclosed almost upon every important question. Whether the subject be foreign or domestic — relative to war
or peace, navigation or commerce — the magnetism of opposite views
draws them wide as the polls asunder." [9]

The importance of parties in the Senate was soon to be replaced
by sectional and economic divisions. The split between the North
and the South over slavery and the tariff was far more important than
party labels.

Within Congress the committee system clearly overshadowed the
importance of parties in the latter half of the nineteenth century.

RISE AND FALL OF PARTY DISCIPLINE. Parties began to appear at the
turn of the twentieth century as an important influence in the Senate.
David Rothman describes the change in their importance from the
post-Civil War period to 1900:

> Senators in the 1870s usually performed their tasks without
> party superintendence. No one had the authority to keep his
> colleagues in line, and positions of influence were distributed
> without regard for personal loyalties. Democratic and Repub-
> lican organizations rarely attempted to schedule legislation or
> enforce unity in voting. In brief, Senators were free to go
> about their business more or less as they pleased. By 1900 all
> this had changed. The party caucus and its chieftains deter-
> mined who would sit on which committees and looked after
> the business calendar in detail. Members were forced to seek
> their favors or remain without influence in the chamber. At
> the same time, both organizations imposed unprecedented
> discipline on rollcalls.[10]

The rise of party discipline in the Senate is explained mostly in
terms of effective leadership within the body. In the 1890s the leaders
of party caucuses ruthlessly used their power to influence members

[9] Roy Swanstrom, *The United States Senate, 1787–1801*, Sen. Doc. 64, 87th
Cong., 1st sess. (Washington, D.C.: U.S. Government Printing Office, 1962),
p. 283.
[10] David J. Rothman, *Politics and Power: The United States Senate, 1869–1901*
(New York, Atheneum, 1969), p. 4.

and bring about a high degree of party discipline. Party leaders determined most of the membership of party committees on committees, which in turn determined the broader membership of Senate committees.

Although parties continued to be important in Senate proceedings during the twentieth century, the tight party discipline that had been created from 1890 to 1900 gradually eroded. The binding Democratic Caucus rule adopted in 1903 was not followed, the Senators resisting intrusion upon their personal spheres of power. The Senate reflected a balance of power between party leaders and individual members. The legislative parties continued to be split between liberals and conservatives, northerners and southerners, and on a variety of other issues and in regional ways. Clashing personalities often contributed to divisions within the congressional parties.

LEADERSHIP ORGANIZATION. As parties gained importance in Senate organization, procedures, and proceedings, their precedence was reflected in the establishment of formal party posts. Until 1911 the only such post was the chairmen of the party caucuses, elected by party members. But caucus chairmen were not necessarily the recognized party leaders. Rhode Island Republican Nelson W. Aldrich, for example, a powerful and dynamic leader of the Senate, was not the chairman of his party caucus. The only formal position he held was the chairmanship of the Finance Committee.

Informal party leadership worked well as long as there were senators with leadership ability recognized and accepted by party colleagues. But such a situation could not exist for long, and to avoid party squabbling and disintegration, both the Democrats in 1911 and the Republicans in 1913 created formal party organizations by designating the chairmen of their party caucuses to be the floor leaders. The Democrats in 1913 and the Republicans in 1915 established formal whips to be assistant floor leaders.

Direct Election of Senators

The constitutional arrangement under which the Senate was to be chosen by state legislatures came under increasing attack during the Progressive Era of reform that began in the 1880s and lasted into the 1920s.

PROGRESSIVE PRESSURE. The Progressives, whose support was drawn from the agrarian areas of the country, mostly in the Midwest, were at first political outsiders in the encapsulated world of Washington that was dominated by the entrenched Republican and Democratic Parties and special interest groups. The Progressives saw in the politics of the nation's capital a game of power and political tradeoffs that prevented or delayed passage of Progressive legislation that sought an expanded role for the federal government in regulation of the economy.

Progressive senators such as Robert M. La Follette of Wisconsin became disgusted with the wheeling and dealing in the smoke-filled rooms on the Senate side of the Capitol and saw in more democracy a cure for a government that they considered to be primarily controlled by vested interests. The Progressive proposals to change the Senate were not new, although after the Civil War only nine resolutions had been introduced in Congress recommending a constitutional amendment to change the method of Senate election. By 1912, 287 proposals for the direct election of senators had been introduced on Capitol Hill. Not surprisingly, the House was far more in favor of bringing direct democracy to the Senate than were the senators, who enjoyed their power because of the support of state party politicians who controlled most of the state legislatures.

Moves to Amend the Constitution

The first resolution to amend the Constitution to provide for direct election of the Senate was reported out of a House committee in 1892. In 1900 the House voted 240–15 in support of the amendment. Increasing popular pressure for a change to direct election, particularly in the Midwest and western states, was reflected in Democratic platforms from 1900 to 1912, and in resolutions by most of the states. The extent of popular backing for the constitutional change was illustrated by a California referendum, in which direct election of senators was approved by a vote of 14 to 1.

As agitation increased in the states for direct election of the Senate, Capitol Hill remained aloof for a while. After the favorable House vote in 1900, no action was taken by either branch of Congress until 1911. In the meantime, many state legislatures agreed to ratify the choices for the Senate made in direct popular primaries, which in effect constituted a system of direct election. By 1910 about half the senators were chosen in this manner.

The reality of a popularly elected majority in the Senate combined with popular support in a majority of the states for a constitutional change finally forced Congress to act, and the 17th Amendment, providing for direct election of senators by the people, was submitted to the states by Congress in 1912 and ratified by the requisite three-fourths of the states in 1913.

The 17th Amendment did not cause a revolutionary change in the Senate. The majority of senators were already being elected by popular vote through the direct primary system. By the time the amendment was fully effective (sitting senators at the time the amendment was ratified were allowed to fill out their terms) in the 66th Congress (1919–1921), most of the senators who had originally been chosen by state legislatures were reelected by the people.

The Filibuster

A unique feature of Senate procedure, reflecting the body's continuing individualism, is the filibuster, which allows senators unlimited time to speak unless cloture is invoked.[11] The clubby atmosphere and collegiality of the Senate had always permitted unlimited speech, although it was tacitly assumed that the privilege would not be abused for the purpose of obstructing majority rule in the body. The Senate's gentlemanly character began to change, however, as the Civil War began and filibusters came to be used occasionally, although at first they were curbed by the parliamentary rulings of the presiding officers.

GROWING USE OF FILIBUSTERS. The last decades of the nineteenth century witnessed more than half a dozen filibusters that often brought Senate proceedings to a standstill. In 1893, a filibuster against repeal of the 1890 Silver Purchase Act extended over forty-six days, thirteen of which were spent in twenty-four-hour sessions. One Populist senator held the floor for fourteen hours. The filibuster exacerbated many senators, who began to express the unheard-of idea that there should be limits upon debate within the body. Massachusetts

---

[11] The word filibuster comes originally from the Dutch *vrijbuiter* (*vrij*, "free," and *buiter*, "booter") or "freebooter." The Dutch word was used to describe privateers and pirates in the sixteenth century, but was taken into English as "filibuster." By the time of the Civil War the word was in common usage in the United States. See William Safire, *Safire's Political Dictionary* (New York: Random House, 1978), pp. 226–227.

Republican Henry Cabot Lodge declared, "To vote without debating is perilous, but to debate and never vote is imbecile." [12] Lodge believed that "there must be a change, for the delays which now take place are discrediting the Senate.... A body which cannot govern itself will not long hold the respect of the people who have chosen it to govern the country." [13]

STURDY TONGUES AND IRON WILLS. Lodge's warning and recommendation went unheeded, however, and filibusters not only continued, but through ingenious parliamentary maneuvering became more successful in obstructing Senate proceedings. Franklin Burdette comments that the beginning of the twentieth century was "the heyday of brazen and unblushing aggressors. The power of the Senate lay not in votes but in sturdy tongues and iron wills. The premium rested not upon ability and statesmanship but upon effrontery and audacity." [14]

The obstructionism of the "sturdy tongues and iron wills" continued into the administration of President Woodrow Wilson, when the Armed Neutrality bill, strongly backed by the White House, was filibustered to death by eleven senators. Seventy-five senators who supported the legislation signed a statement for the record declaring that the legislation would pass if a vote could be taken. President Wilson angrily commented, "The Senate of the United States is the only legislative body in the world which cannot act when its majority is ready for action. A little group of willful men, representing no opinion but their own, have rendered the great government of the United States helpless and contemptible." [15] Wilson called the Senate into special session, demanding that it amend its rule allowing unending debate.

CLOTURE. The Senate responded to Wilson's request by passing its first cloture rule — Rule 22 — limiting debate. The rule provided that a cloture motion could be made by sixteen senators, two days after which a vote of two-thirds of the senators present and voting would limit further debate to one hour for each senator. The Senate

12 Haynes, *Senate of the United States*, vol. I, p. 398.
13 Haynes, *Senate of the United States*, vol. I. pp. 398–399.
14 Franklin L. Burdette, *Filibustering in the Senate* (New York: Russell and Russell, 1965), p. 80.
15 Haynes, *Senate of the United States*, vol. I, pp. 402–403.

voted overwhelmingly to support the cloture rule, 76–3. Cloture was first invoked in 1919 to close debate on the Treaty of Versailles, which had occupied the Senate for fifty-five days.

Between 1917, when Senate Rule 22 was adopted, and the end of 1981, 168 cloture votes were taken, of which 53 were successful. The original Rule 22 made it extremely difficult to limit Senate debate. The hurdle of a two-thirds vote of senators present and voting proved difficult to overcome. Until the cloture rule was changed in 1975 to require sixty votes of the full Senate for cloture, debate had been closed under Rule 22 in only 25 percent of the cloture votes taken. By contrast, since 1975 a majority of cloture votes have been successful.

THE MODERN CONGRESS

Although many contemporary features of Capitol Hill are rooted in the past, Congress has changed significantly. Washington has become the seat of entrenched and fragmented political power in a way that was not foreseen by the framers of the Constitution. And Congress has become, as Morris Fiorina describes it, the keystone of the Washington political establishment.[16] That establishment consists mainly of the powerful chairmen of the more than 300 committees and subcommitees on Capitol Hill, which are connected with top-echelon bureaucrats downtown and lobbyists to form "iron triangles" of political power in the multiple spheres of public policy that link government with the private sector.

Characteristics of the Modern Congress

Through most of its history, Congress has been an arena in which the forces of centralization and decentralization have struggled for supremacy. Powerful speakers and party leaders on both sides of Capitol Hill have sought to establish disciplined congressional parties that would act as a centripetal force in the legislative process. At the same time, party leaders have attempted to mold congressional procedures to consolidate their power over the disparate elements of Congress.

In their drive for centralized power, congressional leaders have

[16] Morris P. Fiorina, *Congress: Keystone of the Washington Establishment* (New Haven: Yale University Press, 1977).

faced a major obstacle in the individual members' personal quest for power. Influence in Congress is one of the highest goals of members. Power can be obtained either through party leadership or by becoming an independent political entrepreneur within the House or the Senate. Because party leadership posts are limited, most congressmen must satisfy their personal power goals elsewhere. Members strive for power by seeking prestigious committee assignments, the chairmanships of committees and subcommittees, and, particularly in the Senate, large staffs.

DISPERSION OF POWER. Despite the occasional efforts made by the House and the Senate to consolidate their committees, an inexorable trend leads toward multiplication of committees. The twenty-two standing committees in the House and fifteen in the Senate were formally created under the rules of each body and cannot be altered without a vote of the full House or Senate. Each standing committee may, however, create an unlimited number of subcommittees with special jurisdictions, powers, and staffs. Although the number of standing committees has been kept within reasonable bounds in recent decades, scores of new subcommittees have been created. Members of the House majority have to wait for two to four terms before becoming a subcommittee chairman, yet in the Senate most freshmen of the majority party are able immediately to take the reins of a subcommittee and enjoy the perquisites of a committee chairman, which include not only legislative and investigative powers, but also expert staff and, for many, extensive foreign travel.

Even though much dispersion of the subcommittees on Capitol Hill directly relates to the individual members' desire to increase their influence in Congress, committee posts may also serve reelection needs. Committee chairmen may sometimes use the powers of their positions both to pursue influence within Congress and to engage in activities increasing their popularity at home. The chairman of an appropriations subcommittee may channel funds to his or her district or state and at the same time use the committee to increase influence within Congress by demonstrating expertise, legislative skills, investigative techniques, and active oversight of the bureaucracy.

Mississippi Congressman Jaime Whitten, elected to the House a month before Pearl Harbor in 1941, has illustrated throughout his long political career the way in which committee chairmanships may serve the dual purposes of power and influence on the one hand, and reelection on the other. Beginning in 1949, Whitten chaired the agriculture subcommittee of the Appropriations committee, using it to wield power over agricultural policy and the Department of Agriculture that had seldom been witnessed in Washington. Whitten soon became known as the "Permanent Secretary of Agriculture." The Mississippi congressman continued to retain his subcommittee chairmanship when in 1979 he assumed the chairmanship of the full Appropriations Committee. Whitten not only achieved extraordinary power on Capitol Hill and throughout Washington by his skillful use of power as subcommittee chairman, but also saw to adoption of agricultural policies benefiting his Mississippi Delta district. He strongly and successfully supported large subsidy payments to cotton farmers, an important part of his constituency. He backed the use of pesticides favored by the farmers against attempts by the Environmental Protection Agency to limit pesticide use. His district returned his favors by reelecting him with comfortable margins, consistently more than 60 percent of the popular vote and sometimes approaching 80 percent.

Numerous other examples come to mind of committee chairmen who used their posts to increase internal power and reelection interests at the same time. L. Mendel Rivers, Democratic representative from the first district of South Carolina for thirty years, including the city of Charleston, never failed to funnel Defense Department money into his district at every opportunity after he became chairman of the House Armed Services Committee, a post he held from 1965 until his death in 1970. Rivers boasted that 35 percent of the payroll in his district came from military installations and defense industries that he directly or indirectly helped to establish and support. A flamboyant southern politician of the old school, Rivers was not only popular at home but an extremely powerful member of the Washington political establishment. He used his committee chairmanship to form links with the Pentagon that made him one of the most important military planners on Capitol Hill. He, like most senior members of Congress, found no contradiction in pursuing power in Washington at the same time as he carefully cultivated the support of his constituents.

CHARACTER OF COMMITTEES. The committees and subcommittees on Capitol Hill are more than extensions of the interests and per-

sonalities of their chairmen. Although it is true that many committees
have been created at the behest of members of Congress, from senior
congressmen in the House to freshmen senators, many committees
have historically been created to meet institutional needs and respond
to political pressures. The standing committees in particular have an
institutional and political character that transcend their chairmen
and members. The House Ways and Means Committee, though
shaped by its chairman, was created in 1795 and exercises the exclusive constitutional prerogative of the House to originate revenue
legislation. Much of the committee's character — the way in which
it operates within the House and its relationships with the Senate —
stems from its important institutional role. Its "strategic premise," as
Fenno describes it,[17] supports both independence and responsibility
to act within a consensus of members. "In return for its extraordinary
independence," writes Fenno, "the committee promises to make decisions that are acceptable to a great majority of House members."[18]

Each of the important committees of Congress has a character
that is in part shaped by history, external political forces, internal
congressional politics, and congressional norms and customs of various kinds. Each of the "little legislatures" or committees on Capitol
Hill has unique characteristics, many of which are determined by
the contrasting forces that impinge upon them. Some committees,
such as Ways and Means, Appropriations, and Rules, serve the institutional goals of the House at the same time as they provide important internal influence for their members. They represent the
House as an institution, a collective force in political struggles with
the Senate, the president, and the external political world generally.
By contrast, the House Interior Committee is one that primarily
serves the reelection goals of members, most of them from the
western states where conservation and water resources, under the committee's jurisdiction, are of such great importance to constituents.
The House Agriculture Committee is also a "reelection committee,"
drawing many members from agricultural districts who enhance their

---

[17] Richard F. Fenno, Jr., *Congressmen in Committees* (Boston: Little, Brown,
1973), Ch. 3.
[18] Fenno, *Congressmen in Committees*, p. 55. Although Fenno's book was published in 1973, his conclusion about the Ways and Means Committee remains mostly valid. The fluctuating importance of the House Budget Committee has injected a new element in the environment of the House that
affects the Ways and Means Committee.

reelection prospects by using the committee to serve their constituents' interests. The commodity subcommittees of Agriculture directly represent the narrow interests of segments of the agricultural community.

The contrasting political environments of committees, and the different roles they perform, add to the fragmentation of power on Capitol Hill. The norms and practices of committees, and their connections with outside constituencies, have a continuity that prevails while committee chairmen, members, and party balances shift. The "strategic premises" and modes of operation of committees, grounded in history, custom, and the politics of individual committees, are respected by old and new committee chairmen and members alike.

CONGRESSIONAL PARTIES. As a collective force on Capitol Hill, congressional parties are typically portrayed as weak and ineffective. By contrast with the highly disciplined parties of European parliaments, particularly the British House of Commons, congressional parties are indeed relatively powerless to dictate policy to members and whip them into line on crucial votes.

Party discipline in the European sense is unknown on Capitol Hill, but congressional parties are a vital and often powerful force in the legislative process. The average member of Congress votes along party lines most of the time. The balance of power, however, especially in the House, has frequently been in the hands of a conservative coalition of Republicans and Democrats who have joined to defeat the policies of the liberal wings of both congressional parties. In the mid-1980s the Conservative Democratic Forum represented 45 to 65 Democratic votes that did not hesitate to join with the conservative Republican minority in the House to form a majority.

The seeming lack of consistency in party voting, and the perceived weakness of party leaders, mask the underlying importance of parties. The committees and subcommittees of Capitol Hill are controlled by members of the majority parties in the House and the Senate. A party change, such as that which occurred in the Senate in 1981 when the Republicans took control for the first time in more than twenty-five years, can have profound consequences for public policy. The support given to the Reagan administration by Senate majority leader Howard Baker and his Republican colleagues was crucial to the president's success. And there was no doubt that the president had better relations with the Senate, which was controlled by his own party, than he had with the House, which had a Democratic majority. Although the conservative coalition in the House buttressed the president's power, the committees remained dominated by loyal Democrats who disagreed with many aspects of the president's program.

SPECIAL GROUPS OR CAUCUSES. In politics the term *caucus* is usually applied to party groups that meet to deliberate about issues and actions. In the House, for example, the Democratic Caucus became an important party force in the early 1970s. The Republican counterpart to the Democratic Caucus, the Conference, meets to ratify committee choices and occasionally discuss issues of public policy.

In addition to party caucuses, a new type of caucus on Capitol Hill represents the collective interests of different groups of members of Congress. The caucuses are informal "parties" on selected issues and are primarily found in the House. A majority of House members have joined the Tourism Caucus, formed to promote tourism. Like many others, the Tourism Caucus has its own staff, housed in the House Annex, close to the Capitol and House Office Buildings. Other caucuses range from the Frostbelt Caucus, formed during the fuel crisis in the 1970s, to the Rural Caucus, Women's Caucus, Black Caucus, Seal Caucus, and even the High Altitude Coalition. Most of the caucuses are bipartisan.

The primary purpose of each caucus is to promote its special interest by developing and introducing legislation through its members, providing staff assistance to members engaged in advocating the group's goals, and, like the congressional parties, striving to accomplish as much voting unity among members as possible on legislation that interests the caucus.

MEMBERS' GOALS. The committees, parties, and special caucuses of Congress, as well as its procedures, have been shaped by the differing goals of individual members. Although it is difficult to assess exactly what motivates candidates to run for Congress, and their objectives once elected, there is agreement among political scientists that members' goals generally are reelection, power and influence within Congress, and good public policy.[19] These goals are not mutually exclusive, but complement one another. Clearly, to achieve power and in-

---

[19] Richard F. Fenno, Jr., *Congressmen in Committees* (Boston: Little, Brown, 1973), p. 1.

fluence on Capitol Hill a member must be reelected, which is also necessary if the member is to help formulate good public policy. Reelection is the sine qua non of a career in Congress. But, though reelection is the essential condition for existence, it is definitely not the only goal sought by members. Nor does the reelection incentive always take precedence over the quest for internal power or good public policy.

The organization of the modern Congress reflects members' goals in many ways. The fragmentation of power among committees and their chairmen helps members to respond to the needs and demands of constituents and at the same time to increase their influence in Congress. The chairman of the Public Works Committee of the House can use his position not only to channel porkbarrel projects into his district, but also to wield influence over other members because his committee is the gateway through which porkbarrel legislation must pass. Many committees serve both reelection and internal power goals.

Regardless of the goals a member pursues, or in what combination, their achievement by most is not enhanced through the integration of committee power, strong party organizations, or parliamentary procedures that limit a member's floor opportunities to debate, amend, and otherwise influence legislation. Reelection, internal power, and good public policy are, within the framework of congressional politics, highly individualistic pursuits. Members do not get reelected by following a party line, or by achieving prominence within the congressional party organization. On the contrary, the reelection possibilities of members are enhanced by their ability to take positions and actions in response to local interests that vary greatly from one district to another. The pluralism of American electoral politics helps to dictate the pluralism of Congress.

The quest for power on Capitol Hill, like the pursuit of reelection, is served by the decentralization of organization and maximum flexibility in parliamentary procedure. Political scientist Lawrence Dodd observes, "Every member wants to exercise power — to make the key policy decisions.... Given this widespread power motive, an obvious way to resolve the conflict among power-seeking congressmen is to disperse power — or at least power positioned as widely as possible." [20]

[20] Lawrence C. Dodd, "Congress and the Quest for Power," in Lawrence C. Dodd and Bruce I. Oppenheimer, eds., *Congress Reconsidered* (New York: Praeger, 1977), p. 272.

Power is dispersed in government and therefore members seeking influence strive to establish their own bases of power in committees and subcommittees. Just as members are not reelected on the basis of party labels, their power does not depend upon their positions in congressional parties or the national party outside of Congress.

The individual pursuit of power in the short run on Capitol Hill undermines the institutional power of Congress, its collective ability to exercise constant and consistent political leadership. Ultimately, the short-term pursuit of power by members may undermine their ability in the long run to shape the course of government by exercising their collective power.[21]

The pluralism of American politics makes the pursuit of members' goals, whether reelection, power, or good public policy, an entrepreneurial activity, and Capitol Hill the bastion of free-enterprise politics.

Environment of Congress

BICAMERALISM. The division of Congress into two branches has had the most profound consequences for congressional operations and public policy. The framers of the Constitution saw bicameralism primarily as a device that would ensure checks and balances within the legislative body itself. The more detached and deliberative Senate was to control the popularly elected House. It was thought that the Senate would be the more conservative body that would have an incentive to rein in the potentially more "liberal" House.

Bicameralism affects the modern Congress in ways that go far beyond the intentions of the framers. That two separate, distinct, and equal legislative bodies exist side by side on Capitol Hill has fulfilled the wishes of the framers by providing legislative checks and balances. Unlike the legislature envisioned by the founding fathers, however, the contemporary Congress does not place the Senate above the House as a conservative Burkean trustee of the national interest. The Senate, now popularly elected, can be as subject to the whims and passions of the people as the House. In fact, recent decades have witnessed relatively greater turnover in the Senate than the House (see Table 2.1), and a Senate that generally supports more liberal legislation than does the House.

[21] Dodd, "Congress and the Quest for Power," p. 272.

table

Table 2.1

Reelection Success of Senate and House Incumbents

Year	No. seeking reelection	No. defeated: Primary	General	Percentage reelected
1962				
Senate	35	1	5	82.9
House	402	12	22	91.5
1964				
Senate	33	1	4	84.8
House	397	8	45	86.6
1966				
Senate	32	3	1	87.5
House	411	8	41	88.1
1968				
Senate	22	4	4	71.4
House	409	4	9	96.8
1970				
Senate	31	1	6	77.4
House	401	10	12	94.5
1972				
Senate	27	2	5	74.1
House	390	12	13	93.6
1974				
Senate	27	2	2	85.2
House	391	8	40	87.7
1976				
Senate	25	0	9	64.0
House	384	3	13	95.8
1978				
Senate	25	3	7	60.0
House	382	5	19	93.7
1980				
Senate	29	4	9	55.2
House	398	6	31	90.7
1982				
Senate	30	0	2	93.3
House	392	10	29	90.05
1984				
Senate	29	0	3	89.6
House	421	3	17	95.2

The broader differences between the House and the Senate have been buttressed by the customs, traditions, and politics of the two bodies that have widened the gap between the two sides of Capitol Hill beyond the relatively simple division of power and responsibilities outlined in the Constitution. Generally, the House is a more hierarchic body, in which committees and subcommittees exert more authority than they do in the Senate. The Senate is far more collegial than the House, its members being more nearly equal in power and its procedures relatively informal. (See Table 2.2.)

The constitutional and political tradition of bicameralism has resulted in a Congress of separate House and Senate worlds. The politics of Capitol Hill often dictates a struggle between the two bodies, each of which constantly strives to maintain its supremacy over the other. Because it is the *internal* politics of Congress that pits the

Table 2.2

The Bicameral Congress: House-Senate Differences

House	Senate
• Two-year term	• Four-year term
• Smaller, equal constituencies (local)	• Larger, unequal constituencies (state)
• 435 members	• 100 members
• Unique constitutional powers: Originates tax bills (Ways and Means Committee important) Impeachment	• Unique constitutional powers: Advice and consent on many presidential appointments (Judiciary, Foreign Relations Committees important) Tries impeached officers, convicts by 2/3 vote Approves treaties by 2/3 vote (Foreign Relations Committee important)
• Rules Committee important	• Rules Committee plays minor role
• Limited debate	• Unlimited debate unless sixty senators vote cloture
• Unequal power among members	• Greater equality among senators
• Committee and subcommittee chairmen more powerful	• Committee and subcommittee chairmen less powerful
• Staff has less power	• Staff very powerful
• Greater specialization of members	• Senators must deal with more policy areas

House against the Senate, it is often impossible for outside pressures from the White House, the bureaucracy, pressure groups, and even voters to smooth the road to agreement between powerful politicians and their aides on opposite sides of the Capitol. The physical separation of the House and Senate chambers, and the even greater distance between the office buildings of the two bodies on the north and south sides of Capitol Hill, reflect the political divisions that are embedded within the bicameral system.

After President Reagan took office his call to the Republican Senate to accept the House version of the budget to avoid a time-consuming conference only raised the hackles of Senate Budget Committee Chairman Pete Domenici (R, NM), Finance Chairman Robert Dole (R, Kansas), and other Senate leaders who resented the White House interference in congressional politics and, more important, naively asking the Senate to go along with the House. Although the aggravation of Senate leaders was increased because a conservative Republican majority was asked to accept a bipartisan House bill, differences and conflicts between the House and the Senate transcend party politics. Powerful House Democrats constantly clashed with their Senate counterparts in the pre-Reagan years when both sides of Capitol Hill were firmly in the grip of Democrat majorities.

The bicameralism of Capitol Hill not only affects its internal politics, but also shapes the way in which coordinate branches, parties and public opinion, interest groups, and the media relate to the legislature.

THE PRESIDENT AND CONGRESS. The White House, particularly in the hands of an active and aggressive president, is always an important part of the environment of Congress. Under the Constitution and by custom and tradition, the presidency has become a focal point of leadership. A strong president, backed by a popular mandate, determines, particularly during the "honeymoon" period in the initial months of a new administration, the major items on the agenda of Congress. President Reagan used his highly effective political skills and talent as a communicator to place his budgetary proposals at the top of the legislative agenda as his administration began. Aided by a conservative Republican Senate, and a House dominated by a conservative coalition of Republicans and Democrats, Reagan was able to force Congress to deal with the budget on his terms.

Although the president is a legislative leader, it would be a mistake to assume that the White House dominates Congress. The honeymoon of a new president with Congress may go smoothly, but inevitably even the more persuasive presidents confront the reality of the constitutional and political separation of powers between the two ends of Pennsylvania Avenue. Presidents can go so far and no further in uniting the White House with Capitol Hill. The seeming popularity of a president during the honeymoon with Congress inevitably masks the underlying conflict between the two branches that is built into the political system and has been sharpened by political tradition. Congressional leaders, and the chairmen of committees and subcommittees, constantly seek to increase their power and status on Capitol Hill and in the broader Washington political establishment. They will follow the president insofar as his interests coincide with their own goals, and insofar as the White House can be used to buttress their power and status. The framers of the Constitution wisely saw that, by giving Congress independent powers and constituencies separate from the presidency, the legislature would inevitably be motivated to retain its independence against incursions by the president.

It is difficult to measure exactly presidential success on Capitol Hill. Clearly, where the White House takes a strong stand on legislation and engages in intensive lobbying, its rate of success is far greater than where its programs are imprecise and its political pressures on the legislative branch are weak. Paul Lenchner's analysis of party unity in Congress reveals "the unifying impact of White House occupancy upon the president's partisans in Congress. To the extent that a sense of common purpose is possible in Washington against the twin obstacles of social pluralism and constitutional dispersion of power, we seem largely dependent upon the chief executive to provide it." [22] When direct pressure from pressure groups is lacking, congressmen have the flexibility to act as trustees. Usually the demands of individual constituents become politically important only when they are mobilized by interest groups and channeled to Congress. When the president takes a firm position on congressional votes, for example, the rate of success of the White House ranges from 50 to 90 percent, with an average success rate of approximately 70 percent. (See Figure 2.1.) Legislative proposals coming from the White House on which

[22] Paul Lenchner, "Congressional Party Unit and Executive-Legislative Relations," *Social Science Quarterly*, 57, no. 3 (December 1976), p. 595.

Figure 2.1

Presidential Success on Votes, 1953–1983[a]

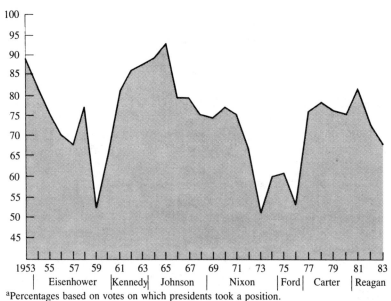

[a]Percentages based on votes on which presidents took a position.
Source: Congressional Quarterly Weekly Report, Vol. 41, No. 52 (December 31, 1983), p. 2783.

the president has not taken a strong position have less than an even chance of passage.[23]

THE BUREAUCRACY AND CONGRESS. Like the presidency and in conjunction with it, the bureaucracy is a source of legislative proposals for Congress. Administrative agencies have legislative expertise and understanding of the problems that arise within agency jurisdictions. Agencies are also the focal point of political constituencies that are

---

[23] The *Congressional Quarterly* has compiled data on the success ratios of presidential proposals to Congress from 1954 to 1973, but the difficulty of compiling the data led to its discontinuance after 1973. According to these data, in only five years from 1954 to 1973 were more than 50 percent of the proposals of the White House to Congress approved, and four of these years occurred during the Johnson administration, from 1964 to 1968, the remaining year being in the Eisenhower administration in 1954. The *Congressional Quarterly* data may be found in Peter Woll and Robert H. Binstock, *America's Political System,* 3rd. ed. (New York: Random House, 1979).

connected as well with the committees of Capitol Hill. The linkage among agencies, committees, and political constituencies form iron triangles of politics that often dictate public policies. Formally, the legislative proposals of administrative agencies must be cleared by the Office of Management and Budget in the Executive Office of the President. Nothing, however, prevents administrators from informally communicating their wishes and needs to their committee chairmen on the Hill. A simple telephone conversation suffices, or casual comments at lunch at the Monocle, or one of the other "in" restaurants on Capitol Hill.

The bureaucracy, often considered to be synonymous with "the Executive Branch" under the control of the president, is in fact considered by Congress to be a fourth branch of the government that is as much an agent of the legislature as it is of the executive. It is not uncommon for committee chairmen to consider agencies under their jurisdiction to be an extension of their own power. They jealously guard the appropriations and authority of the agencies against attempts from "the outside," which includes the president, to curtail agency power. From the vantage point of Congress, the bureaucracy is considered to be a major part of the permanent Washington political establishment. By contrast, presidents come and go, and in recent years the one-term presidency has become common. The bureaucracy, then, is integrated into the politics of Capitol Hill more than is the presidency, although the surface appearance of Washington politics as reported by the press and television might suggest the contrary. After all, the White House is intrinsically far more glamorous and newsworthy than, say, the Consumer Product Safety Commission. The White House has automatic entrée to the press, which never fails to report on the most minute activities of the president and the First Lady. President Reagan's visits to Capitol Hill were major news events covered by national television and the press. By contrast, most newspapers do not assign reporters to administrative agencies, and the actions of bureaucrats are rarely considered newsworthy outside of Washington.

THE SUPREME COURT AND CONGRESS. Although both the president and the bureaucracy directly and continuously interact with Congress, the Supreme Court stays in the background but is nevertheless an important force in determining the broad boundaries of congressional authority. Rarely (though often significantly) has the Supreme Court declared provisions of congressional laws to be unconstitutional. Of the more than 85,000 public and private bills that have been passed, only 122 or 123 provisions have been declared unconstitutional by the Supreme Court.[24] Generally the Supreme Court has supported a vast expansion of congressional authority under Article I of the Constitution, adopting a loose constructionist approach to constitutional interpretation. Since the New Deal, the Court has acquiesced to the exercise of congressional power in the economic sphere while adopting closer judicial scrutiny of congressional laws where they affect civil liberties and civil rights. Concern for individual rights and liberties in part underlay the Supreme Court's decision in June 1983, declaring the legislative veto to be unconstitutional.[25] Congress had used a veto power authorized by the Immigration Law to overrule a decision by the Immigration and Naturalization Service, which had suspended deportation of an alien on the ground that he was of good moral character and his deportation would result in extreme hardship.[26] The Court overturned the legislative veto procedure, on the ground that it violated the constitutional separation-of-powers and checks-and-balances system, in a decision of potentially far-reaching consequences. The case was a rare but signal example of judicial intervention in the legislative process.

Occasionally Congress threatens to curb the jurisdiction of the Supreme Court, an authority it possesses under Article III. The Court, however, has been politically astute in sidestepping issues that would bring it into direct political confrontation with Congress. Although Congress has infrequently curtailed the jurisdiction of the Supreme Court, generally its threats to do so are more hollow than real.

Threats to curb the Court arose in the early 1980s when Republican North Carolina Senator Jesse Helms attempted to garner support for proposals that would limit the jurisdiction of the federal courts over busing, abortion, and other matters on which, in the view of Helms and his conservative colleagues, the Court had acted improperly. Proposals were also made by conservatives to overturn, for example, the Court's historic abortion decision in *Roe* v. *Wade* (1973), by making abortion a crime.

[24] Henry J. Abraham, *The Judicial Process*, 4th ed. (New York: Oxford University Press, 1980), pp. 296–297.
[25] Immigration and Naturalization Service v. Chadha, 77 L. Ed. 2d 317 (1983).
[26] The findings of good moral character and extreme hardship were required by statute to suspend deportation.

Inevitably, there is conflict between Congress and the Court from time to time, yet most constitutional issues on the reach of congressional authority have been resolved. Neither the Court nor Congress is likely to threaten the other's authority significantly in the future. In the day-to-day operations of Congress, the Court remains distinctly in the background, figuratively, as it is, almost literally, in the shadow of the Capitol Dome.

The environment of Congress is shaped not only by the way in which other branches of the government touch upon it, but also by the broader political forces of parties, pressure groups, public opinion, and the press.

POLITICAL PARTIES. Although congressional parties are loosely connected with both national and local party organizations they are at the same time distinctly different. The leadership, caucuses, and conferences of congressional parties attempt to define the policies to guide congressional party members in their voting and other activities. Members of Congress, though, will follow the dictates of their congressional leaders only insofar as they find their interests in accordance with the party leaders' desires. Like parties outside of Congress, the congressional parties are themselves factionalized. For example, sixty-five House members formed the Conservative Democratic Forum after Reagan took office to press for a conservative budget that in some respects went beyond the program of the Republicans in sponsoring cuts in government programs. Other House Democrats, though more liberal than the members of the Conservative Forum, generally found themselves unable to agree on budget, tax, and other policies. The Republicans have exhibited a great deal of cohesion but generally they, like the Democrats, have been split along conservative and liberal lines.

Ideology aside, members of both parties also pursue individual goals of power and status on Capitol Hill, reelection, and good public policy that often place them at odds with their party colleagues. Although members may be helped by congressional parties in their reelection efforts, they are more dependent upon local constituency organizations and are more attuned to the demands of these constituencies than they are to the more exalted and often abstract ideological and power interests of congressional party leaders.

INTEREST GROUPS. Interest groups are often more influential than political parties on Capitol Hill. They influence members in various ways. First, interest groups have become a distinct part of the Washington political establishment. In increasing numbers they have located their offices within easy reach of the Capitol as well as of the bureaucracy downtown. Lobbyists socialize regularly with members of Congress, wining and dining them at lunch and often seeing them informally at the numerous evening social engagements that are so characteristic of the Capital. Skillful lobbyists have become a permanent fixture on the Washington political scene, and they know the intricate and often convoluted ways in which power is exercised in that somewhat Byzantine world. They have a permanency and continuity, complemented by specialization and expertise, that effectively connects them to committee chairmen and powerful Hill staffers.

The influence of lobbyists on Capitol Hill is increased by the close relationship that frequently connects interest groups and administrative agencies. Congressional committees, agencies, and private groups often work closely together in a comfortable collusive arrangement to advance their mutual interests. The internal power, reelection, and good public-policy goals of legislators may be advanced in varied ways with assistance from private interests. Groups can use their expertise and influence in Congress to buttress individual members' internal power and status. At the same time, groups such as the AFL-CIO, veterans, farmers, and various business organizations can marshal their members and finances to aid the election campaigns of congressmen and senators. Members striving to achieve "good public policy," however defined, to be successful must reach out to gain the support of relevant groups within the affected policy arena.

Although Congress is not, as Senator Edward Kennedy charged, "the best that money can buy," there is no doubt that the financial and other resources of interest groups make them an integral part of the congressional process. The decentralization of Congress increases the access and power of interest groups at the same time as it dilutes the influence of political parties in the legislative process.

PUBLIC OPINION. Political parties and interest groups create linkages between public opinion and Congress. National parties are relatively ineffective in transmitting broad public demands to Capitol Hill, whereas interest groups have little difficulty in making known the views of specialized publics. Polls are constantly being taken of public attitudes on a few major policy issues, yet polling results have little direct influence on members of Congress. The questions asked by pollsters of the public are usually phrased most generally, such as: "Should military spending be increased?" "Do you favor the right to abortion?" "Should the government balance its budget?" "Should the government encourage the use of nuclear power?" Not only do the answers to these questions provide little concrete guidance to legislators in the complex task of framing public policy, but national surveys have little bearing upon reelection requirements in the disparate congressional districts of the nation. It is difficult even for congressmen to assess public opinion in their own districts, which almost always contain clashing viewpoints among varied groups. In assessing both national and local public opinion, members of Congress more often than not find themselves making judgment calls without a great deal of evidence. They act more as trustees of their constituencies, doing what they consider to be in the best interests of their districts and states, than as delegates of a clearly defined majority opinion of constituents.

THE PRESS. The press and the mass media are the informational veins and sinews of government. The press translates for the people what the government does, and strives to keep the government officials and members of Congress abreast of what is happening outside their often isolated and insulated worlds. A copy of the *Washington Post* is on the desk of every member of Congress each day, and is avidly read by congressional aides, who are immersed in the political games of Capitol Hill. Moreover, members care particularly about their image in their local and statewide newspapers. Members of the Florida delegation eagerly follow press accounts of their activities in the *Miami Herald* and *St. Petersburg Times*.

Each member of Congress has a press secretary and aide to handle relations with both the national and local reporters. The press, though it often views itself as in an adversary relationship to government, there is in fact often a close and friendly relationship between the press aides of congressmen and the reporters with whom they deal. The accounts of members' activities in statewide and local newspapers are generally favorable. Local newspapers in particular rarely have reporters on the scene in Washington, and rely upon legislators' press releases for information. Such releases always picture the congressman or senator in glowing phrases.

Members of Congress are interested in the national press and television for increasing their power within Congress, while they rely upon the state and local press and media to create a favorable personal image for reelection. Favorable coverage in the *New York Times* or the *Washington Post* boosts a congressman's or senator's reputation for power in Washington, but it is not seen by members as particularly important in gaining votes back home. Coverage by national network television, however, may serve the dual purposes of power within Congress and reelection because state and local constituents are always a part of the viewing audience.

Because the press is vital in achieving both internal power and reelection goals, members often seek to do that which is newsworthy in order to be covered by the press. In the past, senators such as Joseph McCarthy of Wisconsin, John McClellan of Arkansas, and Estes Kefauver of Tennessee gained reputations for power within and outside of Washington by their nationally televised investigations of communism, racketeers, and the drug industry, respectively. During the Vietnam War Arkansas senator W. F. Fulbright became a leading figure in foreign policy through nationally televised hearings by the Senate Foreign Relations Committee, which he chaired. The national press focuses more on the Senate than the House in its quest for newsworthy drama. The Senate Foreign Relations Committee is a favorite beat for ambitious reporters, as are the congressional committees with jurisdiction over the armed services and intelligence activities.

The multifaceted environment of Congress, characterized by pluralistic governmental and private interests impinging upon the legislature, buttresses the individualism and personalized power on Capitol Hill. Bicameralism fragments the legislature, and the separation of powers guarantees legislative independence from executive control and the dispersion of administrative agencies that have become significant underpinnings of decentralized committee power in Congress. Although the Supreme Court may hold congressional legislation to be unconstitutional, it has no direct role in the activities of Congress. The lack of disciplined parties, the pluralism of special interests, and the vagueness of public opinion fortify a decentralized legislature. Interest groups in particular demand representation in Congress, which they achieve as committees are created with jurisdiction over the interests of particular groups. Finally, the needs of a national and vast state and local press, which are entrepreneurial as reporters constantly seek to outdo their peers, nicely fit in with the political entrepreneurial activities of members and aides as they seek to buttress their individual power enterprises within Congress and at the grass roots.

The Functions of Congress

The Constitution gave Congress a variety of functions, and political custom has expanded these to make the modern legislature as complex in tasks as it is in organization, procedures, and environment.

LAW MAKING. As Article 1 opens, the Constitution provides, "All legislative powers herein granted shall be vested in a Congress of the United States, which shall consist of a Senate and House of Representatives." Although the president was given the veto power over congressional legislation, which could be overridden only by a two-thirds vote of both branches of Congress, the Constitution unequivocally delegates primary law-making authority to the Congress. In recognition of this law-making function, members are referred to as "legislators."

In exercising the legislative function members pass bills that have a *general* effect upon the community as a whole, binding citizens to obey the statute. Legislation is *prospective*, applying to future rather than past conduct. Legislation is based upon political values as well as factual judgments.

Much of the activity of Congress is legislative work, but in fact very few bills are passed. Most members' activities have only indirect connections to legislation that is finally passed. In an average Congress approximately 15,000 bills and resolutions are introduced by members, of which fewer than 1,000 are finally passed. More than 5,000 committee meetings and hearings are conducted in an average two-year session, but only a small percentage of such activity results in reported legislation and even less in final passage of a bill. Legislative output in relation to legislative work is very low on Capitol Hill.

Much of the legislative work of the modern Congress consists of authorization and appropriations bills, the passage of which is required for the continued functioning of government programs. Authorizing legislation establishes government programs and usually places a ceiling on expenditures that can be made to finance them. Appropriations bills specify the levels of money outlays within the boundaries that have been set by the authorization bills. Authorization and appropriations bills are the core of much of the legislative process.

The founding fathers were careful to provide that the legislative function would be exercised only by representatives of the people in the House and of the states in the Senate.

THE REPRESENTATIVE FUNCTION. The House, collectively, represents the people more directly than does the Senate. With admitted exaggeration, Ohio Congressman Charles A. Vanik, who represented the 22nd district of Ohio, encompassing the suburbs of Cleveland, from 1954 to 1980, referred to the Senate as a body that primarily represented "trees and cows." [27] The congressman was only half facetiously emphasizing an increasingly significant reality in American politics, that the Senate, due to population shifts and the constitutional requirement that there be two senators from each state, has become a highly "unrepresentative" body when measured against the standard of one person–one vote. The House, since the Supreme Court's decision in *Wesberry v. Sanders*, in 1964, is required to be apportioned on the basis of the one person–one vote rule, which obliges state legislatures after each census to draw congressional district lines so that each district will contain equal numbers of voters.

The representative function, however, is not simply carried out by equal apportionment of legislative districts. The founding fathers recognized the different forms and styles of representation as they constructed the bicameral legislature and assigned popular representation to the House and state representation to the Senate. Congress was not simply designed to represent the people, but was to take state interests equally into account.

The representative styles that are embedded in the Constitution are those commonly referred to as *delegate* and *trustee*. The representative acting as a delegate of the people transforms popular demands into government action. As trustee, however, the legislator takes into account the national interests as well as broader constituency interests that may or may not coincide with the particular demands of voters. Under the Constitution, the House was to be the delegate of popular interests and the Senate both the delegate of the states and the trustee of the national interest. In addition to the delegate and trustee functions, political scientists have defined an additional legislative style called *politico*. The legislator acting as a politico tends to strike a balance between the delegate and trustee styles.

[27] Vanik's remarks were made at a symposium on Congress held at Boston College, January 30, 1981.

In exercising their legislative function, members of Congress often find themselves in a quandary. It would be difficult to find a member of either the House or the Senate who would claim that his or her actions were simply knee-jerk reactions to constituents' demands.[28] Voting decisions by congressmen, like their other pursuits on Capitol Hill, defy easy description and placement in neat categories.[29] Unequivocal mandates for action rarely materialize. In carrying out their *legislative* responsibilities congressmen and senators must use their own judgment to balance what they consider to be the interests of their constituencies with the national interest.

The representative function is performed not only on legislation but also on casework, involving congressional staff in dealing with individual problems constituents are having with the government. Both representatives and senators have local offices staffed by aides who deal exclusively with constituents' problems that, for example, may bring up the failure of government to pay benefits on time, eligibility for government benefits, burdensome government regulations, and matters of immigration and naturalization. Casework involves congressional aides in direct representation of individual constituents' interests.

The role of Congress as a representative of local and state constituencies buttresses another of its major constitutional functions, which is to act as a check upon the president.

CONGRESS AS A CHECK ON THE PRESIDENT. Embattled House Speaker Tip O'Neill chastised the House for blindly accepting President Reagan's budget program, which, the Speaker felt, could well end up being a disaster for the nation. The House, declared O'Neill, had the constitutional and political responsibility for being the nation's lawgiver independently of the president. Never in his long House career, concluded O'Neill, had he seen such an acquiescent body, a

---

28 The little survey evidence we have on representational styles on Capitol Hill suggests that most members identify themselves either as politicos or trustees. See, for example, Roger H. Davidson, *The Role of the Congressman* (New York: Pegasus, 1969), pp. 117–122. See also Warren E. Miller and Donald E. Stokes, "Constituency Influence in Congress," *American Political Science Review*, 57 (March 1963), pp. 45–56.

29 The complexity of voting decisions is documented in John W. Kingdon, *Congressmen's Voting Decisions*, 2nd ed. (New York: Harper and Row, 1981).

condition made more ironic because it was controlled by the Democrats while the White House was Republican.

The important role of Congress as a check upon the president is not greatly emphasized outside of Capitol Hill. Predictably, most presidents desire a cooperative Congress, and attack legislative obstruction of presidential programs as against the national interest. Presidents often attempt to deal with recalcitrant Congresses by going directly to the American people for support in their struggle with Congress. President Woodrow Wilson toured the nation in his unsuccessful attempt to gain Senate ratification of the Treaty of Versailles in 1919. Wilson was convinced that he was right, and that Senate adversaries led by Republican conservative Henry Cabot Lodge were wrong. President Franklin D. Roosevelt frequently addressed the American people by radio in "Fireside Chats," both to explain and to marshal support for the New Deal. The emergency of the Depression, stated Roosevelt, demanded swift action under the leadership of the White House. The responsibility of Congress was not to check the president but to secure rapid passage of the president's program. After Roosevelt, presidents from Harry Truman to Ronald Reagan, in varying degrees and ways, challenged Congress to follow the national interest as the White House defined it.

President Harry S Truman, who had himself lambasted Congress on more than one occasion for failing to follow the right course of action set by the White House, recognized in his memoirs that "The most important thought expressed in our Constitution is that the power of government shall always remain limited, through the separation of powers. This means that each of the three branches of the government — the Legislative, the Judicial, and the Executive — must jealously guard its position. This jealous concern is a good thing. When I was a Senator, I was always anxious to see the rights and the prerogatives of the Congress preserved. If I had ever held judicial office, I would have considered it my duty to keep alert to any possible interferences with the independence of the judiciary. As President, it was my duty to safeguard the constitutional position of the office I held — the presidency of the United States." [30]

It is the constitutional prerogative of the Congress to be the primary legislative body for the nation, a responsibility that it should

[30] Harry S Truman, *Memoirs*, vol. 2: *Years of Trial and Hope* (Garden City, N.Y.: Doubleday, 1956), p. 453.

not relinquish to the president. The White House is always an outstanding source of legislative proposals and helps to set the agenda of
Congress, but it remains an external force in congressional politics.
Except during unusual periods of crisis, Congress has generally fulfilled its responsibility for acting independently of the president and,
if necessary, of checking what it considers to be ill-considered presidential action. Richard M. Nixon, admittedly an extreme case, found
his imperial presidency brought abruptly to an end when he was
forced to resign under the threat of a congressional impeachment
and an almost certain conviction for "High Crimes and Misdemeanors." The resurgent Congress of the post-Nixon years failed to pass
much of the presidential programs of the Ford and Carter administrations. President Reagan found that even with his own party controlling the Senate he had to engage in extraordinary lobbying to
persuade Congress to his point of view on important aspects of his
program, including budgetary cuts and taxation.

The role of Congress in the separation-of-powers system, like its
legislative and representative functions, is essentially constitutional
in origin and character. Congress performs additional functions that
relate to but also go beyond its constitutional responsibilities.

OVERSIGHT OF ADMINISTRATION. The growth of the federal bureaucracy, administering hundreds of programs under statutory authority,
has given Congress great responsibility for overseeing administrative
implementation of its policies. The importance of administrative
oversight has been recognized in various congressional statutes, including the Legislative Reorganization Acts of 1940 and 1970. These
laws charge congressional committees with the responsibility for
engaging in oversight activities of programs under their jurisdictions.

Administrative oversight by congressional committees is particularly
important because administrative agencies are a major independent
law-making force. In creating agencies Congress frequently delegates
essential legislative authority to them, to make what are in effect
new laws to fill in the details of congressional statutes that frequently
are relatively vague. Law making by administrative agencies is called
rule making, and the volumes upon volumes of administrative rules
greatly exceed in quantity the volume of congressional statutes. The
bureaucracy has become far more than a simple adjunct of Congress,
for in many areas of public policy it is a law-making branch equivalent to Congress itself.

The purpose of administrative oversight is to ensure that administrative rule making and other forms of policy implementation are consistent with congressional intent. In statutory areas of relative specificity, such as social security, veterans' benefits, and various distributive policies such as government subsidies to farmers and businesses, the discretion of administrative agencies is reduced. The agencies are directed to carry out programs that Congress has outlined in some detail. In the regulatory realm, however, Congress often passes the burden of reconciling group conflict on to the bureaucracy by charging administrative agencies with implementing "the public interest, convenience, and necessity." Such vague legislative standards leave the agencies with virtually complete discretion to do as they choose. Congressional oversight in the regulatory realm is extraordinarily difficult, because in effect there is no clear legislative intent; otherwise it would have been written into the law. Oversight of regulatory policies must be ad hoc, where members of congressional committees are forced to guess at the intent of the sponsors and backers of regulatory legislation in the past. Such oversight generally reflects the current subjective views of the legislative overseers on what should constitute good regulatory policy.

Although oversight of administration is recognized in theory to be one of the most important activities of Congress, in fact there is little incentive on Capitol Hill to spend time in separate oversight hearings in an attempt to control the bureaucracy. More important to congressmen than oversight hearings are hearings and other activities pertaining to appropriations, authorizations, and development of new legislation. Oversight hearings themselves infrequently become the vehicles for new legislation. Most members of Congress do not see oversight as a useful way to advance their legislative careers, reelection prospects, or good public policy.

Another difficulty in carrying out oversight is that effective surveillance of the bureaucracy requires Congress to be in a more adversarial relationship to administrative agencies than it generally is. The committees charged with exercising the most important oversight of agencies are those within whose jurisdiction the agencies fall, and these are the very committees which handle "their" agencies with kid gloves. If oversight hearings are held they are more friendly than adversary. The chairmen of the Armed Services committees, for example, are not interested in using oversight hearings to undermine the power and prestige of the Defense Department. Senate Labor and Human Resources committee members, and their counterparts on the House Education and Labor Committee, have no incentive to rein in the Labor and the Health and Human Services Departments, which are within their legislative jurisdictions. Perhaps the most effective oversight activities of Congress are conducted by the Government Operations Committee of the House, and the Governmental Affairs Committee of the Senate, which do not have vested-power interests in maintaining close and cozy relationships with administrative agencies.

INVESTIGATION. Investigative hearings, commonly held, for example, by the House Government Operations Committee and the Permanent Investigations Subcommittee of Governmental Affairs in the Senate, as well as by other special committees, are directed at discovering fraud, waste, mismanagement, and inefficiency generally within government and violations of the law within the government and private sectors. Texas Democrat Jack Brooks, for example, while chairman of the House Government Operations Committee, constantly held hearings to ferret out waste and inefficiency in government agencies and departments, ranging from the General Services Administration that is the supply agency for the bureaucracy, to the Defense Department. Investigative hearings may be a form of oversight for government agencies, but generally investigations are pointed more than are oversight hearings at discovering and remedying particular problems of inefficiency and unlawful conduct than at reviewing the implementation of programs as specified by legislative intent.

Because congressional investigations often do not relate to the development or implementation of legislation, a question may be raised about the appropriate use of investigative techniques by congressional committees. In conducting investigations, committees can subpoena witnesses and recommend that they be cited for contempt of Congress if they fail to respond to questions.

Can investigative committees conduct "witch hunts" that are apparently unrelated to the constitutional responsibility of Congress to legislate? The Supreme Court has limited the reach of the investigative powers of Congress and required congressional committees under certain circumstances to respect the civil liberties and rights of witnesses as they are stated in the Bill of Rights. The Court first limited the investigative powers of Congress in *Kilbourn* v. *Thompson* (1881), which had resulted in conviction of a witness before a congressional investigating committee because of his failure to testify on the financial dealings of Jay Cook and Company. The Compulsory Testimony Act of 1857 made it a crime for persons subpoenaed by Congress or one of its committees to refuse to testify or answer questions. Overturning the conviction under the Act in the Kilbourn case, the Court held that Congress does not have a "general power of making inquiry into the private affairs of the citizen," [31] and that the investigative authority of Congress must be limited to matters over which it has jurisdiction. In the Kilbourn case the Court was particularly bothered that the resolution authorizing the investigation did not mention legislation that might result from the inquiry.

After the Kilbourn decision the Court sustained congressional investigations provided they had a legislative purpose or clearly pursued a legitimate end, such as oversight of administration. In the 1927 case of *McGrain* v. *Daugherty* the Court found no legislative purpose in a challenged congressional investigation that had resulted in arrest of a witness who had refused to testify, but upheld the congressional action on the ground that the subject matter of the investigation, the Teapot Dome scandals, implicated the administration of the Justice Department, which was legitimately within the jurisdiction of Congress.

The Court confronted far-reaching problems about the proper scope of congressional investigations because of the probes of the House Committee on Unamerican Activities, created in 1938, and the investigations of Wisconsin Republican Senator Joseph McCarthy, who used his chairmanship of the Senate Government Operations Committee in 1953 to expose what he claimed was widespread Communist activity within and outside of government. Because the Communist investigations had overtones of political repression, First Amendment questions were raised from many quarters, including the American Civil Liberties Union. Moreover, because the result of testimony on Communist activities could have dire consequences for witnesses, they claimed that their right to protection against self-incrimination under the Fifth Amendment should be upheld.

The Court considered the rights of witnesses before congressional committees and the reach of congressional authority to investigate Communist activities in *Watkins* v. *United States* (1957). Watkins had been convicted of contempt because of his refusal to testify fully

---

[31] Kilbourn v. Thompson, 103 U.S. 168, 169 (1881).

before the House Unamerican Activities Committee, declining to testify about the activities of former Communist Party members. Chief Justice Earl Warren wrote the opinion for the Court, which emphasized from the start that the power of Congress to conduct investigations "is inherent in the legislative process. That power is broad. It encompasses inquiries concerning the administration of existing laws as well as proposed or possibly needed statutes." [32] Warren continued, "It is unquestionably the duty of all citizens to cooperate with the Congress in its efforts to obtain the facts needed for intelligent legislative action. It is their unremitting obligation to respond to subpoenas, to respect the dignity of the Congress and its committees and to testify fully with respect to matters within the province of proper investigation. This, of course, assumes that the constitutional rights of witnesses will be respected by the Congress as they are in a court of justice." [33]

Warren concluded, however, that the circumstances of Watkins's conviction violated his constitutional right. First, the authorizing resolution for the Committee on Unamerican Activities was too broad and vague to permit the Court to determine the proper boundaries of the committee's jurisdiction. The committee's charge allowed it to roam freely and with discretion to investigate the political activities of citizens without regard to a legislative end. More important, a witness appearing before the committee, who was subject to criminal sanctions for failure to answer its questions, "is entitled to have knowledge of the subject to which the interrogation is deemed pertinent. That knowledge must be available with the same degree of explicitness and clarity that the due process clause requires in the expression of any element of a criminal offence. The 'vice of vagueness' must be avoided here as in all other crimes." [34] The committee, concluded Warren, had failed to clarify adequately the subject to which the questions asked of the witness were pertinent.

Although the decision of the Court in the Watkins case seemed on its face to question the constitutionality of the House Unamerican Activities Committee, the Court in *Barenblatt* v. *United States* (1959), with Chief Justice Warren dissenting with Justices Black and Douglas, failed to adhere strictly to what seemed to be the Watkins

[32] Watkins v. United States, 354 U.S. 178, 187 (1957).
[33] Watkins v. United States, p. 187.
[34] Watkins v. United States, p. 208.

precedent. The Court upheld the conviction of Barenblatt under the Compulsory Testimony Act for refusing to answer questions by members of the House Unamerican Activities Committee. In presenting his case to the Supreme Court, Barenblatt relied upon the Watkins opinion, arguing that the committee had no authority to conduct investigations into Communist activities. The Court ruled that the mandate of the committee was proper, and that its questions to Barenblatt were pertinent to a legitimate inquiry. In a tone of self-restraint, the Court stated, "So long as Congress acts in pursuance of its constitutional power, the judiciary lacks authority to intervene on the basis of the motives which spurred the exercise of that power." [35]

It is difficult to fully reconcile the Barenblatt and Watkins opinions. Chief Justice Warren did question the authority of Congress to permit investigative committees to be charged as broadly as the Unamerican Activities Committee was. But the committee itself was not specifically ordered to be disbanded because of its vague mandate. The Court decided the Watkins case, as it did Barenblatt, on the technical ground of the pertinency of questions asked of the witnesses. By the time of Barenblatt, the Court was clearly unwilling to interfere with what it considered to be a reasonable exercise by Congress of its responsibilities.

The purpose of legislative investigations is primarily to inform members of Congress about matters pertinent to legislation or oversight. Although Congress clearly must inform itself, it also has a responsibility for informing and educating the public about government activities and proposed public policies.

INFORMING THE PUBLIC. California congressman Clem Miller, killed in an airplane crash while campaigning, had written a series of letters to his constituents that eloquently, accurately, and often poignantly described what it was like to be a freshman congressman. [36] "The job of a congressman in major degree," wrote Miller, "is communicating — making our political world understandable." [37] Above

---

[35] Barenblatt v. United States, 360 U.S. 109, 132 (1959).

[36] The letters were eventually published in book form. See Clem Miller, *Member of the House: Letters of a Congressman*, John W. Baker, ed. (New York: Charles Scribner's Sons, 1962).

[37] Miller, *Member of the House*, p. 62.

all, congressmen must communicate with their constituents to explain the complex world of Washington in which they live and work.

Congressmen inform and educate their constituents with newsletters and the innumerable personal visits they make to their districts. Congressmen and constituents are constantly informing and educating each other. Congressman Clem Miller wrote that during a "recent trip through the district I talked about many things. In line with my policy that the first duty of a congressman is to the area he represents, I attempted to make meaningful reports relating to the everyday concerns of the group I was addressing." [38] Miller continued, "I generally spoke of the coming session of Congress," and "I tried to report congressional realities as seen by a new member. Several times, before sympathetic audiences, I tried to define the limits of congressional abilities, and never with particular success." [39]

Though members of Congress recognize their responsibility for keeping the public informed, the demands of their job make it nearly impossible for them to spend much time educating their constituents. In Washington, the congressman is absorbed in committee hearings, meetings with staff and lobbyists, and the Washington social scene that includes ambassadors' parties and perhaps an occasional breakfast, reception, or state dinner at the White House. On any given day a congressman may very briefly play host to a visiting group of constituents, when a few pleasantries but little else are exchanged.

Outside Washington the schedules of congressmen and senators are also very tight, allowing them almost no time for serious interchange of ideas with constituents. Members race about from one location to another, attending breakfasts, lunches, and dinners, where more often than not they address their audiences not to educate them but to gain their support.

Individual legislators find it difficult to spend much time informing and educating the public, but Congress as an institution has taken steps that facilitate communication between Washington and the nation beyond. The proceedings of the House are now televised and in some localities, as in the metropolitan Washington area itself, may be seen on cable television. Portions of House debates, admittedly somewhat staged, are occasionally part of the evening news

[38] Miller, *Member of the House*, p. 70.
[39] Miller, *Member of the House*, p. 70.

programs of the three major networks. It is highly likely that the Senate will follow the House in allowing television cameras to cover floor proceedings.[40] Even more important, most committee proceedings are open to the public, so that visitors to the Capitol may, provided they arrive early, attend hearings, markup sessions, and even business meetings. The national press and network television also have a strong role in informing the public on daily Capitol Hill events.

The multiple responsibilities and functions of congressmen produce much tension among members who must decide how they are to allot their time. The congressional life is a hectic one, for legislators seek to advance their careers on Capitol Hill at the same time as they strive to build effective constituency organizations to ensure reelection. Members of the House, on the average, visit their districts weekly, usually leaving Washington on Friday and returning late Monday while Congress is in session. Interspersed through the year are many congressional recesses, called "district work weeks" in the House, allowing incumbents to spend more time among constituents. The constituent world, though external to Congress, touches upon and helps to shape the Washington activities of many members, particularly those from marginal districts where incumbents can expect to face strong challenges.

The world outside Congress includes, along with constituents, a powerful Washington political establishment that acts in many respects as a more important force upon Capitol Hill than the voters back home. The linkages between Congress on the one hand and bureaucrats and lobbyists on the other are particularly strong. Astute legislators attempt to cultivate contacts within the bureaucracy and interest groups to help them achieve both power and status in Congress and often as a vital aid to reelection as well.

[40] Television coverage of the House is restricted to the Speaker's podium and a dais below from which members address the House. The television cameras are not permitted under House rules to sweep the chamber, avoiding the embarrassment of catching members asleep, reading newspapers, or otherwise acting in a less decorous manner than is considered desirable to project a proper House image to the public.

PART
II

Inside Congress

CHAPTER THREE

Committees:
Little Legislatures of Capitol Hill

Committees are the focus of power and the major force behind legislation on Capitol Hill. This exchange, between Texas Senator John Tower and Rhode Island Senator John Pastore during a debate over antitrust legislation, makes the point vividly.

MR. TOWER: There is no popular demand for this legislation.

MR. PASTORE: How do you know? Did you talk to the people of the state of New York? Did you talk to the people of the state of Pennsylvania? Who did you talk to? A few oil men down there in Texas?

MR. TOWER: Whom did *you* talk to? How many people have communicated with *you* demanding this legislation?

MR. PASTORE: Who are you trying to kid?

MR. TOWER: Who has demanded it?

MR. PASTORE: Who has demanded it?

MR. TOWER: Yes.

MR. PASTORE: Why, the committees of this Congress! [1]

CHARACTER OF COMMITTEES

Committees in the United States Congress are unlike those in any other national legislature in the world. The lack of disciplined political parties within and outside of Congress not only makes it possible,

[1] Rochelle Jones and Peter Woll, *The Private World of Congress* (New York: Free Press, 1979), pp. 76–77.

but also encourages legislators to carve out their own political careers in any way they can. The quest for personal power on Capitol Hill is mostly responsible for the uniqueness of the system, in which committees are indeed little legislatures, often with exclusive jurisdiction over segments of public policy. Committees and even subcommittees exist in a world of their own. Their chairmen determine when and if they will meet, legislation that will be taken up, investigations that are to be conducted, or oversight proceedings that they will carry out. The chairmen decide who will testify in committee hearings. Committees have almost complete discretion to determine the content of legislation that will be reported out and placed on an appropriate legislative calendar for consideration on the floor, although the leadership in both the House and the Senate and the House Rules Committee become a critical part of the legislative process once bills are reported from committees.

The major or standing committees of Congress, those which by a vote of the House or Senate have been created permanently and continue from one congressional session to the next, have the authority to set up their own subcommittees, which greatly outnumber the parent committees. (See Tables 3.1 and 3.2.) The power of both standing committees and subcommittees depends in large part upon the political skills of their chairmen and the astuteness of their staffs.

The Chairman's Power

A committee chairmanship means many things to a member. It is a symbol of power, a base from which a reputation for power can be built. Louisiana Senator Russell Long became a Capitol Hill legend in the 1970s when he was chairman of the powerful Senate Finance Committee. He constantly upstaged and outmaneuvered his Senate colleagues when they attempted to interfere in his domain. Long let it be known that only he and his committee would determine the content of tax legislation, which vitally affected nearly all areas of public policy.

Even though Long frustrated some of his fellow senators, particularly those such as Edward Kennedy who had a more liberal bent, he received their accolades when he did battle with the House in conference. Long's House counterpart, the chairman of the Ways and Means Committee, guarded the constitutional prerogative of

Table 3.1

Number and Type of House Committees,
Eighty-fourth through Ninety-seventh Congresses, 1955–1982

Congress	Standing committees	Subcommittees of standing committees	Select and special committees	Subcommittees of select and special committees	Joint committees	Subcommittees of joint committees
84th (1955–56)	19	83	2	5	10	11
90th (1967–68)	20	133	1	6	10	15
92d (1971–72)	21	120	3	8	8	15
94th (1975–76)	22	151	3	4	7	17
96th (1979–80)	22	149[a]	5	8	4	5
97th (1981–82)	22	132	3	7	4	6

[a] Includes nine budget task forces and the Welfare and Pension Plans Task Force (of the Subcommittee on Labor Management Relations).

Sources: Compiled from information taken from yearly volumes of Brownson, Congressional Staff Directory; and Congressional Quarterly, Congressional Quarterly Almanac. From Norman J. Ornstein et al., Vital Statistics on Congress (Washington, D.C.: American Enterprise Institute, 1982), p. 98. Reprinted by permission.

Table 3.2

Number and Type of Senate Committees,
Eighty-fourth through Ninety-seventh Congresses, 1955–1982

Congress	Standing committees	Subcommittees of standing committees	Select and special committees	Subcommittees of select and special committees	Joint committees	Subcommittees of joint committees
84th (1955–56)	15	88	3	6	10	11
90th (1967–68)	16	99	3	12	10	15
92d (1971–72)	17	123	5	13	8	15
94th (1975–76)	18	140	6	17	7	17
96th (1979–80)	15	91	5	10	4	5
97th (1981–82)	15	94	5	12	4	6

Sources: Compiled from information taken from yearly volumes of Brownson, *Congressional Staff Directory*; *Congressional Quarterly, Congressional Quarterly Almanac*; Walter Oleszek, "Overview of the Senate Committee System," paper prepared for the Commission on the Operation of the Senate, 1977; and the *Washington Monitor, Congressional Yellow Book*. From Norman J. Ornstein et al., *Vital Statistics on Congress* (Washington, D.C.: American Enterprise Institute, 1982), p. 99. Reprinted by permission.

the House to originate revenue legislation. The chairman of the Ways and Means Committee is considered in the House to be one of its principal representatives to the outside world, and particularly one of its most important team players in the constant battle with the Senate over tax policy. For years Long had been eclipsed by Ways and Means chairman Wilbur Mills (D, Ark.), whose knowledge of tax policy and of House politics made him a formidable foe in conference. Mills's alcoholism drove him to indiscretions, including a bath in the Tidal Basin at the Jefferson Memorial with a stripper nicknamed "The Argentine Firecracker," whom he also joined on the stage of a burlesque theater in Boston. These antics ended his political career, but his replacement, Al Ullman of Oregon, found that he was no match for Long. Committee chairmanships mean power only when they are in skilful hands.

STAFF POWER. Staff directors and other upper-echelon aides frequently determine the course and effectiveness of committees in the broader legislative process. Massachusetts Senator Edward Kennedy, for example, is widely known on Capitol Hill for the skill and aggressiveness of his staff. When he was chairman of the Health Subcommittee and the Administrative Practice and Procedure Subcommittee, his staff dictated most of the investigative and legislative activities that were undertaken. Kennedy's reputation for power in health legislation, and as a leading proponent of airline deregulation, were the result of an expert and politically talented staff. Committee chairmen use their staffs not only to enhance their power within Congress, but also to assist in their campaigns for reelection.

PERQUISITES. The power of committee chairmen extends beyond influence over legislation and staff. Foreign travel, for example, is an important perquisite (perk) of most committee chairmen, who have large travel budgets at their disposal. In 1980, House committees spent $2.5 million on foreign travel and the Senate reported a total travel expenditure of $272,435.[2] The House Foreign Affairs and Armed Services Committees each spent more on travel in 1980 than the entire Senate.[3] Not only chairmen, but members, too, engage in

[2] *Congressional Quarterly Weekly Report*, vol. 39, no. 24 (August 22, 1981), p. 1543.
[3] Foreign Affairs, $450,992; Armed Services, $303,909.

extensive foreign travel at government expense, but it is the chairmen who must approve of the trips. One House subcommittee chairman with long seniority pointed out, "As a chairman you can choose where and when you want to go on foreign trips. When I first got here I wondered how this was done, and now I know. If I want to go any-where, I simply instruct my staff to find a plausible reason and then we go." [4]

New York Representative Stephen Solarz, a member of the House Foreign Affairs Committee, became chairman of its Africa Subcom-mittee and later switched to become chairman of the Asian and Pacific Affairs Subcommittee. He has taken so many foreign trips at government expense that the *New York Post* labeled him the "Junket King." Solarz, who outdistanced his House colleagues in foreign travel long before he became a subcommittee chairman, nevertheless had even more reason to travel as a chairman than he did before. During one session, Solarz made four trips lasting three weeks each, to twenty-five countries in all parts of the world, including the Mid-dle East, Africa, Europe, the Soviet Union, China, Japan, and India. Solarz, who has a reputation for hard work while traveling and in Congress, is quick to reply to critics who accuse him of junketing that his trips are not vacations. In response to a critical account of his Caribbean travels in the *New York Post* in 1981, the congressman said, "Throughout my entire stay in Salvador and Guatemala, wher-ever we went, we went in a caravan of three cars with a dozen secur-ity personnel armed with submachine guns. If you were going to go on a vacation, this is the last place one would have gone at this par-ticular time." [5]

COURTSHIP. Committee chairmanships also bring with them power beyond Capitol Hill. California Representative George Brown, Jr., recalled with pleasure that when he became chairman of the Science, Research, and Technology committee his position gave him greatly improved communication with the top echelon on the executive branch as "Secretaries, Assistant Secretaries, Deputy and Undersecre-taries are almost always available to come over to your office to chat." [6] He added, "I felt highly flattered when [Department of En-

[4] Jones and Woll, *Private World of Congress*, p. 176.
[5] *Congressional Quarterly Weekly Report*, vol. 39, no. 24 (August 22, 1981), p. 1544.
[6] Jones and Woll, p. 195.

ergy Secretary] Jim Schlesinger called me at home and told me he was going to make the appointment of an assistant secretary for the environment, whose responsibilities fall within the jurisdiction of my subcommittee." [7] The congressman's experience of power is common to other committee chairmen who find, especially in the Senate, that they are consulted by the White House before political appointments are made to agencies under the jurisdiction of their committees. Moreover, all chairmen are involved in continuing consultation between the executive branch and Congress. Committee chairmen speak for Congress and express its informal intent in matters of concern to executive departments and agencies.

Committee chairmen join congressional party leaders at the ceremonies that take place when the president signs bills in the White House Oval Office or the Rose Garden. The chairmen often prominently display in their offices the pens handed to them by the president as a tribute to their power. Apart from bill-signing ceremonies, chairmen are invited to state dinners and breakfasts with the president at the White House.

Private organizations and foreign governments invite chairmen to address them in return for large honoraria, and they attend meetings and conferences with all expenses paid. House chairmen are particularly distinguished from other members by special treatment from private groups, which also give significantly more in campaign contributions to them than to ordinary members. Although committee and subcommittee chairmanships are important in the Senate, they do not distinguish members as much as they do in the House. Because there are only one hundred senators in contrast to four hundred thirty-five congressmen, and because a Senate seat is considered to be the highest political office with the exception of the presidency, all senators are treated respectfully within and outside of the body.

EVOLUTION OF COMMITTEES

The framers of the Constitution did not foresee the importance that committees would have in the legislative process. After all, the early Congresses scarcely contained enough members to form committees, although a large number of ad hoc committees were created to draft bills during the formative years. The House Committee of the Whole,

[7] Jones and Woll, p. 195.

however, which is the entire membership of the House sitting as a committee, strictly dominated the legislative process and its small number of select committees. The Senate, too, did not have standing committees as we know them today and, like the House, established temporary committees to do legislative tasks and disbanded them once their work was finished. The twenty-six-member Senate (the first Senate had only twenty-two members because two states had not yet ratified the Constitution) was of the same size as the Senate committees are today, and like the Committee of the Whole in the House, the Senate meeting as a whole conducted the legislative business at hand. Committees in both the early House and Senate were merely adjuncts of the legislative process.

Committees were also less important in early Congresses because of the rapid turnover of members. Washington, which became the nation's capital in 1800, was unattractive both physically and politically. Much of it was uninhabitable and dangerous. Legislators could and often did get lost, especially if they were well lubricated with whiskey, as they attempted to find their way along the twisting and turning dirt path between the Capitol and the White House. Washington weather then, as now, caused its inhabitants to flee in the summer. Congress did not hold regular summer sessions until air conditioning was installed after World War II.

Washington was also a distant place in a time when travel was not by jet, but by horse and carriage and barge. Travel that now takes hours took days and even weeks. Perhaps congressmen would have stayed in Washington in its early years if the political life of the city had been more challenging and rewarding. But the dismal façade of the city, its uncomfortable boarding houses, knee-deep mud, unpleasant weather, shantytowns, and a population of social and political outcasts made the city's and the nation's politics seem dismal as well. The kind of political careerism on Capitol Hill that gave committees and their chairmen prime importance when Woodrow Wilson wrote about Congress in 1885 was entirely absent in the opening decades of the century. Members served in Congress mostly as an unpleasant duty, and most happily returned home after serving one or two terms at most.[8] The isolation of the city, the difficulty of traveling even within it, and the lack of diversions beyond politics

---

[8] More than one-third of the members of Congress consistently failed to return after serving one term for most of the first half of the nineteenth century. See James Sterling Young, *The Washington Community 1800–1828* (New York: Columbia University Press, 1966), p. 90.

created an environment of political overkill that stupefied legislators. Commenting upon the Washington community at that time, James Sterling Young writes, "No less distinctive than the bleakness of its physical setting, was the pronounced antipathy of the governing group toward their community, their disparaging perceptions of their location, and their restiveness in their role as power-holders." The amateur legislators of the early Congresses did not see nobility in the location of power. Rather they disparaged politics in the strongest terms, as "a species of *mania*," "an unprofitable way of life," "at war with my natural taste, feelings, and wishes," a profession in which men "barter their hopes of an independent and peaceful old age for the temporary possession of . . . a bauble." [9] One former legislator summed up his feelings, "It is impossible to conceive the comfortlessness and desolation of feeling, the solitariness and depression of spirits and the constant tension in which [my] two years were passed [in Washington]." [10]

Growing Committee Importance

Committees and their chairmen grew important when Washington became a pleasanter place to live and national politics a more rewarding profession at the end of the nineteenth century. The seniority system and the power of committee chairmen to dominate the legislative process did not fully develop until well into the twentieth century. The seeds of careerism on Capitol Hill, which saw members returning in greater numbers, had been firmly planted when Woodrow Wilson wrote in 1885 in his famous *Congressional Government*, "By custom, seniority in congressional service determines the bestowal of the principal chairmanships [of committees]." [11] The future president wrote his book on Congress when he was a graduate student in political economy at Johns Hopkins University. When he visited Capitol Hill and sat in the galleries of the House and the Senate, he observed and was puzzled because very few legislators were on the floor. Where were they? Wilson's simple observation and question led to an investigation that produced an answer that was startling to many political novices at the time, but soon became common knowledge about Congress: The business of the legislature is con-

[9] Young, *Washington Community*, pp. 51–52.
[10] Young, pp. 51–52.
[11] Woodrow Wilson, *Congressional Government* (New York: Meridian, 1956), p. 82. Wilson's book was first published in 1885.

ducted off the floor in committees, which control the legislative process.

Wilson wrote about the House of Representatives that there are

> no authoritative leaders who are the recognized spokesmen of
> their parties. Power is nowhere concentrated; it is rather delib-
> erately and of set policy scattered amongst many small chiefs.
> It is divided up, as it were, into forty-seven seigniories, in each
> of which a standing committee is the court-baron and its chair-
> man lord-proprietor. These petty barons, some of them not a
> little powerful, but none of them within reach of the full
> powers of rule, may at will exercise an almost despotic sway
> within their own shires, and may sometimes threaten to con-
> vulse even the realm itself; but both their mutual jealousies
> and their brief and restricted opportunities forbid their com-
> bining, and each is very far from the office of common
> leader.[12]

The young Woodrow Wilson was fascinated with the autonomy of committee chairmen. "The chairman of a great committee like the Committee of Ways and Means stands," observed Wilson,

> at the sources of a very large and important stream of policy,
> and can turn that stream at his pleasure, or mix what he will
> with its waters; but there are whole provinces of policy in
> which he can have no authority at all. He neither directs, nor
> can often influence, those other chairmen who direct all the
> other important affairs of government. He, though the great-
> est of chairmen, and as great, it may be, *as any other one man
> in the whole governmental system*, is by no means at the head
> of the government. He is, as he feels every day, only a big
> wheel where there are many other wheels, some almost as big
> as he, and all driven, like himself, by fires which he does not
> kindle or tend.[13]

Wilson concluded that the House was "a disintegrate mass of jarring elements." [14] He judged the Senate as harshly as he did the House, finding that "It has those same radical defects of organization which weaken the House. Its functions also, like those of the House, are segregated in the prerogatives of numerous standing committees. In this regard Congress is all of a piece." [15]

---

12 Wilson, *Congressional Government*, p. 76.
13 Wilson, p. 142. Emphasis supplied.
14 Wilson, p. 145.
15 Wilson, p. 146.

The Congress described by Woodrow Wilson is in many respects the Congress of today. But modern committee chairmen have even more power, because they are chosen not, as in Wilson's time, by the Speaker but by the seniority system, which dictates that the most senior member of the majority party on a committee will become its chairman. Chairmen in both the House and the Senate must be approved by party caucuses, but in only a handful of cases have senior committee members been denied the ultimate political prize of the chairmanship.

Congressional customs and traditions, such as seniority and the division of the legislative process into hundreds of separate committee bailiwicks, have not only buttressed but dictated the power of chairmen and their panels. Wilson wrote, "The privileges of the standing committees are the beginning and end of the rules." [16] The extent of committee power rests in the exercise of it, but formal rules have both reflected and shaped committee power.

The rules of the House and the Senate have formally established committee jurisdictions, powers, and procedures. (See Table 3.3.) Congressional rules determine the number of standing, select, and special committees, and these committees in turn govern the creation of subcommittees. Powerful and often autonomous committees are buttressed by rules that give them exclusive jurisdiction over important areas of public policy along with the necessary powers to initiate and oversee the implementation of legislation.

House rules governing committees differ from those in the Senate, reflecting the different ways in which the two bodies conduct their legislative business. The House is larger and more formal than the Senate, which has accentuated the committees and helped to give subcommittees more power than they have in the Senate. Committees and subcommittees are the focus of power in the House.

HOUSE COMMITTEE ORGANIZATION AND PROCEDURES

Reasons for Creation of Committees

POLITICAL DEMANDS. House committees did not just happen. Many were created in response to the demands of interest groups for representation, combined with recognition of the importance of major

[16] Wilson, p. 62.

Table 3.3

House and Senate Committee Organization

House		
Exclusive committees	*Major committees*	*Nonmajor committees*
Appropriations	Agriculture	Budget
Ways and	Foreign Services	District of Columbia
Means	Banking	Government Operations
Rules	Finance and Urban	House Administration
	Affairs	Interior and Insular Affairs
	Education and Labor	Merchant Marine and
	Foreign Affairs	Fisheries
	Energy and Commerce	Post Office and Civil Service
	Judiciary	Science and Technology
	PublicWorks and	Small Business
	Transportation	Veterans' Affairs

Senate	
Major committees	*Minor committees*
Agriculture	Rules and Administration
Nutrition and Forestry	Veterans' Affairs
Appropriations	Aging
Armed Services	Intelligence
Banking	Small Business
Housing and Urban Affairs	Joint Economic Committee
Commerce	Joint Committee on Internal
Science and Transportation	Revenue Taxation
Energy and Natural Resources	
Environment and Public Works	
Finance	
Foreign Relations	
Governmental Affairs	
Human Resources and Judiciary	

areas in public policy. The committees on Interior and Insular Affairs
(1805), Veterans' Affairs (1813), Agriculture (1820), Banking, Finance, and Urban Affairs (established in 1865 as the Banking and
Currency Committee), Education and Labor (1867), Merchant Ma-

rine and Fisheries (1887), and Small Business (1942) fall into the category of panels that were created mainly in response to the demands and growing importance of outside interests.

INSTITUTIONAL NEEDS. Internal House politics and institutional needs have also spawned committees. The predecessor of the House Administration Committee, formed in 1789, was the first standing committee. The Committee of Ways and Means was created in 1795 to represent the important constitutional role of the House in the initiation of tax legislation. The powerful and prestigious House Appropriations Committee was created in 1865, representing not only the constitutional power of the purse that is shared equally between the House and the Senate, but also the special House role in initiating appropriations bills that has been conceded to it by *custom*.

The House Rules Committee, established in the first Congress in 1789 as a select or ad hoc panel that was authorized at the beginning of each new Congress, was made a standing committee in 1880. The Rules Committee is the legislative gatekeeper of the House. The committee's approval is required for important legislation to reach the floor, although it is possible to bypass the committee under certain circumstances. The Budget Committee, constituted in 1975, also performs the important institutional role of overseeing and coordinating the diverse and complicated budget process. Congressional committees tend to go their separate ways in the legislative process, which includes budget authorization and appropriations. The House Budget Committee and its counterpart in the Senate were established to strengthen the congressional budget process by integrating it. The committees have had only limited success, because the forces of disintegration on Capitol Hill tend to prevail over those of centralization of power.

The expansion of the executive branch led to creation of committees to oversee emerging departments and agencies. Often political pressures spawned committees on Capitol Hill before corresponding executive departments were formed, as with the committees on Agriculture, Education and Labor, and Interstate and Foreign Commerce. But it did not take outside political pressure to make Congress aware of the importance of establishing committees on Foreign Affairs, Military Affairs, and Naval Affairs, the latter two predecessors of the Armed Services Committee, in 1822. By that time the House had already set up a standing committee to deal with expenditures in executive departments, analogous to the contemporary Government Operations Committee.

Types of Committees

STANDING COMMITTEES. At the top of the committee hierarchy in the House are the major, or standing committees. They are permanent and deal with major areas of public policy and internal administration and procedures. Other panels as well may have great power, including both select committees and subcommittees. In the 97th Congress (1981–1982), there were three select and 138 subcommittees.

SELECT COMMITTEES. Appointed by the Speaker, select committees deal with special tasks. Once their work is completed they are supposed to disband; however, some select committees, such as Small Business, which for years was reappointed and recharged with each new session of Congress, have enough political backing to transform them into standing committees. The Select Committee on Aging, which continues to be appointed by the Speaker with a renewed mandate at each new session of Congress, seems to have acquired permanent status as the representative of tens of millions of senior citizens throughout the country. One fiery and colorful chairman, 82-year-old Florida Democrat Claude Pepper, had made the committee an effective voice in legislation affecting the elderly, although the committee itself does not have direct legislative jurisdiction.

SUBCOMMITTEES. The House exemplifies not only committee but subcommittee government. Among the more than 125 subcommittees are panels that approximate the power of the major standing committees. *Formally*, subcommittees are protected by a "Subcommittee Bill of Rights" that was adopted by the Democratic Caucus in 1973. Because the Caucus was a majority of the House, its rules applied to the entire body. Subcommittee chairmen outnumbered the chairmen of the standing committees by a wide margin, and had become a powerful political force in the House. Before 1973, however, they were formally subject to complete control by their parent standing committees. Committee chairmen seeking to aggrandize their power kept a tight rein on subcommittee budgets, staffs, and legislative jurisdiction. Moreover, standing-committee chairmen could control appointment of the chairmen and members of subcommittees.

The bill of rights, which went into effect in 1974, gave subcommittees the independent powers and resources they had so eagerly sought. The authority that standing-committee chairmen had traditionally exercised to select subcommittee chairmen was taken away and given to caucuses of the members of standing committees. Moreover, under the new bill of rights, the entire membership of the standing committees determined subcommittee jurisdiction and the party ratios on the subordinate panels. Subcommittees were also guaranteed budgets and staffs that allowed them to do their work. Legislation falling within the jurisdiction of subcommittees had to be delegated to them, replacing the former practice of giving standing-committee chairmen discretion to withhold legislation. Finally, each standing committee was required to create at least four subcommittees.

Arizona Congressman Morris Udall commented after the House changes that the real power in the body had now been transferred to subcommittee chairmen. Responding to a proposal made by the more junior members of the body that would have prevented full committee chairmen from chairing any subcommittees, Udall said, "You can't put [the real] power in the subcommittee, then prevent the full committee chairman from sharing in the action." [17] When the junior members of the Senate began proposing measures that copied some of the major provisions of the House Subcommittee Bill of Rights, the wily and experienced senior Senator Russell Long of Louisiana, looking over his shoulder at the House experience, echoed the views of many of the powerful chairmen of standing committees when he said, "I have seen what has happened when the chairman [of a standing committee] trespasses on the prerogatives of a subcommittee chairman. I have seen subcommittee chairmen point their finger in a chairman's face and say, 'You so-and-so, I will never speak to you again,' and keep that commitment for years. I do not want that [in the Senate], and nobody else wants it." [18]

The changes in the role of House subcommittees, giving them more nearly equal powers with standing committees in the legislative process, were part of broader modifications affecting committees that occurred in the Congresses of the 1970s.

[17] Jones and Woll, *Private World of Congress*, p. 217.
[18] Jones and Woll, p. 230.

Selection of Committee Members

The increased power of subcommittees represented a decline in the traditional powers of the senior members of the House, most of whom as standing-committee chairmen had ruled the body. That rule was challenged in the early 1970s as an influx of new members sought to make their mark on the legislative process. Moreover, the House leadership decided that its power, too, would be increased if the stranglehold of committee chairmen on legislation and other House activities was loosened. "The Speaker," said Oklahoma Congressman Carl Albert when he occupied the position, "feels the impact of the committee system in a particularly personal way as he attempts to fulfill his responsibilities to the House and to the nation." [19]

The power to appoint chairmen and control committee assignments is one of the most important in the House. Generally, the *informal* rule of seniority has dictated who will become the chairmen of both standing committees and subcommittees. House Democrats for decades gave to their representatives on the powerful Ways and Means Committee the authority to make Democratic committee assignments. Most members of the Ways and Means Committee had achieved great seniority themselves, and giving them control over committee assignments simply reinforced the senior power establishment of the House.[20]

LOOSENING THE GRIP OF SENIOR MEMBERS. The iron grip that senior Democrats had for a long time on House committees began to loosen in the 1970s with the influx of a greater than usual number of new members. Democratic congressmen wanted their congressional party to become more democratic in organization and procedures. Junior members simply wanted a larger share of the action that had always been controlled by senior and mostly southern Democrats. The senior clique of the Democrats in the House had not only frustrated new members by excluding them from the inner circles of power, but had also on more than one occasion thwarted Democratic Party

---

[19] U.S. Congress, House, "Committee Organization in the House," Hearings Before the Select Committee on Committees, 93rd Cong., 1st Sess. (1973), vol. 1 (Washington, D.C.: U.S. Government Printing Office, 1973), p. 4.

[20] The Republicans, who controlled the House for only four years, between 1933 and 1982, gave the power to appoint Republican committee members to a special committee on committees chaired by their floor leader.

leaders, especially the Speaker. The alliance between the emerging majority of newer members and the party leadership, who were well aware that over the long term their power depended upon the consent of a majority of their party in the House, was able to make changes in the early 1970s that diminished what had been the unchallenged power of the senior committee chairmen and the Democrats on the Ways and Means Committee.

For the first time in decades the Democratic Caucus was able to unite and use the principle of majority rule that prevails in all Democratic assemblies. Before the 1970s the fragmentation of power in the House had prevented any meaningful incursions upon the authority of committee chairmen. The seniority rule itself was and continues to be an informal way of resolving the leading question of who will become committee chairmen. The absence of party government on Capitol Hill, a system in which disciplined congressional parties would allocate chairmanships and assign members to committees, makes the seniority rule essential to the resolution of conflict.

The Democratic Caucus could not abolish the seniority rule, nor did it wish to, but it did reduce what had been the arbitrary power of committee chairmen to dominate their panels and determine the course of legislation. After taking away the authority to make committee assignments from the Democratic members of the Ways and Means Committee, the Caucus provided that the more representative Democratic Steering and Policy Committee would have the authority both to nominate chairmen and assign members. The decisions of the Steering and Policy Committee would have to be ratified by the Caucus. Moreover, standing-committee chairmen could chair in addition only one subcommittee. When the rule was adopted in 1971, subcommittee chairmanships were given for the first time to sixteen Democrats who had been elected since 1958. By 1975 members were limited to chairmanship of only one committee.

The battle over the power to make committee assignments, which resulted in giving more junior members greater opportunities to serve on committees of their choice, reflected the prevailing view of members that their political ambitions could be fulfilled only through assignment to committees that suited their interests. No longer could the small clique of Democrats on the Ways and Means Committee control the fate of their more junior colleagues. Not only was the Steering and Policy Committee more responsive to the

Caucus in making committee assignments, but all Democrats were guaranteed a major committee assignment and an important subcommittee post as well. Members have always recognized, as Congressman Clem Miller wrote, that "All House action springs from one committee or another." [21] Miller continued, "As newcomers, without organization, without the sense of trust and interdependence that comes from long association, we lack any locus of power. The interior lines of communication and strength are contained in the hands of those who have been here for many years." [22] Miller was commenting upon the House of the 1960s, which the newcomers of the 1970s modified to give themselves greater access to committee power. The result has been a "more decentralized, autonomous, and leadership-resistant set of standing committees." [23]

SERVING MEMBERS' GOALS. Members seek committee assignments to fulfill their legislative goals of reelection, power and influence within the House, or good public policy.[24] The goals are not mutually exclusive, for legislators always seek reelection at the same time as they strive for power and status on Capitol Hill. Members may use committee posts to advance all three goals. Regardless of the priority of members' goals, some committees continue to be the most sought after in the House because they arc perceived to be prestigious and powerful. Even under the new House rules that give the more junior members greater access to committees, they are by no means guaranteed their first choices.[25]

As Congress convened when Ronald Reagan took office, the usual scramble for committee assignments began. Many new members sought the Budget Committee, which had been an orphan in the past.

[21] Clem Miller, *Member of the House: Letters of a Congressman*, John W. Baker, ed. (New York: Scribner's, 1962), p. 97.

[22] Miller, *Member of the House*, p. 98.

[23] Christopher J. Deering and Steven S. Smith, "Majority Party Leadership and the New House Subcommittee System," in Frank H. Mackaman, ed., *Understanding Congressional Leadership* (Washington, D.C.: Congressional Quarterly Press, 1981), p. 261.

[24] Richard F. Fenno, Jr., *Congressmen in Committees* (Boston: Little, Brown, 1973), p. 1.

[25] See Charles Bullock, "Motivations for U.S. Congressional Committee Preferences," *Legislative Studies Quarterly* (May 1976), pp. 201–212; Malcolm Jewell and Cho Chui-hung, "Membership Movement and Committee Attractiveness in the U.S. House of Representatives," *American Journal of Political Science*, vol. 18, no. 2 (May 1974), pp. 433–441.

The campaign rhetoric and what was to become known as Reaganomics, however, placed budgetary policy at the top of the legislative agenda. The Budget Committee was seen by many new members in particular as an emerging power center. Significantly, the Democratic leadership wanted experienced and savvy legislators to control its side of the committee, and consequently the Steering and Policy Committee appointed no freshman Democrats to the Budget Committee. Reflecting the more conservative tone of Democratic budgetary politics, fiscal conservatives such as Phil Gramm of Texas, who was to become a leader of the Conservative Democratic Forum in opposition to the leadership, was appointed at the same time as the middle-of-the-road Democrat, James Jones of Oklahoma, was made chairman. The failure to appoint any freshman Democrats to the committee disappointed at least one House group, the Congressional Black Caucus, who had sponsored the newly elected black representative from the first district in Chicago, Harold Washington, to represent both the liberal and black views on the panel. Washington, however, who had initiated his campaign for the committee slot only five days before the meeting of the Democratic Caucus to decide committee positions, was unable to garner sufficient support to overturn the nominations of the Steering and Policy Committee.

House Republicans too recognized the growing importance of the Budget Committee. New York Congressman Jack Kemp, the leading House advocate of supply-side economics and a growing power in Republican politics both within and outside of the House, joined the committee. Four Republican freshmen considered themselves lucky to be given seats on the Budget panel by the Republican Committee on Committees.

PARTY RATIOS. The politics of committee assignments involves not only the choice of individual members, but also the determination of party ratios on the committees. Generally the balance between Democrats and Republicans on committees is the same as it is in the House. The majority party determines committee ratios, and sometimes fortifies its power on key committees by giving its members a larger percentage of committee seats than they would be entitled to on the basis of party ratios in the House. For example, though Democrats outnumbered Republicans in the House by five to four in the 97th Congress, the Democratic leadership established

ratios on the Rules and Ways and Means Committees that gave
their party members a two-to-one advantage, and also stacked the
Budget and Appropriations Committees by giving Democrats a three-
to-two edge in seats, a more favorable ratio than they had in the
House. The Republicans vainly attempted to sequester more seats
on the prestigious and powerful committees, but a concerted Democratic effort turned them back. The Republicans charged blatant
unfairness, but House Speaker Tip O'Neill responded that the Republican objections came from "a couple of windbags" who were
practicing "picayune politics." [26] "This Congress," said O'Neill with
a straight face, "has acted with more dignity and more fairness than
any I have ever seen." [27]

SELECTION POLITICS. "Hardball" politics always characterizes the
committee selection process, because the stakes are so high. Because
the seniority rule has generally been followed in the selection of
committee chairmen, political bloodshed has usually been avoided.
New York Democrat Emmanuel Celler, who served in the House for
fifty years (1923–1973), observed at the end of his career, "The
seniority system is the least objectionable of all systems for elevation
of men to chairmanships. We have tried in the history of Congress
all manner and kind of selection, and they have all been discarded
because they were not flawless, they were objectionable." [28] Nevertheless, as Sir John Acton observed in the nineteenth century, "Power
tends to corrupt; absolute power corrupts absolutely." Over the years,
legislators and House leaders outside the circles of power of committee chairmen felt that Lord Acton's maxim was a particularly apt
description of politics on Capitol Hill.

The changes in the House that shifted the nomination and selection of committee chairmen to the Steering and Policy Committee
and Democratic Caucus were a warning to committee chairmen
that they ruled by consent and not by decree. Committee and subcommittee chairmen would have to pay more attention to the interests and demands of committee members. As a warning to chairmen
in the future, the Democratic Caucus, which broadened the selection

[26] *Congressional Quarterly Weekly Report*, vol. 39, no. 5 (January 31, 1981),
p. 223.
[27] Ibid.
[28] *Congressional Quarterly Weekly Report*, vol. 31, no. 1 (January 6, 1973), p.
22.

process for chairmen, also deposed three of the most senior and powerful chairmen in the House, who collectively had served for more than one hundred years.[29] The three chairmen had run their committees arbitrarily, and had exhibited an unusual arrogance of power in the House. The unseating of the three chairmen on the ground that they had become too exclusive in the exercise of their power was unprecedented, for the seniority system had become firmly entrenched.[30]

CHAIRMANSHIP SELECTION. Although no standing-committee chairmen with seniority have been deposed since 1975, mainly because they have respected the interests of committee and subcommittee members, seniority has not automatically guaranteed subcommittee chairmanships. Texas Congressman Bob Eckhardt (D), for example, successfully challenged Virginian David Satterfield to become chairman of the Commerce Subcommittee on Consumer Protection. Satterfield was senior to Eckhardt, but the Texan won on a secret ballot of the full Interstate and Foreign Commerce Committee, 17 to 12.

The battle over the prize of the Health Subcommittee chairmanship in 1978 illustrated that members striving for the power and prestige of a subcommittee chairmanship would not let the seniority rule stand in their way. When Florida Congressman Paul Rogers (D), who had served as chairman of the Health Subcommittee for almost a decade, announced his retirement in 1978, Richardson Preyer (D, NC), was next in the seniority line for the chairmanship. The House Democratic leadership, including Speaker Tip O'Neill, Majority Leader Jim Wright, and Rules Committee Chairman Richard Bolling, strongly supported Preyer. The members of the Interstate and Foreign Commerce Committee, however, were the ones to determine who would become chairman of the Health Subcommittee. One of their members, Henry Waxman, who was serving his third term as representative of the 24th District of California, which included

[29] The three deposed Democratic chairmen were F. Edward Hebert (La.), Armed Services Committee; W. R. Poage (Texas), Agriculture Committee; and Wright Patman (Texas), Banking, Currency, and Housing Committee.
[30] Adam Clayton Powell (D, NY) was stripped of the chairmanship of the Education and Labor Committee in 1967 largely because of allegations of irregularities in the handling of committee funds.

Hollywood and much of the entertainment industry, decided to challenge Preyer for the chairmanship.

Waxman had always won his elections by large margins, his popularity being so great that he needed to spend little on his campaigns. He coasted into office in 1978, spending only $26,000 on his election. Though assured of reelection, Waxman knew that he would have to fight hard if he was to obtain a majority of the votes of his committee for the subcommittee chairmanship. He spent almost as much money on his campaign for the subcommittee post as he had for his reelection, distributing more than $24,000 of his own campaign funds to his committee colleagues to aid them in their 1978 reelection campaigns. The practice was questionable, but not illegal. Rules Committee Chairman Richard Bolling accused Waxman of trying to buy the Health Subcommittee chairmanship. Waxman won, 15 to 12, with seven members voting for him who had received his campaign contributions.[31]

Powers and Roles of House Committees in the Legislative Process

Committees perform most of the functions of Congress. They perform central legislative and representative roles. Most major committees have outside constituencies of interest groups that continually interact with them, providing support, advice, and criticism to help shape public policy. Committees such as Agriculture, Armed Services, Interstate and Foreign Commerce, Veterans, and Select Committee on Aging, represent private interests. The dispersion of committees has greatly increased the influence of outside groups on Capitol Hill.

Referral to Standing Committees

The Speaker, in consultation with the House parliamentarian, refers nearly all bills to the committees that have appropriate jurisdiction. Agricultural legislation goes to the Agriculture Committee, defense bills to the Armed Services Committee, and veterans' benefits legislation to the Veterans' Affairs Committee. Most legislation in the House is assigned to only one committee, although the Speaker may

---

31 The Eckhardt and Waxman stories are based on Jones and Woll, *Private World of Congress*, pp. 82–83.

make multiple referrals when a bill touches the jurisdiction of more than one committee. Legislation affecting personnel policies in the Defense Department falls automatically within the jurisdiction of the Armed Services Committee, but may also be referred to the Post Office and Civil Service Committee. President Carter's energy legislation, sent to the Hill in 1977, was divided among three powerful standing committees, Banking, Finance, and Urban Affairs; Interstate and Foreign Commerce (renamed Energy and Commerce in the 97th Congress); and Ways and Means. Moreover, Speaker Tip O'Neill created a Select Ad Hoc Energy Committee to oversee development of energy policy.

REFERRAL TO SUBCOMMITTEES. Usually the standing-committee chairman refers legislation to a subcommittee, which does most of the work on the bill. Before the 1973 Subcommittee Bill of Rights the standing-committee chairman had virtually complete discretion to control the flow of legislation to subcommittees. Chairmen could effectively kill legislation by refusing to bring it up for consideration before either the full committee or a subcommittee. The rule changes, however, required the consent of the full committee to prevent legislative referral to subcommittees.

Both the formal rules and the politics of the House reinforce the power of subcommittees in the legislative process.[32] In general, after legislation is referred, the subcommittee chairman will schedule hearings if he or she considers the legislation important enough to have a fair chance of passage through the obstacle course of the full committee, the Rules Committee, and on the floor. Subcommittee chairmen are well aware that they can make their legislative mark by successfully developing and guiding legislation to victory. Members are judged by their colleagues on how effective they have been in legislative work. After all, though thousands of bills are introduced in each session of Congress, only several hundred are finally passed. Legislators whose names are attached to the select number of bills that become law gain recognition and accolades not only from their colleagues, but beyond Capitol Hill as well.

[32] See Deering and Smith, "Majority Party Leadership and the New House Subcommittee System"; and Roger H. Davidson, "Subcommittee Government: New Channels for Policymaking," in Thomas E. Mann and Norman J. Ornstein, eds., *The New Congress* (Washington, D.C.: American Enterprise Institute for Public Policy Research, 1981), pp. 99–133.

For example, Michigan Democrat John Dingell, who after his father's death in 1955 took over his seat representing industrial Detroit, used his chairmanship of the Energy and Power Subcommittee to put an indelible stamp on energy legislation. Dingell finally lost his battle to prevent the decontrol of oil, but for years he was the House point man for the opposition, succeeding in delaying decontrol.

Over the years, a host of subcommittee chairmen have enhanced their reputations for power within and outside of Congress by pursuing legislative work. Before he became chairman of the Interior and Insular Affairs Committee, for example, Arizona Democrat Morris Udall used a subcommittee chairmanship to become a leader in the environmental field. Florida Democrat Paul Rogers, before he retired in 1978, actively chaired the Health Subcommittee and became known as "Mr. Health" of Capitol Hill. For almost a decade his name was attached to every major piece of health legislation. Virtually every area of public policy is identified with one subcommittee or another, whose chairmen largely control the flow of legislation.

HEARINGS. Subcommittees conduct public hearings on legislation before it is sent to the full committee. Hearings obstensibly give interested parties, whether members of the public, interest groups, or government officials, a "day in court," an opportunity to express their views. Although hearings are considered by most members to be an essential step in the legislative process, they are primarily of symbolic importance. Usually committee staffs, working behind the scenes, carefully stage hearings to emphasize the views of their chairmen. Friendly witnesses who support the legislation endorsed by the subcommittee chairmen are invited to testify in order to compile a favorable public record. Hostile witnesses, of course, may appear in response to the notice of committee hearings, but their presence is not encouraged. Subcommittee chairmen and their staffs can usually make certain that the balance of testimony favors their positions.

TYPES OF HEARINGS. Committee and subcommittee hearings are conducted not only to review new legislative proposals, but also to consider authorization of money for existing programs, appropriations (direct provision of funds), investigations, and oversight of administrative agencies. Authorization hearings, conducted by committees with legislative jurisdiction, constitute the bulk of their work. Appropriations hearings are conducted by separate appropriations committees and subcommittees. Both legislative and special committees hold investigative and oversight hearings.

The number and scope of committee hearings on any given day while Congress is in session fills pages in the *Congressional Record*. Appropriations subcommittees are constantly holding hearings on the budgets of the agencies under their jurisdiction, and on broader policy matters as well. During one day in the second session of the 97th Congress, the Appropriations Subcommittee on Energy and Water Development continued lengthy hearings on the water-development appropriations bill for fiscal year 1983, while the Subcommittee on Labor-IIHS (Health and Human Services) and Education heard testimony both from members of Congress and public witnesses about programs administered by the Labor, Health and Human Services, and Education Departments. Broader policy matters were reviewed by the Appropriations Subcommittee on Commerce-Justice-State-the Judiciary and Related Agencies, which met in executive session to hear testimony from FBI Director William Webster on policy matters related to his agency. The Appropriations Subcommittee on Defense also held a hearing on drug abuse in the military.

RESULTS OF HEARINGS. Hearings are generally a necessary step in the legislative process, yet relatively few of the innumerable hearings that are constantly being staged by committees result in passage of legislation. Often hearings do not even produce legislative recommendations. The growth of committee staffs, who are constantly seeking issues to place their committees in the limelight and to reflect favorably upon themselves and their bosses, is a major reason for the seemingly endless hearings that committees hold on topics ranging from control of the atmosphere to construction of the Franklin D. Roosevelt Memorial. Sunset legislation, which would establish a timetable for government programs after which they would have to be reauthorized by Congress, has been the subject of committee hearings in both the House and the Senate since 1975. The legislation seems to have no chance of passage, but it has some appeal among staffers and legislators alike, who find that it is challenging and controversial enough to make for lively hearings and interesting legislative proposals. Normally under the jurisdiction of the Rules Committee in the House, sunset legislation was the focus

of extensive hearings held by the Rules Subcommittee on Legislative
Process in 1982.

MARKUP. Once a subcommittee or committee has completed hearings, it takes up the bill section by section in a "markup" session,
during which committee members literally mark up the bill by
adding or deleting provisions. Under the relatively new "sunshine"
rules of Congress, most markup sessions are open to the public, although usually they are purposely held in small rooms tucked away
in the Capitol that are difficult to find; even if found, a member of
the public will have difficulty obtaining a seat because markup sessions are always crowded with committee staff.

Representative Clem Miller (D, Calif., 1959–1962), gave an insider's view of the markup, during which legislation mostly developed
by the staff and closely attuned to the interests of affected administrative agencies is put into final form. Miller wrote,

> The committee staff has a proprietary interest in our bill. The
> bill we went to hearing with was probably its creature to be-
> gin with. Its details were worked out in conference with the
> executive department "downtown." The staff knows every by-
> way in the bill, has hedged against every technical problem,
> and tried to accommodate internal inconsistencies. Where
> even the most specialized congressman must turn his atten-
> tion here and there whether he would or not, our bill is the
> life of the committee staff. It has a professional interest in the
> launching and the seaworthiness of the bill.[33]

With the staff in the background, often closely directing the proceedings, the committee majority and minority members meet in
what Miller called the "preliminary bout" of the markup. The committee chairman is the main figure. "To get through mark-up time
successfully," wrote Miller, "the first obstacle is the subcommittee
chairman. The staff must cope with his preconceptions, prejudices,
and idiosyncracies. However it is done, the chairman must be convinced because he is the decisive influence. His lukewarmness or
coolness will be immediately broadcast far and wide to make trouble
in a widening pool."[34] Miller concluded, "The hostility of the

[33] Miller, *Member of the House,* p. 13.
[34] Miller, *Member of the House,* p. 13.

chairman is almost fatal, and division between the majority members almost equally so." [35]

Successful markup sessions require a great deal of consensus among committee members. A chairman's power is built not only upon his ability to persuade his committee to follow his leadership, but also on creation of an environment of accord.

"After hearings," wrote Congressman Miller in his description of committee proceedings,

> to be sure of some unity, the subcommittee chairman calls a meeting of Majority members to look over some possible changes in the bill. The chairman insists on informality. It is a "discussion." Nothing is to be "final." Your "ideas" are sought. One member wants a much tougher section in one part of the bill. There is a chance of agreement. The staff had anticipated this with some appropriate language. Another member, not primed by a staff man, throws out an innocent suggestion which it turns out the chairman is most opposed to. The "suggestion' is permanently shelved.[36]

Subcommittee chairmen strive for unity among the members of their committees in order to ensure success of the legislation in the full standing committee. The chairman of the full committee, which may hold hearings and always conducts markup sessions of its own, also makes the assent of both majority and minority committee members a primary goal before the legislation is reported. Favorable Rules Committee, and more particularly, floor action, is far more likely when a committee is united behind a bill.

THE COMMITTEE REPORT. Standing committees explain their legislative intent in separate reports on bills prepared by the staff. The "report language" is as important as the bill itself, explaining and filling in the details of the legislation. Reports may contain minority views when committee unanimity has not been reached. Committee reports are important not only in illuminating legislative details for other legislators, but are also considered an authoritative expression of congressional intent by the courts.

The extraordinary efforts made by the members and staff of committees to guarantee legislative victories do not always succeed. In

[35] Miller, p. 14.
[36] Miller, p. 14.

the House, not only is the Rules Committee a potential obstacle, which in the past particularly stymied a wide range of liberal legislative proposals opposed by its conservative membership, but other barriers exist as well. An increasingly powerful Budget Committee must approve authorizations for money. The Appropriations Committee has the final say over exactly how much money actually will be spent. Moreover, many legislative programs in areas such as social security, health care, and energy require the government to raise money through taxes. The Ways and Means Committee has jurisdiction over all tax legislation, and its agreement with the recommendations of other committees may not be easily gained. The politics of consensus, then, must be successfully carried out in a number of arenas outside of the committees that have primary legislative jurisdiction.

Institutional Committees of Special Importance

THE RULES COMMITTEE. The House Rules Committee, which meets in a tiny room on the third floor of the Capitol with a panoramic view of the Mall, was one of the first committees of the House and has periodically dominated the legislative process. The committee became especially powerful after the "revolt" of 1910, when the House removed the authority of the Speaker to determine which bills would be taken up on the House floor. Ironically, the Rules Committee was to become as arbitrary as the Speaker had been in exercising its power over scheduling legislation and the rules under which bills would be debated on the floor.

The Rules Committee became a bastion of conservative Democratic strength from the 1930s through the 1960s, reflecting control of the House by Democratic majorities for the entire period, with the exception of two Congresses, and the seniority that southern representatives were able to build because of the noncompetitiveness of their elections.

Presidents from Franklin D. Roosevelt to Lyndon B. Johnson found the more liberal items on their legislative agendas often stymied by a Rules Committee bent upon preserving the old order. It was the role of the committee within Congress, however, which determined its power and destiny. Although the committee for decades opposed civil rights, labor, and welfare legislation that it considered too liberal, it was reflecting the views of a generally conservative House. The fragmentation of the House, its multiple committee structure and lack of party discipline, and its arcane parliamentary procedures, buttressed the Rules Committee, but its power depended even more upon the support of the House itself. Members used the committee as a public whipping boy to explain why important legislation was not passed, while quietly giving their consent to the committee's power.

When the Democratic membership of the House began to have a more liberal cast in the early 1970s, the party's caucus took measures to reduce the independence of the Rules Committee and to make it more responsive to the majority party. New Democratic Caucus rules provided for secret balloting for committee chairmen. The Caucus immediately deposed three of the most senior committee chairmen, although not touching the Rules Committee, as a warning that henceforth no committee could act independently of the Caucus with impunity. The Rules Committee was singled out and made an arm of the Speaker, who was given the authority to appoint the committee's majority members. The Democratic Caucus clearly saw the Speaker as its representative, regarding enhancement of his power as an increment of its own.

The Rules Committee, although reduced in power, remains an important force in the legislative process. The committee is unlikely to pigeonhole legislation without the consent of the Speaker, but as an arm of the Speaker it is potentially as powerful as it ever was. As Bruce I. Oppenheimer observed, "Unlike the Rules Committees of the 1940s and 1950s, the current committee uses its position in the congressional process to expedite, not to obstruct the proceedings of the institution." [37] The committee continues to hold hearings on legislation to determine what kind of a parliamentary rule to grant. If the committee fails to agree on a rule it is virtually impossible for a bill to be reported to the floor. Because the committee must keep an eye on the Caucus and on the Speaker, the committee's majority members are less likely than in the past to delay or kill legislation. Merely by determining the kind of rule under which the legislation will be considered, however, the committee can have a significant influence. For example, closed rules prohibit floor amendments, deny-

---

[37] Bruce I. Oppenheimer, "The Changing Relationship Between House Leadership and the Committee on Rules," in Mackaman, ed., *Understanding Congressional Leadership*, p. 224.

ing the House the opportunity to change legislation. Open rules, on the other hand, allow amendments that may substantially change a bill. Of course the House may vote to override a rule proposed by the committee, but such action is rarely taken.

The Rules Committee, then, does not substantively change legislation, but continues to affect the legislative process through its power to schedule legislation and decide the floor rules.

THE BUDGET COMMITTEE. The House Budget Committee was created as a relatively weak body, with rotating membership and ten of its twenty-five members being drawn from the Appropriations and Ways and Means Committees. No member can serve on the Budget Committee for more than four years in any ten-year period. Moreover, the chairmanship is supposed to rotate after each Congress. The committee, born from the compromises of the Budget and Impoundment Control Act of 1974, adopted an early strategy of compromise in dealing with vested committee interests.

The Budget Committee was given formal authority to develop the budget resolutions of the House, which, once approved by a majority of members, would establish ceilings for budget authorizations and appropriations. The early advocates of a centralized budgeting process in the House wanted the committee to play a major role, to be the budget czar of the body.

The power of the Budget Committee depends mainly on the persuasive abilities of its chairman, who must conduct delicate negotiations with committee chairmen and House leaders who are used to exercising power in their own right. Connecticut Democrat Robert Giaimo, a twenty-two-year House veteran, chaired the committee from 1976 to 1980, an unusual four-year term permitted by a House waiver of its rules. Giaimo had eagerly sought the post, winning a competition in the Democratic Caucus. He soon found the task of having constantly to deal with the power balance of the House exhausting, and decided not only to give up his committee post, but to leave the House in 1980.

Oklahoma Democrat Jim Jones replaced Giaimo in the 97th Congress. Jones found himself and his committee the center of media attention at a time when President Reagan's budget proposals were at the top of the House agenda. Jones recognized, however, that although the Budget Committee might temporarily be in the driver's seat due to overwhelming White House and public pressures to reduce government expenditures, over the long term the committee would have to negotiate and not dictate budget policy to the long-entrenched committee interests of the House. The permanent chairman of the standing committees might bow to the Budget Committee due to the exigencies of the times, but in the long run they would not support a budget process that threatened their committee sovereignty.

Even Jones's careful stewardship of the Budget Committee during the first session of the 97th Congress, when he did not fully seize the advantage he had to pressure committee chairmen into agreeing to a budget resolution that mostly reflected the views of the Reagan administration, caused a backlash as Congress got under way in 1982. Rules Committee chairman Richard Bolling, commenting upon both White House and Budget Committee pressure, charged, "The Administration's victories last year destroyed the legislative process." [38] Remarking that enmity had been created between the Budget and other committees, Bolling stated, "The Rules Committee is the referee. We're trying to maintain both a budget process and a legislative process." [39]

The Budget and Impoundment Control Act of 1974, which established the Budget Committee, was an attempt to centralize the budget process on Capitol Hill. The Budget Committee, though, has no automatic authority to determine authorizations and appropriations. The chairman knows that the power of a committee extends only as far as its ability to persuade what Woodrow Wilson called the "Feudal Barons of the House," its committee chairmen, to follow its lead. Unfortunately for the prospects of a centralized budgeting process, committee chairmen understandably guard jealously what they consider to be their prerogative to dictate budgetary as well as other policies within their jurisdiction. Most legislators, who themselves look forward to the power of committee chairmanships or of being ranking minority committee members, support the dispersion of House power into committee enclaves. The decentralization of House power is the will of the majority.[40]

[38] Martin Tolchin, "Waiting for a Budget, the Pace Would Suit a Snail," *New York Times*, April 9, 1982, p. A14.

[39] Tolchin, "Waiting for a Budget," p. A14.

[40] See John W. Ellwood and James A. Thurber, "The Politics of the Congressional Budget Process Reexamined," in Lawrence C. Dodd and Bruce I. Oppenheimer, eds., *Congress Reconsidered*, 2nd ed. (Washington, D.C.: Congressional Quarterly Press, 1981), pp. 204–220; Lance P. Leloup, "Process

THE APPROPRIATIONS COMMITTEE. The House established a separate Appropriations Committee in 1865. Previously its functions had been exercised by the Ways and Means Committee. The Appropriations Committee by nature is the focal point of important power. The committee determines the amounts of money that *will* be spent on government programs. The committee and its subcommittees do not legislate per se, nor do they determine how much money *may* be authorized, but in deciding appropriations they profoundly affect a wide range of public policy. The chairman and subcommittee chairmen of Appropriations know that government programs cannot be sustained without their cooperation. They know that Appropriations Subcommittee hearings can effectively legislate without making laws simply by putting administrators on notice that unless they conform to the wishes of the committee they will not receive the funds they desire.

Within the House the Appropriations Committee is one of the most respected and sought-after panels. The congressional power of the purse, one of the most formidable powers Congress possesses, is exercised by the committee. Its chairmen are among the most senior on Capitol Hill, illustrated by the fact that the committee chairman in 1982, Mississippi Democrat Jamie Whitten, was first elected to the House a month before Pearl Harbor in 1941.

Not only does the Appropriations Committee control the checking accounts of administrative agencies in the Treasury, but also it constrains committee action within Congress. Before the creation of the Budget Committee in 1974, the Appropriations Committee was the only body that could rein in the often excessive spending authorizations of the standing committees. The politics of appropriations and authorizations was played out under informal rules and expectations that recognized the central role of the Appropriations Committee in dampening budget authorizations.

The Appropriations Committee continues to be a major House force, although its power has been somewhat eroded by the Budget Committee. The five Appropriations Committee members who have ex officio seats on the Budget Committee, however, give the older

vs. Policy: The U.S. Budget Committee," *Legislative Studies Quarterly,* 4 (May 1979), pp. 227–254; and Allen Schick, "The Three-Ring Budget Process: The Appropriations, Tax, and Budget Committees in Congress," in Mann and Ornstein, eds., *The New Congress,* pp. 288–328.

and more lasting panel a large voice on the newer one. Moreover, though the Budget Committee influences spending ceilings, the Appropriations subcommittees are constantly involved in the day-to-day operations of government, making the specialized determinations that are so critical to public policy. The Appropriations Committee has been overshadowed somewhat by the new budget process, but it remains one of the most critical institutional committees of the House.

THE WAYS AND MEANS COMMITTEE. The House originates revenue bills under the Constitution. The Ways and Means Committee has carried out this responsibility since the beginning of the Republic. The committee is the first step in the difficult and generally highly controversial process of deciding the ways and means of government, the tax and revenue levels that are necessary to sustain government programs.

The Ways and Means Committee, like Appropriations, is one of the supercommittees of the House. It represents the body to the outside world, including the Senate, as it carries out the revenue initiative role.

Tax policy affects almost every committee and every member of the House. The most effective chairmen of the Ways and Means Committee are those who can lead the House in developing tax policy. Skillful politics and tax expertise are essential to the power of the chairmen. The House expects its Ways and Means chairman to be one of its strongest and most astute members.

Effective Ways and Means chairmen take their cue from their predecessor Wilbur Mills, who made the committee not only a dominant force in the House but a powerful representative of the body in its dealings with the Senate. "As I see it," said Mills, "our job is to work over a bill until our technical staff tells us it is ready and until I have reason to believe that it is going to have enough support to pass. Many of our bills must be brought out under a closed rule and to get and keep a closed rule, you must have a widely acceptable bill. It's as simple as that." [41] Institutional committees such as Appropriations and Ways and Means must operate within the framework of a House consensus in order to produce the results that are expected of them.

---

[41] Quoted from John Manley, *The Politics of Finance* (Boston: Little, Brown, 1970), in Fenno, *Congressmen in Committees*, p. 55.

THE ADMINISTRATION COMMITTEE. Unlike the Ways and Means and other institutional committees, the House Administration Committee is not directly a major force in the legislative process. From time to time important legislation, such as campaign-finance proposals and ethics bills, are referred to it; however, most of the time of the committee is spent in overseeing standing-committee budgets. And nothing is dearer to the heart of committee chairmen than their budgets, which fix the number of staff and in general regulate the scope of committee activities.

The Administration Committee's reach goes beyond the budgets of other panels to the management of members' office expenses, including the money available for travel. The committee also assigns office space and hearing rooms, matters that are frequently the subject of intensive negotiation and outright conflict.

Administration Committee chairmen have been known to use their sway over committee and member accounts to boost their power. The politics of Congress often exists for its own sake, in isolation from the outside world, as members seek internal power and recognition from colleagues that they are important in the workings of the House. The chairmen and staff of the Administration Committee are in a strategic position to influence the body through their manipulation of the accounts of the House.

The most notorious chairman of the Administration Committee in recent years was Ohio Democrat Wayne Hays, who built the panel into what one observer called a "frightening base of power." [42] Hays used the committee's power to disburse funds and control office space to "reward his friends and punish his enemies." [43] Hays apparently felt that he had become so invulnerable to attack that he kept his mistress, Elizabeth Ray, on the committee payroll, even though she rarely if ever reported to work. Hays's arbitrary handling of committee funds and office and travel allowances raised the ire of many of his colleagues, but they refused to challenge him openly. Finally, the Democratic Steering and Policy Committee voted secretly, by only 13 to 11, to remove him in 1975. The recommendation, however, was not supported by the Democratic Caucus. Hays had done enough favors for its members to retain their support, and when his position was challenged he carefully cultivated the backing

[42] *Congressional Quarterly Weekly Report*, vol. 34, no. 22 (May 29, 1976), p. 1334.
[43] Jones and Woll, *Private World of Congress*, p. 122.

of the freshman caucus, assuring them that they would have their own meeting room and would be properly taken care of in their quest for office space and allowances.

Hays eventually resigned from Congress in disgrace because of the Elizabeth Ray scandal. Although his successors have not been as flamboyant as he, the Administration Committee remains a powerful force within the House. Its Accounts Subcommittee develops and presents the legislative budget each year, determining allocation of money to committees, staff, and members. Committee budgets in particular are often the focus of acrimonious debate as the Accounts Subcommittee makes its judgments about who gets what. That the amounts involved are not trivial is illustrated by the $68.5 million budget for House committee expenditures in 1981, and $76.2 million in 1982. (See Table 3.4.) The Accounts Subcommittee controls disbursement of the entire amount as it reviews staff salaries, domestic travel, consultant fees, and money for equipment and supplies. The subcommittee controls in a very important sense the lifeblood of the body when it allocates committee funds.

The presentation of committee budgets is always a time for elevated rhetoric between the majority and minority members. The exchanges that took place in 1982 were typical. The Accounts Subcommittee chairman, Frank Annunzio (D, Ill.), a product of the Chicago Democratic machine, told his colleagues that his committee's recommendation should be accepted intact. "I want to warn you," he said, "that if you fool around with these [committee] budgets any more you are going to destroy the committee system in this House because we have reached a zero-base. You will be challenging the integrity of every chairman in this House who came before my subcommittee to present their budget in a frugal, honest manner." [44] Congressman Robert Badham, a California Republican and subcommittee member, replied for his side of the aisle. "Admittedly," he said, "I, along with my minority colleagues, are dismayed by some authorization levels recommended for some committees. Energy and Commerce, as an example for the Department of Energy that is to be phased out, will have few or no bills, tops the scales of committee spending at over $4 million. This excessive amount, in my judgment, is far beyond what any committee should demand or require." [45]

---

[44] *Congressional Record*, 97th Cong., 2nd Sess., March 10, 1982, p. H800.
[45] Ibid., p. H801.

Table 3.4

House Committee Funding (Investigative funds, calendar year 1982, for all House committees except Appropriations and Budget)

Committee	Spent 1981 [a]	Request 1982	Approved by House	% Change 1981–1982 approved
Agriculture	$ 952,112	$ 1,221,249	$ 1,143,122	+20.1
Armed Services	776,676	1,022,500	918,866	+18.3
Banking	2,220,600	2,620,059	2,414,919	+ 8.8
D.C.	236,533	318,289	265,000	+12.0
Education and Labor	2,291,288	2,923,200	2,630,005	+14.8
Energy and Commerce	3,724,496	4,375,761	3,969,000	+ 6.6
Foreign Affairs	1,797,500	2,044,462	1,928,424	+ 7.3
Government Operations	2,099,673	2,648,353	2,230,000	+ 6.2
House Administration	844,038	977,000	977,000	+15.8
Interior	1,156,482	1,341,602	1,249,615	+ 8.1
Judiciary	1,346,751	1,546,750	1,452,336	+ 7.8
Merchant Marine	1,501,526	1,813,330	1,609,104	+ 7.2
Post Office	902,470	1,318,200	963,350	+ 6.7
Public Works	1,707,748	2,030,521	1,840,521	+ 7.8
Rules	425,382	472,500	458,732	+ 7.8
Science and Technology	1,691,236	2,034,400	1,847,000	+ 9.2
Small Business	749,709	893,770	804,680	+ 7.3
Standards of Conduct	108,441	200,000	200,000	+84.4
Veterans' Affairs	333,381	599,104	357,494	+ 7.2
Ways and Means	1,950,146	2,252,000	2,202,000	+12.9
Aging	1,160,773	1,268,725	1,223,680	+ 5.4
Intelligence	867,209	961,000	938,700	+ 8.2
Narcotics	522,000	540,000	540,000	+ 3.4
Subtotal	$29,366,170	$35,422,775	$32,163,548	+ 9.5
Information Services	6,893,000	8,200,000	7,441,725	+ 8.6
Total	$36,259,170	$43,622,775	$39,605,273	+ 9.2

[a] May not include some outstanding 1981 bills.

Source: House Administration Committee, *Congressional Quarterly Weekly Report*, vol. 40, no. 14 (April 3, 1982), p. 734.

In the end, the majority always prevails, and the budgets are always increased, particularly allocations for a staff that some critics say threatens to overwhelm Congress itself.

The institutional committees of the House both represent and buttress the broader system in which committee autonomy is preserved and committees and their staffs are constantly increased. The Rules Committee, which to outsiders has often seemed an arbitrary overlord, directs the business of the House in a way that preserves a system in which there are well over 100 semisovereign committees and subcommittees. Left on their own, the committees would destroy themselves in internecine warfare. The Appropriations and Budget Committees prevent the prodigal ways of other panels from destroying the legislative process. The Ways and Means Committee represents the House by performing its important constitutional role as the originator of revenue legislation. The committee is an integrative force in the highly decentralized House, where tax legislation affects the interests of virtually every committee. Finally, the Administration Committee, although acting as watchdog for House accounts, sustains the committee system by giving a sympathetic ear to the constant demands of committee chairmen for increased budgets. The power of the Accounts Subcommittee is based on its ability to achieve a consensus of powerful chairmen, which it accomplishes through an incremental budgeting approach that allows for the constant increase in committee funds.

Although committees are the heart and soul of the legislative process in the House, there are parliamentary procedures for bypassing committees under unusual circumstances.

Bypassing Committees

The majority rules in democratic assemblies. The power of House committees is mainly based upon the lack of a cohesive majority that would require a disciplined party. Committees cannot be completely arbitrary, however, for if there is a majority consensus, parliamentary procedures exist for bypassing the normal committee process.

THE CONSENT CALENDAR. Members place noncontroversial bills on the Consent Calendar, which is called on the first and third Mondays of each month. When a bill is called from the Calendar it becomes law if no objection is made. To prevent passage of a Consent Calendar bill three members must object. Because most members do not have the time to review legislation that is placed on the Calendar, the House has appointed six official "objectors," three from each party, to review the Calendar and remove potentially controversial or substantively important legislation that would normally go through the regular process of committee consideration and floor debate.

THE DISCHARGE PETITION. Congress adopted the discharge rule in 1910, which provides that a member may move to discharge a bill that has been before a committee for thirty days, or for seven days before the Rules Committee. A constitutional majority of the House, 218 members, must sign the discharge petition, which is then placed on a Discharge Calendar. After seven days, during which the committee holding the bill is given the chance to act, any member who signed the petition may move to discharge the legislation from the committee. A simple majority vote is required to carry the motion.

The House has discharged only twenty-five bills since 1909, of which twenty passed the House. Only two became law, however, the Fair Labor Standards Act of 1938 and the Federal Pay Raise Act of 1960. The House is clearly reluctant to use the Discharge Petition to circumvent its committees. The majority of the House has consistently respected the legislative jurisdiction of its standing committees. Committee hearings and markup are considered to be essential steps in the legislative process. More than 50 percent of the Discharge Petitions that have been signed by the required majority were introduced in the first decade after the rule was adopted in 1910, as part of the revolt that decentralized power in the House. Although occasionally Discharge Petitions are filed, the procedure is largely dormant.

House reforms in the 1970s, which made the Rules Committee an adjunct of the Speaker, and other committees more responsive to the Democratic Caucus, make the Discharge Petition and other methods for bypassing committees less important than in the past to attainment of committee accountability. No longer can the Rules Committee cavalierly bottle up legislation. Nor can the chairmen of other panels arbitrarily pigeonhole bills they dislike. Although the power of standing-committee chairmen has been somewhat reduced, subcommittees have proliferated and their chairmen have demanded and received a great deal of independent power to control the legislative process. The support of both standing and subcommittee chairmen remains essential to passage of legislation.

SUSPENSION OF THE RULES. Standard parliamentary procedure allows all democratic assemblies to suspend their regular rules for doing business by a two-thirds vote of the members present. Often a formal vote is not taken, and the Speaker or presiding officer simply asks for the yeas and nays; if no substantial opposition is audible, the motion passes. Although suspension of the rules could technically be used to bypass regular committees, generally it is committee chairmen themselves who ask the Speaker to take up measures under suspension to avoid delay in the Rules Committee and in the normal scheduling process for bills. The House has increasingly used suspension of the rules to bring legislation to the floor, due to the increasing press of business that accumulates until the end of sessions when there is not enough time to consider pending bills under normal procedures.

CALENDAR WEDNESDAY. On Wednesdays standing committees may call up measures which they have reported but which have been stalled in the Rules Committee. To bring up a bill, though, a committee chairman must be recognized by the Speaker, who calls the committee roll in alphabetical order. The House generally dispenses with the procedure altogether by unanimous consent, or allows little time to call the roll when it is used. Committees may have to wait weeks before they are recognized. Even if a bill is called to the floor through the Calendar Wednesday procedure, only two hours is allowed for debate, which is rarely enough to gain the necessary consensus to pass complex legislation. Originally installed in 1909 to circumvent the Speaker's control over the scheduling of legislation, the Calendar Wednesday rule has fallen into disuse. Since 1950 it has been successfully used in the passage of only two bills, the Fair Employment Practices Act of 1950 and the Area Redevelopment Act of 1960.

THE PRIVATE CALENDAR. The Private Calendar, like the Consent Calendar, contains noncontroversial legislation which has been reported from committees but which may go directly to the floor without first having to be approved by the Rules Committee. Committee consideration of legislation that finds its way to the Consent and Private Calendars is generally only a formality. No hearings or markup sessions are held, and no committee reports are issued. Committee chairmen as a courtesy to members report noncontroversial and private bills, which are automatically transferred to their appropriate calendars. Private bills, like those on the Consent Calendar, are scrutinized by three especially appointed "objectors" from each party.

The Private Calendar lists bills granting relief to citizens that would ordinarily not be available to them under the law. The legislation is "private" in the sense that it governs only a named individual and does not have a general effect. Private bills typically grant relief from strict immigration-law requirements to relatives or spouses of American citizens, allowing them to enter the country. Other immigration-law matters, such as the expulsion of resident aliens, may also be the subject of private bills. Another major category of private legislation gives compensation to private parties who have been injured by government action. In the past, the doctrine of "sovereign immunity," which held that the government cannot be sued for compensatory damages for actions taken within the boundaries of its authority that protected its property, the public purse, or were necessary to effective public administration, made it virtually impossible for private individuals to recover damages for government torts. Although the government now permits itself to be sued under certain circumstances, many private bills still deal with awarding damages to individuals injured by the government. For example, the family of a CIA agent who died while testing LSD for the agency was given compensation through a private bill.

RIDERS TO APPROPRIATIONS BILLS. A *rider* is generally a *nongermane* provision that is added to a bill. Riders that are attached to appropriations and tax legislation are virtually immune to a presidential veto, because all presidents are reluctant to overturn the money and revenue legislation that is necessary to run the government. President Franklin D. Roosevelt spoke for all presidents in expressing his frustration with riders, commenting in 1938: "Regardless of the merits or demerits of any such riders [to tax and appropriation bills] the manifest fact remains that this practice robs the Executive of legitimate and essential freedom of action in dealing with legislation." [46]

Riders are used not only to circumvent the possibility of a presidential veto, but to bypass committees and normal legislative procedures. Texas Republican James Collins expressed the views of many of his conservative House colleagues when he pointed out, "For twenty-five years Congress has been controlled by liberal Democrats and you can't get any type of freedom from [business] regulation out

---

[46] William Safire, *Safire's Political Dictionary* (New York: Random House, 1978), p. 613.

of their committees. The only recourse we have is to go to the appropriations bill [and add riders]." [47] One Republican staffer who was particularly adept at helping his congressman burden appropriations bills with riders, commented approvingly about the process, "It's vampire politics. You bite, draw blood, and let it fall where it will." [48]

Ironically, the House has long had a rule of germaneness governing all legislative amendments. Technically the rule makes many riders, particularly those which mandate existing administrative agencies to implement new policies, out of order. The House has increasingly suspended the rule, however, by unanimous consent or a two-thirds vote to allow legislative riders. More common than legislative riders have been limitation riders, which restrict use of government funds for existing programs. The rule of germaneness does not have to be suspended for limitation riders to appropriation bills, because they are directly relevant to expenditure of funds in the broad categories included in such legislation. The germaneness rule actually encourages appropriations riders, because appropriations bills cover every government program.

SENATE COMMITTEE ORGANIZATION AND PROCEDURES

Committees are as vital to the operation of the Senate as they are to the House. (See Table 3.3.) The Senate, however, is a smaller and more collegial body than the popular chamber, making senators as individuals more powerful in their own right than are representatives. In the past, junior senators were all but ignored until they passed the initiation rites of the body, which often took years.[49] Senior committee chairmen invariably dominated the body. They are still very powerful, but junior senators now can more easily make their mark on the legislative process, and committee chairmanships are not essential for recognition in the body.

Senators also attach less significance to subcommittee chairmanships than do representatives. "Subcommittee government" characterizes the House but not the Senate, where nearly all majority-party

---

[47] *Congressional Quarterly Weekly Report*, vol. 38, no. 44 (November 1, 1980), p. 3252.
[48] Ibid., p. 3251.
[49] Donald R. Matthews, *U.S. Senators and Their World* (New York: Vintage, 1960).

members have their own subcommittee chairmanships, placing them roughly on an equal footing. In contrast, it takes years for majority-party House members to obtain a subcommittee chairmanship, which is a factor in making it a valuable prize.

Committee Jurisdictions

The Senate organizes its committees in much the same way as the House does, dividing jurisdiction over federal programs among them. As in the House, a manual provides the organizational and procedural framework for committees.[50] The jurisdictions of standing committees are set forth in great detail. For example, the *Manual* provides:

> [The] committee on Human Resources, to which committee shall be referred all proposed legislation, messages, petitions, memorials, and other matters relating to the following subjects:
>
> 1. Measures relating to education, labor, health, and public welfare
> 2. Aging
> 3. Agricultural colleges
> 4. Arts and Humanities
> 5. Biomedical research and development
> 6. Child labor
> 7. Convict labor and the entry of goods made by convicts into interstate commerce
> 8. Domestic activities of the American National Red Cross
> 9. Equal employment opportunity
> 10. Gallaudet College, Howard University, and St. Elizabeths Hospital
> 11. Handicapped individuals
> 12. Labor standards and labor statistics
> 13. Mediation and arbitration of labor disputes
> 14. Occupational safety and health, including the welfare of miners
> 15. Private pension plans
> 16. Public health
> 17. Railway labor and retirement

---

[50] *Senate Manual*, Senate Doc. 95-1, 95th Cong., 1st Sess. (Washington, D.C.: U.S. Government Printing Office, 1977).

18. Regulation of foreign laborers
19. Student loans
20. Wages and hours of labor

Such committee shall also study and review, on a comprehensive basis, matters relating to health, education and training, and public welfare, and report thereon from time to time.[51]

Appointment to Committees

Party leadership committees, the Democratic Steering Committee and the Republican Committee on Committees, assign members to committees, taking into account political considerations, such as the preferences of committee chairmen and the individuals seeking assignments, and whether or not individual senators should be "rewarded" for their loyalty to the party leadership. In the past, powerful Senate leaders, such as Lyndon B. Johnson, were singlehandedly able to reward or punish members by controlling new committee assignments. Johnson, as majority leader and chairman of his party's steering committee, determined who received the choice committee seats. Rowland Evans and Robert Novak, in their classic work on Johnson, wrote that in order to build his network of power,

> Johnson stretched the meagre power resources of the majority leader to the outer limits. The mightiest of these was his influence over committee assignments. Still, it was not comparable to the absolute power enjoyed by Nelson Aldrich a half century before. As chairman of the Democratic Steering Committee, Johnson steadily widened the breach in rigid seniority rules, working delicately with a surgical scalpel, not a stick of dynamite.[52]

Johnson could not unilaterally violate the seniority rule in making committee assignments, but relied upon political persuasion and finesse in a body that was controlled by an "inner club" of senators who were members of a collegial elite. Within the club Johnson could move his players around to get the results he wanted. His

---

[51] Ibid., pp. 36–37, sec. 25.1L.
[52] Rowland Evans and Robert Novak, *Lyndon B. Johnson: The Exercise of Power* (New York: New American Library, 1966), p. 111.

use of power to influence committee assignments cut both
ways. "Good" liberals, such as Humphrey, could be prema-
turely boosted into the Foreign Relations Committee, and a
"bad" liberal, such as Kefauver, could be made to cool his
heels for years. A "bad" liberal, such as Paul Douglas, could
be barred from the Finance Committee for eight long years,
while five fellow members of the Class of '48 (Kerr, Long,
Frear, Anderson and Johnson himself) and one from the
Class of '50 (Smathers) were finding places there. Senators
who dared to function too far outside the Johnson Network
waited long to get inside the prestige committee.[53]

When Mike Mansfield (D, Mont.) became majority leader in
1961, he adopted a more democratic leadership style than had Lyndon Johnson.[54] He "appears to have preferred operating as but one
member of the 17-member Democratic Steering Committee."[55] Senators could no longer obtain choice committee assignments simply
by being in the favor of the majority leader. They had to lobby for
themselves, persuading the Steering Committee and the chairmen of
the committees to which they wished to be assigned to give them
the seats they wanted. The democratization of the Senate that occurred during the era of Mike Mansfield in the 1960s extended into
the 1970s as both majority and minority leaders recognized that they
could no longer keep a tight hold on the reins of power. As the
Senate became more individualistic, not only was the power of party
leaders reduced but committees themselves were no longer the
tightly knit group that could readily control legislative outcomes.
Both Johnson and Mansfield, despite their different leadership styles,
recognized and respected the power of committees. Majority leader
Lyndon B. Johnson remarked in 1960, "The only real power available
to the leader is the power of persuasion. There is no patronage; no
power to discipline; no authority to fire senators like a president can
fire his members of the cabinet.... It's persuasion with colleagues on
both sides of the aisle. Anything the Senate may do requires a majority vote. About all the leader can do is recommend."[56]

Senator Mike Mansfield, when he was majority leader in 1963,

53 Evans and Novak, *Lyndon B. Johnson*, p. 113.
54 Robert L. Peabody, *Leadership in Congress* (Boston: Little, Brown, 1976),
pp. 340ff.
55 Peabody, *Leadership in Congress*, p. 341.
56 Peabody, p. 339.

lamented, "What power do the leaders have to force these committees to twist their arms, to wheel and deal, and so forth and so on, to get them to rush things up, or to speed their procedure? The leaders in the Senate, at least, have no power delegated to them except on the basis of courtesy, accommodation, and a sense of responsibility." [57]

The Senate of the 1980s is more individualistic than the Senate of Lyndon B. Johnson or Mike Mansfield. Committees continue to be powerful, but are less respected by the members than in the past. Wisconsin Democrat Gaylord Nelson, who served in the Senate for three terms before he lost his bid for reelection in 1980, commented on the changing character of the Senate as the 1980s opened: "The institution was stronger twenty years ago because people went along with chairmen, and chairmen went along with each other. That put more strength in the hands of the leadership. During the course of my time, that all broke down." [58] Former Republican Senator James Pierson added, "It's every man for himself. Every senator is a baron. He has his own principality. Once you adopt that as a means of doing business, it's hard to establish any cohesion." [59]

Committee Procedures

Senate and House committee procedures are much the same. After legislation is assigned to committees by the parliamentarian, who interprets committee jurisdiction that is formally stated in the *Senate Manual*, the legislation usually goes to subcommittees for hearings. Of course, not all legislative recommendations are given hearings, for committee and subcommittee chairmen determine for themselves which proposals they want to take up formally in their committees. Automatically taken up are appropriation and authorization bills, which occupy a major portion of committee time.

As in the House, after hearings are held committee reports are issued, written by the staff members who have been most intimately involved with the legislation. Once a committee has reported a bill it goes to the majority leader, who determines in consultation with

---

[57] Peabody, pp. 339–340.
[58] *Congressional Quarterly Weekly Report*, vol. 40, no. 36 (September 4, 1982), p. 2181.
[59] Ibid.

his aides when, and sometimes if, it will be scheduled for floor debate. The majority leader generally assesses the mood of the Senate on the legislation and attempts to schedule floor debate only on legislation that has wide backing. Controversial legislation gets to the floor, but the majority leader strives to reduce controversy to a minimum. After all, from the standpoint of the leadership, there is little point in wasting Senate time on bills that have little chance of passage.

Institutional Committees

The Senate, like the House, has several committees of special consequence because they help to carry out the unique constitutional role of the body. Under the Constitution the Senate alone is given the authority to ratify treaties, and to approve of presidential appointments to the Supreme Court, the lower federal judiciary, the heads of executive departments, and other officials Congress designates.

The Senate's exclusive constitutional authority to approve of treaties reflected a desire by the founding fathers to give the Senate a key role in foreign policy making generally. Indirect election of the Senate, whose members were chosen by state legislatures, the six-year term of office, and the requirement that members be thirty-five years of age, were all designed to produce a body that could properly take the national interest into account in making foreign policy. The Senate was not to be subject to the whims of a fickle electorate. It was to be the deliberative body of the legislature, which could make foreign policy with knowledge, secrecy, dispatch, and consistency.

FOREIGN RELATIONS COMMITTEE. Created in 1816, Foreign Relations soon became the most prestigious panel in the Senate. Treaties, international affairs, the State Department, and diplomatic nominations fell within its jurisdiction. The most illustrious members of the Senate have served on the committee, including Daniel Webster and John C. Calhoun in the nineteenth century, and in the twentieth, Robert A. Taft. Examples of strong chairmen who made the committee a major foreign-policy force were Massachusetts Republican Henry Cabot Lodge, who used his committee post to defeat the Treaty of Versailles in 1919. Idaho Republican William Borah was on the committee at the time, and helped to lead the forces in opposition to the treaty. Later he became chairman of the committee and an important foreign-policy voice in the 1920s in support of isolationism.

The tribute given to Borah when he died in 1940 reflected the prestige that could accrue to a member of the Foreign Relations Committee. Harold L. Ickes, President Franklin Roosevelt's Secretary of the Interior, recalled that Borah "was given a state funeral at 12:30 Monday in the Senate chamber and the President and the Cabinet attended. Every member of the Supreme Court was there, as well as the two ex-justices, Sutherland and Van Devanter. Many ambassadors and ministers representing foreign countries were also there." [60] Ickes observed, "Borah's death leaves a real gap in the Senate. He was an outstanding man and a great senator. Curiously enough, although he served in the Senate for some thirty-three years, his name is not attached to any legislation. However, I do not urge this to his discredit because he ably and conscientiously filled the role of critic, especially in international matters. A man like that can be just as useful, and perhaps even more so, than one like Senator Wagner [D, NY], who pushes through fine legislation to improve our social and economic conditions." [61]

Ickes's comments reveal not only the prestige that Foreign Relations Committee members may have, but also that such prestige does not have to be attached to legislative achievement. Increasingly, as treaties become less important in the conduct of international relations, the role of the committee has become that of critic. Committee members often act unofficially as roving ambassadors representing the country abroad, and at home they may view themselves as surrogate secretaries of state who rightfully should have a voice in foreign policy making.

Senators consider a strong Foreign Relations Committee to be essential in maintaining the constitutional role of their institution. Viewed with admiration and respect are strong Foreign Relations Committee chairmen; weak chairmen are an embarrassment.

JUDICIARY COMMITTEE. Joining the Foreign Relations Committee in performing an important institutional role is the Judiciary Committee. All presidential nominations for federal judgeships must pass

---

[60] Harold L. Ickes, *The Secret Diary of Harold L. Ickes*, vol. 3, *The Lowering Clouds, 1939–1941* (New York: Simon and Schuster, 1955), p. 116.
[61] Ickes, *Secret Diary*, pp. 116–117.

through the committee. The committee's authority to review nominations to the Supreme Court gives it unusual distinction. It carries out the unique constitutional role assigned to the Senate, which has exclusive authority to approve of federal judicial appointments.

OTHER COMMITTEES. Several other committees perform important institutional responsibilities in the Senate, but none are as important as Foreign Relations and Judiciary. The Rules and Administration Committee deals with the budgets of Senate committees, holding hearings on their budgetary recommendations and shaping the final legislative budget for the body. The committee also has jurisdiction over other matters of internal interest, such as assignment of office space, committee organization, and support agencies insofar as they have to do with the Senate, such as the Government Printing Office, which publishes the *Congressional Record,* and the Library of Congress. The committee does not wield the same kind of power in the Senate that the Rules Committee of the House possesses. Senate legislation reported from committees goes through the majority leader's office directly to the floor, where unlimited debate is allowed unless cloture is invoked.

Finally, the Senate's exclusive authority over Cabinet and other presidential nominations to executive posts initially resides in the committees that have jurisdiction over the departments and agencies involved. For example, the Armed Services Committee must first clear nominations to the Defense Department before they go to the floor. Committees vote on nominations, and their rejection of nominees does not necessarily prevent final Senate confirmation, but is an almost insurmountable obstacle to final approval.

Joint Committees

Congress has created joint committees, which include members appointed from both bodies, to examine and administer matters that interest each. The Joint Economic Committee, created in 1946 after passage of the Full Employment Act during that year, investigates and makes recommendations on national economic policies. The Full Employment Act formally recognized the role of the federal government in maintaining economic prosperity and full employment, and the Joint Economic Committee represents Congress' role in that process. Members of both the House and the Senate serve on the

Joint Economic Committee, as they do on all joint committees, and the chairmanship rotates from the House to the Senate from one session of Congress to the other. The Joint Economic Committee, like other joint committees, does not have legislative responsibilities, but its recommendations can influence the legislative process.

The remaining three joint committees on the Library, Printing, and Taxation, respectively, oversee the operation of government in the areas under their jurisdiction. The Joint Library Committee, for example, oversees the operation of the Library of Congress and the Botanic Gardens. Public printing is under the jurisdiction of the Printing Committee, and the administration and effectiveness of tax measures are reviewed by the Joint Committee on Taxation.

Conference Committees

Conference committees are ad hoc joint committees created to resolve Senate and House differences on legislation. When the Senate and the House have different versions of legislation, each unacceptable to the other body, conference committees may be created to resolve their differences. Conference committees are not automatically established. But, time permitting, the leadership of each side of Capitol Hill will set up conference committees on important and timely legislation.

Formally, the Speaker of the House and the presiding officer of the Senate appoint members of conference committees, but informally they act in consultation with the chairmen of the committees involved. Under House rules, a majority of its delegation to a conference committee must support the position of the House. Senate members are freer to compromise. Conference committees often substantially reshape legislation, but they must act within the boundaries of consent on each side of Capitol Hill in order for their final recommendations to be adopted.

FUNCTIONS OF COMMITTEES

Committees serve the goals of members of Congress, and the needs of the institution as well. Congress is the primary legislative body, and committees are essential in the legislative process. But committees also perform many tasks and functions that may only indirectly relate to legislation. Aside from serving the goals of members for reelection and internal influence on Capitol Hill, committees perform, in addition to their legislative activities, oversight, investigative, and representative functions.

Reelection of Members

Reelection, internal power and influence on Capitol Hill, and "good public policy" are the three primary goals of members. Richard Fenno has pointed out, "All congressmen probably hold all three goals. But each congressman has his own mix of priorities and intensities — a mix which may, of course, change over time." [62]

Generally, the more junior the representative or senator the more effort he or she will devote to building a secure electoral base back home. Particularly important for reelection is credit-claiming for specific benefits channeled to districts and states. Some committees facilitate credit-claiming more than others. Members whose primary goal is reelection seek seats on committees that have jurisdiction over important interests in their districts, so that they may claim credit for committee-generated benefits flowing to their constituents.

For example, the House Agriculture, Interior and Insular Affairs, Merchant Marine and Fisheries, and Public Works and Transportation Committees provide their members with excellent opportunities to claim benefits for their districts. The Agriculture Committee is divided into commodity subcommittees that serve the special economic interests of agricultural districts. Perfect vehicles for credit-claiming are the subcommittees on Cotton, Rice and Sugar; Livestock, Dairy and Poultry; Tobacco and Peanuts; and Wheat, Soybeans and Feed Grains.

A good example of a credit-claiming congressman who uses his position as chairman of the Tobacco and Peanuts subcommittee to credit-claim is North Carolina Democrat Charles (Charlie) Rose. Elected in 1972, Rose immediately sought and obtained a seat on the Agriculture Committee, but he had to wait until 1981 to become chairman of the Tobacco and Peanuts subcommittee. Both crops are vital to his district, and his constituents are well aware that their congressman is a leading supporter of subsidies for tobacco and peanuts. He has succeeded in passing legislation that directly benefits his district, making him a creditable credit-claimer.

[62] Fenno, *Congressmen in Committees*, p. 1.

Appropriations Committee seats and subcommittee chairmanships also can give a member of Congress a good credit-claiming base. Mississippi Democrat Jamie Whitten, elected in 1941, used his chairmanship of the agricultural subcommittee on appropriations, which he obtained in 1949, to become the "Permanent Secretary of Agriculture." So important are agricultural interests in his district that Whitten continued as the subcommittee chairman when he finally achieved the full Appropriations Committee chairmanship in 1979. He used his influence over the years to support cotton subsidies, which were important in his district, and, in accordance with the views of his rural constituents, he opposed controls over pesticides. Because the Appropriations Committees on both sides of Capitol Hill have final control over the amount of money that will be spent by the federal government, powerful committee members, by channeling funds to their states and districts, gain important constituent support.[63]

Internal Power

Committees serve not only the electoral needs of members, but also their goals of internal power and influence, particularly in the House. Members seek the prestige committees on both sides of Capitol Hill, which especially means the institutional committees, to elevate their status with their colleagues. A seat on the House Ways and Means Committee, for example, elevates its holder above the ordinary members of most other committees.

Both the House and the Senate divide their committees into categories of importance, limiting Democratic representatives to one seat on "exclusive" committees, and senators to two "major" committee slots.[64] House Democrats are generally limited to one standing-committee chairmanship. Committee chairmen are not permitted to be chairmen of more than one subcommittee of their committee, nor can they chair a subcommittee on another committee. Other

---

[63] The case of Pennsylvania congressman Daniel J. Flood illustrates how a congressman can become almost invulnerable to electoral attack through effective credit-claiming based upon the chairmanship of an appropriations subcommittee. See 263–264.

[64] An exception to the House rule on exclusive committees is that the Democrats have allowed their members of the Ways and Means and Appropriations Committees to sit also on the Budget Committee.

Democrats are limited to one subcommittee chairmanship, with the exception of Budget Committee members, who are exempt from the rule. House Republicans have rules similar to those of the Democrats, although their members have more flexibility in committee assignments.

Senators of either party are allowed to sit on two major committees and one minor committee. They are limited to one full committee chairmanship, and may chair only one subcommittee of each committee on which they serve.

The party rules of the House and the Senate that limit the committee positions members may hold distribute the opportunities they have for gaining power and influence. Both the House and the Senate have responded to the recurrent demands of a majority of members over the years to increase their access to the committees of their choice. Committee chairmanships still require seniority, but seats on prestigious committees may be obtained by junior congressmen or senators.

Good Public Policy

Finally, committees serve the "good public policy" goals of members. Legislators can help to make good public policy on almost any committee, but there are a few committees that members choose because they are more interested in the advancement of Senate work they consider to be in the national interest than in always responding to the parochial interests of their districts. In the House, a congressman may join the Agriculture Committee to advance his constituent interests, and the Ways and Means Committee to gain a reputation for power with his colleagues, but will seek a seat on the Foreign Affairs, Education and Labor, or perhaps the Budget Committee primarily to make good public policy. Richard F. Fenno observes that

> members of the Education and Labor and Foreign Affairs Committees express . . . a strong personal interest in and a concern for the content of public policy in their committee's subject matter; in short, they want to help make good public policy. Congressmen who seek membership on these two committees do so, they say, because these committees deal with "interesting," "exciting," "controversial," and "important"

subjects. . . . Some members on each committee see membership as positively helpful to them in their districts; more view
membership as having either no effect (mostly Foreign Affairs) or an adverse effect (mostly Education and Labor) on
their reelection. And none cites influence in the House as a
relevant reason for seeking membership.[65]

New York Democrat Stephen Solarz is a good example of a good-
public-policy-oriented congressman who has used the House Foreign
Affairs Committee as a platform for his views. Solarz's 13th district,
stretching from northern Brooklyn to the beaches of Coney Island,
was redrawn in 1980, and there was some talk that the congressman's normally huge margins of victory might be reduced; however,
Solarz won in 1982 by 81 percent of the vote, making his once-safe
district even safer. His electoral popularity has allowed him to pursue
a House career that does not have to center on electoral activities.
His seat on the Foreign Affairs Committee could be viewed as an
electoral plus because it gives Solarz a greater opportunity than
other members of Congress to appeal to the majority of Jewish
voters in his district by supporting the cause of Israel. The congressman's interest in foreign policy goes far beyond Israel, however. He chaired the Africa Subcommittee for two years before he
became in 1981 the chairman of the Asian and Pacific Affairs Subcommittee. He spends much of his time traveling around the world
informing himself about foreign-policy matters. Solarz has also pursued good public policy as a member of the House Budget Committee, where he has been the proponent of innovative economic ideas.

The importance of committees to the goals of representatives and
senators provides a strong underpinning for the committee system,
and for the status quo. It is far easier to expand committees on Capitol Hill than to reduce their number or change their jurisdiction
through reorganization.

Representation of Special Interests

Many congressional committees were established in response to group
demands for representation on Capitol Hill. A myriad of subcommittees represent interests that span the political landscape. Major com-

---

[65] Fenno, *Congressmen in Committees*, p. 9.

mittees with important legislative jurisdiction that were created, not in direct response to political demands but to do the necessary business of government, include the Armed Services Committees on both sides of Capitol Hill, the Energy and Commerce Committee (formerly the Interstate and Foreign Commerce Committee) in the House and the Commerce Committee in the Senate, and even the original Agriculture Committees (established in the House in 1820 and in the Senate in 1825). Inevitably, these committees represent important economic and political interests. The committees and subcommittees of Congress join administrative agencies in representing a pluralistic political universe. Interest groups provide support for continuation of committees on Capitol Hill, as they do for retention of administrative agencies that represent them.

Even a cursory view of the committee landscape reveals the multitude of special interests that are represented. On both sides of Capitol Hill special committees deal with: Agriculture; Banking, Housing, and Urban Affairs; Education and Labor; Small Business; Public Works and Transportation (House) and Environment and Public Works (Senate); Veterans' Affairs; and Aging. Subcommittees, special and select committees, expand special-interest representation. The Select Indian Affairs Committee survived attacks on its independence when the Senate committee system underwent reorganization in 1977. Hearings before the Senate Rules and Administration Committee on the reorganization plan saw representatives of Indian tribes who vigorously argued for continuation of "their" committee.

Subcommittees pinpoint special-interest representation. Most interests that have even a minimum of political clout are represented on Capitol Hill. Subcommittees on the Family Farm, the Handicapped, the Consumer, the Merchant Marine, Aviation, Surface Transportation, Financial Institutions, Housing and Urban Affairs, Insurance, Coastal Personnel and Modernization, the Panama Canal and the Outer Continental Shelf, Elementary, Secondary and Vocational Education, Retirement, Income and Employment are among the hundreds of subcommittees buttressing plural-interest representation.

Oversight of the Executive

The Legislative Reorganization Act of 1946 formally recognized the oversight responsibilities of standing committees, charging them with overseeing the administrative agencies under their jurisdictions. Keeping administrative agencies responsible to the intent of Congress is the purpose of legislative oversight. Once Congress enacts programs they must be administered by executive departments and agencies that may go their own way unless Congress exercises continuous supervision over them through its committees.

Committee hearings and investigations, annual authorizations and appropriations, informal contacts between congressional staff and bureaucrats, General Accounting Office audits, special congressional staff studies carried out by support agencies such as the Congressional Budget Office, and Senate confirmation proceedings help Congress to exercise oversight. Although since 1946 Congress has emphasized oversight in resolutions reminding committees of their oversight responsibilities, effective oversight performance is at best sporadic. Oversight does not particularly help members of Congress to reach their reelection or internal-influence goals. Oversight does not help members of Congress to credit-claim or take positions, the activities that are so important for reelection. Nor does oversight particularly advance a member's Capitol Hill career, which is helped more by time spent on developing legislation, on policy expertise, or pursuing internal congressional matters, such as party leadership positions or seats on prestigious committees. Oversight has an outside focus, but a reputation for power can be gained only by concentrating upon the internal world of Capitol Hill.

Members who care about good public policy also find oversight less important than development of legislation and policy expertise. They are understandably more interested in congressional policy making than in administrative implementation, even though the way in which a program is administered helps to shape public policy.

Political scientist Morris Ogul observed, after extensive investigation of legislative oversight, "Despite their evident sincerity in acknowledging a general obligation to oversee, few members felt any strong stimulus to fulfill this obligation regularly. The gap between expectations and behavior was large." [66] Congressmen "assigned a relatively low priority to oversight and hence spent little time on it." [67] Moreover, "congressional committees give oversight a priority

[66] Morris F. Ogul, *Congress Oversees the Bureaucracy* (Pittsburgh: University of Pittsburgh Press, 1976), p. 181.
[67] Ogul, *Congress Oversees the Bureaucracy*, p. 182.

second to lawmaking and ... committee staff persons spend a small percentage of their time on it." [68] "Members calculate personal gains and losses before they undertake oversight activity. In this gain-loss calculus, oversight is frequently seen as less central than legislating and serving one's district more directly." [69]

It is clear that even though committees are primarily legislative bodies, the "little legislatures" of Capitol Hill may perform many valuable functions beyond originating and developing legislation. They are the major focus of congressional politics. Party leaders know that their effective exercise of power on Capitol Hill depends upon their ability to persuade the largely independent committees to follow their lead. Even presidents know that in dealing with Congress they must accommodate not only its leaders but also the chairmen of key committees, who are often viewed as the heads of sovereign bodies. Like foreign leaders, committee chairmen are often invited to state dinners and other White House functions, in a presidential effort to gain their support.

COMMITTEE REFORM

At any one time committee organization and procedures reflect power relationships on Capitol Hill, and the power of outside groups as well, as they strive to buttress their access to legislators through committee representation. The committee status quo is inevitably supported by a powerful political infrastructure within and outside of Congress. Committee chairmen and their staffs and ranking minority members do not want to relinquish their positions, and they zealously fight any attempt to reorganize their committees in a way that would diminish their power. Outside interests, both private groups and administrative agencies and departments, do not want to see their access to Capitol Hill diminished by reduction in power or even elimination of "their" committees. The iron triangles of politics, formed by the mutually supported relationship between committees, agencies, and special interests, represent and defend the status quo.

[68] Ogul, p. 182.
[69] Ogul, p. 182.

Reform and Power

Reform, then, is a political issue, dealing in allocation of power. Those whose power within and outside of Congress is enhanced by the committee system want to preserve it, and those whose power is diminished by the status quo want to change it. From time to time congressional party leaders have proposed committee reorganization to reduce fragmentation and facilitate their ability to lead. Outside of Congress, groups that do not feel they are adequately represented on Capitol Hill have also argued in favor of reorganization of the committee system that excludes them. Those whose channels of influence to the "little legislatures" of Capitol Hill are obstructed join with party leaders in an effort to reduce committee bastions of power. They feel, as do the party leaders, that their power can be enhanced only by reducing the fragmentation of legislative power caused by the ever-growing number of committees and subcommittees.

The quest for personal power is not the only reason behind proposals for the "reform" of the committee system. The power of Congress itself may be at stake, as it confronts a constitutionally unified presidency capable of taking swift and forceful action without formal congressional approval. Congressional party leaders, and even committee chairmen themselves, confronted with an "imperial" presidency, have occasionally joined forces to preserve the power of Congress by reducing its committee fragmentation. The Legislative Reorganization Act of 1946, which reduced the number of standing committees, increased congressional staff, and strengthened the congressional party system, was an important example of congressional response to what was viewed as excessive executive power. The Budget and Impoundment Control Act of 1974 was another example of legislation designed to increase congressional strength in relation to the executive. The 1974 law created budget committees on each side of Capitol Hill, and a congressional budget office to strengthen the ability of Congress to shape the federal budget, most of which was under the control of the president and his Office of Management and Budget. The 1974 statute also prevented permanent presidential impoundment of appropriated funds without congressional approval. It was passed mainly in response to the presidency of Richard M. Nixon, who carried the constitutional powers of the office to their limits and even beyond.

Committees remain the keystone of the congressional power establishment regardless of attempts to reduce their independence, powers, and number. They prevail because they serve the incentives of legislators for reelection, internal power and influence on Capitol Hill, and good public policy. Political pluralism is a reality on Capitol Hill as it is in the broader political system. Within and outside of Congress, pluralism makes disciplined political parties impossible, inevitably enhancing committee power.

CHAPTER FOUR

Congressional Parties and Other Internal Influences

Though committtees are predominant on Capitol Hill, other groups help to shape the legislative process and influence members, including party leaders, state delegations, special caucuses, and the burgeoning congressional staff. Party leaders can and do exert pressure upon members even though their organizations are undisciplined. Also important may be broad party ideologies, for members vote along party lines far more than is commonly believed.

State delegations may also influence members who find that on many matters they share interests with their fellow state representatives. A variety of special interests are also reflected in nonparty caucuses whose members are encouraged to back their causes. Finally, congressional aides are ubiquitous on Capitol Hill, instantly giving advice to members and often acting on their own in the legislative process.

IMPORTANCE OF PARTIES

The general importance of congressional parties regardless of their lacking discipline has been reviewed.[1] Political parties became important on Capitol Hill in the latter part of the nineteenth century.

Ebb and Flow of Party Discipline

Historian David Rothman writes that even by the mid-1840s party influence began to increase significantly in the Senate: "Then the

[1] See Chapter Two.

[party] majority composed, discussed, and approved the committee slate in caucus and submitted it to the Senate for the formality of a vote. Rank held firm and chairmanships became the exclusive privilege of the dominant party. Moreover, the majority also determined the minority proportion on the committees, allowing the rival caucus to fill the quota." [2]

Party discipline was lacking in the House, however, throughout the nineteenth century. Woodrow Wilson, when he observed and wrote about Congress as a young graduate student in 1885, was struck by the fragmentation of power in the House. He was much enamored of the British system, in which party discipline prevailed in the parliamentary parties. Wilson wrote,

> Congress cannot, under our present system, have that serious purpose of search into the merits of policies and that definite and determinant party — or if you will — partisan aim without which they can never be effective for the instruction of public opinion, or the cleansing of political action. The chief of these reasons, because the parent of all the rest, is that there are in Congress no authoritative leaders who are the recognized spokesmen of their parties. Power is nowhere concentrated; it is rather deliberately and of set policy scattered amongst many small chiefs. It is divided up, as it were, into forty-seven seignories, in each of which a standing committee is the court-baron and its chairman lord-proprietor. These petty barons, some of them not a little powerful, but none of them within reach of the full powers of rule, may at will exercise an almost despotic sway within their own shires, and may sometimes threaten to convulse even the realm itself; but both their mutual jealousies and their brief and restricted opportunities forbid their combining and each is very far from the office of common leader.[3]

In twentieth-century Congresses party discipline has ebbed and flowed as the party leaders, sometimes joined by rank-and-file party members, have vied with committee chairmen for control over the legislative process. Party caucuses, when unified, can exercise and have exercised significant power. In 1911 the House Democratic Caucus succeeded in binding its members by a two-thirds vote to support its

[2] David J. Rothman, *Politics and Power: The United States Senate, 1869–1901* (New York: Atheneum, 1969), p. 13.

[3] Woodrow Wilson, *Congressional Government* (New York: Meridian, 1956), p. 76. Wilson's work was originally published in 1885.

positions on the floor on important matters of public policy. In 1974 a "resurgent" Democratic Caucus flexed its muscles in deposing three senior committee chairmen who allegedly had acted contrary to the wishes of the majority of House Democrats. But such bursts of party discipline and power are rare on Capitol Hill. More powerful and persistent than the forces of centralization are those of decentralization, which buttresses the fragmented committee system.

HOUSE PARTY LEADERSHIP

In the House, the Speaker and the Majority Leader attempt to direct the majority party with the aid of "whips" and the chairmen of the Rules and Ways and Means Committees. The party's Steering and Policy Committee is also an important adjunct of the leadership, as is the chairman of the Democratic Caucus. Party leaders are ex officio chairmen and vice chairmen of important party committees, such as the Steering and Policy Committee, which is chaired by the Speaker and vice-chaired by the Majority Leader and the chairman of the Caucus. House Speaker Tip O'Neill sees "effective leadership in the post-reform House as dependent upon including as many Democrats as possible in the process and giving them a stake in the leadership's success.... Getting the junior members involved is considerd especially important because of their numbers and their tendency toward independence." [4]

The House Republican minority has its own leadership organization. (See Figure 4.1.) The Conference, which is the caucus of all Republican members, elects its own minority leader, who serves as the chairman of the party's committee on committees; it makes Republican committee assignments. Republicans have a separate Policy Committee, which attempts to advise party members and leaders as well on policy positions that the Republicans should adopt.

The Democratic Majority

Since the New Deal the Democrats have been the House majority except in two sessions (1947 to 1949 and 1953 to 1955). To facilitate

---

[4] Barbara Sinclair, "Majority Party Leadership Strategies for Coping with the New U.S. House," in Frank H. Mackaman, ed., *Understanding Congressional Leadership* (Washington, D.C.: Congressional Quarterly Press, 1981), pp. 197–198. See also Barbara Sinclair, *Majority Leadership in the U.S. House* (Baltimore: Johns Hopkins University Press, 1983), pp. 142–146.

Figure 4.1

Party Organization in the House of Representatives

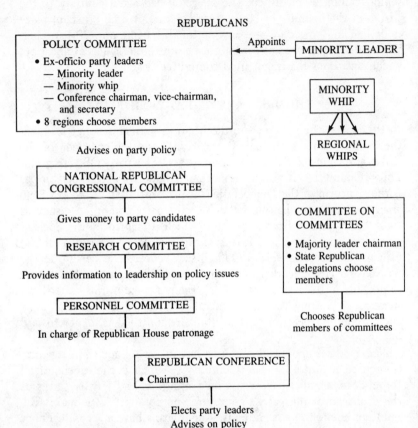

REPUBLICANS

POLICY COMMITTEE
- Ex-officio party leaders
  — Minority leader
  — Minority whip
  — Conference chairman, vice-chairman, and secretary
- 8 regions choose members

Appoints ◄ MINORITY LEADER

MINORITY WHIP

REGIONAL WHIPS

Advises on party policy

NATIONAL REPUBLICAN CONGRESSIONAL COMMITTEE

Gives money to party candidates

COMMITTEE ON COMMITTEES
- Majority leader chairman
- State Republican delegations choose members

RESEARCH COMMITTEE

Provides information to leadership on policy issues

Chooses Republican members of committees

PERSONNEL COMMITTEE

In charge of Republican House patronage

REPUBLICAN CONFERENCE
- Chairman

Elects party leaders
Advises on policy

DEMOCRATS

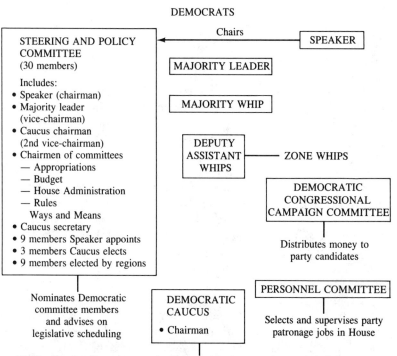

STEERING AND POLICY COMMITTEE
(30 members)

Includes:
- Speaker (chairman)
- Majority leader (vice-chairman)
- Caucus chairman (2nd vice-chairman)
- Chairmen of committees
  — Appropriations
  — Budget
  — House Administration
  — Rules
  Ways and Means
- Caucus secretary
- 9 members Speaker appoints
- 3 members Caucus elects
- 9 members elected by regions

Chairs

SPEAKER

MAJORITY LEADER

MAJORITY WHIP

DEPUTY ASSISTANT WHIPS —— ZONE WHIPS

DEMOCRATIC CONGRESSIONAL CAMPAIGN COMMITTEE

Distributes money to party candidates

Nominates Democratic committee members and advises on legislative scheduling

DEMOCRATIC CAUCUS
- Chairman

PERSONNEL COMMITTEE

Selects and supervises party patronage jobs in House

Ratifies Steering Committee nominations of committee members and chairmen or may substitute own nominations and appointments

Nominates Speaker

Helps to set party policies

Determines committee size and procedures, and ratios of Democrats to Republicans

our discussion we will describe the organization of majority party leadership as it is under the Democrats, recognizing, of course, that a Republican majority would install its own leadership.[5]

THE SPEAKER. The principal difference between the House majority and minority parties is the former's control over the speakership. The Speaker is elected by the full House, and its majority always puts into the position one of its leaders.

The speakership is unique in several ways. First, it is a *constitutional* office, provided for in Article I, Section 2. The Speaker, chosen by the members, *presides* over the body. No comparable constitutional position exists in the Senate, where under the Constitution the vice president presides. The President Pro Tempore is a constitutional position in the Senate, selected by the members, but the position has not become one of important power because its occupant, unlike the Speaker of the House, does not have sole authority to preside if he so chooses. Moreover, the traditional Senate emphasis upon equality of power among its members resulted historically in de-emphasizing the power and importance of its presiding officers, who today are usually junior members rotating at each hour as acting Presidents Pro Tempore.

A tradition of strong House Speakers characterized the nineteenth century. The 1910 "revolt" reduced the Speaker's independence and made him accountable to his party members on Capitol Hill.[6] Ohio Republican Nicholas Longworth, when he became Speaker in 1925, commented on the relationship between his new position and his party: "I believe it to be the duty of the Speaker, standing squarely on the platform of his party, to assist insofar as he properly can the enactment of legislation in accordance with the declared principles and policies of his party and by the same token to resist the enactment of legislation in violation thereof." [7]

Political scientist Robert Peabody stresses in his study of House leadership the role of the Speaker as a representative of his party. A "potential candidate [for the speakership] cannot deviate far from the mainstream of his party's ideological orientation if he hopes to be-

---

[5] See Sinclair, *Majority Leadership in the U.S. House* for a comprehensive discussion of party leadership in the House.
[6] See pp. 41–45.
[7] George B. Galloway, *History of the House of Representatives* (New York: T. Y. Crowell, 1961), p. 144.

come a leader." [8] Speakers and other party leaders "have served an apprenticeship in terms both of years of experience and, more generally, occupancy of lesser party positions. Hence, the rise in importance of a hierarchy of party offices, which, in turn, has led to the emerging or established patterns of leadership succession." [9]

Skillful Speakers who know how to accommodate their party's members are guaranteed long tenure. One of the most astute politicians of the twentieth century, Texas Democrat Sam Rayburn, was Speaker for seventeen years.[10] His successor, John W. McCormack of Massachusetts, was in office for nine years, from 1962 to 1971. Oklahoma Democrat Carl Albert followed McCormack and was Speaker until his retirement in 1977. Thomas P. O'Neill of Massachusetts, who followed Albert, seemed assured of the job as long as he wanted it.

The political skill and personality of the House Speaker determine his tenure. In this condition he is like other congressional leaders. Robert Peabody observes:

> Every leader in Congress, as in other organizations, brings to office a unique set of characteristics: age, ambition, education, health, personal skills, prior political and professional experience—in sum, a personality. Not only does this personality affect the opportunities he may have to obtain a leadership position, they also, in part, influence the extent to which he can maintain office and perhaps even alter the scope and the potential of a given party position. A leader's personality, his strengths and liabilities, also is the single most important variable that affects his ability to withstand or succumb to a challenge.[11]

A skillful Speaker has considerable power over members of his own party and over House proceedings as well. But personal style is paramount to leadership, as the legendary Sam Rayburn pointed out in 1950. "The old day of pounding on the desk and giving people hell is gone," commented Rayburn. "A man's got to lead by persuasion and kindness and the best reasons — that's the only way he can lead

[8] Robert L. Peabody, *Leadership in Congress* (Boston: Little, Brown, 1976), p. 47.
[9] Peabody, *Leadership in Congress*, p. 475.
[10] He served 1940–1947, 1949–1953, and 1955–1961. The Republicans controlled the House during the intervening years.
[11] Peabody, p. 498.

people." [12] The Speaker's formal powers were increased in 1975, when he was given authority to select the Democratic members of the Rules Committee, and when through the Steering and Policy Committee, which the Speaker chaired, appointments to other committees were made. Nevertheless, an effective Speaker must exercise the arts of political persuasion to bring his colleagues into line. The increasing fragmentation of power among committees has made the Speaker's job more difficult. Majority Leader Jim Wright observed in 1980 that

> The leadership's task must have been infinitely less complicated in the days of Mr. Rayburn and Mr. McCormack. In Mr. Rayburn's day, about all a Majority Leader or Speaker needed to do in order to get his program adopted was to deal effectively with perhaps twelve very senior committee chairmen. They, in turn, could be expected to influence their committees and their subcommittee chairmen, whom they, in those days, appointed. . . . Well, now that situation is quite considerably different. There are, I think, 153 subcommittees [in Congress]. . . . We have relatively fewer rewards that we can bestow or withhold. I think that basically all the leadership has nowadays is a hunting license to persuade — if we can. But if it makes the task harder, perhaps it also makes it more interesting. It wouldn't be any fun if it were easy.[13]

THE MAJORITY LEADER. The Democratic Caucus elects its Majority Leader. The Speaker is the chief, the five-star general, but the Majority Leader is his principal assistant, a four-star general with power in his own right. Until 1899 the chairman of the Ways and Means Committee served as the majority party's floor leader, although occasionally the Speaker appointed someone else to the position. The majority-party caucus assumed the power to elect its floor leader as part of its 1910 revolt against the dominance of the Speaker. The Majority Leader, with the backing of the caucus, could overshadow the Speaker, as Majority Leader Oscar Underwood did during the Wilson administration. George Galloway wrote in his history of the House, "As floor leader, Underwood was supreme, the Speaker a fig-

---

[12] *Guide to Congress*, 3rd ed. (Washington, D.C.: Congressional Quarterly, 1982), p. 383.

[13] Christopher J. Deering and Steven S. Smith, "Majority Party Leadership and the New House Subcommittee System," in Mackaman, ed., *Understanding Congressional Leadership*, pp. 288–289.

urehead." [14] Underwood was an exception, however, and later Speakers, such as Sam Rayburn, restored the supremacy of the office.

The Majority Leader assists the Speaker in developing party policy, scheduling legislation for floor debate, and meeting with committee chairmen to expedite bills the leadership considers to be important. The Majority Leader has an advantage on the floor because he is the first to be recognized, giving him vital control over what legislation is first introduced.

PARTY WHIPS. Next in line in the Democratic Party hierarchy in the House is the Majority Whip. Under him is an extensive whip organization, appointed by the leadership, including deputy and at-large whips, and twenty-two regional whips representing the different geographic areas of the country.[15] The whips are as effective as their ability to persuade. They help the leadership in getting out the party vote on partisan issues. The whip's office prepares notices of important pending legislation in order to alert members. The leadership and the whip hold regular meetings to discuss scheduling of legislation and matters pertaining to party discipline. One Democratic House member observed:

> The policy on our side is set through the leadership and Whip system.... The Speaker, the Majority Leader, the Whip and all the Assistant Whips meet and adopt a position on issues, not on everything. But they adopt a position.... Then the guy who is working the door [of the House] gives a thumb-up or thumb-down to let you know what they have decided when you come in to vote.[16]

Congressman Clem Miller described the way party whips operated when he was in the House, which was at the end of the tenure of Sam Rayburn as Speaker in 1961:

[14] George B. Galloway, *History of the House of Representatives* (New York: T. Y. Crowell, 1961), p. 108.
[15] See Lawrence C. Dodd and Terry Sullivan, "Majority Party Leadership and Partisan Vote-Gathering: The House Democratic Whip System," in Mackaman, ed., *Understanding Congressional Leadership*, pp. 227–260; Robert L. Peabody, "House Party Leadership in the 1970s," in Lawrence C. Dodd and Bruce I. Oppenheimer, ed., *Congress Reconsidered*, 2nd ed. (Washington, D.C.: Congressional Quarterly Press, 1981), pp. 137–155.
[16] John F. Bibby, ed. *Congress off the Record: The Candid Analyses of Seven Members* (Washington, D.C.: American Enterprise Institute, 1983), p. 30.

To get members to the floor and keep them there for a right moment is the job of the Whip organization. The Democratic Whip calls the zone Whips representing regions throughout the country. His secretary speaks to other secretaries. Perhaps they can reach their members. Perhaps they cannot. Perhaps they care; perhaps they do not. If he is reached, the member is told to come to the floor for an important vote. Irritably, he shuffles the work on his desk. The call may be followed by another of even greater urgency, 'til he is told, "The Speaker wants to see you on the floor *at once!*" [17]

By the end of the 1970s, Massachusetts Congressman Joe Moakley, an at-large whip, lamented the lack of party discipline that made his job more difficult. "At one time you'd blow a whistle and say this is what the party wants and the members would line up and say 'Yes sir, yes sir, yes sir,' but today they get elected on Monday and they are giving a [floor] speech on Tuesday." [18] Junior members are no longer willing to accept the discipline that they observed during the days of Rayburn when they were told that "To get along, you have to go along." [19]

CAUCUS CHAIRMAN. All House Democrats constitute the Caucus, which if unified under an effective chairman can dominate party affairs. The Caucus during the twentieth century has been largely dormant, however, reflecting the inability of a majority of its members consistently to agree on policies and actions. Periodically the Caucus has come to life, exerting discipline over its members and controlling the House. After the "revolt" of 1910, in which the authority of the Speaker, then Illinois Republican Joseph Cannon, was sharply reduced, the Democrats regained control of the House and through their Caucus bound members to vote for any legislation supported by a two-thirds Caucus vote. But "King Caucus," as the Republicans labeled their Democratic colleagues, soon lost its power because of the unwillingness of its leaders to put party over personal interests, a perennial condition on Capitol Hill.

Under the leadership of California Congressman Philip Burton,

[17] Clem Miller, *Member of the House: Letters of a Congressman*, John W. Baker, ed. (New York: Scribner's, 1962), pp. 52–53.
[18] Ann Cooper, "House Democratic Whips: Counting, Coaxing, Cajoling," *Congressional Quarterly Weekly Report*, vol. 36, no. 21 (May 27, 1978), p. 1306.
[19] Richard Bolling, *House Out of Order* (New York: Dutton, 1965), p. 48.

the Caucus reasserted itself in the mid-1970s. For a brief period it actively asserted its authority to approve of committee chairmen after they had been nominated by the Steering and Policy Committee. The seniority rule traditionally had dictated the choice and continuation of chairmen, but in 1975 the Caucus, under Burton's leadership, took the unprecedented step of deposing three of the most senior committee chairmen in the House. The action was a brief demonstration of the Caucus's power and was not repeated. Burton's use of the Caucus to wield personal power inevitably caused a member backlash, and soon what had promised to be a resurgent caucus quieted down under Burton's successor, Washington Democrat Thomas Foley. The Caucus did not become king because its members were unwilling to accept a monarch as their leader. Party leaders, too, such as House Speaker Tip O'Neill, did not want an active Caucus that would challenge them.

Louisiana Democrat Russell Long, who since the beginning of his House career has aspired to leadership positions, reactivated the Caucus in 1980 when he became its chairman. Working closely with the leadership, Long sought to increase the weight of the Caucus in party councils. Long's personal style helped to account for the increased effectiveness of the Caucus. "Gillis Long is probably the best internal politician in the House," commented Caucus Staff Director Alvin From, "He might not be the great national spokesman, but he knows how to bring people together." [20] Missouri Democrat Richard Gephardt added, "He's a believer in cohesion and consensus between the disparate elements of the party. People don't feel threatened by him. They feel willing to open up and talk with him. People trust him." [21]

Long even took the unusual step of providing a link between the congressional party and Democrats outside of Congress. He created the National House Democratic Caucus, chaired by himself and former chairman of the National Democratic Committee, Robert S. Strauss. "We had two parties," said Long, "Congressional and National. I felt it was good to pull the two together." [22] The National Caucus planned to hold meetings throughout the country to solicit

[20] *Congressional Quarterly Weekly Report*, vol. 41, no. 41 (October 15, 1983), p. 2117.
[21] Ibid., p. 2118.
[22] Ibid., p. 2119.

ideas and concerns from party leaders. Long hoped that the Caucus would have an influence upon the 1984 Democratic platform.

The future of the internal caucus remains in doubt. Its effectiveness will depend upon the skill of its chairman, who can serve, under its rules, for only four years. Moreover, the Caucus can be of consequence only when the mood of party members favors centralization rather than fragmentation of power. The party's presidential defeat and the election of a Republican Senate majority for the first time in almost two decades struck a note of fear for House Democrats, many of whom felt that they had to pull together in order to survive. The post-1980 environment favored an active and relatively unified Caucus, which Long sought to lead. But the Louisiana Democrat knew that consistent party discipline was impossible. "If we try to get everybody to vote a party line," said Long, "you end up tearing it up." [23]

A party staffer who has been around Capitol Hill for a long time, Democratic Study Group Director Richard Conlon, echoed the Long view that the Caucus had to be used carefully in order to survive. Any attempts to make it too dominant, like those which occurred during the reign of Phil Burton, would cause its dismantlement by other party leaders, whose positions and power would be threatened. "When we first got the Caucus going in 1969," observed Conlon, "everyone was aware of the fact that we had a new flower here. But it's like a wild flower growing in the rocks; its chances to survive are 50-50. We've been nurturing it, but if it goes crazy, it will die." [24]

Former Caucus Chairman Thomas Foley agreed. "The Democratic Caucus never should be what it once was or what it is today in some state legislatures," he said. "It should never make collective judgments for the party. We left that role several years ago, and we're never going back." [25]

Adjunct Party Leadership Committees

Both *party* and *institutional* House committees assist the leadership.

STEERING AND POLICY COMMITTEE. The principal party panel, chaired by the Speaker and vice-chaired by the Majority Leader and the chairman of the Caucus, is the Steering and Policy Committee.

[23] Ibid.
[24] Ibid.
[25] Ibid.

It makes Democratic committee assignments and assists in scheduling legislation. The committee-assignment function of the committee was once lodged in the Democratic members of the House Ways and Means Committee, a procedure that was changed in 1974 to make the appointment process more accountable to the Speaker and the Caucus. Ways and Means Democrats had generally been a conservative clique that was out of touch with the party's rank and file. The appointment power of the Ways and Means Democrats had gone unchallenged for decades, mostly because of the stability of the House and its domination by southern conservatives. An influx of new members in the dramatic elections of 1974, which took place just after Watergate and vastly increased the House Democratic majority, undermined the system of the past and made change inevitable. The new House Democrats demanded that the leadership be responsible to them, which required that the authority to make committee assignments be lodged in a representative party committee that in turn would be accountable to the Caucus. In addition to the leadership, the twenty-four-member committee includes twelve members who are elected by congressmen representing different regions of the country. The Speaker appoints eight members, attempting to buttress the representative character of the committee. For example, he may appoint a freshman, a woman, and a member of the Black Caucus. The Speaker has also used his appointment power to increase the number of party leaders on the committee, selecting, for example, deputy whips.

CAMPAIGN AND PERSONNEL COMMITTEES. Assisting the leadership in addition to the steering and policy committees are the Democratic Congressional Campaign and Personnel Committees. The former assists the Democratic candidate in strategic electoral planning, and raises and disburses money to help Democrats in their electoral battles. The committee's chairman is an unofficial part of the House leadership. An active chairman can be an important force not only in House politics, but also in national party councils. California Democrat Tony Coelho pushed himself to the forefront of national Democratic politics when he took over the post in 1980. "It seemed a thankless post when he got it," wrote Michael Barone, "but Coelho made something of it. He raised unprecedented sums of money. He developed the ongoing direct-mail fundraising that the Democrats desperately needed but had neglected in the 1970s. He provided unprecedented kinds of aid to candidates. He modeled much of his operation after the successful work of Republicans, and unblushingly. The Democrats picked up 26 House seats in 1982, his first election year as chairman." [26] The Republicans considered Coelho to be a significant enough threat to target him, unsuccessfully, for defeat in 1982 by giving $100,000 to his opponent.

The Personnel Committee is a relatively minor leadership-dominated party panel that makes and supervises House patronage appointments. The Speaker is an ex officio member, and the chairman in the 98th Congress, Massachusetts Democrat John Moakley, is an aspiring party leader. Moakley served on the Rules Committee and could some day, as its third-ranking member, become chairman.[27]

Linkage Between Party Leadership and Institutional Committees

Finally, the House leadership relies upon the critical institutional committees of the body for assistance. Since 1974 the Rules Committee, whose Democratic members are appointed by the Speaker, assist the leadership in guiding legislation from committees to the floor. Before 1974 the committee acted independently of the Speaker, and there was often a major leadership obstacle as it went its own way in defiance of the Speaker and Majority Leader's wishes. When the Rules panel had the independent authority to assign Democrats to committees as well as to obstruct legislation, it was in many respects more important than the leadership itself.

The Ways and Means, Budget, and Appropriations Committees also have important leadership responsibility as they carry out the constitutional role of the House to originate revenue legislation (Ways and Means), and to exercise what is generally recognized informally as the responsibility initially to shape appropriations. Also considered part of the leadership is the Budget Committee, whose members are partially drawn from the Appropriations and Ways and Means Committees. Tenure on the Budget Committee, however, is limited, making it a less desirable panel than the other institutional

---

[26] Michael Barone and Grant Ujifusa, *The Almanac of American Politics, 1984* (Washington, D.C.: National Journal, 1983), p. 115.

[27] He could do so in the unlikely event that the second-ranking member, Gillis Long, who for a long time has sought to become the Rules chairman, steps aside, perhaps to assume another leadership post.

committees for pursuing a House leadership career. Freshmen with an eye to future leadership often attempt to get on the Budget Committee initially, knowing that their chances for a seat are far better there than on the other institutional committees that have few junior members. Once a congressman gains seniority, however, he or she will seek to transfer to the prestigious committees.

House Speaker O'Neill worked closely with the institutional committee chairmen in the 98th Congress. Ways and Means Chairman Dan Rostenkowski, a brusque but effective Chicago politician raised in the old machine politics school of Chicago Mayor Richard J. Daley, had been given the choice in 1980 of becoming either Majority Whip or chairman of Ways and Means. He chose the latter post, encouraged by O'Neill, who wanted a party loyalist in the position. Rostenkowski makes it no secret that he aspires to the speakership, and he knew that the chairmanship of Ways and Means would give him an opportunity to demonstrate his leadership skills and marshal broad party support. Faced with a difficult situation, with a popular Republican president and an astute Senate adversary, Kansas Republican Robert Dole, chairman of the Finance Committee, Rostenkowski nevertheless made his mark, although it was a minimal one. Massachusetts Democrat James Shannon, himself a member of the committee, commented, "I can't imagine anyone taking over that committee under more difficult circumstances than he did. But he has done a very good job in taking a committee that had a tendency to go its different ways, and build coalitions." [28] Shannon, like many other representatives, was already assessing the leadership style of the burly Ways and Means chairman. "He's a tough guy," said the Massachusetts congressman, "He'll do everything he can to reach out to attract your support. But if you don't deliver on your end, he'll remember that, too." [29] Another committee member commented, "All he cares about is control of the committee. As far as his interest in tax law, he couldn't care less." [30]

Ways and Means is a leadership committee not only because it exercises the constitutional prerogative of the House to originate revenue legislation, but because revenue bills vitally affect the interests of every member. In the same position is the Appropriations

[28] *Congressional Quarterly Weekly Report*, vol. 41, no. 4 (January 29, 1983), p. 194.
[29] Ibid., p. 195.
[30] Ibid.

Committee (which informally has exercised the power to originate
legislation in its sphere), which decides how money will be spent,
another matter vital to the entire House. The committee is so powerful that its subcommittees have been called "The College of Car-
dinals." [31] The committee's chairman, Mississippi Democrat Jamie
Whitten, took over the post in 1979 with the backing of House
Speaker O'Neill, fending off an attempt by House liberals to unseat
him because of what they viewed as his anticonsumer and antien-
vironmental record as chairman of the Appropriations Subcommittee
on Agriculture. Whitten has worked closely with the leadership ever
since. One leadership aide commented, "The Appropriations committee has an institutional sense of itself as among the power centers in the House. It has a disdain for others that is bred from its
image of itself as experts, while all others are amateurs. Whitten
brings some of that to the job." [32]

Finally, the Budget Committee, installed by the 1974 Budget Act
to oversee both revenue and spending legislation, can exercise, under
an effective chairman, an important leadership role. Since its incep-
tion the Budget Committee has been less rather than more powerful
in a body where all committees strive to retain their independence
and power. The Ways and Means and Appropriations Committees
continue their dominance over the budgetary process, but major incursions upon their prerogatives have been made by the Budget
Committee from time to time. The Budget Committee's independence and assertions of power have at times strained relationships
with the Appropriations Committee and the leadership. Friction also
has occasionally developed between the Budget Committee and House
authorizing committees when their independence is being threatened.
It seems likely that the Budget Committee claims to power will be
brief, as the leadership joins with Appropriations and Rules Committee members to curb its authority.

Minority Leadership — the Republicans

Parallel to the organization of the majority party is that of the minority, although they exhibit major differences mainly because of the

[31] *Congressional Quarterly Weekly Report*, vol. 41, no. 24 (June 18, 1983), p. 1210.
[32] Ibid., p. 1212.

status of the minority party. Lack of control over the speakership and committees severely reduces the minority leadership's influence in the legislative process.

THE MINORITY LEADER. The duties of the Minority Leader correspond to those of the Majority Leader, including the scheduling of legislation. The Minority Leader, like his majority counterpart, has to deal with strong and independent personalities as he attempts to guide his party. A Republican representative commented about Minority Leader Robert Michel (Ill.): "[He] did a very specific thing the day he won [his election as minority leader]. He got up and made a speech in part of which he said that he really saw himself as an orchestra leader and that he had 191 people playing in the orchestra and that he wanted to coordinate the flow of all the talent on his side of the aisle. I walked up to him after that speech and said if you really mean that, I want to sign on and be helpful." [33]

Personal qualities and style primarily determine the Minority Leader's power. His potential resources are not inconsiderable, but he must know how to mine and use them. Of particular importance to him is his relationship with the Speaker and other members of the majority leadership. A good relationship means consultation on such important matters as scheduling legislation, floor management of bills, allocation of staff, office, and committee space, and other important internal matters. The two leaderships also meet to determine party allocations of committee seats — how many Democrats and Republicans will be assigned to each committee — the ratios being approximately the same as between the two parties in the House.

A president of the same party increases the Minority Leader's power and status. White House briefings and consultations become a part of his routine, because the president looks to him for leadership on Capitol Hill. When the minority is the "out" party, facing a Democratic president, the Minority Leader often takes it upon himself to speak nationally for the party, sometimes in cooperation with his Senate counterpart.[34]

---

[33] Bibby, ed., *Congress off the Record*, p. 31.
[34] In the early 1960s, House Minority Leader Charles Halleck (R, Ind.), joined with Senate Minority Leader Everett Dirksen (R, Ill.) in what was called the "Ev and Charlie" show that periodically went on television to represent the Republican Party after President John F. Kennedy delivered his State of the Union messages and other speeches.

PARTY ORGANIZATION AND COMMITTEES. A whip organization and
staff assist the Minority Leader, who is also chairman of a committee that assigns Republicans their committee seats.

The party has a separate Policy Committee on which the Republican leaders, except for the Minority Leader, sit to debate and determine party policy positions. One member commented about the
committee:

> It's a place where we debate issues fairly extensively and very
> openly. Then we vote. The members of the policy committee
> vote. Virtually any member is welcome to come to the meet-
> ing, but only members of the policy committee can vote to
> take a position. And basically what it does is give an oppor-
> tunity to air views and then to signify where the leadership
> and the majority of the party are going. But there is no sense
> of being bound by it all.[35]

The National Republican Congressional Committee is also a part
of the leadership that, like its Democratic counterpart, assists both
party incumbents and challengers with financial donations and
strategic-planning sessions.[36]

THE CONFERENCE. Analogous to the Democratic Caucus is the
Republican Conference, but it is far less active and important in
party affairs. A Republican freshman observed about the Conference,
"It doesn't meet very often.... It's generally poorly attended unless
there is some very hot issue to debate, and there is never any resolution in the Conference. There's no vote of any kind. We never take
a position as a conference. We let the policy committee do that." [37]
The Conference chairman, however, can use his post, as can the
chairman of the Democratic Caucus, to bolster his position in the
party and even to gain recognition beyond Capitol Hill. Illinois
Republican John Anderson was Conference chairman before he resigned his congressional seat to run for the presidency in 1980. Although at first he irritated many conservative Republicans because
of his liberal stand, he was able to fend off several challenges to his
Conference chairmanship, and by the time he left Congress he had

[35] Bibby, pp. 29–30.
[36] In the 98th Congress, the Republicans also created Task Forces to investigate
different policy areas.
[37] Bibby, p. 30.

won the respect of his party. New York Congressman Jack Kemp, a nationally prominent Republican known for his support of supply-side economics, succeeded Anderson, using the post to boost his leadership of House Republicans.

CONGRESSIONAL PARTIES AND THE RANK AND FILE IN THE HOUSE

That congressional parties lack discipline has become a political cliché, which, like most clichés, fails to take into account many underlying realities. Members, of course, do not have to vote with their parties, because failure to do so rarely has adverse political consequences. Indeed, the opposite may occur. David Mayhew has forcefully argued that a congressman's reelection drive is aided by the lack of party discipline, for it allows him to be flexible in taking positions that will appeal to his constituents. "What is important to each congressman, and vitally so," writes Mayhew, "is that he be free to take positions that serve his advantage. There is no member of either house who would not be politically injured, or at least who would not think he would be injured — by being made to toe a party line on all policies (unless of course he could determine the line). There is no congressional block whose members have identical position needs across all issues." [38]

Though members want to be free of party positions that would be unappealing to their constituents, position taking is not too important in most electoral campaigns. More critical are credit claiming and advertising, which merge into a home style that usually has little to do with Capitol Hill activities. Incumbents can easily and with minimal finesse cast what they do in Congress as achievements for their districts. Peer rather than electoral pressures more often than not determine members' allegiance to their party.

Party Unity Voting

Determining the extent to which an average member of Congress votes with his or her party on partisan issues is one way of measuring party influence. Issues supported by a majority of party members

[38] David R. Mayhew, *Congress: The Electoral Connection* (New Haven: Yale University Press, 1974), p. 99.

are considered to be partisan. When party leaders and a majority of members advocate a course of action, only peer pressure influences members to get into line. Party leaders know that members will not vote against their district, and they also know that voters' demands on many issues are nonexistent or nebulous, allowing the representative to choose which way to vote. One member described how the leadership exerts influence:

> Well, I've heard the pitch a couple of times on the floor. The Speaker or the majority leader will come over to the recalcitrant member who has voted the wrong way and explain to him, you know, "We know your district; you can do this. You can give us this one. This isn't going to hurt you back home, and we need it. Look, if we can turn around six votes here, we've got this thing and we've got the guys here who think they're ready to go." It's just very straightforward. . . .[39]

Internal incentives encourage representatives to vote with their parties unless they involve a clear-cut conflict of interest with their districts. Party leaders can influence their House careers in many ways, from committee seats to supporting their campaigns for reelection. "I don't play follow-the-leader," said one junior member, "but I do have the support of Tip O'Neill. He came to the fundraiser for me in November. I have just been appointed by Tip as one of the congressional observers on a presidential commission. I don't know if I am being rewarded, but I have a good feeling about what I'm doing, and I don't think it's because the leadership expects it or demands it. I am doing it because I happen to concur in a lot of instances."[40] Reading between the lines, we find that the congressman in question was both helped and flattered by the attention of the Speaker, who knew well the twin incentives of members for reelection and internal power and influence.

In recent decades, party unity scores on both sides of the aisle in the House and the Senate have ranged from a low of 57 percent, recorded by the Democrats in the late 1960s and early 1970s, to a high of 76 percent, achieved by both parties in the early 1980s. (See Tables 4.1 to 4.3.) Although party unity scores are quite high, rarely are more than 50 percent of the votes partisan, with a majority of the members of one party voting against a majority of the other, and often no more than 36 percent of the votes are partisan. By contrast,

[39] Bibby, p. 27.
[40] Bibby, pp. 26–27.

Table 4.1

Votes in Congress Showing Party Unity, 1953–1981
(percentage of votes)

Year	House	Senate
1953	52	n.a.
1954	38	47
1955	41	30
1956	44	53
1957	59	36
1958	40	44
1959	55	48
1960	53	37
1961	50	62
1962	46	41
1963	49	47
1964	55	36
1965	52	42
1966	41	50
1967	36	35
1968	35	32
1969	31	36
1970	27	35
1971	38	42
1972	27	36
1973	42	40
1974	29	44
1975	48	48
1976	36	37
1977	42	42
1978	33	45
1979	47	47
1980	38	46
1981	37	48

Note: Data indicate the percentage of all recorded votes on which a majority of voting Democrats opposed a majority of voting Republicans. n.a. = not available.
Sources: Congressional Quarterly Almanac, various years; and *Congressional Quarterly Weekly Report,* vol. 40 (January 9, 1982). From Norman J. Ornstein et al., *Vital Statistics on Congress* (Washington, D.C.: American Enterprise Institute, 1982), p. 168.

at the end of the nineteenth century 90 percent of the votes were partisan, and party unity scores regularly were 90 percent or greater.[41]

[41] Charles O. Jones, *The United States Congress* (Homewood, Ill.: Dorsey, 1982), p. 234.

THE CONSERVATIVE COALITION. Regional differences exist in both congressional parties, and none is more important than the traditional North-South split in the Democratic Party. Generally, northern Democrats have been far more liberal than their southern colleagues. Conservative Democrats, most of whom have been southern representatives, join with Republicans to form what has been called the Conservative Coalition. The ability of the coalition to sway Congress from one session to another varies, but its overall record of success has been impressive. Table 4.4 illustrates the broad base of support for the Conservative Coalition on both sides of Capitol Hill.

Clearly significant in congressional voting are regional influences. Northern and southern Democrats have traditionally been sharply divided over civil rights, with northern liberals supporting an extended federal role and the southerners opposing government interference. Regional influences have divided the parties on other issues as well, such as government management of the economy and social welfare.

Influences on Party Voting

Influences beyond regional identification and interests affect party discipline. Leadership style, whether or not the president is of the same party as a member; positioning in the minority or majority party; the extent to which a representative's district is safe; and peer pressure of various kinds that may affect a member's career on Capitol Hill and electoral chances beyond are all factors that help to determine party allegiance.

LEADERSHIP PRESSURES. "I don't even think about the leadership in the sense of a threat," commented one member. He continued, "I've voted against the leadership position on some very key issues." [42] Another added, "I don't worry about what the leadership is going to think. I truly feel that what I'm doing is that I'm voting what's right and that makes a difference for me. I think my vote has been with the leadership in a good number of instances. I don't play follow-the-leader, but I do have the support of Tip O'Neill." [43]

Regardless of the disclaimers that they follow their party leaders,

[42] Bibby, *Congress off the Record*, p. 26.
[43] Bibby, pp. 26–27.

Table 4.2

Party-Unity History

Composite party-unity scores showing the percentage of time the average Democrats and Republicans voted with their party majority in partisan votes in recent years:

Year	Democrats	Republicans
1983	76%	74%
1982	72	71
1981	69	76
1980	68	70
1979	69	72
1978	64	67
1977	67	70
1976	65	66
1975	69	70

Source: Congressional Quarterly Weekly Report, vol. 41, no. 52 (December 31, 1983), p. 2791.

Table 4.3

Party Scores

Party-unity and opposition-to-party scores below are composites of individual scores and show the percentage of time average Democrats and Republicans voted with their party majority in disagreement with the other party's majority. Failures to vote lower both party unity and opposition-to-party scores. Averages are closer to House figures because the House has more members.

	1983		1982	
	Dem.	*Rep.*	*Dem.*	*Rep.*
Party unity	76%	74%	72%	71%
Senate	71	74	72	76
House	76	74	72	69
Opposition	17%	20%	20%	21%
Senate	22	20	23	19
House	17	19	19	22

Source: Congressional Quarterly Weekly Report, vol. 41, no. 52 (December 31, 1983), p. 2791.

Table 4.4

Support for Party on Votes in Congress, 1954–1981
(percentages)

Year	House			Senate		
	All Demo-crats	Southern Demo-crats	Repub-licans	All Demo-crats	Southern Demo-crats	Repub-licans
1954	80	n.a.	84	77	n.a.	89
1955	84	68	78	82	78	82
1956	80	79	78	80	75	80
1957	79	71	75	79	81	81
1958	77	67	73	82	76	74
1959	85	77	85	76	63	80
1960	75	62	77	73	60	74
1961	n.a.	n.a.	n.a.	n.a.	n.a.	n.a.
1962	81	n.a.	80	80	n.a.	81
1963	85	n.a.	84	79	n.a.	79
1964	82	n.a.	81	73	n.a.	75
1965	80	55	81	75	55	78
1966	78	55	82	73	52	78
1967	77	53	82	75	59	73
1968	73	48	76	71	57	74
1969	71	47	71	74	53	72
1970	71	52	72	71	49	71
1971	72	48	76	74	56	75
1972	70	44	76	72	43	73
1973	75	55	74	79	52	74
1974	72	51	71	72	41	68
1975	75	53	78	76	48	71
1976	75	52	75	74	46	72
1977	74	55	77	72	48	75
1978	71	53	77	75	54	66
1979	75	60	79	76	62	73
1980	78	64	79	76	64	74
1981	75	57	80	77	64	85

Note: Data represent percentage of members voting with a majority of their party on party-unity votes. Party-unity votes are those roll calls on which a majority of a party votes on one side of the issue and a majority of the other party votes on the other side. The percentages are normalized to eliminate the effects of absences, as follows: party unity = (unity)/(unity + opposition). n.a. = not available.

Sources: Congressional Quarterly Almanac, various years; and *Congressional Quarterly Weekly Report,* vol. 40 (January 9, 1982). From Norman Ornstein et al., *Vital Statistics on Congress* (Washington, D.C.: American Enterprise Institute, 1982), p. 169.

Figure 4.2

Staff of Members and of Committees in Congress, 1891–1981

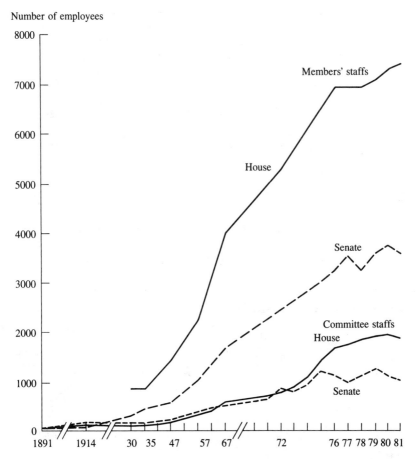

Number of employees

Source: From Norman J. Ornstein, et al., *Vital Statistics on Congress* (Washington, D.C.: American Enterprise Institute, 1982), p. 111.

an active and persuasive Speaker, strong Majority and Minority Leaders, dedicated and vigorous Whips clearly influence party voting strongly. One representative admitted that should the Speaker ask him to "give one for the Gipper," to put the party over the top on a close vote, "I would give the vote to the leadership." [44] John Kingdon writes,

> One might expect party leaders to be a potential source of influence on legislative voting for a number of reasons. One is that they control a number of sanctions which can be used against diffident party members, such as committee assignments, passage of pet pieces of legislation, favorable or unfavorable scheduling of bills, and a host of minor favors. Party leaders might also be expected to possess vital brokerage and other interpersonal skills, as attested by their election by their party's colleagues. Both party leaders and ranking committee members, furthermore, have considerable potential for public exposure, which might be expected to enhance their influence in the House. [45]

Kingdon found, however, that during the late 1960s when he studied Congress, "as an actor that might have some weight in the decisional calculus of congressmen, their party leadership is singularly unimportant." [46] Committee chairmen and ranking minority members determined the legislative agenda and their parties' line more than did the regular party leaders.

How to determine what the party line should be is an obvious difficulty faced by congressional leaders. A freshman Republican in the House commented, "One thing that surprised me — and maybe this is unique to the minority or the Republican party — is how few issues they really take a position on." [47] The comment was made before the election of Ronald Reagan in 1980, which led to greater Republican cohesiveness and strengthened the party line under White House leadership.

A presidency of the opposite party, though it helps the House minority to settle upon a program, poses a dilemma for the majority party, which has difficulty in agreeing upon policy in the absence of presidential leadership. A Democratic Whip commented in the first days of the Reagan administration:

> I'm now one of the multitude of assistant whips, and we meet every Thursday morning in the office of Tom Foley [Democratic Whip]. We sat down last Thursday morning. What is

[44] Bibby, p. 27.
[45] John W. Kingdon, *Congressmen's Voting Decisions*, 2nd ed. (New York: Harper and Row, 1981), p. 111.
[46] Kingdon, *Congressmen's Voting Decisions*, p. 112.
[47] Bibby, *Congress off the Record*, p. 27.

our response [to Reagan's program]? What is our program? We now have the president's [Reagan's] program before us. What is our program? Then somebody said, "Well, maybe the Democrats on the Budget committee will come up with something. They're going to be holding hearings; they'll come up with the Democratic program." That's absurd. That's why I participated today in the announcement of a new Democratic think-tank to help come up with some new programs and ideas.[48]

Presidential guidance and agenda setting, especially when done in consultation with congressional leaders, help immeasurably in determining a party's line on Capitol Hill. Congressional leaders and certainly committee chairmen are frequently at odds with each other, unable to agree on what course of action the party should take. Presidential prodding helps to bring them together. Effective presidential leadership continues to bolster party-unity voting even after the honeymoon period ends.[49]

PRESIDENTIAL PERSUASION. Clinton Rossiter, in his classic work, *The American Presidency*, called the president both "Chief Legislator," and "Chief of Party." But the president's relations both with Congress and with his party on Capitol Hill are tenuous at best. Even when the president takes a strong stand, cajoling, pleading, and attempting by any means to persuade his own party members on Capitol Hill to follow his lead, about the most he can hope for is the backing of 70 percent of his party. (See Table 4.5.) Moreover, presidents seem to have little effect upon party-unity voting on Capitol Hill, which remains relatively constant for each party regardless of whether or not it occupies the White House.

The data seem to be clear. What do the members themselves say about presidential influences upon their party voting? John Kingdon concluded on the basis of his survey of member attitudes,

For all the leadership which the executive branch and administration supposedly give to Congress, individual congressmen pay them remarkably little heed in their voting decisions. Administration officials are mentioned spontaneously in the interviews one-quarter of the time. In fully 61 percent of the

[48] Bibby, p. 27.
[49] See Paul Lenchner, "Congressional Party Unity and Executive-Legislative Relations," *Social Science Quarterly*, vol. 57, no. 3 (December 1976), pp. 589–596.

Table 4.5

Support for the President's Position on Votes in Congress,
by Party, 1954–1981 (percentages)

Presidents and years	House			Senate		
	All Democrats	Southern Democrats	Republicans	All Democrats	Southern Democrats	Republicans
Eisenhower						
1954	54	n.a.	n.a.	45	n.a.	82
1955	58	n.a.	67	65	n.a.	85
1956	58	n.a.	79	44	n.a.	80
1957	54	n.a.	60	60	n.a.	80
1958	63	n.a.	65	51	n.a.	77
1959	44	n.a.	76	44	n.a.	80
1960	49	n.a.	63	52	n.a.	76
Kennedy						
1961	81	n.a.	41	73	n.a.	42
1962	83	71	47	76	63	48
1963	84	71	36	77	65	52
Johnson						
1964	84	70	42	73	63	52
1965	83	65	46	75	60	55

Note: Percentages indicate number of congressional votes supporting the president divided by the total number of votes on which the president had taken a position. The percentages are normalized to eliminate the effects of absences, as follows: support = (support)/(support + opposition). n.a. = not available.

Sources: Congressional Quarterly Almanac, various years; and *Congressional Quarterly Weekly Report,* vol. 40 (January 2, 1982). From Norman J. Ornstein et al., *Vital Statistics on Congress* (Washington, D.C.: American Enterprise Institute, 1982), pp. 166–167.

decisions, the administration is of no importance whatever, and is of minor importance in 21 percent, of major importance in 14 percent, and is determinative in 4 percent of the cases. As compared to other actors in the system, the administration thus seems to exercise rather little influence on congressmen's decisions.[50]

Members of the president's party feel some pressure to toe the party line dictated by the White House, but continue to maintain their independence. One representative commented:

[50] Kingdon, *Congressmen's Voting Decisions,* pp. 177–178.

	House			Senate		
Presidents and years	All Demo- crats	Southern Demo- crats	Repub- licans	All Demo- crats	Southern Demo- crats	Repub- licans
1966	81	64	45	71	59	53
1967	80	65	51	73	69	63
1968	77	63	59	64	50	57
Nixon						
1969	56	55	65	55	56	74
1970	64	64	79	56	62	74
1971	53	69	79	48	59	76
1972	56	59	74	52	71	77
1973	39	49	67	42	55	70
1974	52	64	71	44	60	65
Ford						
1974	48	52	59	45	55	67
1975	40	48	67	53	67	76
1976	36	52	70	47	61	73
Carter						
1977	69	58	46	77	71	58
1978	67	54	40	74	61	47
1979	70	58	37	75	66	51
1980	71	63	44	71	69	50
Reagan						
1981	46	60	72	52	63	84

I still will make my decision based upon what I think is right, but I support the president, and if I can support him I will. . . . If there are no valid arguments for me not to support him, I will support him. If there is no real strong interest in my constituency . . . or I feel that it's the right thing, I will support him. He's my president, and he's the leader of my party, and I feel the same way about the leadership, but, again, it's not a follow-the-leader type of thing.[51]

[51] Bibby, *Congress off the Record*, p. 38.

Some congressmen seem to be relieved when their party does not occupy the White House, giving them greater freedom to take positions that will be appealing to constituents, and helping them to avoid being identified with unpopular presidential programs. After the election of Ronald Reagan in 1980, a House Democrat commented:

> All my friends keep saying to me, "Gee, it must be terrible now to be a Democrat in Congress. It must feel very lonely, and it must be a much more difficult role." It's much easier now to be a Democrat in the House. The burden — to the extent that you feel the burden of the country, and I think that we frequently did feel it when we had to go to the wall on some tough issues [when the president was of our party] is lifted totally now. It's really going to be relatively easy to explain things back home. Last night, I met with two different groups of constituents out in the district who were upset about two different elements of the Reagan program. It's so much easier for me now than it was six months ago, to say, "Gee, yes, isn't that terrible, look what they want to do to us." [52]

ELECTORAL DEMANDS. Electoral competition affects the willingness of congressmen to adopt party positions that may be unpopular or difficult to explain back home. Representatives "who are least secure electorally are substantially less likely to consider party leadership in their decisions than those who are secure. Fully 71 percent of the insecure congressmen show party leadership as unimportant, compared with 56 percent of the most secure. Apparently in the traditional case of party versus constituency, greater electoral security permits a congressman to pay more attention to his party leaders." [53] Weak congressional parties particularly serve the electoral needs of marginal incumbents, those who face tough battles for reelection.

ORGANIZATIONAL FRAGMENTATION. Dispersed rather than integrated power networks characterize Congress. Fragmentation even exists within the party leadership organizations themselves. In the House, for example, the chairman of the Democratic Caucus has occasionally challenged the Speaker and the Majority Leader. Although an arm of the Speaker, the Rules Committee may independently flex

[52] Bibby, p. 39.
[53] Kingdon, *Congressmen's Voting Decisions*, p. 114.

its muscle in a legislative contest. Autonomous committees, with their satellite staffs, are the real centers of congressional power. State delegations and special caucuses add to the organizational disintegration of Congress and to the difficult task of maintaining a meaningful degree of party cohesion.

Finally, in the congressional election process as well as on Capitol Hill, parties are overshadowed. Candidates generally do not depend upon local party organizations to put them into office. Candidate parties have replaced the traditional local party organization. One member commented, in an admittedly rather extreme statement, "The party is no damn good . . . they can't organize and they can't raise money . . . I don't have anything to do with the party organization. . . . They have their function. They give you a vehicle to run on. The real function of the party is to have someone to meet the candidate for Congress when he comes into a strange town." [54]

A typical freshman member commented, "I was not the party's favorite candidate, and my toughest race was the primary, where I had to run against the guy who was an incumbent state treasurer. I had to build my own organization to do it and sort of go around the party." [55] After election, though, the same congressman cultivated the party. "I never go into a county before I have talked to the chairman," he said, "and, basically, I raise money for the party and try to make them my own organization." [56]

Another congressman summed up his feeling that local party organizations have little influence in the House: "You can look around the floor of the House and see a handful — twenty years ago you saw a lot of them — today, you can see just a handful of hacks that were put there by the party organization, and there are very, very few of them left. [The House is mostly comprised of] people who went out and took the election." [57]

Political Consequences of Lack of Party Discipline

Woodrow Wilson, in his classic *Congressional Government*, stated what became a recurrent theme in political science: Governmental accountability and responsibility require disciplined political parties to bridge the gap between the government and the people.

[54] Richard S. Fenno, Jr., *Home Style* (Boston: Little, Brown, 1978), p. 176.
[55] Bibby, *Congress off the Record*, p. 43.
[56] Bibby, p. 43.
[57] Bibby, p. 43.

Parties are a necessary integrative force in politics, without which the collective responsibility of government cannot exist; that is, the people will not be able to hold the government as a whole accountable for its actions. The absence of party discipline produces a system in which government is fragmented, not only between the president and the Congress, but among congressional committees and executive departments and agencies. Under such circumstances governmental accountability is to specialized interests rather than to a national constituency.

Political scientist Gary Jacobson, examining the modern Congress, echoed the Wilsonian theme, "As long as members are not held individually responsible for Congress's performance as an institution, a crucial form of representation is missing. Responsiveness is insufficient without responsibility. Political parties are the only instruments we have managed to develop for imposing collective responsibility on legislators." [58]

Jacobson concluded that the lack of party government has "contributed to political drift, immobilism in the face of tough, divisive problems like energy and inflation, shrill single-issue politics disdaining compromise, enfeebled leadership, and growing public cynicism and distrust of politicians and of political institutions." [59]

Disciplined political parties seem unlikely in the future, for the forces of political disintegration are not waning. A host of factors continue to contribute to the decline of political parties, including the rise of political action committees, the media and political consultants, and the demise of local political bosses, which make it possible for and even encourage candidates to develop their own individual organizations and styles to elect and sustain them.

OTHER INTERNAL INFLUENCES IN THE HOUSE

The lack of party discipline on Capitol Hill has encouraged and enhanced the influence not only of committees but of other groups, including special caucuses, state delegations, and, some feel most important of all, staff.

[58] Gary C. Jacobson, *The Politics of Congressional Elections* (Boston: Little, Brown, 1983), p. 190.
[59] Jacobson, *Politics of Congressional Elections*, p. 191.

Special Caucuses

Different caucuses, most of which are called the Legislative Service Organizations (LSOs), have been organized to represent special interests.[60] Perhaps best known is the Black Caucus, but a host of others represent economic, regional, and ethnic interests. Caucuses generally reflect rather than influence the views of their members, although an active caucus leadership can help to bring members into the fold who otherwise might have been disinclined to give their support.

INTRAPARTY CAUCUSES. Although most caucuses cross party lines, several have been formed within the parties essentially to represent more liberal or conservative views than the average party member holds. The Democratic Study Group (DSG), for example, was created in 1959 to represent liberal party members who felt that their leaders and committee chairmen were far too conservative. The DSG tried to mobilize party support behind John F. Kennedy's New Frontier program, and Lyndon B. Johnson's Great Society, although it eventually became an antiwar group in the late 1960s. The DSG strongly backed the party's reform in the early 1970s that activated the Democratic Caucus, increased the Speaker's power, and took authority away from Ways and Means Democrats to assign committee seats to party members.

The DSG has its own staff, which is actively engaged in developing legislation and in briefing members. The group even organized its own political action committee in the 1970s to provide funds for liberal House candidates. The DSG's influence ebbs and flows depending in large part on the liberal and conservative balance within the party. But over the years the group has had a major influence both on party organization and on legislation.

The DSG is an intraparty group that has exhibited unusual con-

---

60 For an analysis of the increase in caucus activity since 1975, see Steven Webb Hammond, Arthur G. Stevens, Jr., and Daniel P. Mulhollan, "Congressional Caucuses: Legislators as Lobbyists," in Allan J. Cigler and Burdett A. Loomis, eds., *Interest Group Politics* (Washington, D.C.: Congressional Quarterly Press, 1983), pp. 275–297. See also Burdett A. Loomis, "Congressional Caucuses and the Politics of Representation," in Lawrence C. Dodd and Bruce I. Oppenheimer, eds., *Congress Reconsidered*, 2nd ed. (Washington, D.C.: Congressional Quarterly Press, 1981), pp. 204–220.

tinuity in the constantly changing world of caucus politics. Other intraparty groups have exerted power, but they have had limited staying power. After the election of Ronald Reagan in 1980, conservative Democrats organized the Conservative Democratic Forum (CDF), whose fifty to fifty-four members were instrumental in the passage of Reagan's program in a Democrat-controlled House. While the "Boll Weevils," as the CDF members were known, were working for Reagan, Republican liberals, known as the "Gypsy Moths," approximately twenty Republican moderates from the North, joined the Democrats in opposition to some of Reagan's economic programs, particularly those involving major spending cuts for social programs. A more lasting Republican moderate caucus is the Wednesday Group, which originally met on Wednesdays, to develop policies that would reflect the party's center.

NONPARTY CAUCUSES. An extraordinary variety of interests and degrees of formality characterize caucuses that welcome lawmakers who share their special interests, regardless of party affiliation. More than seventy special-interest caucuses have been organized on Capitol Hill. The House requires that they register, but the Senate, which has created just slightly more than a dozen caucuses, does not require their registration. The House Administration Committee decided in 1981 that caucuses accepting contributions from outside sources should not be allowed to use House facilities or public funds.[61] The congressional Black Caucus, Hispanic Caucus, and the Travel and Tourism Caucus had each raised more than $100,000 through their fundraising efforts. By 1983 only the Hispanic Caucus decided to continue accepting outside funds, requiring it to move out of its congressional offices.

Caucus proliferation reflects the political pluralism of Capitol Hill and of the polity beyond. Caucus leaders "lobby" their fellow members just as interest-group lobbyists on the outside attempt to sway Congress. The Black Caucus, for example, takes stands on many kinds of issues that affect black Americans: opposing spending cuts in social programs and aid to South Africa, and supporting the Martin Luther King holiday that finally passed Congress in 1983. On another front, the Women's Caucus has supported the Equal Rights Amendment over the years, and other policies, such as increased child support, which it feels benefit women.[62]

[61] The rule went into effect in January 1983.
[62] See, for example, *Congressional Quarterly Weekly Report*, vol. 41, no. 49 (December 10, 1983), pp. 2627–2628.

The Women's, Black, and other Caucuses also play the power game in Congress, knowing that passage of legislation favorable to their interests depends in large part upon control over key posts. One junior congresswoman remarked:

> The Women's caucus asked me if I would go for a spot on Ways and Means. We had lost — when I say "we," I mean the women had lost their sole representative on Ways and Means. But there were two people from my state, who were senior members [of the delegation], who were vying for it, and I was a bit concerned that in [the first two weeks] I was down here, I might antagonize the entire state delegation. So I stayed away from that, and I went for the committees that I did choose.[63]

The newly arrived congresswoman's remark referred to yet another important internal congressional influence, the state delegation, which may be able to sway its members more than special caucuses do.

State Delegations

All the representatives from a state, regardless of party, constitute the state delegation. In the House, active state delegations bury internal conflicts as much as possible and work together for the benefit of their states. "We have a wide ideological spectrum," said Representative Jim Wright of Fort Worth, Texas, speaking about his delegation, "but we're able to close ranks and work together for any program that benefits any part of the state." [64]

Not all delegations are like the Texans, who over the years have stuck together to become a formidable force in House politics, controlling major leadership positions and committee assignments. Some delegations rarely meet, others gather infrequently to discuss issues that affect their states. State delegations in no way control the votes of their members, although informal pressures can be exerted. Even during the days when Texan Sam Rayburn was Speaker of the House, dominating its proceedings and leading his delegation, one Texas congressman said,

> Unless the issue is of special concern to the state, we frequently split almost directly down the middle. The Speaker

[63] Bibby, *Congress off the Record*, p. 5.
[64] Martin Tolchin, "The Texas Delegation Has One Client: Texas," *New York Times*, March 4, 1983, p. A18.

almost never attempts to influence any member against his
own best judgment or conviction. There are some members
of the delegation he just can't reach. Some members owe their
allegiance to the Southern coalition, others like to think for
themselves. We do stick by our colleagues if someone is jumping on one of them — or Texas if people are jumping on
Texas. Generally many of us incline to follow the judgment
of the Texan on the given committee that has considered the
bill, but that is not absolute.[65]

Speaking about the same period in the House, another member recalled about his state delegation:

The state delegations are not very powerful. We used to meet
together, though not too regularly, for informal discussions
of issues with no attempt to bind members. There are few
meetings of the delegation as a whole now, but we are a
fairly close working group, and by informal means we manage
to cooperate closely. There are many phone calls between
members, we sit together on the floor, things of that sort. We
also work very closely with our senators.[66]

A congressman's internal power and electoral success may be enhanced by a cohesive state delegation that supports his quest for
choice committee assignments and leadership positions, while helping him to boost his constituency support. Large delegations in particular have more influence in the House if their members stick
together. "On some matters," said one congressman from a large
delegation, "we get together and decide what to do so that we have
greater bargaining leverage with the leadership." [67] Another commented, "We like to keep the delegation solid whenever we can. Because it gives you more leverage in the House. He could say he was
trading with a substantial bloc of votes, not just his own." [68]
Outside of Congress on the electoral front, congressmen frequently
find it to their advantage to have voted with their delegation and to
have maintained good relationships with their delegation colleagues.
Political scientist John Kingdon comments, "Many congressmen feel

[65] Charles L. Clapp, *The Congressman: His Work as He Sees It* (Garden City, N.Y.: Anchor, 1964), p. 47.
[66] Clapp, *The Congressman*, p. 47.
[67] John W. Kingdon, *Congressmen's Voting Decisions*, p. 89.
[68] Kingdon, p. 89.

uncomfortable about voting out of step with the rest of the delegation. Newspapers all over the state regularly print delegation box scores, and it can be something of an embarrassment to find oneself voting against the rest of the state's congressmen. Such occurrences can also be used against one in the next campaign." [69]

Congressmen also use their state delegations as a sounding board to assess constituents' attitudes. "A congressman often does not know just what his constituents think about a given issue," states Kingdon. "Given such uncertainty about such an important actor in the system, congressmen can use the state delegation as a convenient constituency substitute." [70]

State delegations, particularly the larger ones, affect their members' voting and committee assignments, but they are merely one of many internal influences. Most powerful are delegations with strong regional identities and many common interests, such as the Texas delegation. Speaker Sam Rayburn remarked about the group's power, "We pick 'em young, we pick 'em honest, we send 'em there, and we keep 'em there." [71] Other large state delegations, without a regional identity and political traditions like those of Texas, such as California and New York, have exhibited little cohesion and only minor influence in House politics.

Fellow Congressmen

Congressmen influence each other in various ways, outside the formal context of committees, parties, special caucuses, and state delegations. Members create informal communications networks with their colleagues to help them assess how they should act to optimize their power within Congress and their electoral chances as well. Junior congressmen in particular seek the advice of more senior legislators who themselves have credibility in the House for their understanding of the legislative process and of the power games that are played within it. But all members, junior and senior, find that they cannot stretch their time to enable them to make independent judgments on the countless matters that come before them.

Members cue off each other in roll-call voting and position taking.

[69] Kingdon, pp. 89–90.
[70] Kingdon, p. 90.
[71] Tolchin, "The Texas Delegation," p. A18.

In the days before electronic voting came to the House, members formed separate lines on teller votes to be counted for or against a bill or motion. "They may rush in from the cloakroom," commented a staffer, "look who is in the teller line, and if there are three or four people they know in the line, they'll just join it. They may not even know what they're voting on." [72] After electronic voting came in the early 1970s, cuing became even easier, for members could now look at the electronic board that registered the votes of members to decide what to do. When the final roll-call bells sound, congressmen have fifteen minutes to get to the floor to register their vote. Typically, an undecided legislator will arrive toward the end of the voting period, glance up at the electronic board to see how his colleagues have voted, and then register his or her vote by cuing, following the lead of respected members with generally similar political views.

Congressmen pay particular attention to the actions of leading members of committees that have considered bills, following their lead especially in technical areas requiring expertise to understand the issues. Commenting on the military, space, and nuclear energy programs, one congressman said, "On things like this — ABM, anything having to do with the Space Program or atomic energy — I rely on the committee. You have to be a nuclear physicist or a Ph.D. or something to even understand what's involved. A common member of Congress can't make an independent judgment on it no matter how hard he tries." [73]

BARGAINING. Congressmen trade favors for their mutual advantage. Porkbarrel legislation particularly, which channels benefits to local districts, reflects multiple trade-offs as representatives support each other's pet projects.

Collegiality and respect among congressmen facilitates bargaining. Former member Clem Miller observed that "There is a compelling need for respect — to be held in respectful esteem by your colleagues. . . . When a bill of great importance to a member is in process, he wants to be able to hear, 'I'll vote for it because it's Jim's bill. Jim's a great guy,' not 'If Jim's for it, I'm against it.' " [74]

Individualism characterizes the congressional process, requiring and

---

[72] Kingdon, *Congressmen's Voting Decisions*, p. 98.
[73] Kingdon, pp. 97–98.
[74] Miller, *Member of the House*, p. 120.

Table 4.6

Personal Staffs of Members of the House and the Senate, 1891–1981

Year	Employees in House	Employees in Senate
1891	n.a.	39
1914	n.a.	72
1930	870	280
1935	870	424
1947	1,440	590
1957	2,441	1,115
1967	4,055	1,749
1972	5,280	2,426
1976	6,939	3,251
1977	6,942	3,554
1978	6,944	3,268
1979	7,067	3,612
1980	7,371	3,746
1981	7,487	3,638

Source: Norman J. Ornstein, *Vital Statistics on Congress* (Washington, D.C.: American Enterprise Institute, 1982), p. 110.

buttressing informal bargaining and communications among members. Parties, state delegations, and committees, however, may shape and channel the ways in which congressmen relate to each other. Members primarily cue from their fellow congressmen in one or the other of these groups. Increasingly, members have not only relied upon their fellow congressmen for advice, but also upon their ever-growing staffs.

CONGRESSIONAL STAFF—
THE "UNELECTED REPRESENTATIVES"

Congressional staffers are in many respects surrogate congressmen.[75] Both personal and committee staffs have grown enormously over the years. (See Figure 4.2 and Table 4.6.) Congressional aides have increasingly shaped the legislative process, often determining the content of legislation itself. An active and expert staff is a symbol of power on Capitol Hill, especially in the Senate. Staffers also assist members in their reelection campaigns, working out of both Wash-

[75] See Michael J. Malbin, *Unelected Representatives: Congressional Staff and the Future of Representative Government* (New York: Basic Books, 1980).

ington and district offices to cultivate good relations with constituents, performing the role of ombudsman as they help voters overcome their problems with government.

Eric Redman's *The Dance of Legislation* has for many years introduced students of Congress to the innovative and powerful role played by congressional staff. Political scientist Richard Neustadt introduces the book:

> Imagine yourself fresh from college, a Rhodes Scholarship ahead of you, temporarily in Washington as junior staffer for a senior senator and given scope by him to try to put a bill through Congress: a good bill — a health bill — a bill you care about. Imagine that, and you are in Ric Redman's shoes. . . . From there, [the book] takes you on Ric's way precisely as *he* went — first-person, present tense — racing and stumbling, sometimes fumbling, in pursuit of action on his bill until its fate is sealed.[76]

Redman's account illustrates the central role that even junior staffers may play in shaping legislation.

Senior and experienced aides, however, are usually the ones who are most influential on Capitol Hill. Redman himself describes how one long-time staffer, Harley Dirks, Chief Clerk of the Appropriations Committee, wielded power behind the scenes:

> Like other Appropriations Committee clerks, Dirks is unknown to the public and to much of the Washington press corps. Tourists do not call at his office (although senators and Secretaries do), and at Appropriations hearings members of the audience sometimes whisper, "Who is that man sitting next to the chairman?" . . . The only outsider . . . who has ever sensed Dirks's true influence was an academic researcher who interviewed him in connection with a study attempting to correlate Appropriations figures with senators' backgrounds. Amused, Dirks simply jotted down for his visitor his own prediction of dollar amounts, by program, in an Appropriations bill the senators themselves had not yet even discussed. When the bill finally passed, Dirks's projections corresponded uncannily with the approved figures.[77]

[76] Eric Redman, *The Dance of Legislation* (New York: Simon and Schuster, 1970), p. 11.
[77] Redman, *Dance of Legislation*, pp. 45–46.

Staff Functions

Harrison W. Fox, Jr., and Susan Hammond, in their pioneering work on congressional staff, concluded that

> staffs perform much of the congressional work: they perform almost exclusively the constituent-service function; do most of the preliminary legislative research; help generate policy ideas; set up hearings, meetings, and conferences; carry out oversight activities — program evaluations, investigations, etc.; draft bills; and meet and talk with executive, interest, and constituent groups on substantive matters. The member spends most of his or her time chairing hearings; debating, conferring with colleagues and voting on the House or Senate floor; talking to constituents; marking up bills; and directing and working with his personal and committee staff.[78]

John Kingdon observes that although members themselves do not admit that their staffs dictate *voting* decisions on the floor, a high probability exists that a congressman's vote will reflect his or her staff position. The staff is "a good predictor of the vote and . . . of substantial importance in congressmen's decisions, at least as important as their constituencies." [79]

Reasons for Staff Influence

The origins of and one reason for the modern congressional staff may be found in the Legislative Reorganization Act of 1946. At the time, a consensus formed on Capitol Hill that Congress had too long been in the shadow of a dominant presidency, and that something needed to be done to streamline congressional organization and procedures and to provide expert staff to help the legislature cope with the complexities of policy making in a technical age. Congressional scholar Ernest Griffith points out the dilemma:

> The principal difficulty faced by Congress in carrying out its contemplated functions may be put in question form. How can a group of non-specialists, elected as representatives of the

[78] Harrison W. Fox, Jr. and Susan Webb Hammond, *Congressional Staffs: The Invisible Force in American Law Making* (New York: Free Press, 1977), p. 143.
[79] Kingdon, *Congressmen's Voting Decisions*, p. 203.

electorate, really function in a specialized and technological age? For surely no one will deny that the overwhelming majority of the great problems facing the government are complex to such a degree that the most skilled specialization and the most profound wisdom are none too great to deal with them.[80]

Griffith wrote after passage of the Legislative Reorganization Act, which he found "marked the real birth of a full-fledged congressional staff." [81] Before the 1946 law, Wisconsin Senator Robert M. La Follette, Jr., one of its principal authors, had written in *The Atlantic*:

> The question of adequate and expert staff is of vital importance. Undoubtedly one of the great contributing factors to the shift of influence and power from the legislative to the executive branch in recent years is the fact that Congress has been generous in providing expert and technical personnel for the executive agencies but niggardly in providing such personnel for itself.[82]

La Follette's call for additional staff was met in the 1946 law, which provided for professional committee staffs for the first time, and increased funds for personal staffs as well. Oklahoma Democrat Mike Monroney, who sponsored the bill in the House, had commented during the committee hearings on the legislation: "The fact that we struggled along for ten, fifteen, or twenty years with incompetent committee assistance, that is, insufficient committee assistance, to say the least, would lead to the conclusion that the membership of Congress recognizes the crying need for this technical assistance." [83] The problem, said Georgia Democrat Robert Ramsback, is that "None of these committees has been adequately staffed.... The members of the staff [of the Agriculture Committee] are helpful, and attentive, and sincere, but they have no special training for what they are doing, they have no special knowledge of the problems of agriculture, they are merely a clerical staff." [84]

---

[80] Ernest F. Griffith, *Congress: Its Contemporary Role*, 3rd ed. (New York: New York University Press, 1961), p. 67.
[81] Griffith, *Congress: Its Contemporary Role*, p. 84.
[82] Cited in George B. Galloway, *Congress at the Crossroads* (New York: Thomas Y. Crowell, 1946), p. 157.
[83] Fox and Hammond, *Congressional Staffs*, p. 21.
[84] Fox and Hammond, p. 21.

The Reorganization Act of 1946 only partially solved the urgent congressional need for professional staffing. Congress passed yet another reorganization act in 1970 that increased committee and personal staff. In the following decade House and Senate allowances for personal staff doubled.

Staff as an Adjunct and Symbol of Power

Although the initial impetus for more staff was presidential-congressional conflict and the imbalance of power between the two branches, the quest for personal power on Capitol Hill gave members an incentive to buttress their personal and committee staffs. Senators in particular, who have to spread themselves so thin in dealing with the same workload as the House, though they are far less numerous, rely upon staff not only to provide expert advice but to be their surrogates in the internal politics of the Senate. As senators jockey for position and power their staffers act as strategists and advance troops. The mark of a good senator is an excellent staff; and a reputation for power often depends upon an aggressive staff who help to make a senator a leading political and legislative force.

Alaska Senator Mike Gravel (D), a perennial outsider while he was in the body, lamented in 1975, "We are all supposed to be equal in the Senate and the only way we can truly make ourselves equal is, of course, to have equal chance to gain the knowledge and acquire the information that we need to discharge our obligations as senators in our legislative roles. . . . In a rational democracy, power is dependent upon knowledge. What we talk of here is the ability to acquire knowledge through the use of staff." [85]

Edward Kennedy of Massachusetts is a senator whose reputation for power on Capitol Hill was built mostly through his staff. *Washington Post* reporter Stephen Isaacs referred to Kennedy and a number of his colleagues as well when he wrote about "the sight of many senators scrambling after staff bodies like hunters in pursuit of prey, hungering for the impact that extra staff person or two, or three, or even dozens can give to them and their political careers." [86] Kennedy

---

[85] Quoted in Rochelle Jones and Peter Woll, *The Private World of Congress* (New York: Free Press, 1979), p. 139.

[86] Cited in Jones and Woll, *The Private World of Congress*, p. 130, from the *Washington Post*, February 16, 1975, p. A8.

garnered staff through various subcommittees he chaired, generally gaining energetic and expert aides who put him at the forefront of legislation in areas such as health and deregulation.[87]

Staff is less important in the House than in the Senate: "Congressmen pride themselves on running their own show and put down senators for their heavy reliance on staff coaching." [88] Staff is nevertheless crucial to a representative who wants to carve out a career on Capitol Hill, and have good relations with constituents. New congressmen usually make every effort to hire experienced Hill people, and aides conversant with the often arcane ways of the Washington political world. One freshman congressman told how the core of his staff came from the retiring Republican senator from his state: "I was fortunate enough to pick up, for my experienced Hill personnel, people who had worked for as much as twelve years for the Republican senator, who had just retired and had very competent people. And I hired three of his people to work for me back in the state. I picked up his top press and legislative person to work for me here." [89]

House members focus particularly upon building their district staff to do casework and maintain close relations with constituents. A greater percentage of House than Senate staff is based in home offices.

Influence of Staff

"Congress needs help" has always been the cry of proponents of the steady increase in congressional staff. Clearly Congress needs staff to do its job. But staffers are more than mere assistants. They perform the functions of Congress itself, and act as intermediaries not only among the members themselves but also between the legislature and the other branches of government, interest groups, and constituents.

Ironically, as staff has grown so too has the workload of Congress. Staffers seek high marks for themselves by generating legislation and actively engaging in a wide array of activities. Without them not only would less legislation be developed, but legislative, investigative, and oversight hearings would be cut back. Press releases would be reduced to a minimum. Members themselves would have to be more directly engaged in the legislative and deliberative process. They

[87] See Jones and Woll, pp. 55–75.
[88] Jones and Woll, p. 130.
[89] Bibby, *Congress off the Record*, p. 11.

might have to draft and even themselves sign letters to constituents, which in the modern age of staff and technology are drafted by aides, reproduced on electronic typewriters, signed by auto-pens with the congressman's John Hancock, and sent to unsuspecting constituents who often feel they have received a letter from the member himself or herself. One long-time staffer commented, "My congressman's predecessor had two girls on his office staff when he first came to Congress — no AA [administrative assistant]. He supervised the office himself, and gave whatever had to be done to the girls. He also might end up typing something himself. He *never* sent out press releases." [90]

Another experienced aide observed, "Why, the previous incumbent, who served for eighteen years, replied to his letters by longhand. . . . Now, government is much more complicated and people are baffled — but they are also much more sophisticated and conscious of pending legislation. The staff *has* to act as liaison with them." [91]

In a heated Senate debate over staffing in 1975, Senator Herman Talmadge (D, Ga.), told his amused colleagues:

> If we would fire half the Senate employees we have, fire half the staff and not permit a paper to be read on the floor of the U.S. Senate, we would complete our business and adjourn by July 4. (Laughter)
>
> The Senator from Georgia knows that when you get more staff and more clerks they spend most of their time thinking up bills, resolutions, amendments. They write speeches for senators, and they come in here on the floor with senators. Unanimous consents are obtained for so-and-so to sit. He is their protégé, telling the senator how to spend more money.[92]

Staffers, acting as entrepreneurs, try to sell new ideas for legislation to their bosses, for their mutual benefit. Members who sponsor important legislation, particularly bills that gain press attention, boost their reputations in Congress and outside. The staffers responsible for the new ideas in turn gain recognition on Capitol Hill for their influence. Sometimes the press finds a good story in staff power, highlighting the importance of staff directors and other well-placed aides.

For example, Richard Halloran wrote, "The staff of the House

[90] Fox and Hammond, *Congressional Staffs*, p. 4.
[91] Fox and Hammond, p. 4.
[92] Fox and Hammond, p. 5.

Armed Services Committee is considered by its admirers to be among the strongest and most powerful committee staffs on Capitol Hill and by its critics to be among the most arbitrary and autocratic." [93] Halloran reported, "There is widespread agreement that members of the committees' professional staff have more influence on military budgets, weapons, research and development than do members of the committee itself. That makes them among the most influential people in Washington in determining the military posture of the United States." [94]

The "high priests" of legislation often aptly describes congressional staff.[95] Senator Ernest Hollings (D, SC), when he was chairman of the Legislative Appropriations Subcommittee, suggested that the staff may control members more than vice versa:

> There are many senators who feel that all they are doing is running around and responding to the staff. My staff fighting your staff, your staff competing with mine. It is bad. . . .
> Everybody is working for the staff, the staff, staff; driving you nutty. In fact, they have hearings for me all of this week. . . . Now it is how many nutty whiz kids you get on the staff to get you magazine articles and get you headlines and get all of the other things done.[96]

Carping about staff power is a periodic Capitol Hill phenomenon engaged in by a few members and critics of Congress. Most legislators, however, continue to seek more staff, knowing that without experienced aides their effectiveness will be reduced in Congress and on the campaign trail. Staff power diminishes somewhat the personal role members play in the legislative process, and in representing constituent interests. Congress itself, though, could not function effectively as a lawmaker or in representing voters' interests without staff support.

Michael J. Malbin concludes in his first-hand account of the role of staff, that the "unelected representatives" are essential to proper congressional performance, but they reduce the deliberative character

---

[93] Richard Halloran, "Military Panel Staff: Roots of Power," *New York Times,* June 28, 1982, p. A13.

[94] Halloran, "Military Panel Staff: Roots of Power," p. A13.

[95] The term was applied to the staff of the House Armed Services Committee. See Halloran.

[96] Cited in Fox and Hammond, *Congressional Staffs,* pp. 4–5.

of the body. Deliberation requires direct rather than indirect communications among members. The staff too frequently, according to Malbin, acts as interpreters between legislators, short-circuiting direct communication and preventing members from gaining a true feel or sense of the positions of his colleagues.[97]

Malbin argues that "For a process of legislative deliberation to function reasonably well, at least three distinct requirements must be satisfied. The members need accurate information, they need time to think about that information, and they need to talk to each other about the factual, political, and moral implications of the policies they are considering. The new use of staff undercuts each of these." [98]

Congressional staffs also have an effect upon substantive policy. Acting as entrepreneurs, the impetus of staff "is to build coalitions by having programs respond, at least symbolically, to more demands, rather than let them die their natural death. The result is increasingly inclusive, increasingly complex legislation, that can only be understood by an expert. Needless to say, this increases the power of permanent Washingtonians with the necessary expertise, such as former staffers." [99]

That the staff is one of the most important internal influences on the legislative process seems clear. It is equally clear that for the democratic process to work, legislators must control their staffs, and must be directly engaged in shaping public policy and overseeing its implementation by the bureaucracy. Staffers can indeed become unelected representatives, wielding power behind the scenes that may distort the democratic responsiveness of the institution. Most staffers are as politically sensitive as their bosses, however, and the reality of their power must be accepted as a condition for an effective Congress.

SENATE PARTY LEADERSHIP

Important on both sides of Capitol Hill are the personal styles of party leaders, but particularly in the Senate, which traditionally has been characterized by far more informality and collegiality than has prevailed in the House. The Senate lacks the institutional committees

---

[97] Michael J. Malbin, *Unelected Representatives* (New York: Basic Books, 1980), p. 241.
[98] Malbin, p. 242.
[99] Malbin, p. 250.

that act as adjuncts of the leadership. No Rules Committee has the authority to be the leadership's gatekeeper for legislative proposals that come from other committees. The Speaker appoints the members of the majority party on the Rules Committee, a power that no Senate leader has with respect to any committee. The House leadership is also represented on the Budget Committee, which has become increasingly important in the 1980s as an overseer setting policy guidelines for expenditure and tax legislation. Senate leadership has no representation on its Budget Committee, which is chosen by normal Senate procedures. Nothing in the Senate compares to the Speaker of the House, a constitutional position the occupant of which has extraordinary power to control House proceedings *provided* a majority of House members acquiesce.

Majority and Minority Leaders

Party caucuses elect their leaders in the Senate as they do in the House. (See Figure 4.3.) Personal styles and the environment of the Senate determine the character of party leadership. Robert Peabody observes, "Other than his formal prerogative to initiate legislation and to move to adjourn the Senate, a majority leader, like all other senators, is left to rely on his style, his personality, and his powers of persuasion." [100] Lyndon B. Johnson, who dominated the Senate as majority leader in the 1950s more than any leader before or since, commented, "The only real power available to the leader is the power of persuasion. There is no patronage; no power to discipline; no authority to fire senators like a president can fire his members of the Cabinet." [101]

Lyndon B. Johnson and Minority Leader Everett Dirksen were nevertheless able to hold sway over their parties, not only because of their highly effective personal styles, but also because of the cooperative environment in a Senate that was collegial and, some think, controlled by an inner club of senior members who revered the institution and its ways. Senate folkways of apprenticeship, legislative work, specialization, courtesy, reciprocity, and institutional patriotism held

[100] Robert L. Peabody, *Leadership in Congress* (Boston: Little, Brown, 1976), p. 339.
[101] Peabody, *Leadership in Congress*, p. 339.

the body together, giving it a distinctive character that could be exploited by skillful leaders.[102]

Whether or not an inner club, linked to the leaders of both parties and controlling Senate proceedings during the 1950s and into the 1960s, ever really existed, which is a matter of debate, it is clear that beginning with the majority leadership of Senator Mike Mansfield (D, Mont.) in 1961, the Democratic leadership circle broadened to include most members. Political scientist Nelson Polsby, who first seriously questioned the whole idea of an inner club, pointed out that the concept "vastly underplayed the extent to which *formal* position — committee chairmanships, great seniority, and official party leadership — conferred power and status on individual senators almost regardless of their clubability. Second, it understated the extent to which power was spread by specialization and the need for cooperative effort." [103] Polsby concluded, "We can think of the internal politics of the Senate not as a small group of powerful men, surrounded by everybody else, but as a group which divides labor and power — unequally to be sure, but still significantly — among almost all of its members." [104]

Everett Dirksen, Johnson's counterpart on the Republican side, held tight reins over his party as Minority Leader from 1959 to 1969, after which Senate Republicans began to reflect the heightened individualism that Mansfield had spawned on the other side of the aisle. Dirksen and Johnson had almost singlehandedly used their formal party organization in combination with astute leadership styles to buttress their power and bring about party cohesion.

But Senate leadership, over the long run, cannot be a one-man show. "Top party leadership in the Senate," observes Peabody, "is, almost without exception, collegial in nature. Even the strongest floor leader surrounds himself with loyal lieutenants. He must, of necessity, cooperate closely with the majority of his committee leaders. The majority leader usually has to co-opt the support of the minority

---

[102] See Donald R. Matthews, *U.S. Senators and Their World* (New York: Vintage, 1960) for a discussion of Senate norms and folkways.

[103] Nelson W. Polsby, "Goodbye to the Inner Club," *Washington Monthly* (August 1969), pp. 30–34.

[104] Cited in Robert L. Peabody, *Leadership in Congress*, p. 349, from Nelson W. Polsby, *Congress and the Presidency* (Englewood Cliffs, N.J.: Prentice-Hall, 1964), p. 45.

Figure 4.3
Party Organization in the Senate

REPUBLICANS

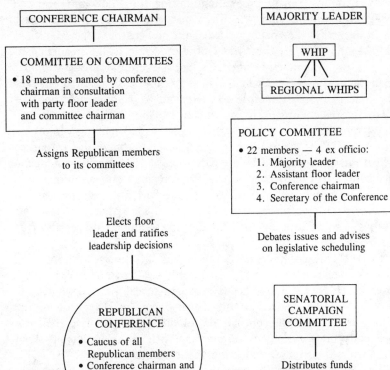

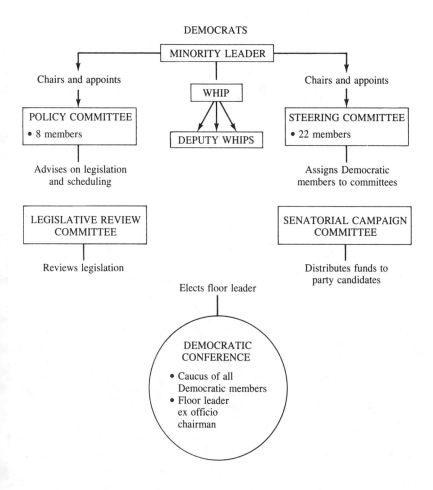

leader if the scheduling of legislation and other business of the Senate is to go forward smoothly." [105]

A major challenge to Senate party leaders has always been the highly individualistic character of the body, which, in the view of many senators, has become its dominant feature. Former Senator Gaylord Nelson (D, Wis.), argues, "The institution was stronger twenty years ago because people went along with chairmen, and chairmen went along with each other. That put more strength in the hands of the leadership. During the course of my time, that all broke down." [106] Former Senator James Pearson (R, Kansas), echoed Nelson's opinion: "It's every man for himself. Every Senator is a baron. He has his own principality." [107]

Leadership Committees

Assisting the floor leader of each party is a policy committee that helps to schedule legislation, a Committee on Committees (Steering Committee on the Democratic side) that makes party committee assignments, and a Senatorial campaign committee that raises funds for party candidates. The Democratic floor leader, unlike his Republican counterpart, chairs both his party's steering and policy committees, enhancing his influence over committee assignments and the scheduling of legislation. (See Figure 4.3.)

As Majority Leader, for example, Lyndon B. Johnson buttressed his informal power network by using his position as chairman of the Steering Committee to reward his friends and punish his enemies through committee assignments. Journalists Roland Evans and Robert Novack wrote, "To build his network of influence, Johnson stretched the meager power resources of the majority leader to the outer limit. The mightiest of these was his influence over committee assignments." [108] The authors recount how Johnson used his power to control committee assignments to prevent a change in the Senate's cloture Rule 22, which required a two-thirds vote of the senators present to

---

[105] Peabody, p. 325.
[106] *Congressional Quarterly Weekly Report*, vol. 40, no. 36 (September 4, 1982), p. 2181.
[107] Ibid., p. 2179.
[108] Rowland Evans and Robert Novak, *Lyndon B. Johnson: The Exercise of Power* (New York: Signet, 1968), p. 111. First published in 1966 by the New American Library, Inc.

close debate. For decades the rule had facilitated filibusters by *both* conservatives and liberals, but liberal senators spearheaded a move for change in the 1950s because they felt the rule allowed a conservative minority to control the Senate. As the 86th Congress convened in 1959, Senate liberals gathered their forces once again to attack Rule 22. Johnson did not want the split among Democrats that he felt controversy over the rule would provoke. He called the freshmen Democrats, the class of 1958, to his office to explain the importance of avoiding conflict, and to persuade them to vote for Rule 22. "But behind the soft argument," observed Evans and Novack, "was an unspoken threat. Muskie and all the other freshmen knew that committee assignments would not be doled out to them until *after* the Rule 22 questions were settled. There was, then, a large question of how a freshman senator who voted against Lyndon B. Johnson, majority leader, would fare when committee assignments were made by Lyndon B. Johnson, chairman of the Democratic Steering Committee." [109] The liberal motion was defeated, with the freshmen splitting 8 to 7 in favor of Johnson's position.

Democratic majority leaders have not since Johnson's day used their formal positions as chairmen of the Steering Committee to dictate committee assignments. Mike Mansfield ushered in a new democratic style of leadership in 1961. His loose leadership reins helped to spawn the increasing individualism of the Senate that became so manifest in the 1970s and 1980s. Robert Peabody found that "Mansfield appears to have preferred operating as but one member of the 17-member Democratic Steering Committee. Unlike Johnson, who took an active role in selecting his Democratic whips, Mansfield remained completely neutral in the whip contests of 1965, 1969, and 1971. 'It's been my policy not to take a stand ahead of time, to let the caucus decide, and to lean toward those who have been in office. That's been my consistent practice.' " [110]

The Democratic floor leader is also chairman of the policy committee, a position that, like his chairmanship of the Steering Committee, he can use to enhance his influence over the legislative process. Personal style determines how or if the policy committee will be used as part of the leadership organization. The committee was dormant when Lyndon B. Johnson became majority leader in 1953. It had vir-

[109] Evans and Novak, *Lyndon B. Johnson*, p. 217.
[110] Peabody, *Leadership in Congress*, p. 341.

tually no staff, and all it did was to inform Senate Democrats how party members had voted on roll calls. But Johnson had plans for the committee. Evans and Novack write, "Having watched the Policy Committee fail to function during his four years in the Senate, Johnson began to view it as a potentially powerful political instrument, a top strategy board of senators with staff guidance from outside experts that would compete for ideas and policies with the executive branch of the government. With his reflective ability to relate everything to himself and his own political power, Johnson quickly saw that a revitalized policy committee could become the private preserve of the leader, reinforcing his power and adding to his control over the entire Democratic membership." [111] In the ensuing years he built the committee and its staff into an effective instrument of his power.[112]

The policy committee continued, at least for a time, to be an important leadership adjunct after Johnson left the Senate. During Mike Mansfield's tenure as Majority Leader the committee advised him on legislation and floor scheduling. It "met twice a month to debate policy and to issue statements on matters ranging from tax reform to the withdrawal of forces from Vietnam." [113] Commenting on the role of the committee, Mansfield said, "When the Democrats were in charge, we bowed to the President. Under Nixon, we function primarily as a policy determining commitee." [114] When Robert Byrd (D, WVa), became majority leader in 1977, the policy committee became less important, rarely meeting as a group. Byrd essentially used its staff as part of his office to prepare background material on legislation, make voting assessments, and write memoranda for news conferences.[115]

The same factors that determine the power of Democratic floor leaders also shape the influence of Republican leaders. Generally Senate Republicans have grown even more loosely organized than the Democrats. The floor leader does not have the advantage of being chairman of the Committee on Committees, which makes Republican committee assignments, nor is he chairman of the policy commit-

---

111 Evans and Novak, p. 73.
112 Peabody, *Leadership in Congress*, p. 337.
113 Peabody, p. 338.
114 Peabody, citing Andrew J. Glass, "Congressional Report: Mansfield Reforms Spark 'Quiet Revolution' in Senate," *National Journal*, Reprint #16 (Minneapolis: Winston, 1972), p. 9.
115 *Guide to Congress*, p. 400.

tee. Regardless of formal authority or the lack thereof, the influence of both floor leaders primarily depends on their persuasive abilities.

When Howard Baker (R, Tenn.), became the Republican Majority Leader in 1981, he adopted a consultative style to strengthen the sense of collegiality among his Republican colleagues. Being in the majority for the first time since 1953 strengthened Republican team spirit, which was given an added boost by Ronald Reagan's presidency. *New York Times* reporter Martin Tolchin observed that though Senate Republicans wanted Reagan to succeed, "The explosive personal and ideological mix in the Senate had to be harnessed, and, for that task, Howard Baker was the key. 'If you're looking for somebody who could put us all in a pot and make us come to a boil,' said Senator Dole, 'he's the one. He's the chef.' " [116] Reagan himself commented, "I'm frank to say that I don't think we could have had the successes that we've had up there without his leadership." [117] Democrats, too, admired Baker's style, Tennessee Senator Jim Sasser saying admiringly, "He's a genius at finding the compromise point and pushing it through." [118]

Other Leadership Organization

As in the House, the Senate parties elect whips who assist their floor leaders. The prestige bestowed upon whips, who since World War II have effectively used the position as a ladder to become floor leader, is the primary reward of the office. The whips generally leave to their staffs the job of keeping party members abreast of floor action, and rounding them up to vote. [119]

Other leadership positions of more or less importance, depending upon the vigor with which they are pursued by their occupants, are the Republican Policy Committee on Conference chairmanships that are separate from the party's floor leader and the chairmanships of the senatorial campaign committees. The Democratic Floor Leader is ex officio the chairman of the conference, and uses it in various ways to solidify or expand his power. While he was majority leader, Robert

---

[116] Martin Tolchin, "Howard Baker: Power in the Senate," in Peter Woll, ed., *Behind the Scenes in American Government*, 4th ed. (Boston: Little, Brown, 1983), p. 225.

[117] Tolchin, "Howard Baker," p. 225.

[118] Tolchin, p. 225.

[119] Peabody, *Leadership in Congress*, p. 331.

Byrd convened the conference only at the beginning of sessions to select party leaders. As Minority Leader, Byrd more actively used the conference and its staff, holding weekly luncheon meetings to which members were invited, and creating task forces in different spheres of public policy. The ways in which conference chairmen use their staffs, for which they have a budget of approximately $415,000 yearly, largely determine the importance of the conferences. While Byrd was trying to make the Democratic conference staff more active in issue development, Republican Conference Chairman James McClure of Idaho was using his staff in the 98th Congress (1983–1984) to publicize the activities of his party colleagues by providing expert assistance of all kinds to their press secretaries.

Conclusion

In the end, political parties are supposed to bridge the gap between people and government. They are the only means available in democracies to aggregate interests and reflect the will of the people. Congressional parties are, however, but one of many internal influences on Capitol Hill. Party discipline is absent mostly because the members want it that way. They desire the flexibility to deal with their constituents. They want to be tied to parties only when it benefits their chances for reelection. How members of Congress deal with constituents in the pluralistic world of electoral politics is the subject of the following chapters.

PART
III

Congressmen and Constituents:
The Electoral Connection

Setting of Congressional Elections

The folklore of American democracy preaches that Congress is a captive of the forces in electoral constituencies, particularly individual voters. In the House of Representatives the Constitution provided a body that was to have, Alexander Hamilton said, "a due dependence upon the people." Members of the House were to be directly accountable to their electoral constituencies, an accountability that was to be greatly strengthened by the short two-year term of office in contrast to the six-year term of the Senate. Contemporary political scientists have persuasively argued that the organization, procedures, and norms of Capitol Hill, particularly in the House, are predominantly shaped by the reelection incentive of members.

CONGRESSIONAL ELECTIONS AND CONSTITUTIONAL DEMOCRACY

Under the Constitution, there was to be a direct electoral connection between the House of Representatives and the people. The two-year term of office in combination with direct elections was to ensure democratic accountability in the popular branch. The indirect election of the Senate by state legislatures, together with its six-year term and powers that were at least equal to those of the House, were designed, however, to create a legislature that was not entirely under popular control.

The influence of elections in bringing about democracy was also reduced under the Constitution because of the equal representation of states in the Senate. State interests were to balance popular interests, and a more deliberative Senate was to check the popular passions of the House.

Even though there was no question that the Constitution, by providing for equal apportionment of the House among the states on the basis of their populations, supported the "one person-one vote" rule for the lower chamber, equal apportionment was not relevant to the Senate. Popular election of senators after 1913 did not alter the malapportionment of that body. States such as Alaska, Nevada, and Wyoming, with populations of fewer than 500,000 and voter registrations of approximately 250,000, choose the same number of senators as California and New York, with populations of more than 20 million and registered voters numbering 10 and 7 million, respectively.

The electoral system in the Constitution was clearly not designed solely to make the voice of the people dominant in government. Elections were also viewed as an important mechanism to ensure checks and balances within Congress, and between Congress and the president. Elections, then, had both a positive and a negative effect in the democratic process. Elections connected people with government, but ensured that popular demands would be filtered and checked.

Elections in Democratic Theory

Elections serve a different function in democratic theory than they perform under the Constitution. Simply stated, in a democracy elections not only allow voters to choose their representatives, but are supposed to facilitate transmission of the broader will of the people to government. Democratic governments are to act in accordance with popular mandates, enacting public policies that conform to the wishes of the majority of the people.

THE LIBERAL-DEMOCRATIC MODEL. The best summation of democratic theory is to be found in the classic work of British philosopher Sir Ernest Barker.[1] Barker described democratic government as "government by discussion." Based on the premise of the rationality of

---

[1] Ernest Barker, *Reflections on Government* (London: Oxford University Press, 1942).

voters and their ability to act politically in terms of their self-interests, government by discussion is rationally organized.

In the liberal-democratic model the principal instrument of rational politics is to be political parties, which develop and sharpen issues and present meaningful alternative programs to the public. When voters go to the polls, they are to focus more upon party programs than upon the personal characteristics and styles of the individual candidates. They are to choose a party and vote for candidates on the basis of party labels. Voters select their party after extensively discussing and rationally considering which party best serves their interests.

After completion of elections it is the duty of the victorious party to implement its program through the national legislature. The executive, too, is to be the instrument of the majority party, and is to work closely with the legislature to ensure that the will of the majority of the people is carried out.

Elections and party government are closely linked in much of democratic theory. Though it is difficult to generalize about democratic theory, the views of Barker reflected the political philosophy of late nineteenth-century and twentieth-century Britain and, to a lesser extent, the Continent. Democracy was simply seen as impossible without effective parties, and elections were always to be organized around the contrasting programs more than the candidates of parties.

Just as the practice of American politics has always contrasted with the politics of other nations, democratic theory in the United States has also differed. No consistent philosophy of democracy has been stated that would lead to acceptance of the liberal-democratic model of government, in which parties are so prominent. The pluralism of American politics has, except for a few periods in history, diminished the importance of national parties. Elections remain, as designed by the founding fathers, a divisive force that helps the checks-and-balances system to work. The different constituencies of the House, the Senate, and the president continue to buttress conflict between the president and Congress, and within the legislative branch itself.

CONSTITUTIONAL REQUIREMENTS. Judging elections from the standpoint of the standards of *constitutional* democracy is far different from evaluating elections in terms of democratic theory. The dispersion of congressional constituencies, and the different terms for members of the House and the Senate, make it very difficult for Congress to develop disciplined legislative parties with contrasting stands on large issues of public policy. Party weakness also results from the separation of powers between the president and Congress. This result was the intent of the framers of the Constitution, who did not want direct democracy in any form and carefully constructed the system to prevent it.

The fragmented and multifaceted electoral connection between Congress and the people is consistent with the principles of the Constitution. Elections generally do not unite the president and Congress, or the House and the Senate, under the banner of a national popular mandate. Occasionally, elections do transmit broad national interests to Washington, uniting the president and Congress at least for a short time to enact a legislative program responsive to popular demands. The New Deal and Great Society programs of Presidents Franklin D. Roosevelt and Lyndon B. Johnson, respectively, occurred after unusual electoral mandates were given by the people. The dramatic increase in the relative strength of the Republican Party that occurred in the late 1970s and resulted in the Republican Senate and Reagan presidency in 1981, buttressed Republican victories on Capitol Hill in the initial phase of the Reagan administration. On issues of budget cutting and tax reduction there seemed to be a popular mandate supporting the Reagan administration. The congressional elections of 1980 reflected public concern about these overriding national issues, helping to defeat liberal legislators and elect Republicans and conservative Democrats who supported Reagan's program.

Types of Elections

Elections reflect the attitudes of voters about the personalities, styles, and effectiveness of candidates, and about political issues. Elections also may reflect public apathy in low voter turnout. Clearly, elections differ in their political consequences, some being far more important than others.[2]

[2] See Barbara Sinclair, "Agenda and Alignment Change: The House of Representatives, 1925–1978," in Lawrence C. Dodd and Bruce I. Oppenheimer, eds., *Congress Reconsidered*, 2nd ed. (Washington, D.C.: Congressional Quarterly Press, 1981), pp. 221–245.

CRITICAL ELECTIONS. V. O. Key, Jr., wrote in 1955 that even

> the most fleeting inspection of American elections suggests
> the existence of a category of elections in which voters are, at
> least from impressionistic evidence, unusually deeply con-
> cerned, in which the extent of electoral involvement is rela-
> tively high, and in which the decisive results of the voting
> reveal a sharp alteration of the preexisting cleavage within
> the electorate. Moreover, and perhaps this is the truly differ-
> entiating characteristic of this sort of election, the realign-
> ment made manifest in the voting in such elections seems to
> persist for several succeeding elections.[3]

Key described as "critical" elections that are characterized by relatively long-term realignments of voter attitudes. At the national
level, for example, the sweeping victory of Franklin D. Roosevelt
over Herbert Hoover in 1932, coupled with the election of huge
democratic majorities in the House and the Senate, represented a
major electoral shift in voter attitudes that lasted many years.[4]

DEVIATING AND REINSTATING ELECTIONS. Although sharp shifts have
occurred in voter attitudes in other elections in the twentieth century, as in 1952 when Dwight D. Eisenhower swamped the relatively
unknown Adlai Stevenson, such changes have not been lasting. Major
short-term electoral shifts have been characterized as "deviating elections" that invariably are followed shortly by "reinstating elections,"
in which voters return to their permanent party allegiances in making
electoral choices.[5] Electoral continuity results from "maintaining
elections" that perpetuate voter alignments.

IDENTIFYING TYPES OF ELECTIONS. It is relatively easy to classify
elections in theory, but far more difficult to identify elections that

---

[3] V. O. Key, Jr., "A Theory of Critical Elections," *Journal of Politics*, vol. 17
(February 1955), pp. 3–18, at pp. 3–4.
[4] Nationwide, Roosevelt received 57.42 percent of the popular vote in contrast
to Hoover's 39.64 percent. Roosevelt's national margin did not reflect the
truly extraordinary shifts in voter attitudes that occurred from 1928 to 1932
in many states, particularly southern and border states. For example, in 1928
Texas gave Hoover 51.7 percent of the vote, but in 1932 Hoover received only
11.2 percent against Roosevelt's 88.2 percent. The House of Representatives
in 1932 had 310 Democrats and 117 Republicans; the Senate 60 Democrats
and 35 Republicans.
[5] Angus Campbell, Philip E. Converse, Warren E. Miller, and Donald C. Stokes,
The American Voter (New York: John Wiley, 1960), Ch. 19.

fall into the categories of "critical," "deviating," and "reinstating." [6]
The Eisenhower victories of 1952 and 1956, for example, were easily
identified as deviating elections for several reasons, including the
magnet of Eisenhower's attractive personality and the fact that the
voters chose the former general without changing their partisan
loyalties at the congressional and state levels of politics. Eisenhower's
coattails resulted in razor-thin Republican majorities in the House
and the Senate in the 83rd Congress (1953–1955). [7] But thereafter
the Democrats took control of Congress by increasing margins
throughout the Eisenhower years. The election of 1960, in which
John F. Kennedy won the national popular vote by less than 1 percent, has been characterized as "reinstating" because the underlying
Democratic national majority reasserted itself even though Kennedy's Catholicism cost him Democratic votes in the South. [8]

The typology of elections, from "critical" to "reinstating," is defined by changes in party alignments among voters. A critical election, for example, cannot and does not occur unless a relatively
permanent change in voter alignments has been reflected in electoral
choice. Much has been made in recent years of the decline of parties,
characterized by ticket splitting, voting for personalities rather than
party programs, and the general failure of voters to organize their
political viewpoints along party lines.

The disintegration of political parties, argue those who support
the thesis, was hastened at the turn of the century by major changes
in the rules of the game by which elections were conducted. Mis-
guided political reformers, seeing in parties and their bosses a dia-
bolical manipulation of the American electorate, wanted to "purify"
the political process by making it nonpartisan. The Australian or
secret ballot was introduced, significantly reducing the power of machine politics. Direct primaries and nonpartisan local elections were
further blows to effective party politics. Moreover, the effective dis-
enfranchisement of black and poor whites limited the possibilities
for developing a party system in which the contrasting views of important groups of voters could be represented.

---

[6] See Walter Dean Burnham, "Insulation and Responsiveness in Congressional
Elections," *Political Science Quarterly*, vol. 90 (1975), pp. 411–435.
[7] In the House, Republicans 221, Democrats 211; in the Senate, Republicans 48,
Democrats 47.
[8] Philip E. Converse, Angus Campbell, Warren E. Miller, and Donald C.
Stokes, "Stability and Change in 1960: A Reinstating Election," *American
Political Science Review*, vol. 55 (June 1961), pp. 269–280.

Elections and Congressional Politics

Different types of elections affect Congress in contrasting ways. Critical elections ending in long-term realignment of the electorate along party lines will inevitably be reflected in changes in party balances on Capitol Hill. After the election of Roosevelt in 1932 the former Democratic minority became a consistent majority that dominated Congress with few exceptions for more than forty-five years. Democratic control of Congress, however, did not mean consistent legislative support for the policies of Democratic presidents and the national party platform. In fact, the Democrats who controlled the leadership positions and committee chairmanships of Capitol Hill were more often than not conservative southerners. They had the necessary seniority to become committee chairmen, posts that were beyond the grasp of the relative newcomers in the party whose votes were necessary to give the party control over Congress.

LACK OF DISCIPLINED PARTIES. Because congressional parties are not disciplined, and are often in conflict with a president of the same party, it is difficult to measure the effect of critical and other elections upon the congressional process. That process consists not only of policy formulation, but involves a wide range of other activities, including casework and other forms of constituent relations, investigations, and administrative oversight. In democratic theory the most important influence elections can have on the legislature is to give it a direction in public policy. But elections cannot give mandates to Congress if the majority of members are not responsive to the same popular mandate that elects the president.

Linkage between the people and Congress through elections requires not only disciplined parties on Capitol Hill, but a connection between those parties and the same parties outside of Congress. However effective congressional party organizations might be in aggregating the disparate forces of Capitol Hill, they cannot be effective democratic instruments unless they are responsive to outside constituencies. In the twentieth century much of Congress became a highly professional body, developing its own norms of behavior and rules of procedure, many of which became barriers between the legislature and the external political world. Congress became a world unto itself.

EFFECTS OF SENIORITY RULE. One of the most important aspects in producing a professional Congress was the seniority rule, which had its roots in late nineteenth-century practice but which did not reach its peak of rigidity until after World War II.[9] Under the seniority rule, committee chairmen, who must be of the majority party in the House or the Senate, are chosen according to their years of service on the committee. Party changes see the ranking minority members of committees, who are the most senior members of the minority party on the committees, moving up to the chairmanship.

Seniority is important not only in selecting committee chairmen, but also in determining congressional party leadership positions and in selecting a Speaker of the House who is also an important leader of his party. In the nineteenth century it was possible to become Speaker after a tenure of six or seven years. In the twentieth century informal tenure requirements for Speakers have steadily grown and now twenty years or more of House service is generally required to become Speaker. Moreover, to move up to the position, one must have held a position of Majority or Minority Leader, which itself requires long years of service to build the necessary political support within the House. Thomas O'Neill of Massachusetts served twenty years in the House before being elected Majority Leader in 1973, and therefore had served twenty-four years before becoming Speaker in 1977. Sam Rayburn of Texas, one of the most astute Democratic leaders of the House in the twentieth century, served as Majority Leader from 1937 to 1940 after twenty-four years in the House. In 1940, after twenty-eight years of House service, he became Speaker.

The seniority rule and seniority requirements for leadership positions have greatly affected the way in which Congress responds to elections. In the 1950s and early 1960s, for example, the seniority rule placed in the major positions of power on Capitol Hill conservative southerners who stalemated civil rights legislation and other liberal programs that were not to their liking. The House Rules Committee, dominated by conservatives and chaired by the eccentric Virginia Congressman Howard "Judge" Smith, easily prevented liberal attempts to pass civil rights legislation. Admittedly, a majority of the House was not in favor of moving ahead in protecting civil rights during the 1950s and early 1960s, and the Rules Committee reflected far more of a House consensus than is generally thought. Neverthe-

---

[9] For a pre-1970s examination of the seniority system, see Barbara Hinckley, *The Seniority System in Congress* (Bloomington: Indiana University Press, 1971).

less, the often obstructionist tactics of Smith and the majority of the Rules Committee so frustrated House Speaker Sam Rayburn that in 1961 he successfully sought expanded membership for the committee to dilute the entrenched power of Smith and his committee majority. After 1961 the dominant role of the Rules Committee began to recede somewhat, and committee conservatives were not able to prevent passage of major civil rights legislation in 1964 and 1965, nor could they stop the Johnson steamroller that resulted in wideranging liberal legislation to cope with the economic and social problems of the nation. In 1974 the Rules Committee was further altered to make it an instrument of the Speaker.[10]

The seniority rule itself did not make Congress unrepresentative, but simply left it responsive to the interests and needs of senior committee chairmen. *Their* constituencies were far better served than those of the average congressman. *Their* interests, in reelection, internal power, or good public policy, were far more likely to be advanced on Capitol Hill than were the same pursuits of other congressmen. Because senior members by definition came from nonmarginal congressional districts and states, in which they did not have to face real challenges from within their own party or the opposition party, they were relatively free to pursue internal power and good public policy. Generally the South considered its elected representatives and senators in Washington to be part of a governing class that would be left undisturbed to act as trustees for the interests of constituents and of the nation. Before the 1960s the one-party South limited competition to Democratic Party primaries, and the relative ineffectiveness of most party challenges and the lack of two-party competition was a major factor in the superior seniority of most southerners on Capitol Hill.

Although southern control of committee chairmanships, which lasted from the New Deal of the 1930s into the Johnson years of the 1960s, often produced a conservatism that clashed with liberal presidents such as Franklin D. Roosevelt, Harry Truman, and John F. Kennedy, more than a few southern chairmen supported the New Deal and in some cases liberal legislation that went beyond it. Senator Lister Hill, an Alabama Democrat chosen in a special election in 1938 to replace Hugo L. Black, whom President Roosevelt had appointed to the Supreme Court, was an avid supporter of the New

[10] For further discussion of the Rules Committee, see Chapter 3.

Deal. After serving sixteen years in the Senate he became chairman of its Labor and Public Welfare Committee and its health subcommittee, positions he held for fourteen years until his retirement in 1968. Hill was the son of a distinguished surgeon, and was named after Lord Lister, a famous British physician. During the Eisenhower years, when the electoral climate was relatively conservative, Hill became the Senate spokesman for trend-setting health legislation that was distinctly out of tune with the times. Virtually unopposed in Alabama until he was nearly defeated in 1962 by a Republican challenger, Hill was free to pursue good public policy on Capitol Hill and build his reputation as a major Senate power. When he retired, the *New York Times* commented editorially that "Lister Hill has done more for the health of Americans in modern times than any man outside the medical profession." Hill, the editorial continued, "has been a tireless protagonist of the generous research budgets for the National Institutes of Health. He was co-author of the Hill-Burton Act, which over the past twenty-one years has made possible the building of thousands of new hospitals and clinics. More recently, he has worked on legislation to aid the mentally retarded and to build more medical schools." [11] Though Hill had the support of the American Medical Association, whose members benefited by his support of hospital and medical research, his actions were not connected with his electoral constituency. His pursuit of good public policy, much of it liberal, almost cost him his seat in 1962, when he defeated Republican challenger James Martin by 50.9 to 49.1 percent of the vote. By contrast, in 1956 he was unopposed, and had not been seriously challenged in his prior Senate career.

Congress and Electoral Change

Although the framers of the Constitution institutionalized conflict between the president and Congress by constructing contrasting electoral constituencies, through most of the nineteenth century voters elected candidates of the same party to the White House and Congress. Insofar as electoral change was reflected in new party alignments, Congress was part of that change. Capitol Hill did not become professional until the 1880s, and consisted mostly of amateur citizen-legislators who rarely served for more than two terms and generally were more than delighted to get back to their private pur-

[11] *New York Times*, January 27, 1968, p. 28.

suits after serving two years in the distant, uncomfortable, and often seemingly inaccessible capital city.

WEAKENING OF PARTY LINKAGE. By contrast with the nineteenth century party linkage between president and Congress due to the relatively consistent voting patterns of the electorate, the twentieth century has witnessed growing disparity between the party results of presidential and congressional elections. (Table 5.1) Republican William Howard Taft confronted a Democratic-controlled House during the last two years of his presidency (1911–1913). Woodrow Wilson also had to face a Congress of the opposite party in his last two years, and the Republican-controlled Senate defeated his pet project, the Treaty of Versailles. The Republican presidents of the 1920s lived happily with lopsided majorities in both the House and the Senate until 1931, when the House shifted to a slim Democratic majority in the waning years of the Hoover administration. The critical election of 1932 united the president and Congress again under the Democratic label, a situation that lasted until the 80th Congress (1947–1949), in which the Republicans controlled the House and the Senate by wide margins under the administration of Democrat Harry S Truman.

Beginning with the Eisenhower administration in 1953, the chasm between voting patterns for Congress and the presidency began to widen. Eisenhower had slim Republican majorities on both sides of Capitol Hill in the 83rd Congress (1953–1955), but the Democrats took control of Capitol Hill for the remaining years of the Eisenhower administration and retained power in Congress until the Senate shifted to the Republican Party in 1980 to coincide with the election of Republican Ronald Reagan. In recent decades the American voter seems perfectly willing to engage in ticket splitting in congressional elections, not only choosing candidates of opposite parties for the White House and Congress, but within Congress selecting candidates of different parties for the House and the Senate.

IMPORTANCE OF CONGRESSIONAL ELECTIONS. The relatively disparate and seemingly erratic behavior of voters, at least as reflected in their allegiances to parties, makes it very difficult to assess the importance of congressional elections in the broader picture of electoral change.[12]

---

[12] For a comprehensive overview of the literature on congressional elections, see Barbara Hinckley, *Congressional Elections* (Washington, D.C.: Congressional Quarterly Press, 1981).

Table 5.1

Ticket Splitting between Presidential and House Candidates,
1900–1980

Year	Districts[a]	Districts with split results[b]	
		Number	Percentage
1900	295	10	3.4
1904	310	5	1.6
1908	314	21	6.7
1912	333	84	25.2
1916	333	35	10.5
1920	344	11	3.2
1924	356	42	11.8
1928	359	68	18.9
1932	355	50	14.1
1936	361	51	14.1
1940	362	53	14.6
1944	367	41	11.2
1948	422	90	21.3
1952	435	84	19.3
1956	435	130	29.9
1960	437	114	26.1
1964	435	145	33.3
1968	435	139	32.0
1972	435	192	44.1
1976	435	124	28.5
1980	435	143	32.8

[a] Before 1952, complete data are not available on every congressional district.
[b] Congressional districts carried by a presidential candidate of one party and a House candidate of another party.

Sources: *Congressional Quarterly Weekly Report*, vol. 36 (April 1978), p. 9; Walter Dean Burnham, *Critical Elections* (New York: Norton, 1970), p. 109; and Michael Barone and Grant Ujifusa, *The Almanac of American Politics 1982* (Washington, D.C.: Barone, 1981). From Norman J. Ornstein et al., *Vital Statistics on Congress* (Washington, D.C.: American Enterprise Institute, 1982), p. 53.

Is there any electoral connection at all, in terms of the policy preferences of voters, between Congress and the constituents? V. O. Key, Jr. pointed out that it

> can be a mischievous error to assume, because a candidate wins, that a majority of the electorate shares his views on public questions, approves his past actions, or has specific expecta-

tions about his future conduct. Nor does victory establish that the candidate's campaign strategy, his image, his television style, or his fearless stand against cancer and polio turned the trick. The election returns establish only that the winner attracted a majority of the votes — assuming the existence of a modicum of rectitude in election administration. They tell us precious little about why the plurality was his.[13]

Although it may be difficult to assess the meaning of elections, V. O. Key concluded that "Voters are not fools. To be sure, many individual voters act in odd ways indeed; yet in the large the electorate behaves about as rationally and responsibly as we should expect, given the clarity of the alternatives presented to it and the character of the information available to it." [14] Voters select candidates using the information available to them, and insofar as they are misled it is because political candidates fail properly to inform the electorate about pressing public issues and governmental problems that may affect the voters' interests. The electorate is constantly attempting to cut through the obfuscation and veneer of political campaigns to make intelligent choices based upon self-interest. But presidential and congressional candidates, surrounded by public-relations advisers and media consultants, frequently continue to concentrate on developing and projecting a popular and attractive style and an appealing personality in order to win votes. Both candidate and voters may lose sight of concrete public-policy issues.

The ability of Congress to reflect national electoral change depends both upon the organization, procedures, and incentives of the Capitol Hill community — which extends beyond members to staffers, lobbyists, and bureaucrats — and upon the habits of voters themselves. Is there a connection between the Washington careers of members and their aides, between the activities of lobbyists and bureaucrats on Capitol Hill, and the broader electorate beyond Washington? Are the election campaigns of congressmen and senators geared to and capable of aggregating the pluralistic interests of the wide variety of constituents at the same time as they are responsive

---

[13] V. O. Key, Jr., *The Responsible Electorate* (Cambridge, Mass.: Harvard University Press, 1966), p. 2.

[14] Key, *The Responsible Electorate*, p. 7. Although Key's conclusion was based upon his view and analysis of presidential elections, it is reasonable to conclude that he would have stated the same opinion about congressional elections.

to local and state needs? Are voters in fact given a meaningful choice of candidates and parties to enable them to express their political preferences?

Congressional elections do reflect national political and economic trends, but not because of voting behavior. Voters continue to make their choices mainly by assessing candidates' personalities and styles, rather than their handling of issues. It is the way that incumbents and potential challengers themselves assess the influence national trends may have upon their reelection or election prospects that affects the aggregate results of congressional elections measured by party balances on Capitol Hill. Incumbents of one party who sense political ties moving against them may, for example, retire early, diminishing the prospects for continued party control of their district or state. Potential challengers similarly may be encouraged to run and their backers may be given incentives to make generous donations to their campaigns, if they feel that the political winds are in their favor. Political scientist Gary Jacobson concludes that

> although national issues may not count for a great deal in individual voting decisions, they do influence the strategic decisions of congressional elites. Strategies generate choices across states and districts that systematically reflect national forces. Responding to candidates and campaigns, voters respond systematically, if indirectly, to national forces as well. Collectively, congressional elections hold the administration's party responsible for the general state of economic and political life.[15]

ENVIRONMENT OF CONGRESSIONAL ELECTIONS

A number of major changes have taken place in the environment of congressional elections, beginning in the early 1960s and extending into the 1980s. The reapportionment revolution of the 1960s forced states to apportion their congressional districts equally, threatening the security of many incumbents who over the years had built effective constituency organizations to ensure their congressional tenure. Reapportionment did not prevent political gerrymandering, but it

[15] Gary C. Jacobson, *The Politics of Congressional Elections* (Boston: Little, Brown, 1983), p. 156. See also Gary C. Jacobson and Samuel Kernell, *Strategy and Choice in Congressional Elections* (New Haven: Yale University Press, 1981).

did upset the status quo and give state legislatures the opportunity to change political balances. The constitutional requirement for equal apportionment of legislative districts, which applies at both the national and state levels of government, is based upon the right to equal political participation. The Constitution requires not only the one person-one vote ratio, but equal access to the ballot for racial minorities. The Constitution also proscribes gender discrimination in voting.

The formal environment of congressional elections is shaped by statutory as well as constitutional rules. The most important law pertaining to congressional campaigns is the Federal Election Campaign Practices Act, passed in 1971 and amended three times from 1974 to 1979. The law provides for the reporting of campaign contributions and expenditures to the Federal Election Commission, and limits the amount of money that individuals and groups can give to congressional candidates. The act has affected the way in which interest groups operate in congressional campaigns, and has indirectly spawned hundreds of political action committees throughout the United States to channel the funds of corporations, labor unions, and other political groups into the campaign coffers of congressmen and senators. Other laws affecting political campaigns are, for example, the Hatch Act of 1940, which proscribed direct political activities of public employees in campaigns. Finally, Congress itself has established codes of ethics defining the political activities of members in ways that affect their electioneering.

In addition to the formal context of political campaigning, many types of informal institutions and practices mold congressional campaigning. The politics of the presidency, interest groups, and political parties touch upon congressional campaigns in many ways. Voters' attitudes and behavior are major determinants of the character and results of election to Congress.

Constitutional Context

The Constitution initially defines the context of congressional elections by providing for equal representation of state populations in the House, and two senators for each state regardless of population in the Senate. Elections in the House must occur every two years. Since the 17th Amendment was adopted in 1913, the voters in the states have chosen their senators directly to serve for six years. One-third of the Senate, as provided by the original Constitution, is chosen every two years. Original constitutional provisions also determine the qualifications of voters and of candidates.[16]

EQUAL POLITICAL PARTICIPATION. Although equal political participation in congressional elections was implied in the Constitution, it was not until 1964 that the one person-one vote rule was applied to congressional districting.[17] Moreover, equal political participation in the electoral process for minorities was not guaranteed until the 15th Amendment was adopted in 1868, providing that no state could deny or abridge the right to vote of any person "on account of race, color, or previous condition of servitude." The purpose of the 15th Amendment was to guarantee equal voting rights for blacks, but those rights for blacks and other minorities were achieved only after a long and often bitter political struggle that culminated in the success of the civil rights movement in the 1960s. A series of Supreme Court decisions before the 1960s, coupled with the Voting Rights Act of 1965, formally guaranteed equal participation to minorities and provided machinery for enforcement of voting rights.

Although most states had granted suffrage to women by the turn of the century, a few states remained in which women could not vote. The 19th Amendment, adopted in 1920, prohibited gender discrimination in voting. No longer accepted was the view, stated by the Supreme Court in 1873, that "Man is, or should be, woman's protector and defender.... The paramount destiny and mission of woman are to fulfill the noble and benign offices of wife and mother. This is the law of the Creator." [18] That philosophy was the underpinning of the Court's holding in 1875 that "The Constitution of the United States [did] not confer the right of suffrage upon any one ... the constitutions and laws of the several states which commit that important trust to men alone are not necessarily void." [19] A constitutional challenge to the 19th Amendment on the ground that it violated state autonomy was rejected by the Court in 1920.[20]

---

[16] See Chapter 1 for a discussion of the original constitutional framework of Congress.

[17] *Wesberry v. Sanders*, 376 U.S. 1 (1964).

[18] *Bradwell v. State*, 83 U.S. 130, 141 (1873), upholding a state prohibition upon the practice of law by women.

[19] *Minor v. Happersett*, 88 U.S. 162 (1875).

[20] *Leser v. Garnett*, 258 U.S. 130 (1920).

Although the 19th Amendment granting female suffrage had an immediate effect, the 15th Amendment, passed long before, did not at first prevent state discrimination against blacks in voting. The states could not openly discriminate, but they could and did write laws that in effect prevented blacks from voting. Literacy tests and poll taxes were favorite state discriminatory devices against blacks, which also discouraged many poor whites from voting.

END OF RACIAL DISCRIMINATION IN VOTING. The tolerant attitude of the Supreme Court toward state laws that in effect if not on their face discriminated against blacks in voting began to change in the 1920s. The Court held in 1927 that the equal-protection clause of the 14th Amendment prohibited states from enacting laws under which blacks could be excluded from party primaries.[21] Soon after, however, the Court permitted political parties to act as voluntary associations, where no state legislation governed their activities, so that they could exclude blacks from both primaries and conventions.[22] Finally, in 1944, the Court held in *Smith* v. *Allwright* that primaries were an integral part of the general election process and that "the recognition of the place of the primary in the electoral scheme made clear that state delegations to a party of the power to fix the qualifications of primary elections is delegation of a state function that may make the party's action the action of the state."[23] Even where political parties were not governed by state law, concluded the Court, they could not establish white primaries.

The adoption of the 24th Amendment in 1964 expanded federal protection against voting discrimination by prohibiting poll taxes in federal elections. The philosophy that underlay the 24th Amendment was the same as that articulated by the Supreme Court two years after the amendment's adoption, when the prohibition upon poll taxes was extended under the equal-protection clause of the 14th Amendment to state and local elections. Justice Douglas wrote for the Court that a state violates equal-protection requirements "whenever it makes the affluence of the voter or payment of any fee an electoral standard. Voter qualifications have no relation to wealth nor to paying or not paying this or any other tax."[24] The end of the

---

[21] Nixon v. Herndon, 373 U.S. 536 (1927).
[22] Grovey v. Townsend, 295 U.S. 45 (1935).
[23] Smith v. Allwright, 321 U.S. 649, 660 (1944).
[24] Harper v. State Board of Elections, 383 U.S. 663, 666 (1966).

poll tax expanded the franchise for blacks, who were disproportionately poor in the states where the tax applied, as well as for other
minorities and poor white voters.

The Voting Rights Act of 1965 complemented the constitutional
protections of equal political participation for minorities. The law
abolished literacy tests for five years, a ban that was made permanent
in 1970, and authorized the Attorney General to initiate suits in
federal courts to prevent voting discrimination in states or political
subdivisions where less than 50 percent of the black voters were
registered. States and political subdivisions in which literacy tests and
low voter registration indicated discrimination were required, under
the "pre-clearance" provisions of the law, to obtain Justice Department approval of any election-law changes. The pre-clearance provision applied to nine states and portions of thirteen others in 1982,
when the requirement for pre-clearance was scheduled to expire.

The effect of Supreme Court decisions extending voting rights,
congressional voting legislation, and the civil rights movement generally has been to increase black voter registration greatly throughout
the southern and border states. Equal political participation in voting
has become a reality both for racial minorities and for women. The
effect on Congress has been to increase the representation of blacks
and women on Capitol Hill, primarily in the House of Representatives.

ONE PERSON-ONE VOTE. Another aspect of equal participation is the
constitutional requirement that one person's vote be equal to another's. Before reapportionment was ordered by the Courts in the
1960s there was great disparity among the populations of congressional and state legislative districts, giving some voters far more
weight in the political process than others.

The original provision of the Constitution for equal apportionment of the House on the basis of state populations, and the equal-
protection clause of the 14th Amendment added in 1868, would
seem to require on their face population equality within congressional
districts throughout the nation. The Constitution did not require
states to divide themselves into congressional districts, but once they
did, a strong inference can be made from the Constitution that the
districts should have been kept equal in population. Just as the founding fathers accepted the principle that the states should be equally

represented in the House, they undoubtedly would have extended the principle of one person-one vote to congressional districts had those been required by the Constitution.

The first major challenge to inequality in congressional districting reached the Supreme Court in the *Colegrove* v. *Green* case in 1946. It challenged congressional districting in Illinois, under which, for example, a Chicago district with a population of more than 900,000 contrasted with a district in southern Illinois with a population of slightly more than 100,000. Each district, of course, elected only one congressman, severely diluting the weight of the Chicago voters relative to their counterparts in rural areas. In 1946 a political science professor at Northwestern University, Kenneth W. Colegrove, challenged the state legislation that had created the Illinois districts, charging that the law denied voters the equal protection of the laws guaranteed them by the 14th Amendment. The Federal District Court dismissed Colegrove's claim and he appealed to the Supreme Court, which affirmed the lower court's judgment by a 4 to 3 vote.[25]

It was not until *Baker* v. *Carr* in 1962 that the Supreme Court finally declared that the federal courts did have jurisdiction over electoral reapportionment cases. The Baker case, however, involved a challenge under the equal-protection clause to the malapportionment of state and not congressional legislative districts. But the Court's grant of jurisdiction to review state legislative districting was a clear precedent for cases involving congressional districting as well. There was no doubt that the Baker decision would open the door to lawsuits throughout the nation challenging the malapportionment of both state and congressional electoral districts on equal-protection grounds. And, when the courts reached the merits of such cases, it was equally inevitable that they would sustain the challenges because of the gross malapportionment of electoral districts in so many states. A year after the Baker case, Justice Stewart wrote in a case overturning the Georgia county unit system on equal-protection grounds that within electoral constituencies "there can be room for but a single constitutional rule — one voter, one vote." [26] Eventually the one person-one vote rule was applied by the federal courts to require the

25 Colegrove v. Green, 328 U.S. 549, 556 (1946).
26 Gray v. Sanders, 372 U.S. 368, 382 (1963).

remapping of virtually every state legislative district, including those for both branches of state legislatures.[27]

The Court ruled that congressional districts must conform to the one-person–one-vote rule in *Wesberry v. Sanders* in 1964. The Court relied upon the Baker precedent to grant jurisdiction but, as it had not in Baker, it then ruled on the substantive issue of congressional apportionment. In the Wesberry case the malapportionment of congressional districts in Georgia had been challenged on the grounds that they violated Article I, Section 2 of the Constitution, which provides that "The House of Representatives shall be composed of members chosen every second year by the people of the several states." Moreover, the plaintiffs argued that the unequal distribution of population among the congressional districts violated the command of the equal-protection clause of the 14th Amendment. It was the state that had drawn the congressional districts which, stated the plaintiffs, constituted state action denying equal protection of the laws. The Supreme Court, however, did not invoke the equal-protection clause to decide the Wesberry case, but instead relied upon its interpretation of Article I, Section 2. Justice Black's majority opinion in the Wesberry case stated that, "Construed in its historical context, the command of Article I, sect. 2, that Representatives be chosen 'by the People of the several States,' means that as nearly as is practicable one man's vote in a congressional election is to be worth as much as another's." [28] At the time of the Wesberry case there were enormous differences in the voting strengths of different congressional districts throughout the nation. Differences between the largest and smallest districts were often more than 400,000 voters, and in Michigan the largest congressional district had 600,000 more voters than the smallest one.

The result of the Wesberry decision is that every ten years, after the census is taken, state legislatures, and in a few cases state commissions, must redraw district lines to conform to the one-person–one-vote rule. Throughout the country all congressional districts now contain approximately 500,000 persons.

GERRYMANDERING. The constitutional requirement for equality of population among electoral districts, with the exception of the

[27] See Reynolds v. Sims, 377 U.S. 533 (1964).
[28] Wesberry v. Sanders, 376 U.S. 1, 7–8 (1964).

United States Senate, does not apply to gerrymandering, which is the purposeful drawing of district lines to limit the voting power of particular groups of people. Practiced by state legislatures and local elected bodies as well, gerrymandering usually is carried out by the majority party to disadvantage the opposition party by minimizing its voting strength. State legislatures gerrymander in drawing the lines of state and congressional electoral districts. Local legislative bodies, such as city councils, usually gerrymandered to optimize the electoral strength of incumbents.

The term gerrymander is derived from the name of the governor of Massachusetts in 1811, Elbridge Gerry, who signed a redistricting bill, passed by the state legislature, which contorted district lines. The overall pattern of districts was said to resemble a salamander, and those unkind to the governor, who had actually signed the redistricting bill reluctantly, came to call the electoral map a gerrymander. The odd configurations of gerrymandered districts have led to colorful descriptions, as in the "monkey-wrench" district of Iowa, the "dumbbell" district of Pennsylvania, the "horseshoe" district of New York, and the "shoestring" district of Mississippi. The term gerrymandering has also been transposed in colorful ways to apply to other governors: the reapportionment of electoral districts in New York State in 1961 was referred to as "Rockymandering," after the governor, Nelson Rockefeller.[29]

The ancient and honorable tradition of gerrymandering in American politics has generally been left untouched by the Supreme Court, which finds no constitutional objection to reapportionment based upon political considerations. The Court will not, however, permit electoral districting based upon race, which clearly is aimed at reducing the voting strength of a racial minority. For example, in *Gomillion* v. *Lightfoot* (1960), the Court overturned on equal-protection grounds an Alabama law that had redrawn the city boundaries of Tuskegee in a way that virtually excluded all the black voters from the town. The famed black college, Tuskegee Institute, was banished from the city limits. The Alabama act was unanimously passed without debate by the legislature for the obvious purpose of preventing an emerging black majority from taking over the government of

---

[29] For the background and historical development of the term gerrymander, see William Safire, *Safire's Political Dictionary* (New York: Random House, 1978), pp. 255–256.

Tuskegee. Justice Frankfurter's opinion for the unanimous Court distinguished the circumstances of the case from those which arose in *Colegrove v. Green:*

> ... The appellants in Colegrove complained only of a dilution of the strength of their votes as a result of legislative inaction over a course of many years. The petitioners here [in the Gomillion case] complained that legislative action deprived them of their votes and the consequent advantages that the ballot affords. When a legislature thus singles out a readily isolated segment of a racial minority for special *discriminatory* treatment, it violates the 14th amendment.[30]

The most common use of gerrymandering is not to discriminate racially but to manipulate district lines so as to maximize the voting strength of the party controlling the legislature, which is doing the redistricting. State legislatures have always had to do some redistricting because of the constitutional requirement for a decennial census, after which seats in the House of Representatives are reallocated on the basis of population shifts from state to state. It was not until the Supreme Court required the one-person–one-vote rule for all electoral districts, however, that the redrawing of district lines became a major activity of state legislatures after each census was taken. State legislatures are required to maintain equality of population within both congressional and state legislative districts, which every ten years opens up vast possibilities for gerrymandering to maximize the strength of the parties in power within the states at the time. The strategic importance of the gerrymandering power to a political party was illustrated by the major Republican effort in the 1980 elections to capture state legislatures, knowing that success would enable them to gerrymander districts to maximize their party strength in Congress as well as at the state level for the next ten years.[31]

---

[30] Gomillion v. Lightfoot, 364 U.S. 339, 346 (1960). Emphasis supplied. The district court, upon remand of the case, declared the Alabama acts to be unconstitutional and ordered the boundaries of Tuskegee to revert to what they had been before.

[31] Although the Republicans made a massive national campaign effort to increase their control of state legislatures, they won only modest gains. They picked up slightly more than 200 of the 5,900 state legislative seats that were contested. After the election they held 39 percent of the nation's 7,482 state legislative seats. The Republican effort had little effect upon the control of state legislatures. They gained control of five chambers, but lost control of

The Supreme Court sustained political gerrymandering in *Gaffney* v. *Cummings* (1973), which involved an equal-protection challenge to political districting in Connecticut that was designed not to give an advantage to one party over another, but to optimize the safety of the seats of the incumbents of both parties by gerrymandering the districts to maintain in the legislature representation that approximated the statewide strengths of the Democratic and Republican parties. The Court generously viewed the underlying purpose of the plan to be one of providing "political fairness" between the parties. The Court, however, upheld the plan not because of its "political fairness," but because it considered the apportionment of state, and by implication congressional, electoral districts to be inevitably political and within the jurisdiction of state legislatures, provided apportionment schemes did not unreasonably vary from the one-person–one-vote rule.[32]

In response to the charge by the plaintiffs that the Connecticut apportionment plan was "a gigantic political gerrymander, invidiously discriminatory under the 14th amendment,"[33] the Court replied: "It would be idle, we think, to contend that any political consideration taken into account in fashioning a reapportionment plan is sufficient to invalidate it.... Politics and political considerations are inseparable from districting and apportionment.... The reality is that districting inevitably has and is intended to have substantial political consequences."[34]

As in the Connecticut plan, most redistricting ends up protecting

the Alaska Senate, in which they had had a majority but which after 1980 was evenly divided between the parties. After the 1980 elections the Republicans controlled 34 of the 98 partisan state legislative bodies — 17 state senates and 17 lower houses. In the 41 states where the legislatures draw the new congressional and state legislative district lines, Republicans had complete control in only three and a majority of one house in 22. In effect the Republican effort, which poured $3 million into campaign chests to capture state legislatures, did not alter the balance of power between parties at the state level that had existed before 1980.

[32] The Gaffney case also involved a challenge to the apportionment scheme on the ground that it did violate the one-person–one-vote standard; however, the Court found the population variations among the districts to be reasonable, commenting that mathematical equality did not have to be maintained among the populations of electoral districts. "Minor" deviations from the equal-apportionment principle were permissible, concluded the Court, and in such cases state legislatures did not have to justify their reapportionment plans.

[33] Gaffney v. Cummings, 412 U.S. 735, 752 (1973).

[34] Gaffney v. Cummings, pp. 752–753.

incumbents. Making seats safe for one party usually means making them safe for the other as well. When Democratic Representative Phillip Burton headed a California commission charged with coming up with a redistricting plan after the 1980 elections, he gerrymandered with a vengeance in favor of the Democrats, but by doing so he made the newly drawn Republican districts almost politically invulnerable to Democratic attack. He "dumped" the state's Republican voters into 17 districts, leaving the remaining 28 seats safe for the Democrats.

Gerrymandering virtually eliminates two-party competition in the majority of congressional districts. Incumbents pressure state legislatures or reapportionment commissions for changes to protect them, especially if they see their victory margins being reduced by increasingly successful challengers. For example, Democratic Congressman Abraham Kazen, Jr., had served the 23rd district in Texas for eight terms without being seriously challenged. He won the 1978 and 1980 elections by 90 and 70 percent of the vote, respectively. In 1982, however, Republican challenger Jeff Wentworth, a county commissioner, spent $400,000, almost twice as much as Kazen, obtaining 34 percent of the vote. The incumbent thought he saw the handwriting on the wall in the form of growing Republican strength in San Antonio and its suburbs, which were in his district. He persuaded the Democratically controlled state legislature to solve his dilemma by gerrymandering both Wentworth's home and most of San Antonio out of his district for the upcoming elections in 1984. Wentworth commented, "I would be running door to door [in 1984] but for the fact that I did so well in 1982 that Kazen went to the Texas legislature and asked them to move me out of the district." [35]

Political gerrymandering continues to be an important reality in American politics. Because Congress has not assumed the responsibility for determining the shape of its own electoral districts, a power it has under Article I, Section 4,[36] state legislatures and politics continue to define congressional districting. The one-person–one-vote rule prevails, but party balances in Congress are subject to the ever-dynamic forces of state politics.[37]

[35] *Congressional Quarterly Weekly Report*, vol. 42, no. 12 (March 24, 1984), p. 650.

[36] Article I, Section 4 provides that "The times, places, and manner of holding elections for Senators and Representatives, shall be prescribed in each state by the legislature thereof; but the Congress may at any time by law make or alter such regulations, except as to the places of choosing Senators."

[37] For further discussion of gerrymandering and redistricting, see Bernard Grofman, Arend Lijphart, Robert B. McKay, and Howard A. Scarrow, *Represen-*

Party Competition in Congressional Elections

Formal equality in voter participation in elections, under the one-person–one-vote rule, is an important part of the electoral process but does not automatically make votes count in a meaningful way. Presumably, voting is most meaningful in an environment of party competition, where the electorate is given a real choice between candidates and the programs they advocate. The environment of congressional elections, however, particularly in the House, is not one of party competition but of emphasis upon the personal styles and organizations of individual candidates.

SEPARATION OF CONGRESSIONAL AND LOCAL POLITICS. The electoral world of the member of Congress is distinctly and often sharply different from the world of local party politics, which concentrates upon developing effective organizations to elect persons to local and, for ambitious political machines, state offices. Particularly powerful local political machines, such as that which was run by Mayor Daley of Chicago, field candidates for all levels of political office. For the most part, however, the arena of local and state politics is sufficient to absorb energies and satisfy the power drives of local and state politicians and their backers.

Richard Fenno commented upon the separation between local party politics and congressional elections in his study of the home styles of eighteen congressmen. "Only two of the eighteen members studied," wrote Fenno, "were originally recruited by the local party organization. And eight began their careers by challenging the party organization. Most of the eighteen coexist with the party because of party indifference to the congressional office or because the party leaders value the proven independent strength of the congressmen as a resource. Most primary constituencies consist of people whose loyalties are to the congressman rather than to the party." [38] Most members of the House, concluded Fenno, do not seek to integrate their personal organization with the local party. Congressional candidates support "separate organizations pursuing separate tasks. The task of

---

tation and Redistricting Issues (Lexington, Mass.: Lexington Books, 1982). For an in-depth study of reapportionment in California, see Bruce Cain, *The Reapportionment Puzzle* (Berkeley: University of California Press, 1984). In addition, see Alan I. Abramowitz, "Partisan Redistricting and the 1982 Congressional Elections," *Journal of Politics*, vol. 45 (1983), pp. 767–770.
[38] Richard Fenno, *Home Style* (Boston: Little, Brown, 1978), p. 113.

the congressman's personal organization is to keep him in Congress. The task of the local party organization is to keep the party in control of local offices." [39]

The minimal role of local party organizations in congressional elections makes congressional campaigning highly personal, reflecting the individual styles and organizational abilities of the candidates and their advisers. Individual-candidate parties vie with each other for electoral support.

BLURRING PARTY LABELS. The personal and individual electoral contests for Congress confuse the party picture. Although the 435 congressmen and 100 senators are neatly labeled either Republican or Democrat, the party designations at the state and district levels have different connotations and implications than they have in national politics and in the political world of Washington. In congressional elections party labels are important as the first touchstone of identification with the electorate, which generally perceives of politics as being divided along Democratic and Republican lines. Voters expect candidates to have one of the major party labels, even though the electorate may act erratically and seemingly inconsistently in simultaneously, for example, voting for a congressman of one party and a senator of the other.

Party labels are important for candidates not only as a bridge to voters, but also as a way of gaining organizational support from state and local party committees, activists, and members, without whose support it would be impossible to be elected. In marginal districts, where two-party competition prevails because electoral strength is divided about equally between the parties, candidates must reach beyond the strength of their own party voters to capture independents and swing voters in the opposition party.

Candidates also rely upon parties to help them with campaign financing. The Democratic and Republican congressional campaign committees and national committees make financial contributions strictly along party lines. The resources of the national committees, however, are limited so that they are rarely able to contribute the $10,000 maximum ($5,000 each for primary and general elections) allowed under the Federal Campaign Practices Act. In the 1980s, however, national, state, and local Republican Party committees have

[39] Fenno, *Home Style*, p. 113.

been able to bring considerable resources to bear on congressional campaigns, giving in some cases $70,000 to $100,000 worth of resources to campaigns they feel should be particularly important. M. Margaret Conway writes, "Since 1977 . . . the Republican party's national-level committees have demonstrated the role that political parties could play through making direct contributions to targeted congressional contexts and supporting a number of activities that could have a significant impact on election results." [40]

State and local parties too may contribute to candidates, but they, too, must keep their contributions within the $10,000 limit. Because successful congressional campaigns usually cost well over $100,000, candidates for the most part are forced to find their own sources of funds outside their parties, which restricts the influence party committees can have over their own candidates in the electoral process, and, once elected, in government.

INTEREST GROUPS IN THE ELECTORAL PROCESS

The ever-increasing financial needs of congressional candidates, whose campaigns are affected by the same inflation that pervades the general economy, has given a growing number of interest groups the opportunity to influence electoral politics by making financial contributions to candidates of their choice. Interest groups also seek to influence congressional elections by persuading candidates that they can control the votes of their members, a claim that is more myth than reality. Myth or not, candidates do not want to take the chance of alienating large groups of voters who *may* make the difference in who wins or loses.

Financing Congressional Elections

Running for Congress has become an extraordinarily expensive undertaking that is beyond the financial capacities of nearly all candidates. In 1978, Texas Republican John Tower spent more than $4 million in his successful campaign to retain his Senate seat. Expenditures of several million dollars are not uncommon in Senate

---

[40] M. Margaret Conway, "PACs, the New Politics, and Congressional Campaigns," in Alan J. Siegler and Burdett A. Loomis, eds. *Interest Group Politics* (Washington, D.C.: Congressional Quarterly Press, 1983), p. 143.

races. In 1980 incumbent California Democrat Alan Cranston spent $3 million to defeat Paul Gann, whose statewide reputation had been boosted by his coauthorship of the tax-cutting Proposition 13, which limited property taxes throughout the state. In 1980 incumbent Democratic senators Birch Bayh and George McGovern spent more than $2 million in their unsuccessful campaigns for reelection. New York Republican Alfonse D'Amato spent $1.7 million in 1980 to defeat Democratic candidate Elizabeth Holtzman, who spent more than $2 million on her unsuccessful efforts. Jacob Javits was in the same race, garnering only 11 percent of the vote, but he spent $1.8 million. By 1984, expenditures in the millions of dollars were common in Senate campaigns, and it was not uncommon for more than half a million to be spent by House candidates.

SENATE VS. HOUSE. Although Senate campaigns are generally more expensive than House races, expenditures of several hundred thousand dollars are common in campaigns for the House. In 1980, Arizona Democrat Morris Udall spent more than $500,000 in his successful campaign to defeat the Republican challenger, Richard Huff, a Tucson real estate developer whose campaign cost more than $700,000. Texas Democrat Jim Wright, the House Majority Leader, spent more than $600,000 to defeat his Republican challenger, Jim Bradshaw, a former mayor pro tempore of Fort Worth who had strong conservative backing. Bradshaw's campaign cost more than $400,000. Texas Democrat Bob Eckhardt's bid for his eighth consecutive term in Congress in 1980, to represent the Eighth Congressional District of Houston, was unsuccessful even though he spent more than $300,000. Eckhardt, at 67, faced an unknown 28-year-old attorney, Jack Fields, from Humble. Fields's conservative backers contributed more than $650,000 to his campaign. Fields was strongly supported by the "New Right" and by a wide range of national business political action committees. Moreover, the mainly blue-collar complexion of the district had changed by 1980 and included significant new numbers of Republican voters who had moved into the suburbs on the district's northern boundaries.[41]

The most remarkable expenditure of money in a congressional election occurred in 1980 in the 27th district of California, which

[41] Fields won by 52 to 48 percent of the vote. Eckhardt had won in 1978 by 62 to 38 percent, and in 1976 by 61 to 39 percent.

stretches from the Pacific Palisades in the north to Palos Verdes in the south, encompassing many beach towns. Included in the district are Santa Monica in the north, the newly chic Venice, Marina del Rey, and Hermosa and Redondo beaches in the south. In 1976, in the spirit of California and Hollywood politics, the district elected television commentator Robert K. Dornan, an enthusiastic and eccentric conservative Republican who happily endorsed conservative causes not only in his district but in other parts of the nation as well. At one time he joined in a campaign against what some conservative organizations considered to be improper textbooks used in West Virginia. He spent more than $400,000 in his successful 1976 campaign, in which his liberal Democratic opponent spent more than $600,000. In a scenario that could have been written in Hollywood, Dornan was challenged in 1978 by Carey Peck, son of actor Gregory Peck, who had developed a taste for Congress as a former Capitol Hill aide. Peck's credentials were not only his unabashed liberalism in a marginal district that was split more or less evenly along liberal and conservative lines, but his good looks that mirrored those of his famous father. Although Dornan was himself the nephew of actor Jack Haley, who had played the Tin Woodman in *Wizard of Oz*, his show-business credentials were not of a high enough order to prevent a serious challenge from Peck. The forces of liberalism and conservatism joined in mortal combat in the 27th district of California in 1978, Dornan and Peck both spending about $300,000 in their quest for victory. Dornan barely won, 51 to 49 percent.

The 1978 contest between Dornan and Peck set the stage for 1980. Dornan, who received a 100 percent favorable rating from the conservative National Association of Businessmen for his congressional performance, but only a 5 percent favorable ranking from the liberal Americans for Democratic Action and Committee on Political Education of the AFL-CIO, prepared for the rematch with a vengeance. Expenditures in Dornan's campaign set an all-time record for a House race, amounting to $1,386,330. Although Peck's campaign chest was no match for the Dornan treasury, he spent more than $450,000 in his campaign, one of the highest totals of any congressional campaign in the record-spending year 1980. Although Peck was endorsed by the *Los Angeles Times*, Dornan again won by the slim margin of 51 to 47 percent, with a Libertarian candidate receiving the remaining 2 percent.

The high cost of congressional campaigns has persistently raised questions about the connection between money and politics. Common Cause, the self-proclaimed Citizens' Lobby, closely monitored campaign financing with the help of the records that are kept by the Federal Election Commission, to which all campaign receipts and expenditures must be reported. Common Cause assumes, as do many political observers, that there is a danger members of Congress will be more responsive to the interests of important contributors to their campaign than to the broader public interests. Although the American people, as Senator Edward Kennedy said, may have the "best Congress that money can buy," they may not have a Congress that heeds the interests of unorganized citizens and groups that do not significantly contribute to congressional campaigns.

How CAMPAIGN MONEY IS SPENT. The growing expenditures for campaigns are due to the increasing complexity of electioneering. Congressional candidates, particularly those running for the Senate, hire large campaign staffs and consultants to give them a competitive edge over opponents, who, of course, do the same. In modern campaigns it is de rigueur to have an outside political consultant, a pollster, a computer firm, an advertising agency, a film-maker, a speech writer, and a direct-mail organization. Rising campaign expenditures for these and other services have created a bull market for consultants of all stripes.

High campaign expenditures are also a consequence of the large political constituencies of congressional candidates. The electorate expanded in the 1960s and 1970s following voter-registration drives that enfranchised large numbers of blacks who had previously stayed on the sidelines. Moreover, the vote was extended to persons over eighteen years of age by the adoption of the 26th Amendment in 1971, adding more than 20 million voters to the nationwide electorate. Demographics, too, played an important part in the growing electorate, as the bumper baby crop of the 1950s began to reach voting age in the 1970s.

Although turnout in congressional elections is relatively low, candidates nevertheless never know who votes and who does not. They must deal with their constituencies as a whole, recognizing that each voter is a potential source of support or opposition. The decline of party machines and the general lack of organized party backing for candidates also makes the electoral task more difficult and expensive. No longer can most candidates rely upon a strong local-party organization to provide them with funds and campaign workers. Youthful volunteers have replaced the professional party workers of the past. Though the volunteers themselves are free, the campaign organization must pay for their support, providing them with office space, telephones, canvassing materials, and instruction, and an occasional party to keep up their spirits.

Finally, campaign expenditures continue to increase because of the high cost of advertising space in the electronic and print media, and the expense involved in using computers. All the costs of campaigning, including the salaries of advisers, the costs of sophisticated technological services and equipment, printing costs, telephone services, transportation, and even paper clips and postage stamps, have been affected by inflation.

Political Action Committees (PACs)

Although candidates may raise some of the funds they need from individuals and direct-mail solicitation, or if they are wealthy, from their own pockets, the bulk of campaign money is contributed by interest groups through their political action committees, called PACs.

CHARACTERISTICS OF PACs. Political action committees are the adjuncts of corporations, labor unions, professional associations, trade associations, and other interest groups. The committees receive funds from their parent groups and in turn make contributions to political candidates. The purpose of PACs is to raise political funds on a voluntary basis from a wide range of group members, stockholders, and employees, and aggregate these smaller contributions into larger amounts that in turn are contributed to favored condidates and political party committees. Corporations and labor unions are prohibited by law from making direct contributions that would involuntarily use the funds of members or employees to support political candidates. Although unions and corporations solicit funds from their members for the treasuries of their political action committees, however, they stipulate that such contributions are to be made voluntarily, which technically overcomes the legal proscription upon direct political contributions.

Although political action committees are limited under the Campaign Practices Act from contributing more than $10,000 to any candidate or party committee, the aggregate sums given by PACs

have become the major source of campaign contributions for most
candidates. The number of PACs has grown from 516 in 1974 to
more than 3,000 in 1984.[42] (See Figure 5.1.) Nearly all major corporations, labor unions, and trade and professional associations have
joined the PAC bandwagon.

ORIGINS OF PACs. Though PACs became fashionable in the 1970s
mainly to overcome the restrictions of the campaign-finance laws of
1971, 1974, 1976, and 1979, which limited contributions to individual
candidates, making it more difficult for interest-group power to be
felt in the political process, such committees were organized long
before the 1970s. Since 1925, corporations and labor unions have
been forbidden to make direct contributions to political campaigns,
a proscription which was often ignored, but which encouraged early
creation of PACs by labor unions, if not by corporations. The flamboyant leader of the United Mine Workers, John L. Lewis, created
the first PAC in 1935 as an adjunct of his union. In 1955 the Committee on Political Education (COPE) of the AFL-CIO grew out
of the merger of the two principal labor-union organizations of the
country. Thus, COPE became the model for future PACs. In the
decades before PACs burgeoned into the 1970 PACs, COPE used
the funds it received from the AFL-CIO, designated as voluntary contributions by its members, to support pro-labor candidates throughout the nation.

The AFL-CIO actively engaged in congressional campaigns, not
only through contributions but also by soliciting its members' votes
for favored candidates, but corporations did not have political action
committees of their own and generally operated behind the scenes of
the political process to support candidates of their choice. Some corporations found ways to channel funds to candidates secretly to avoid
the prohibition against direct political contributions from corporate
treasuries. A favored way of circumventing the law was donating services. Airlines and the telephone company would bill candidates
for their services, but there would be a tacit understanding that the
bills would not be paid. Contribution of services was explicitly for-

42 The Campaign Practices Act amendments of 1974 limiting campaign contributions and continuing the legal proscription upon direct contributions by
corporations and labor unions encouraged development of PACs to give interest groups a broad aggregate influence in the political process.

Figure 5.1
PAC Growth

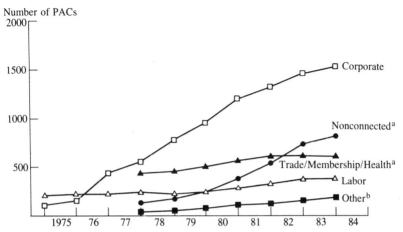

Number of PACs

[a]From January 1975 through December 1976, the FEC did not identify categories of PACs other than corporate and labor PACs. Therefore, numbers are not available for Trade/Membership/Health PACs or Nonconnected PACs.

[b]Includes PACs formed by corporations without capital stock and cooperatives. Numbers are not available for these categories of PACs from January 1975 through December 1976.

Source: Federal Election Commission Record, vol. 10, no. 3 (March 1984).

bidden by the Campaign Practices Act. Sometimes corporations were not so subtle, making direct under-the-table payments, as ITT did in 1972, when it contributed $400,000 to underwrite the Republican National Convention. When questioned about the contribution before the Senate Judiciary Committee, President Nixon's nominee for attorney general, Richard Kleindienst, said he had no opinion on its legality, causing syndicated Washington columnist Jack Anderson to reply:

> ... Mr. Kleindienst is a man who has trouble recognizing a crime when he sees one. Let us make no mistake about it. The contribution of $400,000 by a corporation to support a political convention is crime. It directly and clearly violates the Corrupt Practices Act, which specifies that it is "unlawful for ... any corporation ... to make a contribution or expenditure in connection with any ... political convention."

Yet when questioned about this, Mr. Kleindienst said he
didn't have an opinion. He protested that it was "customary" for political conventions to receive such donations.[43]

Nixon and his lieutenants were particularly adept at "persuading"
corporations to donate large amounts of money to Republican coffers. Revelation of the Nixon practices was a major reason for the
1971 and 1974 Campaign Practices laws.

CAMPAIGN FINANCE LAWS. Ironically, though the Campaign Practices Act was meant to reduce the importance of interest-group
money in political campaigning, exactly the opposite happened. Prior
to the Federal Election Campaign Act of 1971 the letter of the law
prohibited direct corporate and labor union contributions to political campaigns, but the spirit of the law went further in supporting
the idea that campaign financing by powerful interest groups was
undemocratic. The campaign acts of the 1970s continued to proscribe
direct corporate and labor-union campaign contributions, adding the
$1,000 limit upon individuals and the $5,000 ceiling on contributions
by organizations. Moreover, the laws included donation of services in
the category of campaign contributions, the price of services being
equated to money contributions. An airline offering free tickets to
candidates would be considered to have donated money to their
campaigns in the amounts the tickets would normally cost.

Though seemingly extending regulation of campaign expenditures,
campaign acts of the 1970s contained provisions that not only recognized the importance of interest groups in campaigns, but actually
encouraged formation of political action committees. Corporations
and unions were permitted to use their funds to engage in partisan
communications with their employees and members. Funds could
also be used in nonpartisan registration drives directed at particular
constituencies, which could, of course, increase partisan registration.
For example, union drives to register their members would normally
increase the voting base of the Democrats, though many blue-collar
workers vote Republican, as they did in supporting Ronald Reagan
in 1980.

[43] *Congressional Quarterly Weekly Report*, vol. 30, no. 11 (March 11, 1972),
p. 567.

The most important part of the campaign laws supporting PACs allowed corporations and unions as well as other interest groups to create segregated funds, composed of voluntary contributions from employees and members, to be used for political purposes. Moreover, corporations and unions were allowed to use their treasury funds in establishing and administering PACs, and for fundraising expenses incurred in raising voluntary contributions from employees, members, and stockholders. In effect, the new campaign laws gave a legitimacy to PACs that they had not had.

To no one's surprise, it was the AFL-CIO that vigorously lobbied for the new provisions explicitly supporting PACs. The giant labor organization did not want to see its Committee on Political Education jeopardized by the Nixon and Watergate backlash that led to the new campaign restrictions. In order to solicit Republican backing for its position, the AFL-CIO enlisted the support of corporations who would benefit from the law that allowed PACs.[44]

GROWTH OF PACs. Corporate PACs, which had not been in existence before the campaign laws of the 1970s, slowly began to burgeon as corporations realized they had a potent weapon at their disposal for influencing political campaigns. Political action committees spread far beyond the corporate and union spheres in the 1980s to encompass every major interest group in the country. In 1980, 1,200 corporate and 300 union committees registered with the Federal Election Commission (FEC). Professional and trade associations, along with other interest groups, doubled the number of corporate and union PACs on the list. Truly dazzling in scope and imagination is the computer printout of PAC registrations with the FEC. Along with the FEC-recognized corporate and union interests, such as the AFL-CIO, American Airlines, AT&T, Coca-Cola, and General Dynamics Corporation, are the American Federation of Musicians, Carpenters' Committee on Political Action, Florida Sugar Cane League, and the Western Egg and Poultry Action Committee. There is even an Oral and Maxillofacial Surgery Political Action Committee.

---

[44] At first, government contractors were excluded from the provisions allowing PACs and political activity, but they were permitted to create PACs under the 1974 amendments to the law.

Table 5.2

PAC Spending in 1981–82 (in millions of dollars)

	1979–80		1981–82		
	Raised	*Spent*	*Raised*	*Spent*	*Contributed*
Corporate	$ 32.1	$ 30.7	$ 44.3	$ 42.2	$28.8
Labor	25.9	25.3	36.3	35.8	20.4
Non-connected	34.6	32.4	62.6	62.2	10.7
Trade/health/member	33.9	32.5	43.1	41.8	22.6
Cooperative	2.8	2.7	4.0	3.7	2.1
Non-stock corporate	1.0	1.0	2.6	2.0	1.1
Total	$130.3	$124.6	$192.9	$187.7	$85.7

Source: National Journal (February 12, 1983), p. 344.

PAC INFLUENCE. Political action committee donations to congressional candidates have grown from $22.6 million in 1976 to more than $70 million in 1982. (See Tables 5.2 and 5.3.) Even though the committees cannot give more than $10,000 to any individual candidate for the primary and general election combined ($5,000 for each election), the aggregate influence of committee gifts can be very great indeed. Corporate PACs in particular are stepping up their contributions to elect mostly conservative Republican candidates. Incumbents have usually received the lion's share of PAC donations on the assumption that a bird in hand is worth two in the bush (see Fig. 5.2), but the increased PAC gifts to Republican challengers in 1980 may have helped the swing to a Republican majority in the assumption that a bird in hand is worth two in the bush (see Table 5.3.)

Labor unions remain a significant financial resource in congressional campaigns, but corporate PACs are rapidly assuming a dominant role. A spokesman for the AFL-CIO Committee on Political Action, contrasting business and labor resources, wrote, "We have just a finite number of unions and we've reached our level." [45] On the other hand, potential resources of corporations and their trade associations are virtually limitless.

[45] *Congressional Quarterly Weekly Report*, vol. 38, no. 47 (November 22, 1980), p. 3405.

Figure 5.2

PAC Contributions to 1982 House and Senate Candidates
(in millions of dollars)

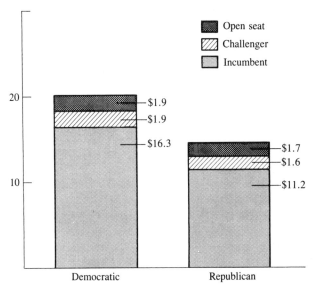

Source: *Federal Election Commission Record*, vol. 8, no. 11
(November 1982).

TARGETING CANDIDATES. The PACs make contributions not only to congressional candidates and particularly key committee chairmen (see Table 5.4), but also may conduct campaigns on their own to elect or defeat specific candidates. In 1980, for example, the National Conservative Political Action Committee (NCPAC) spent only $128,169 in the form of direct contributions to congressional candidates. In the 1980 campaign, however, NCPAC spent $4.5 million, $1.2 million of which went to attack liberal Senate incumbents. The group appeared to have extraordinary success in changing the composition of the Senate, for its liberal Democratic targets were defeated — Frank Church of Idaho, John Culver of Iowa, Birch Bayh of Indiana, and South Dakota Senator George McGovern. The NCPAC was not totally successful, however, for it also targeted incumbent Democratic Senators Allen Cranston of California and Thomas F. Eagleton of Missouri. Cranston won by an extraordinarily

Table 5.3

PAC Contributions (in millions of dollars) to House and
Senate Candidates in Each Party in 1982 Elections

	Corporate	*Labor*	*Political*	*Association*	*Other*	*Total*
House						
Republicans	$10.0	$ 0.6	$2.6	$ 8.6	$0.8	$22.7
Democrats	6.1	12.2	2.5	6.5	1.3	28.6
Senate						
Republicans	5.2	0.3	1.3	2.5	0.2	9.5
Democrats	2.2	4.0	1.1	2.0	0.3	9.6
Total						
Republicans	15.2	1.0	3.9	11.2	1.0	32.2
Democrats	8.2	16.1	3.6	8.5	1.7	38.2

Source: Federal Election Commission as reported in *National Journal* (January
15, 1983), p. 129.

large margin, 59 to 39 percent, and Eagleton defeated his opponent
52 to 48 percent.

Evangelical groups, particularly the Moral Majority, spent an un-
disclosed amount of money in the 1980 elections to influence congressional races. They claimed a role in the defeat of senior Democratic Representatives John Brademas of Indiana and Bob Eckhardt
of Texas. There are no limits upon the amounts interest groups can
spend on congressional campaigns in supporting or opposing particular candidates, provided that no direct contributions are made to the
candidates themselves.

Table 5.4

Political Action Committee Gifts to Key Congressional
Committee Chairmen 1978–1980

Congressman	*Key committees*	*Gifts*
Sen. Robert Dole (R, Kans.)	Finance	$ 328,055
Sen. Pete Domenici (R, N.M.)	Budget	152,585
Sen. Mark Hatfield (R, Oreg.)	Appropriations	89,925
Rep. Jim Jones (D, Okla.)	Budget	130,450
Rep. Dan Rostenkowski (D, Ill.)	Ways and Means	159,100
Rep. Jamie Whitten (D, Miss.)	Appropriations	97,925
Total for all chairmen		$6,513,208

Source: Reprinted from *Common Cause* press release.

Influence of Interest Groups on Congress

The influence that interest-group contributions have in congressional campaigns and upon Congress itself can only be a matter of speculation. Moreover, the extent to which the positions of interest groups and the endorsement of particular candidates influence the votes of group members is difficult to determine. Too many variables make the difference in congressional races to attribute success or failure to any one.

As we discuss interest-group and PAC power, we must keep firmly in mind that interest groups are a vital and legitimate part of the political process. They are important conduits of political demand, and lend their expertise to government in the formulation of legislation and public policy. David Truman and other group theorists forcefully argue that interest groups are the core of the Democratic process, without which it could not function.[46] Nevertheless, a major strand in American political thought accepts James Madison's *Federalist* 10 premise that faction is inherently evil, opposed to the national interest.

Critics of PACs, with Common Cause at the forefront, charge that they have divorced officeholders from their constituents by making candidates dependent upon them. The PACs are pictured as having extraordinary influence on officeholders, cumulatively exercising an extraordinary effect upon government. Singled out for attack are corporate and business-related PACs, whose numbers and contributions have grown at a startling rate, critics feel. The PACs, they say, have undermined political parties and generally circumvented the democratic process.

Political scientist Herbert Alexander, an expert on campaign financing, is highly skeptical about the stereotypical view of PACs that so often appears in the media, the literature of Common Cause and other groups, and in political campaigns themselves.[47] Taking a hard look at the evidence, Alexander found that the charges against PACs cannot be sustained. For example, far more campaign funds are raised from individuals than from PACs. Moreover, PAC money

---

[46] David B. Truman, *The Governmental Process* (New York: Alfred A. Knopf, 1951).

[47] Herbert E. Alexander, *The Case for PACs*, a Public Affairs Council Monograph published by the Public Affairs Council, 1220 Sixteenth St., N.W., Washington, D.C., 1983.

itself represents individual contributions. Campaign-disclosure laws prevent PACs from unduly influencing the political process, and PAC contributions are strictly limited. Corporate, labor, and other types of PACs are not monolithic. Finally, although corporate PACs have increased, they are not generally among the top campaign contributors. Labor unions are a far more important source of money for candidates.

It is not difficult to find *apparent* relationships between the campaign largesse of PACs and the tone of Congress. The American Medical Political Action Committee (AMPAC) of the American Medical Association continues to be one of the largest contributors to congressional campaigns. Perhaps not coincidentally, Congress often favors AMA positions. The association carefully picks candidates who agree with its views, and, as one AMPAC official stated, "Our candidates do not view government as the answer to our problems." [48] The AMPAC generally opposes liberal candidates on the assumption that sooner or later a liberal Congress might vote for national health insurance or even greater government involvement in medicine.

Liberal Democrat Morris K. Udall of Arizona, for example, found himself the target of an unsuccessful AMPAC effort to defeat him in 1980, even though he had supported the AMA's position on hospital cost containment the year before by voting against the Carter administration bill to control hospital costs. Udall's vote was not enough to gain AMPAC's support, however; it gave him nothing while contributing the maximum $10,000 to his Republican opponent, Tucson real estate developer Richard H. Huff. The AMPAC agreed with Huff's charge that Udall was an "ultra-liberal." Although Huff spent more than $600,000 on his campaign, Udall easily won, 58 to 40 percent.

The AMPAC failure to defeat Udall in the 1980 elections illustrated that a powerful PAC cannot by itself determine the outcome of an election. There is little doubt, though, that many PACs are extraordinarily successful in choosing winning candidates. In the 1980 elections, more than 80 percent of the candidates supported by the PACs of the National Automobile Dealers Association, National Association of Realtors, and International Paper Company were

---

[48] *Congressional Quarterly Weekly Report,* vol. 38, no. 47 (November 22, 1980), p. 3408.

successful. Much of the funds given by these organizations went to incumbents who already had an electoral advantage because of their higher name recognition, perpetual campaign organizations, and general fundraising capabilities; contributors lean toward candidates who have a track record of electoral success and who may already be in positions of power on Capitol Hill. The preference that PACs have for incumbents is illustrated by the generally larger share of contributions they give to them (see Table 5.3).

IMPORTANCE OF BUSINESS PACs. The growing success of business PACs relative to labor unions was illustrated by their greater success in the 1980 elections.[49] More than 65 percent of candidates backed by business PACs won, whereas only 49.2 percent of candidates supported by COPE, the PAC of the AFL-CIO, won. The United Automobile Workers PAC was slightly more successful than COPE, with a 62 percent win rate.

The growing success of business PACs has not been matched by independent conservative organizations, such as the National Conservative Political Action Committee (NCPAC), and the Gun Owners of America. In 1980, for example, both organizations went after Democratic incumbents, giving challengers the lion's share of their contributions. Moreover, NCPAC gave only a miniscule proportion of its money directly to candidates, dispersing more than $1.2 million in independent expenditures. The NCPAC strategy that directly challenged the Democratic incumbents on a wide scale failed dismally in the House, although the organization did claim credit for unseating a handful of powerful liberal Senators.

In the final analysis, PAC power seems to be tenuous at best. Contributions flow, members of Congress vote, but there is no necessary connection between the two. In fact, PAC contributions may put congressmen on the spot to vote *against* the interests involved lest they be accused of being the group's captive. Candidates may even refuse contributions to avoid being connected with their donors. Congressional scholar Alan Ehrenhalt, for example, points out that the oil PACs have difficulty in spreading their largesse widely because of the reluctance of many congressmen to accept it. "The 'Seven

---

[49] On the power and importance of business PACs, see Robert H. Salisbury, "Interest Groups: Toward a New Understanding," in Cigler and Loomis, eds., *Interest Group Politics*, pp. 354–369.

Sisters' of the oil industry," writes Ehrenhalt, "have plenty of money to give to candidates, and most of them have PACs. But in the past few years there have been few members of Congress outside Texas or Oklahoma who wanted their campaign finance reports to show $5,000 each from political arms of Exxon, Gulf and Amoco." [50] He concludes that "The major oil companies have been the muscle-bound giants of the campaign finance system." [51]

Above all, seeming correlations between campaign contributions and congressional behavior should be viewed cautiously. The AMA poured $1.6 million into congressional elections in 1978. A year later the House rejected hospital cost controls. Apparently the AMA contributions made the difference. However, "The strongest supporters of hospital cost controls tended to blame another group — the local hospital board whose 'pillar of the community' status made their lobbying more important than any contribution from the Medical Association PAC." [52] A proponent of the controls lamented, "Every leader in the community is on a hospital board. We could never compete with that kind of lobbying." [53]

Group Influence on PAC Members' Votes

Interest groups attempt to wield power in the electoral process not only through the contributions of their PACs, but also by persuading their membership to vote in what the leaders consider to be the interest of the groups. Labor unions, such as the AFL-CIO and the United Automobile Workers, corporations such as Standard Oil of Indiana and the International Paper Company, professional associations such as the American Medical Association, trade associations such as the National Association of Realtors, and evangelical groups comprising the Moral Majority, are among the wide range of interests with expressed candidate and policy positions. Interest-group leaders make every effort to persuade their memberships that they should vote according to the "party line" of the group. The members of labor unions are bombarded with propaganda from their leaders rat-

[50] *Congressional Quarterly Weekly Report*, vol. 41, no. 14 (April 9, 1983), p. 723.
[51] Ibid., p. 723.
[52] Ibid., p. 723.
[53] Ibid., p. 723.

ing members of Congress according to their pro-labor votes and endorsing candidates or challengers. The potential labor vote of an organization such as the AFL-CIO can make the difference in marginal elections *if* the membership votes in the same way. If labor unions could combine the votes of their memberships and their families they would sway close to 50 million voters throughout the nation, a potentially formidable congressional and presidential electoral force. Even more powerful would be the veterans' organizations which, if the families of veterans are counted, would control more than 70 million voters.

The Moral Majority too would be an unusually potent force in politics if it could sway the votes of its members. In 1980 George Gallup found that approximately 30 million voters consider themselves to be strict believers in the Bible, a constituency that the Moral Majority considers its own. Moreover, 21 million additional voters are "born again" Christians, many of whom are a potential constituency for the Moral Majority. Fundamentalist Christian groups, like interest groups in the economic, labor, professional, and other spheres, engage in wide-ranging propaganda to influence the outcomes of congressional elections.

RATING LEGISLATORS. Fundamentalist groups such as the Moral Majority and the Religious Round Table distributed more than a quarter million copies of a Family Issues Voting Index, printed by the Christian Voters Victory Fund, to influence the 1980 congressional elections. The index is similar to other rating reports published and distributed by evangelical groups, such as the Christian Voice "Report Card" of "Fourteen Key Moral Issues." Houston preacher Harold L. Champion published his own voting guide, rating congressional candidates according to their views on family, business, and farm issues. In the entrepreneurial spirit, Champion sold his books to gatherings of Christian conservatives for $3.95, as many as 10,000 copies at one meeting in Dallas.

The Moral Majority and the evangelical political movement rate congressmen on many issues to determine the degree of proper legislative conduct, which is identified as being pro-family, religion, and "freedom." Points are subtracted from congressional ratings where members favor the Equal Rights Amendment, abortion, busing to achieve racial balance, sex education, penalties for segregation in private education, and even for support of the Department of Edu-

cation. Congressmen are praised and their scores raised for supporting a balanced budget and restoring prayer in the public schools.
Christian Voice added foreign-policy issues to the ratings game, ap-
plauding legislators who defended Taiwan "from an attack by god-
less Communist China," and who opposed sanctions against Rhode-
sia, a "pro-American nation under attack by atheist Marxist forces." [54]

The Moral Majority's ratings of congressional candidates followed
the precedent set by other interest groups decades before politization
of the evangelical right. The liberal Americans for Democratic Action and the Committee on Political Education of the AFL-CIO
began to rate congressmen on a scale of "liberalism" in the 1950s.
The techniques of the ADA and COPE were soon taken up by a
wide range of groups that began to rate members of Congress on positions and votes on issues critical to the groups. Rating congressmen became the favorite game of an increasing number of interest
groups in the 1960s and 1970s. The eyes of many interests peered
over the shoulders of legislators as they went about their daily Capitol Hill activities, penetrating the inner sanctums of Congress that
for decades had been relatively sacrosanct and private. Before 1970
even the voting records of congressmen were easily obscured, for
they could shield their contradictory stands in votes taken in the
committee of the whole on the one hand, and on the record vote on
the other. [55]

Legislators generally are fully cognizant of the stands of labor unions
and business or trade groups on bread-and-butter issues. The AFL-CIO
takes positions in advance of votes in Congress to apprise members
of the stand of big labor. Corporations and trade associations do the
same. When groups such as the Moral Majority, Americans for

---

[54] *Congressional Quarterly Weekly Report*, vol. 38, no. 36 (September 6, 1980),
p. 2631.

[55] Before 1971 there was no accurate way to keep a public record of votes in the
House Committee of the Whole, which was the House sitting as a committee. Any one hundred members constitutes a Committee of the Whole, which
appoints its own "chairman," who temporarily replaces the Speaker. Legislation reported by the Committee of the Whole is then considered by the full
House. Until 1971 the Committee of the Whole voted by voice, divisions or
head counts, and by having tellers informally count members as they filed past
them. Recorded teller votes began in 1971, and electronic voting in 1973,
methods of voting that applied both to the Committee of the Whole and to
the full House, making it far more difficult to conceal a member's stand in
the Committee of the Whole.

Democratic Action, Ralph Nader's Public Citizen, and the conservative Americans for Constitutional Action rate legislators, however, they often apply highly subjective criteria of liberalism, conservatism, and "morality." Texas Senator Lloyd Bentsen (D), for example, whose congressional record would certainly place him in the conservative or moderately conservative category, received roughly the same rating from both the liberal Americans for Democratic Action (ADA) and the highly conservative Americans for Constitutional Action (ACA) in 1980. The ADA judged Bentsen's record to be 39 percent favorable, and the ACA gave him 43 percent. The two groups were far less ambiguous on Texas Republican John Tower (R), the ADA rating him at 6, the ACA at 91.

Congressional Response to Ratings

The often complex and confusing ratings game played by interest groups confuses many members of Congress. Suppose that a legislator wants to take a group reading on the issue of creating a Department of Education. The Education Department, the smallest in the federal government, was established by Congress at the urging of President Carter and powerful members of Congress itself, including then Connecticut Senator Abraham Ribicoff (D), chairman of the Senate Governmental Affairs Committee, which had to approve of the new department, and Texas Representative Jack Brooks (D), chairman of the Government Operations Committee. The new department was the smallest in the Cabinet, but became a symbol of a burgeoning bureaucracy and improper interference by the federal government in education, a matter that in the view of conservatives should appropriately be under the jurisdiction of state and local governments. Ronald Reagan called for abolition of the department in his 1980 presidential campaign. The Education Department issue, however, was not one that neatly divided liberals from conservatives, for it was supported by many conservative southern Democrats on both sides of Capitol Hill. Georgia Senator Sam Nunn (D), who was carefully developing a conservative image in economic and defense policies, proudly became a principal sponsor of the Education Department in the Senate.

The positions of interest groups on the Education Department issue, and their subsequent ratings of legislators according to their vote for or against the department, were often ambiguous. Legislators had no doubt that the department was supported by education lobbying groups throughout the nation, including public school teachers and college professors. The AFL-CIO's COPE, however, opposed the Education Department bill that was finally passed by the House, but took no position when the conference report to create the separate department was before the Senate. The Americans for Constitutional Action took no position on the House bill, but rated Senators negatively if they voted in favor of accepting the conference report establishing the department.

Group Power in Electoral Politics

Legislators seek a middle ground in dealing with possible interest-group influence upon their electoral constituencies. Although large groups, such as the AFL-CIO and the evangelical Christians associated with the Moral Majority, like to claim credit for the victories of representatives they support, rarely can one interest group marshal enough members to affect electoral outcomes. Interest-group money is far more likely to positively affect campaigns than the proselytizing of group leaders among their memberships in behalf of particular candidates.

Both the "New Right" and the Moral Majority claimed credit for Democratic losses, particularly in the Senate, in the 1980 elections. The candidates themselves, however, on both winning and losing sides, belittled the importance of the National Conservative Political Action Committee (NCPAC) and the Moral Majority. None of the victorious candidates in the major Senate races attributed their success to the massive amounts of money ($1.2 million) NCPAC spent to defeat their opponents. Republican Representative James Abdnor, who unseated Democratic Senator George McGovern in South Dakota, expressed views that were representative of other victorious senatorial candidates. Abdnor's press secretary stated, "I don't think if NCPAC had not existed it would have made any difference in the outcome." [56] Abdnor even filed a complaint with the Federal Election

[56] *Congressional Quarterly Weekly Report*, vol. 38, no. 46 (November 15, 1980), p. 3372.

Commission charging that NCPAC had used his name without authorization.

An aide to Representative Stephen D. Symms, the Idaho Republican who defeated Democratic Senator Frank Church, declared that NCPAC activities backfired in favor of Church because of clearly erroneous charges made against the incumbent. "I think if anything, groups such as NCPAC probably hindered Steve Symms," said the aide, adding "I think people get tired of trash." [57]

Republican Representative Dan Quayle, who defeated incumbent Senator Birch Bayh in Indiana, recalled that on the eve of the election it appeared that "new right groups might cost the Republicans the election" in South Dakota, Iowa, and Idaho.[58]

Not everyone agreed that NCPAC's influence in the 1980 elections was insignificant. Lance Tarrance, a Houston pollster hired by Republican Representative Charles E. Grassley to aid in his campaign against incumbent Democratic Senator John C. Culver, emphasized that NCPAC had an important effect early in the campaign even before Grassley had been nominated. The NCPAC projected Culver as a feverish liberal who was busy spending public money for projects that could be better handled by the private sector. Moreover, Culver was portrayed as overly liberal on foreign-policy issues, and on such critical domestic issues as abortion. "In 1979, it was not altogether clear to people where Culver was ideologically," commented pollster Tarrance. "He was seen as slightly liberal . . . by the summer of 1980 Culver was perceived as very, very liberal. That was not the result of Grassley's campaign. He was busy getting the nomination." [59]

McGovern aide George Cunningham suggested that NCPAC's preprimary activities might have had a profound effect upon the Senator's chances, causing his favorability rating to drop 20 percent before McGovern even got started.

The Moral Majority's role in the 1980 congressional campaigns was as controversial as the activities of NCPAC. Like NCPAC, the Moral Majority claimed credit for many congressional victories, including that of Republican Senator Jeremiah Denton, a rear admiral who had been a prisoner of war in North Vietnam for seven years, over

[57] Ibid., p. 3372.
[58] Ibid., p. 3372.
[59] Ibid., p. 3373.

the state's Public Service Commissioner, Jim Folsom, Jr. With the help of the Moral Majority, Denton outspent Folsom by a margin of almost three to one ($855,346 to $356,647). The Moral Majority held rallies that appealed to the voters in the fundamentalist Bible Belt state of Alabama. Denton's administrative assistant commented that although Folsom tried to make the Moral Majority an issue, "it was clear he was not in touch with the voters." [60]

The NCPAC and the Moral Majority arrived with much fanfare on the political scene at the end of the 1970s. Whether they will be a short- or long-term phenomenon remains to be seen. In the meantime, the more traditional interest groups of business and labor continue to help determine electoral outcomes by their financial contributions and by attempting to influence their members, employees, and stockholders.

Presidential Influence on Congressional Elections

Congressional elections inevitably feel the force of the presidency. First, very marginal candidates may be able to ride into office on the coattails of the successful presidential candidate. Second, and related to the coattails effect, turnout generally is significantly higher in presidential than in congressional elections. Larger turnouts may have a variety of effects, depending upon the congressional district involved. Voter turnout above the norm may reflect a move toward political change in the district, and a challenge to the incumbent. Democrats usually benefit from large voter turnouts in urban areas, because voters at the lower end of the socioeconomic scale, far more heavily Democratic than Republican, are generally far less inclined to vote than the better-educated and wealthier Republicans.

PRESIDENTIAL COATTAILS. No easy generalizations can be made about the effect of presidential coattails upon congressional elections. Generally the influence of presidential coattails has been vastly exaggerated, the false assumption often being made that popular presidents are responsible for the victories of their parties in the House or the Senate. Popular presidential candidates always help some members of their parties in congressional races, but the aggregate influence of presidential coattails on the balance of power between the parties on

[60] Ibid., p. 3373.

Capitol Hill is at best minimal.[61] In fact, Walter Dean Burnham argues that congressional incumbents "have become quite effectively insulated from the electoral effects, for example, of adverse presidential landslides. As a result, the once-notable phenomenon, the so-called coattail effect, has virtually been eliminated."[62] Unusually popular presidential candidates, such as Franklin D. Roosevelt, Dwight D. Eisenhower, and Lyndon B. Johnson, undoubtedly helped more than a few party members in their congressional races. But the average presidential contender has little effect at the congressional level.

President Reagan's coattails had minimal influence upon the 1980 congressional elections. The presidential race probably influenced congressional contests more because of voters' displeasure with President Carter than as a result of Reagan's popularity. Carter ran substantially behind Democratic House candidates in every region of the country, and received more votes than only three of the thirty-three Democratic Senate candidates, all of whom lost.[63] Even when Carter was successful in 1976, he drew more votes than only one of the twenty-one Democratic winners, Jim Sasser of Tennessee, and only twenty-two of the 292 Democratic House victors, most of whom would have won without Carter on the ballot.

President Reagan's coattails in 1980 benefited only a few senatorial candidates, and were mostly irrelevant in Republican races for the House. In the Senate contests, Reagan may very well have helped Arizona Republican Barry Goldwater to win by 1 percent of the vote, for Reagan ran far ahead of Goldwater in the incumbent sena-

---

[61] The usual method of calculating presidential coattails is to measure the extent to which presidential candidates run ahead of or behind members of their party in congressional contests. It may be assumed but not proven that a presidential candidate who runs far ahead of a congressional candidate helps the congressional contender, and unpopular presidential candidates who poll far fewer votes than members of their congressional parties may have a negative effect.

[62] Walter Dean Burnham, "Insulation and Responsiveness in Congressional Elections," *Political Science Quarterly*, vol. 90, no. 3 (Fall 1975), pp. 412–413. George Edward's analysis of congressional elections between 1952 and 1976 reveals that "By 1972 no coattail effect was apparent." See George C. Edwards III, *Presidential Influence in Congress* (San Francisco: W. H. Freeman, 1980), p. 73.

[63] Jim Folsom, Jr., of Alabama, who lost to Jeremiah Denton 47–50 percent; incumbent Herman Talmadge of Georgia, who was defeated by Mack Mattingly (51–49 percent); and Edward T. Conroy of Maryland, who was swamped by incumbent Charles McC. Mathias, Jr. (66–34 percent).

tor's state. Reagan may also have helped Florida Republican Paula Hawkins win her Senate seat by a 4 percent margin, Reagan having won the state by 16 percent. The Reagan candidacy, however, apparently had little effect upon most Senate races or in House elections. Voters, characteristically, were perfectly willing to overlook the Reagan candidacy and ignore party considerations to vote for popular members of Congress and for contenders who had effective campaign organizations well lubricated by PAC and other contributions. Many of the states won by Reagan elected Democratic senators.

Reagan's coattail effect seemed particularly minimal in the 1980 House elections. He carried only 51 percent of the vote nationwide, an insufficient victory margin to sway many House contests. Although Reagan outpaced most Republican contenders as a vote getter, in many eastern and midwestern congressional districts Reagan ran behind Republican challengers who captured seats from the Democrats. He outpaced challengers by wide margins in only a few western and southern districts.[64]

If presidential elections remain as close in the future as the Reagan-Carter contest of 1980, presidential coattails will continue to have an insignificant influence upon congressional elections. Candidates for Congress, incumbents and challengers alike, will rely upon their own personalities, issues, organizations, and finances in electoral contests. The increasing personalization and fragmentation of electoral politics, in which candidate parties and organizations count more heavily with voters than the regular national, state, and local parties, are very likely to make the coattail effect an anachronism, although occasionally an extremely charismatic and popular presidential candidate may be able to influence close congressional races.

Constituent Attitudes

Congress does not have a national constituency, but only state and local constituencies. The fragmentation of the electoral process, both a cause and effect of party disintegration, is one reason that presiden-

---

[64] Reagan outdrew successful Republican challengers David Dreier in the 35th district of California, receiving 62 percent of the vote to Dreier's 52 percent; in the second district of New Mexico, obtaining 60 percent of the vote over write-in candidate Joe Skeen, who obtained 38 percent; in the first district of Utah, drawing 77 percent against James Hansen's 52 percent. In Virginia's eighth district Reagan polled 56 percent against Stanford Parris's 49 percent.

tial coattails generally do not have much effect upon contests for congressional seats. The electorate does not vote for Congress in the aggregate, but only for individual candidates, whose personalities and styles determine voter preferences more than party identification and issues.

Congressional candidates develop their own styles and organizations to fit the demands of their constituencies. Constituents' attitudes are eclectic, varying greatly from one region of the country to another and even between contiguous electoral districts.

Congressional candidates do not know exactly how constituents' attitudes will affect their electoral chances. Inevitably there is a great deal of guesswork in congressional campaigns, as candidates, their staffs, and public-relations advisers attempt to assess voter opinion. Pollsters are hired to conduct surveys of constituents' opinions so that campaigns can be conducted efficiently to maximize the vote-getting opportunities of the candidates.

Voters' attitudes are diverse and often unfathomable, particularly on issues of public policy. Congressional candidates concentrate upon style and organization more than substance of general policy because they know the fickle attitude of most voters, and the pluralism of the interest groups in their vast constituencies. Political scientists Warren E. Miller and Donald E. Stokes pointed out in an earlier study of constituency influence in Congress, conducted when the populations of House districts were fewer than one-half the 500,000 persons who now comprise them, that less than 20 percent of the electorate had even read or heard anything about candidates running in their district.[65] Legislators cannot relate to their districts and states as a whole, but must focus upon pockets of individual and group opinion when they attempt to assess the public-policy attitudes of their constituencies:

> ... The communication most congressmen have with their districts inevitably puts them in touch with organized groups and with individuals who are relatively well-informed about politics. The representative knows his constituents mostly from dealing with people who do write letters, who will attend meetings, who have an interest in his legislative stance. As a result, his sample of contacts with a constituency of

---

[65] Warren E. Miller and Donald E. Stokes, "Constituency Influence in Congress," *American Political Science Review*, vol. 57 (March 1963), pp. 45–56.

several hundred thousand people is heavily biased; even the
contacts he apparently makes at random are likely to be with
people who grossly overrepresent the degree of political information and interest in the constituency as a whole.[66]

The eclecticism of voters' attitudes on issues and the concentration
of most voters on personality and style has resulted in widespread
ticket splitting among parties. A significant proportion of the electorate simply does not use party identification as the basis of voting
decisions. Congressional candidates cannot rely upon local party
organizations to put them into office. Individual candidates have
become political entrepreneurs in their quest for congressional seats.

[66] Miller and Stokes, "Constituency Influence in Congress," pp. 54–55.

CHAPTER SIX

Campaigning for Congress

The framers of the Constitution devised the two-year House term to keep representatives close to the people, to make legislators forever sensitive to and dependent upon the demands of grass-roots voters. The founding fathers would undoubtedly have been happy to see the almost continuous campaigning of congressmen, even in nonmarginal districts where incumbents are virtually assured of reelection by margins exceeding 60 percent of the vote. The framers envisioned a House in which elections would be competitive, and rapid turnover among members common. The House, however, even more than the Senate, has become an institution in which "careerism" is a primary incentive for members, causing incumbents to use all the advantages of their congressional seats to ensure their reelection. Though members constantly seek power and status within Congress, they know that they cannot pursue their congressional careers without a firm electoral base that will provide them with the necessary seniority to become committee and subcommittee chairmen, or party leaders on Capitol Hill.

Some political scientists, such as David Mayhew, argue that the primary incentive of House members is reelection. The frequency of House elections is a constant reminder to members that they have no time to relax and deliberate in an atmosphere free of immediate constituent demands. On the other side of Capitol Hill, senators have six years of lead time before they must face reelection, making it seem less imperative to maintain campaign organizations and constantly engage in reelection activities. But senators are, like their House counterparts, highly sensitive to constituents' demands, and many members of the upper chamber are almost as frenetic about remaining in the good graces of a majority of their constituents as are members of the House.

CAMPAIGN STRATEGIES AND TECHNIQUES

David Mayhew places congressional campaigning in the neat categories of advertising, credit claiming, and position taking.[1] Richard Fenno writes in his study of the home style of members of Congress that the reelection activities of legislators are often sharply differentiated from their Washington careers. Members attempt to build effective constituency organizations, allocating considerable resources, such as staff, and a great deal of their own time to cultivating support. The home styles of congressmen differ, depending on how they allocate resources, present themselves to their constituents, and explain their Washington behavior.[2]

ADVERTISING. Advertising is "any effort to disseminate one's name among constituents in such a fashion as to create a favorable image, but in messages having little or no issue content. A successful congressman builds what amounts to a brand name, which may have a generalized electoral value for other politicians in the same family." [3] Members advertise through newsletters sent to constituents, in opinion columns for newspapers, and in radio and television reports conviently recorded in studios maintained on both sides of the Capitol at public expense. Incumbents also send out mail questionnaires soliciting the views of their constituents on broad policy issues, which have the direct effect of advertising the names of legislators without committing them to any policy position.

Members advertise when they visit their districts by attending social events, appearing on local television and radio shows, conducting forums where constituents can air their opinions, and more personally in their meetings with constituents in district offices.

Political advertising is designed to package and present candidates in an appealing way in the hope that voters will "buy" them. A legislator's appearance takes precedence over his or her substantive stand on issues. Senator Lawton Chiles (D) of Florida, for example,

---

[1] David Mayhew, *Congress: The Electoral Connection* (New Haven: Yale University Press, 1974), pp. 49–73.
[2] Richard F. Fenno, Jr., *Home Style: House Members in Their Districts* (Boston: Little, Brown, 1978), p. 50.
[3] Mayhew, *Congress: The Electoral Connection*, p. 49.

rose from an obscure state senatorship to win his Senate seat in 1970 by walking the 500 miles between Pensacola in the northern panhandle of the state to the offshore island of Key West in the south. Chiles was branded the "Walking Senator," and visitors to his Senate office are symbolically reminded of his brand name by his original walking boots, prominently displayed on a table directly behind the Senator's desk. Much to the chagrin of political candidates who eschew physical exercise, the campaign walk, particularly in Florida, has become a popular way for candidates to advertise. Governor Robert Graham carried out his own version of the walk during his successful 1978 gubernatorial campaign in Florida.

Almost all members of Congress use their Washington offices to advertise to the multitude of constituents who drop in each year. The offices of legislators are frequently decorated, some from floor to ceiling, with pictures depicting the member's career, shaking hands with congressional leaders and presidents, attending bill-signing ceremonies in the Oval Office or the White House Rose Garden. Appealing family scenes are depicted and attractive spouses are highlighted. Even before reaching Florida Congressman Bill Nelson's (D) office in the Cannon Building, visitors are dazzled by the United States flag and the flag of Florida standing in the marble corridor on opposite sides of the door leading to the reception room. Inside pictures are displayed of the congressman walking along the beach in a pose that reminds one of the 1960s portrayals of John and Robert Kennedy, stressing physical prowess and thoughtful contemplation.

Campaigns for Congress, like those for the presidency, continue to act on the assumption of the late Canadian media philosopher Marshall McLuhan that "the medium is the message." Party ideologies and organizations cannot be counted on to win victories for their candidates. Those seeking congressional seats, like politicians everywhere, must project attractive, warm, and forceful images to an electorate that often will more readily support symbols than substance. Powerful images are appealing to voters; strong commitment to ideologies and issues always raises the possibility of alienating enough voters to cause defeat.

CREDIT CLAIMING. Legislators constantly seek personal credit from their constituents for government benefits that flow to congressional districts and states. Porkbarrel projects, such as dams, conservation work, defense contracts, and military bases; government grants to local communities, colleges, and universities; and government funds for disaster relief are all examples of the pork in the barrel. The annual Rivers and Harbors bill, which authorizes appropriation of billions of dollars for dams, highways, bridges, and federal buildings, is the paradigm of porkbarrel legislation.[4]

The porkbarrel tradition dates to the nineteenth century, when numerous bills for rivers and harbors were passed. The first omnibus bill was passed in 1899, and members have been "bringing home the bacon" ever since. Speaker John Nance Garner (D, Texas) commented on the porkbarreling activities of his northern brethren, "Every time those damn Yankees get a ham bone, I'm going to get a hog."[5]

The size of the congressional pork barrel invariably angers presidents, who often threaten to veto the excessively expensive and, in their view, wasteful projects. The pork barrel, however, is dear to the hearts of all members of Congress. Presidential veto threats are ignored, and presidents themselves recognize that should they veto an omnibus Rivers and Harbors bill, the veto would almost certainly be overridden by the necessary two-thirds vote on both sides of Capitol Hill.

Members are sympathetic to the pleas of colleagues to support porkbarrel legislation. On several occasions members of the House have candidly stated before the chamber that their reelection depended upon approval of funds for local projects. A responsive and sympathetic House approved the porkbarrel amendments of Representatives Kenneth Gray (D, Ill.) in the 1950s, and D. R. (Billy) Matthews (D, Fla.) in 1960 after the congressmen told their colleagues their reelections depended upon the approval of projects for their districts.[6]

---

[4] William Safire writes that the term "pork barrel" is probably "derived from the pre-Civil War practice of periodically distributing salt pork to the slaves from huge barrels." (*Safire's Political Dictionary* (New York: Random House, 1978), p. 553). Safire quotes from C. C. Maxey, who wrote in *National Municipal Review* in 1919: "Oftentimes the eagerness of the slaves would result in a rush upon the pork barrel, in which each would strive to grab as much as possible for himself. Members of Congress in the stampede to get their local appropriation items into the omnibus River and Harbor bills behaved so much like negro slaves rushing the pork barrel, that these bills were facetiously styled 'pork barrel' bills, and the system which originated them has thus become known as the 'pork-barrel system'" (p. 553).

[5] Neil MacNeil, *Forge of Democracy: The House of Representatives* (New York: David McKay, 1963), p. 143.

[6] MacNeil, *Forge of Democracy*, p. 143.

Powerful members of Congress frequently promise in their campaigns that they can deliver more pork to their districts or states than their opponents can. One of the most colorful and skillful manipulators of the pork barrel was Ohio Congressman Mike Kirwin (D), a canny politician with only a third grade education who represented the 19th district, which includes the cities of Youngstown (population 140,000) and Warren (population 63,000). Kirwin began his career in the turbulent days of the New Deal, winning his first election with the aid of Roosevelt's coattails in 1936. His Capitol Hill career spanned 34 years, ending with his death in 1970 at age 83. Kirwin shamelessly pushed porkbarrel projects for his district, including a proposal for an Ohio River–Lake Erie canal, known affectionately as "Mike's Ditch." The project, promoted by Youngstown industrialists, was opposed by nearly everyone else, including the mayors of Cleveland and Pittsburgh, the New York State Power Authority, and the governor of Pennsylvania, who called the canal "utterly worthless." [7] When the project came up for a vote in the House, flamboyant representative John Bell Williams (D, Miss.) roared, "Yesterday, we voted 3.5 or 3.6 billion to throw away [on foreign aid]. Let's build this ditch for Mike!" [8] The House, temporarily stunned by the rhetoric, shouted its approval. Planning began, but after Kirwin's death the project was abandoned.

Kirwin used his position as chairman of the Appropriations Subcommittee on Public Works to dispense pork. The committee was renamed the Energy and Water Development Subcommittee in the 97th Congress, and is now chaired by Alabama Democrat Tom Bevill. The Alabama congressman continues the tradition of his predecessors, liberally advocating Rivers and Harbors bills. During the Carter administration, for example, Bevill did not hesitate to report out of his committee porkbarrel legislation against the express wishes of the White House, which had vetoed or cut many of the projects.

Congressmen who chair appropriations subcommittees are the staunchest guardians of the pork barrel, the contents of which they largely control. As gatekeepers of the public purse, it is these chairmen who determine the amount of money that will be spent for public programs and projects, and often have an important say in *where* public funds will be distributed. Congressman Daniel Flood (D, Pa.),

[7] *Guide to Congress*, 3rd ed. (Washington, D.C.: Congressional Quarterly, 1982), p. 586.
[8] *Guide to Congress*, p. 586.

was for years chairman of the Labor-HEW Appropriations Subcommittee, and the number-two man on the Defense Subcommittee. He used both positions to send as many federal dollars as possible to his 11th congressional district, which included the formerly prosperous anthracite mining area around Wilkes-Barre in northeastern Pennsylvania.

As the anthracite industry declined, the prosperity of the 11th district vanished, to be replaced by higher than usual unemployment and economic stagnation. The district was desperately in need of federal money, and its voters were deeply appreciative of the federal largess, which they correctly attributed to Flood's Washington machinations. The congressman, a former Shakespearean actor, played his congressional role as if he was always on stage. He was a dashing figure, dressing with flair, a white handkerchief always displayed in his left-hand jacket pocket, sometimes accompanied by a boutonniere. To some, his waxed mustache made him look a little like a handsome Dracula, but to his admirers it simply added to his image as a dramatic and powerful congressman.

Flood was both dramatic and powerful after Hurricane Agnes devastated his district in 1972, flooding the Susquehanna Valley, causing loss of both life and property. Flood immediately stepped in and took command, using his influence with the Pentagon to bring in supplies by helicopter and even to commandeer a C5A transport to fly in a fireboat from Boston Harbor. Very few congressmen before or after Flood engaged in such theatrical credit claiming, which enabled Flood easily to be reelected in 1978 even after he had been indicted on criminal charges after his administrative assistant, Stephen Elko, accused him of taking money in return for using his influence in Washington. The congressman had become such a local hero that the major newspaper in his district did not even print any of the charges against him. After his indictment on ten counts of bribery and three counts of perjury his popularity, mainly due to his credit-claiming activities, enabled him to be reelected in 1978 by 58 to 42 per cent of the vote, a smaller margin of victory than he had had in the past, but nevertheless an outstanding electoral performance. Flood's election in 1978, however, was his last. After congressional leaders forced him to resign his subcommittee chairmanship, which he had used so effectively to build power both in Washington and at home, he became a broken man. Following his conviction on bribery charges he resigned his House seat.

POSITION TAKING. Members of Congress enjoy advertising and credit claiming because they do not have to take a stand on controversial issues of public policy. An important rule of electoral politics is that strong positions on issues are bound to alienate some segments, often important ones, of the electorate. Position taking, states David Mayhew, is "the public enunciation of a judgmental statement on anything likely to be of interest to political actors [voters]." [9] Position taking is done both on Capitol Hill and at home in congressional districts and states. Members take positions through roll-call voting, committee hearings, and

> speeches before home groups, television appearances, letters, newsletters, press releases, ghost-written books, *Playboy* articles, even interviews with political scientists. On occasion, congressmen generate what amounts to petitions; whether or not to sign the 1956 Southern Manifesto defying school desegregation rulings was an important decision for Southern members. Outside the rollcall process the congressman is usually able to tailor his positions to suit his audiences. A solid consensus in the constituency calls for ringing declarations. [10]

Congressmen find it easy to take positions supporting God, country, and motherhood, though not necessarily in that order, but concrete issues almost always pose problems. Legislators find it particularly difficult to take positions on explosive emotional issues, such as abortion, busing, and school prayer. North Carolina Senator Jesse Helms (R) became one of the most unpopular members of Congress because of his persistent efforts to force his colleagues to vote on such controversial issues as abortion. When Helms was first elected to the Senate in 1972 his colleagues dismissed him as an ineffective extremist whose fanatical views placed him far outside of the political mainstream. Helms had little difficulty in advertising, having raised an astonishing $7.5 million for his 1978 election campaign, in which he defeated his Democratic opponent by 55 to 45 percent of the vote. Credit claiming, too, is a Helms specialty, and the senator is widely known in his state as the defender of tobacco subsidies on Capitol Hill. Helms's conservative stands appeal to the Bible-belt and right-wing elements in his North Carolina constituency, giving him a

---

[9] Mayhew, *Congress: The Electoral Connection,* p. 61.
[10] Mayhew, pp. 63–64.

solid electoral base. Helms knows, however, that his extreme views on many issues are unpopular with a large number of his constituents. He raised his massive 1978 campaign chest to make certain that every North Carolinian knew who their senator was, and what he had done for the state. Helms's strategy was aimed at winning the votes of constituents who did not fully agree with his extremist views.

Helms's position taking on Capitol Hill makes him a maverick. Few members of Congress want to be forced to vote on the controversial issues Helms raises. Legislators do not want to be put into no-win situations where they will be damned if they do and damned if they don't. Members who vote for or against abortion inevitably alienate either right-to-life groups, who may target them for defeat in the next election, or pro-abortion groups. The Moral Majority targets legislators who vote to support the right to abortion, and who vote, for example, against permitting prayer in public schools.

Utah Senator Orrin Hatch (R) commented upon the difficulties of position taking after he became chairman of the Labor and Human Resources Committee, and of the Constitution Subcommittee of Judiciary in the 97th Congress. The Utah senator found, like many other Republicans, that being a member of the majority party gave him great power on Capitol Hill, but was a mixed blessing at home. Hatch's chairmanships put him in the middle of intense controversy over the Reagan administration's proposed cuts in social programs, and constitutional amendments dealing with such issues as abortion. After his election in 1976 Hatch became a faithful follower of the conservative creed, voting with the Conservative Coalition more than 90 percent of the time. He began to move more to the center, however, after assuming his powerful committee chairmanships, seeking judiciously to balance liberal and conservative forces that were completely at odds over the extent to which the federal government should support social welfare and the right to abortion. Hatch maintained his conservative posture, but recognized that if legislation was to be reported out of his committee he would have to bend on his formally rigid views.

When Hatch proposed a constitutional amendment that would give joint authority to the federal and state governments to regulate abortion, the right-to-life groups, which favored an absolute ban on abortion, vehemently attacked him. As he was about to open hearings on his amendment the Ad Hoc Committee in Defense of Life labeled the Utah senator "a symbolic Hamlet miscast as Horatio-at-the-Bridge, with the enemy poised to pour across." [11] When Hatch refused to join North Carolina Republican senator John East in conducting controversial hearings on legislation to determine when life begins, the ultimate purpose of which was to prohibit abortions, he further angered right-to-life groups while receiving muted praise from women's-rights groups. Hatch not only sought a compromise on the abortion issue, but also was a leader in working out a compromise that permitted many federal social-welfare programs to remain intact instead of being handed over to the states to be administered under block grants.[12]

Hatch recognized that his Washington activities might not play well at home. "I have a difficult time in Utah," he stated. "My folks out there don't realize I'm chairman of two of the most volatile committees. This places me in the middle of controversy. . . . Utahans don't like controversy, but I cannot avoid it. I have to take positions." [13]

Hatch won in 1982, which made him luckier than other incumbent senators who before had lost largely because of their position taking. Iowa senator Roger W. Jepsen (R), for example, unseated incumbent Senator Dick Clark (D), in 1978 mostly because of the unpopular positions Clark had taken favoring abortion and the Panama Canal Treaty. The Catholic voters of Iowa, who formed the core of the Democratic Party there, were constantly reminded by Jepsen and right-to-life groups that Clark had consistently voted in favor of the use of federal funds for abortions. Clark had been not only a popular, but a highly effective senator, defending the farm interests of his state as a member of the Agriculture Committee. Clark had tasted the heady atmosphere of Capitol Hill as an aide to then Iowa Congressman John Culver (D), who was elected to the Senate in 1974 and who, like Clark, was defeated in 1980 primarily because of his liberal record in the Senate. In his 1972 campaign Clark gained widespread popularity by his walk across the state, which transformed him

[11] *Congressional Quarterly Weekly Report*, vol. 39, no. 41 (October 10, 1981), p. 1956.
[12] The federal government gives money to the states in the form of block grants, with which the states have spending discretion in particular policy spheres, such as education and social welfare.
[13] Ibid., p. 1956.

from an unknown congressional aide to a popular and successful candidate. His early success and popularity, however, could not overcome what Iowa voters apparently considered to be excessive liberalism.

Congressmen try to avoid raising issues that evoke widespread controversy, and yet they inevitably must take positions on many kinds of matters in the hundreds of roll-call votes they are called upon to make. Major issues confronting recent Congresses have included draft registration, the MX missile, cuts in social programs ranging from food stamps to aid to the elderly, deregulation, and cuts in programs administered by such agencies as the Occupational Safety and Health Administration (OSHA) and the Environmental Protection Agency (EPA), hospital cost controls, the windfall-profits tax on oil, increased defense expenditures, and the Chrysler loan guarantee. Although members are constantly voting on many issues, and their votes are often reported in local newspapers, in congressional elections the most important positions taken by legislators are those they choose to emphasize and publicize. Challengers, though, invariably call the attention of voters to the controversial stands of incumbents.

The 1980 congressional elections revealed again how incumbents may be trapped by the controversial positions they have taken. Idaho Democrat Frank Church, for example, was attacked by his opponent, Congressman Stephen Symms, and by the National Conservative Political Action Committee (NCPAC) and an independent committee called Anyone But Church, (ABC), for many "liberal" positions. The contest was filled with acrimonious exchanges between the veteran Senator Church, who had served Idaho in the upper chamber since 1956, and Symms, who was an extreme conservative. The challenger, an apple grower when first elected to the House in 1972, supported such conservative causes as deregulation, increased defense expenditures, and the Kemp-Roth tax bill. The congressman opposed the Equal Rights Amendment and supported the amendment of Henry Hyde (R, Ill.) to prohibit use of federal funds to finance abortions.

Symms knew that Church was vulnerable on many of the positions he had taken. As chairman of the Senate Foreign Relations Committee, Church had supported the Panama Canal Treaty. He had also headed a special Select Intelligence Committee to investigate the CIA, enabling his opponent to accuse him of crippling the intelligence agency. Church had voted against the neutron bomb and supported legislation to pardon draft resisters who had opposed the

Vietnam War. Church knew that his constituency was more conservative than most, and on domestic issues he took positions that he knew would be supported by a majority of voters. He opposed gun control and voted for prayer in public schools. He opposed publicly funded abortions except to save the life of the mother or in cases of rape or incest. He even went so far as to support a constitutional amendment to give states the final authority to legislate abortion policy.

Church was an effective campaigner. On the campaign trail he could be found riding a bucking bronco at the local rodeo. He was a persuasive and often spellbinding speaker, who enjoyed meeting with his constituents. His record of constituency service was unmatched. He had helped thousands of voters with their problems with the federal government over his long Senate tenure.

Church spent close to $2 million in his campaign, but found in the end that his highly visible name and activities on behalf of his constituents were insufficient to overcome a "left-wing" image based upon positions he had taken in foreign policy. The election was the second closest Senate race in the nation, with Symms winning by only 4,262 votes. Symms was undoubtedly helped by Reagan's coattails, the Republican candidate polling 66 percent of the Idaho vote against 25 percent for Jimmy Carter.

Position taking is often perilous, but unavoidable. Congressmen invariably find that on occasion they must take a stand that will lose them the votes of some constituents. The home styles of most legislators stress name recognition, service to constituents, and the need to build an effective organization capable of delivering the votes. Members of Congress may be vulnerable because of the positions they have to take. The resources available to congressmen, however, give them a distinct advantage over challengers in the electoral process.

ELECTORAL ADVANTAGE OF HOUSE INCUMBENTS

Ronald Reagan won only 46 percent of the vote in the 30th congressional district of New York in 1980, while Republican congressman Barber B. Conable, Jr., who had represented the district since 1964, won 72 percent of the vote. The district was a Republican stronghold, but it is its congressman of more than twenty years who was by far the most popular Republican in the district. Conable's strength represented not only an engaging and highly effective political style, but also the electoral advantages of incumbency. He ran unopposed in Republican primaries, and the closest election he faced in the previous decade, against Midge Costanza, later to become an aide to President Jimmy Carter, he won by a margin of 59 to 41 percent of the vote. The voters of Conable's upstate New York district had returned him to Capitol Hill in election after election during a period when the House was controlled by the Democrats and the possibility of Republican rule seemed remote. By 1978, however, Conable had reached the important position of ranking Republican on the Ways and Means Committee, a perch that enabled him to lead his congressional party and influence tax legislation. Conable, even more than his constituents, relished the prospect of Republican rule, which made him one of the important leaders of the House.

The secret of Conable's electoral successes was in its broadest sense the power of incumbency.[14] House members, unlike Senators, have had greater than 80 percent success in reelection races. (See Figure 6.1.) Power in the House requires greater seniority than in the Senate because generally Representatives are easily reelected. The wide victory margins enjoyed by Congressman Conable are typical of a majority of the House. (See Table 6.1.)

Representative Tip O'Neill, who became Speaker of the House in 1978, has represented his Cambridge, Massachusetts district since 1952. O'Neill, admittedly a masterful politician, characteristically wins by more than 70 percent of the vote. O'Neill's chief lieutenant in the 97th Congress, majority leader Jim Wright of Texas, had served in the House without interruption since 1954. He had never been seriously challenged in the 12th district, which surrounded Fort Worth, until 1980, when the Republicans, encouraged by their victory in the gubernatorial election of 1978 when William (Bill) Clements defeated Democrat John Hill by 50 to 49 percent, decided to make an all-out effort to unseat Wright. The incumbent, however, won easily over Republican challenger Jim Bradshaw, the mayor pro tem of Fort Worth. Wright had not only attained great power and high status in the House, but had served his constituency well

---

[14] See Albert D. Cover and David R. Mayhew, "Congressional Dynamics and the Decline of Competitive Congressional Elections," in Lawrence C. Dodd and Bruce I. Oppenheimer, eds., *Congress Reconsidered*, 2nd ed. (Washington, D.C.: Congressional Quarterly Press, 1981), pp. 62–82.

Figure 6.1

Incumbent Success in Winning Another Term

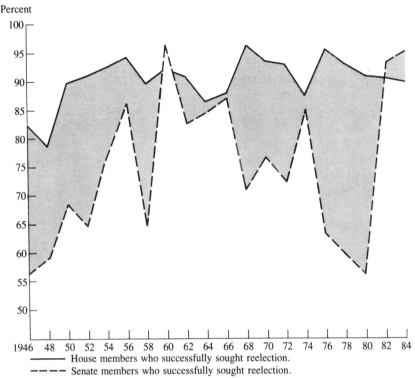

House members who successfully sought reelection.

Senate members who successfully sought reelection.

Note: Figures reflect incumbents running in both primary and general elections.

Source: Congressional Quarterly Weekly Report, vol. 38, no. 14 (April 5, 1980), p. 907; vol. 40, no. 45 (November 6, 1982), pp. 2779–2783.

as a senior member of the Public Works Committee before he became Majority Leader in 1976. The name Wright was a household word in and around Fort Worth. Wright's power in Washington and vigorous home style enabled him to defeat Bradshaw handily by 60 to 40 percent. By 1982 Wright's victory margin had returned to its normal range when he defeated his opponent by 69 to 39 percent of the vote.

The consistent and generally overwhelming electoral victories of congressmen such as Conable, O'Neill, and Wright, resulting in

Table 6.1

Decline in Marginality in House Elections, 1956–1978

Year	Proportion of incumbents winning at least 60 percent of the major party vote	N
1956	59.1%	403
1958	63.1	390
1960	58.9	400
1962	63.6	376
1964	58.5	388
1966	67.7	401
1968	72.2	397
1970	77.3	389
1972	77.8	373
1974	66.4	383
1976	71.9	381
1978	78.0	377
1980	72.9	392

Source: Data for 1956–72 elections were taken from David R. Mayhew, "Congressional Elections: The Case of the Vanishing Marginals," *Polity* 6 (1974): 316–317. Data for the 1974 and 1976 elections were taken from the relevant editions of Richard Scammon's *America Votes* series. Data for 1978 were taken from *Congressional Quarterly Weekly Report*, November 11, 1978, pp. 3283–3290. From Lawrence C. Dodd and Bruce I. Oppenheimer, eds., *Congress Reconsidered*, 2nd ed. (Washington, D.C.: Congressional Quarterly Press, 1981), p. 63.

congressional careers that often span thirty or more years, reflect not only political astuteness but also the intrinsic advantages of incumbents in electoral politics. More than 90 percent of the incumbents who ran for reelection won in all but two election years (1964, 1966) from 1950 through 1980. In the two exceptional years more than 85 percent of the incumbents were victorious.

Challenges Discouraged

The *expectation* of incumbent victories is so great that serious challenges are discouraged. Prospective challengers do not want to become involved in contests that they often believe they cannot win, and more important, potential financial backers do not want to throw their money away on losers. The simple belief in the power of incumbents buttresses the concrete advantages they clearly possess as members of Congress. Major changes in national political and economic conditions can make incumbents more vulnerable than usual as challengers and their backers are encouraged to enter the electoral hustings. For example, the Watergate fiasco was blamed on the Republicans, and resulted indirectly in more Democratic challenges in the 1974 elections to Republican congressional incumbents. At the same time, some Republican incumbents, facing stiff opposition, decided to retire rather than take the chance of losing. But even shifting national trends do not always significantly dent the inherent advantage of incumbents, for they can manipulate them for their own purposes, passing the blame elsewhere and taking positions to capitalize on the political tides.[15]

Incumbents are always far better able to undertake the necessary activities to ensure reelection. One does not have to go as far as David Mayhew, who argues that Congress exists solely for the purpose of reelecting its members, to agree with him that much of the organization, procedures, and opportunities of Capitol Hill help the electoral chances of incumbents.

Members of Congress can engage in the three principal reelection activities — advertising, credit claiming, and position taking — far more easily than challengers. Incumbents have enormous resources to aid them in developing and financing campaign organizations. Incumbency is a magnet for power seekers, and for those attempting to influence government. Political consultants, pollsters, expert staff, publicity, and money are attracted to those already in power. Moreover, incumbents tend to support each other regardless of party. Members of a state delegation in Congress, for example, often support each other within and outside of Congress. Powerful state politicians and state legislatures tend to heed the wishes of congressional incumbents in redistricting. A mystical bond often unites those in power against the external world. Politics is a profession (it has been called the second-oldest profession) whose members recognize that they are in an exclusive club, one that is often reviled by outsiders. If those in power do not protect each other, they may all, regardless of party, fall victim to an unsympathetic citizenry. Republicans and Democrats alike on Capitol Hill are private allies in the constant quest for reelection, regardless of public statements to

---

[15] See Gary C. Jacobson and Samuel Kernell, *Strategy and Choice in Congressional Elections* (New Haven: Yale University Press, 1981).

the contrary. Legislators know that many advantages they enjoy as incumbents are subject to nonpartisan sharing. Members of the majority always have an advantage simply because they are in power, but minority members too are given staff and other resources at government expense that are invaluable in the electoral arena.

THE MONEY ADVANTAGE. Incumbents have distinct advantages over challengers in attracting money. Political action committees, the main source of congressional campaign funds, support incumbents far more than they do challengers, who have far more difficulty in crossing the monetary threshold required to conduct an effective campaign. The more powerful representatives are, the greater their ability to attract financial support. Money is, perhaps, the key to understanding why House incumbents generally have such a great advantage. House races do not have the same visibility as contests for the Senate. House challengers are generally not very well known in the districts where they plan to run, and rarely attract funds from sources outside the district. Political action committee money seeking to influence public policy is far more likely to focus upon the Senate than the House, giving Senate challengers a distinct advantage over their House counterparts. In 1980, for example, the National Conservative Political Action Committee spent most of its money to support Senate rather than House challengers. It is an uphill battle for anyone seeking to unseat a congressman.

Money may make the difference in congressional elections. Political scientist Gary Jacobson found that House incumbents "typically raise and spend 60 to 80 percent more than do their opponents." [16] Spending is much closer in contests where incumbents are held to less than 60 percent of the vote. Significantly, successful challengers outspend incumbents.

Michigan Republican Guy VanderJagt, chairman of the National Republican Congressional Committee, which gives staff aid and money to Republican incumbents and challengers, points out that "You have to spend an awful lot of money to get people to focus on the differences between candidates." [17] Commenting on the advantages of incumbency, VanderJagt continued, "There is no excuse

[16] Gary Jacobson, *Money in Congressional Elections* (New Haven: Yale University Press, 1980), p. 52.
[17] *National Journal*, September 23, 1978, p. 1509.

for an incumbent losing his job. His voting record usually doesn't matter if the challenger does not have substantial resources." [18] VanderJagt's committee found that challengers who unseated incumbents in 1976 spent an average of $290,000, far more than the average challenger's expenditure of $60,000.[19]

FEDERAL ELECTION COMMISSION. Campaign finance laws are designed to treat incumbents and challengers equally, requiring them to report campaign contributions and expenditures. The Federal Election Commission was created in 1974 to enforce the Federal Election Campaign Act. The Commission makes rules to fill in the details of the legislation, and determines violations and what enforcement actions if any will be taken against persons who fail to comply with the law.

Congressional candidates and contributors have challenged overregulation by the FEC. Minnesota Republican Bill Frenzel, whose district lies in the Minneapolis-St. Paul metropolitan area, is outspoken in his attacks on the agency. "The FEC," charges the congressman, "is remorseless in trying to stifle politics. If it continues to be so picky, it might find itself with a good deal less authority." [20] The FEC does seem on occasion to be overzealous. When Hawaiian Democrat Cecil Heftel requested the FEC's assent to give macadamia nuts to other members of Congress, the commissioners seriously studied the matter and formally ruled that the gift would not be a contribution under the law that had to be reported.

The FEC also favors incumbents, charge its critics. Bill Burt, national director of the Libertarian Party, spoke for many political outsiders and challengers when he asserted that the FEC is "there to protect the incumbents." [21] John R. Bolton, an attorney who represented the plaintiffs in *Buckley* v. *Valeo* (1976), which challenged the constitutionality of the campaign finance law, feels that the Commission "proceeds against the least powerful and least popular federal candidates. [I]n effect, it is prosecuting the widows and orphans of the political process." [22]

[18] Ibid., p. 1509.
[19] Ibid., p. 1510.
[20] *Congressional Quarterly Weekly Report*, vol. 38, no. 16 (April 19, 1980), p. 1025.
[21] Ibid., p. 1025.
[22] Ibid., p. 1025.

A *Congressional Quarterly* investigation of the records of the FEC in 1979 found that the bulk of the enforcement actions were taken against nonincumbents. In one three-month period, only two incumbent senators and six incumbent representatives were investigated for noncompliance with the law, in contrast to eight Senate and fifty-two House challengers.[23] One of the challengers, Allard Lowenstein, who was a former congressman, had to pay a $250 civil penalty for failing to file a report on his contributions and expenditures ten days before the 1978 New York primary.

It seems unlikely that the FEC purposely harasses nonincumbents, yet those already holding congressional seats have an advantage in dealing with the FEC because of their experience and staff resources. As one FEC lawyer stated, "It may be that more of these fringe candidates don't know or don't care about filing than is true of incumbents, but we have no choice." [24]

PROPOSED FINANCING OF CONGRESSIONAL CAMPAIGNS. Common Cause has advocated federal financing of congressional campaigns to dampen the influence of interest group, particularly corporate, money in congressional elections. But federal financing would remove the enormous advantage incumbents have in fundraising. Congress has been willing to provide for financing presidential campaigns but has consistently rejected use of federal money in its own elections. Such a system, which would allocate money equally to incumbents and challengers, would distinctly threaten the major money advantage House incumbents now possess.

STAFF. House members receive an allowance of more than $400,000, and senators from $700,000 to well over a million dollars, which is used for the employment of staff, travel, printing newsletters, and engaging in many activities that are often specifically geared to reelection.

Congressional aides in Washington and in the district offices of congressmen are constantly involved in "casework" and in communicating with constituents about their concerns. A congressman's district office in particular acts as a buffer between people and government, seeking to soften the often harsh and adverse influence of

[23] Ibid., pp. 1024–1025.
[24] Ibid., p. 1025.

government upon citizens and helping citizens find their way through the maze of government policies and procedures. Each case handled by a congressional staffer that, for example, cuts government red tape, or prevents unwarranted bureaucratic action, gains a vote and even more from the inevitable ripple effect successful casework causes. "Pork barreling and case work" writes political scientist Morris Fiorina, "are basically pure profit." [25] Congressmen as well as aides may become involved in casework, as when former Congressman Wayne Hays, best known because he kept his mistress on the federal payroll, "stormed clear to the seventh floor of the State Department and into Secretary of State Dean Rusk's office to demand, successfully, the quick issuance of a passport to an Ohioan." [26]

Washington and district staff are involved not only in casework, but in handling myriad activities relating to their bosses' reelection. Press aides paint their congressmen in the best possible light, and carefully cultivate the local press, including radio and television, to give legislators publicity. Incumbents are usually far more newsworthy than challengers, particularly in the period between elections when congressmen use the media to advertise their names.

Generally a staff that grows in expertise from one term to another advises congressmen in their position-taking, advertising, and credit-claiming activities to maximize electoral opportunities. More senior congressmen vigorously pursue their careers on Capitol Hill while leaving to aides the details of constituency relations. Effective staff legwork can go a long way to ensure the reelection of members.

PERQUISITES. Staff is only one of the many perquisites of Congress that bolsters the electoral chances of incumbents. Members can frank campaign literature to constituents in the guise of newsletters. Each year Congress reimburses the Postal Service approximately $50 million for close to 100 million pieces of franked mail, which always increases during election years. Common Cause, recognizing the "unfair" advantage the franking privilege gives to incumbents, sued in the U.S. District Court for the District of Columbia to force Con-

---

[25] Morris P. Fiorina, *Congress: Keystone of the Washington Establishment* (New Haven: Yale University Press, 1977), p. 45. For a contrary viewpoint, see the exchange between John C. McAdams, John R. Johaness (coauthors), and Morris Fiorina in *American Journal of Political Science*, vol. 25, no. 3 (August 1981), pp. 512–604.

[26] "Hays Improves Rapidly from Overdose," *Los Angeles Times*, June 12, 1976, Part 1, p. 19. Cited in Fiorina, p. 45.

gress to limit use of the frank. Common Cause charged that the abuse of the frank violates the Constitution by giving money to incumbents without providing it to challengers. The constitutional challenge to the frank was unsuccessful, and its use or abuse, depending upon one's perspective, continues.

Members can not only freely send letters and newsletters to constituents, but also may send free or at minimal charge Washington memorabilia and souvenirs. Members receive thousands of requests for flags that are flown over the Capitol, and they are only too happy to send the flags for $10. The flags have become so popular that there is a three-month backup of constituent "orders." Constituents are not interested in the flags themselves, but only in those which literally have been hoisted and flown on the flagpoles of the Capitol. The problem is that there are not enough personnel to raise the flags or flagpoles to accommodate the deluge of requests. One congressional aide suggested an ingenious way of meeting the problem. He recommended that Congress hire small aircraft to fly over the Capitol with hundreds of flags trailing behind, which would later be sent to constituents with the truthful statement that they had been "flown over the Capitol." Another observer proposed having a C5A military transport to "fly" flags over the Capitol. No aircraft, however, are permitted to fly over the Capitol.

Congressional aides are busy not only sending flags to constituents, but also making certain that voters receive the full-color, glossy photo "We the People" calendars published by the Capitol Historical Society. Congressmen attach their names to the calendars and frank them to their constituents. A subcommittee of the House Administration Committee approved expenditure of $532,000 to buy 950,000 calendars to be sent in 1982 in preparation for the elections. Pennsylvania Democrat Joe Gaydos, chairman of the Administration Committee's Subcommittee on Contracts, commented, "No other comparable document receives such acclaim. We print a very limited number. I wish we could double or triple it." [27]

INCUMBENCY IN THE SENATE

Senate incumbents do not enjoy many of the electoral advantages of incumbency that characterize the House. The electoral success

[27] Congressional Quarterly, Inc., *Congressional Insight*, vol. V, no. 41 (Oct. 9, 1981).

rates of House incumbents have consistently been above those of the Senate, except in 1960, when 96 percent of the senators seeking reelection won. By contrast, only 61 percent of the senators seeking reelection in 1980 were victorious, but on the House side 92 percent of the incumbents who ran were reelected.

Senior members of the Senate were particularly hard hit in the 1980 elections, reflecting what seems to be a trend toward increasing Senate vulnerability. For the first time since 1932 the chairman of the prestigious Appropriations Committee was defeated when Washington Senator Warren Magnuson, with 36 years of Senate seniority and 44 years of experience on Capitol Hill, was decisively defeated by his younger Republican opponent Slade Gorton. Magnuson spent $1.6 million to Gorton's $900,000, but was unable to overcome the issue of age. Magnuson was seventy-five and did not appear to be in the best of health.

Magnuson's defeat, combined with those of other senior members, including Georgia Democrat Herman Talmadge, chairman of the Agriculture Committee, who had served for 24 years; Idaho Democrat Frank Church, chairman of the Senate Foreign Relations Committee, who was also first elected in 1956; Wisconsin Senator Gaylord Nelson, who had come to the Senate in 1962; and George McGovern of South Dakota, also elected in 1962, represented 155 years of Democratic Senate service. Democratic incumbents were not the only victims as Republican Jacob Javits of New York, with 24 years of Senate tenure and eight years in the House, was ignominiously defeated in the Republican primary by Alfonse D'Amato, a politician unknown outside of Nassau County and the town of Hempstead, where he was presiding supervisor, by 56 to 44 percent. D'Amato crushed Javits, who ran as an Independent in the general election, 45 to 11 percent. (Democrat Elizabeth Holtzman received 44 percent of the vote.) When the dust settled over the 1980 elections the Senate had lost a total of 209 years of congressional experience.

The greater vulnerability of Senate than House incumbents is due to the Senate's arena of politics, broader and more exposed than that of the House. The plum of a Senate seat is second only to the presidency in national politics, increasing the number of serious challenges to Senate incumbents. Aspiring members of the House in particular seek to move to the "upper body" because of Senate status and prestige on Capitol Hill and beyond. Five of the eighteen members of the 1980 Senate freshman class had served in the House.

Senators are targets not only for aspiring politicians, but also, because of their visibility, of interest groups and voters seeking political change. The relatively broader Senate constituencies result in weaker and more amorphous political support than generally characterizes House districts. The ombudsman's role that representatives perform so effectively through casework in their districts and in Washington is more difficult for Senators to perform because of the size of their constituencies and the multiple responsibilities placed upon them in the Senate. Credit claiming too can be better pinpointed in congressional districts than in entire states. Finally, because senators are more vulnerable targets than most members of the House, challengers to Senate seats can more readily raise adequate funds to mount effective campaigns.

Challengers

Former Tennessee Senator Bill Brock, who as chairman of the Republican National Committee spearheaded the successful Republican takeover of the Senate in 1980, commented that it was far more difficult to field strong Republican challengers to oust House Democratic incumbents than to find strong and attractive candidates to contest Senate incumbents. "People really think they can make a difference in the Senate," said Brock, "because it has so much prestige and the aura of power. People tend to look on the House as more of a zoo. They question how much they can accomplish there." [28]

Even the most powerful members of the Senate can be defeated, as the 1980 elections proved. Illustrious Senate careers are no guarantee of tenure on Capitol Hill. The landscape of Senate politics is rife with examples of strong and often successful challenges to powerful incumbents. Senate survivors of electoral battles can rarely rest on their laurels, for formidable challenges are very likely to face them once again.

Amateurs and professionals alike seek Senate seats. In California, where anything goes in politics and appearances are often more important than realities, incumbent senators are likely to be challenged by sports figures, movie stars, and popular personalities of all kinds both in and outside of politics. The senior California Senator Alan

Cranston (D), founder of the liberal California Democratic Council, a statewide volunteer group that had clout in the party in the 1950s and early 1960s, was preparing to challenge incumbent Republican Thomas Kuchel in 1968 when Kuchel was defeated in a primary by Max Rafferty, a highly conservative superintendent of public instruction who was known throughout the state as the man who wanted to return California education to the three R's, Reading, 'Ritin', and 'Rithmetic. Cranston defeated Rafferty 53 to 47 percent and, though his own initial victory resulted from the incumbent's primary defeat, he has had no difficulty in winning reelections by large margins.

Cranston momentarily seemed secure, but incumbent California senators have been more vulnerable than those of any other state because of the fluidity and unpredictability of state politics. S. I. Hayakawa (R), facing a formidable challenge in 1982, retired. Republican Pete Wilson won the seat against former governor Jerry Brown after a tight race. Californians like change in their second Senate seat, which has often attracted colorful personalities. Hayakawa had won his seat in 1976 by defeating Democratic incumbent John Tunney, who had a playboy image and a practiced Kennedy style. Tunney, son of the famous prizefighter Gene Tunney, found that his eastern accent and Kennedy ways were considered somewhat disingenuous by many California voters. Tunney himself had defeated Republican incumbent George Murphy, the Hollywood actor and tapdancer, in 1970, mainly because of newspaper publicity revealing that Murphy had received a retainer of $20,000 a year from Technicolor, Inc. while he was in the Senate. Tunney, who barely won his 1976 primary against political activist Tom Hayden, was politically wounded and unable to recover sufficiently to defeat Hayakawa, who was known for his dramatic and often spirited opposition to student radicals at San Francisco State College in 1968. Once again Californians wanted a change, and Hayakawa provided it. Not only did Hayakawa promise change, but he had a refreshing frankness. How could voters resist a candidate who argued that we should keep the Panama Canal "because we stole it fair and square"? Hayakawa's retirement in 1982 and Pete Wilson's victory continued what seemed to be the California tradition of putting a new face into one of its Senate seats each term while continuing to reelect Senator Alan Cranston who has served without interruption since 1962.

Many Senate challengers have had political experience in the House or in state politics, but the glamor of a Senate seat attracts political novices as well. Astronaut John Glenn (D, Ohio) broke into politics by running for the Senate, at first unsuccessfully, when he was defeated in the Democratic primary by Howard Metzenbaum in 1970; the latter lost the general election to Republican Robert Taft, Jr. Glenn defeated Metzenbaum in the 1974 primary and won an overwhelming Senate victory, defeating his Republican opponent by 65 to 31 percent. Senator Jesse Helms (R, NC) had virtually no political experience when he was elected to the Senate in 1972. He had served on the Raleigh city council from 1957 to 1961, and had been a staff aide in the Senate for two years in the early 1950s. The base from which he launched his successful bid for the Senate was not political, however, but in television and radio. He had become well known throughout the state as a Raleigh television commentator and through his own show on the Tobacco Radio Network.

The visibility and prestige of the Senate, which draws challengers from many quarters, also makes incumbent senators targets for popular discontent.

Reasons for Greater Electoral Exposure

Senators are big political game. Interest groups are willing to spend vast sums to defeat senators who do not share their views. The stakes are simply higher in Senate than in most House elections. Not only do most senators exercise more real political power than the average congressman, but also they are symbols of prestige and status that draw attention from broad-based political interest groups such as the Moral Majority and the National Conservative Political Action Committee. Single-issue politics focuses more on the Senate than the House. The NCPAC, for example, concentrated its resources in the 1980 elections on Senate races and almost ignored House contests.

WEAKER POLITICAL BASES. Senate constituencies are larger, more diverse, and more fluid than those of the House. State legislatures that redistrict House seats more often than not protect incumbents. Approximately 75 percent of the House districts have become noncompetitive along party lines.[29] In 1978, a banner year for incumbents, there was little or no opposition to members seeking reelec-

---

[29] See David R. Mayhew, "Congressional Elections: The Case of the Vanishing Marginals," *Polity*, vol. 6 (Spring 1974), pp. 295–317; and Albert Cover and David Mayhew, "Congressional Dynamics and the Decline of Competitive Congressional Elections," in Dodd and Oppenheimer, *Congress Reconsidered*, pp. 62–82.

tion in more than one-third of the districts. Seventy-eight percent of the incumbents won at least 60 percent of the vote. From 1956 to 1980, marginal House seats have declined, but competitiveness in Senate elections has remained the same or increased. Only seven, or 27 percent of the Senate incumbents who ran in 1980 received as much as 60 percent of the vote.

The decline in the number of one-party states has increased party competition in Senate elections. No longer can Democratic incumbents from the South take their seats for granted. In 1980 Republicans captured Senate seats in Alabama, Georgia, and North Carolina. Mississippi was a solidly Democratic state in Senate elections until 1978, when Republican Thad Cochran won the seat of the retiring James Eastland in a three-way race. For thirty-one years Mississippi had been represented by conservative Democrats James Eastland and John Stennis. While changes in the formerly solid Democratic South were giving Republicans increased successes in their bids for Senate seats, Democrats were making inroads in formerly solid Republican states such as Vermont, which elected its first Democratic senator, Patrick J. Leahy, in 1974.

The spread of party competition in Senate elections adds to the insecurity of incumbents. Ironically, while "party" competition is growing in Senate elections, political parties themselves have become increasingly factional and unable to aggregate the diverse and constantly changing interests and demands of the electorate. Even though party competition is prevalent in Senate elections, incumbent Senators cannot rely upon a solid party core back home to renominate and reelect them. Senators must worry not only about the opposition party, but about primary challenges from members of their own party. Senators, like congressmen, must create their own "candidate parties" under the umbrella of one of the major parties. Senate contests, like those for the House, have become increasingly personal. But senators, unlike representatives, find it far more difficult to create a consistently effective home style.

POSITION-TAKING VULNERABILITY. Former Maine Senator William D. Hathaway, defeated in 1978 after only one term in the Senate after serving four consecutive terms in the House, remarked, "I was just as liberal in the House as I was in the Senate, but I wasn't criticized for it then because I got the grants and whatever else it took." [30]

[30] *Congressional Quarterly Weekly Report*, vol. 38, no. 14 (April 5, 1980), p. 905.

Hathaway himself had won his Senate victory over incumbent Margaret Chase Smith, who had been elected to the Senate in 1948 after eight years in the House. Because Maine has only two congressional districts, popular congressmen are effective Senate challengers, as Hathaway found when he was resoundingly defeated by Representative William S. Cohen in 1978 by 50 to 35 percent of the vote. Cohen, like Hathaway, built a strong constituency base as Hathaway had done before him, and attacked the incumbent Hathaway on controversial positions the incumbent Senator had taken, including support for the Carter administration's compromise on what most Maine citizens considered to be the totally unjustified Indian land claims of the Passamaquoddy and other tribes.

Congressmen, like senators, must take positions, but if representatives do their jobs as ombudsmen for their districts, and develop a reputation through credit claiming for local projects, they are very likely to be reelected regardless of having taken some unpopular positions.

Voters often feel that congressmen are elected for constituent service and senators are chosen in the hope that they will cope effectively with overriding issues of national policy. Political consultant Joe Rothstein states that "When people consider voting for a Senator, they are looking for someone who has some power to effect change and deal with the paramount issues that affect their lives." [31] Former Senator Hathaway comments, "Senators are perceived as being more responsible for what is wrong." [32] When the voters are in a mood to throw the rascals out, they find the Senate a more logical target than the House.

PRESS COVERAGE. The press contributes to the electoral vulnerability of the Senate while generally protecting and reinforcing the popularity of congressmen in their districts. Representatives can more easily control their media coverage, a critical factor in electoral success.[33] Congressmen use their in-house media resources, including television and radio recording studios, to project a favorable image at home. Local press coverage of representatives is often nothing

---

[31] Ibid., p. 906.
[32] Ibid., p. 906.
[33] See Gary Jacobson, "The Impact of Broadcast Campaigning on Electoral Outcomes," *Journal of Politics*, vol. 37 (1975), p. 774.

more than reprints of congressmen's press releases. Rarely does the local press comment unfavorably on the activities of their representative, and even when congressmen have been indicted on criminal charges the local press has rushed to their support. The Wilkes-Barre, Pennsylvania *Times-Leader*, largest daily newspaper in the district of Congressman Daniel Flood, did everything possible to cast the congressman in a favorable image after he was indicted on criminal charges, including the taking of bribes in return for influence. The paper went out of its way to emphasize Flood's widespread district support.[34]

Senators are exposed to far more critical press scrutiny than members of the House. Senators appear on network news programs, and their positions are widely publicized. Senate Minority Leader Robert Byrd announced his opposition to the sale of AWACS planes, highly sophisticated reconnaissance aircraft, to Saudi Arabia. On the eve of the Senate vote in 1981, his announcement was immediately broadcast on national television as an important news event. Both President Reagan and the news media concentrated almost solely upon the Senate during the controversial debates over the administration's plan to sell these planes.

Senators are national news, and their activities are publicized in the national press and news media. Senate challengers, too, attract widespread press coverage, in sharp contrast to the scant media attention that is usually given to House challengers. The press attention to Senate races can increase the vulnerability of incumbents and help to publicize their opponents.

MONEY. The perceived vulnerability of Senate incumbents, combined with the attractiveness of Senate seats, makes it far easier to raise money to challenge senators than to unseat representatives. Potential contributors feel they can have a major impact on government by influencing the outcome of Senate elections. Challengers draw upon the resources of the political opponents of Senate incumbents, as well as upon contributors, who want to play safe by donating to both sides.

---

[34] Michael J. Robinson, "Three Faces of Congressional Media," in Thomas E. Mann and Norman J. Ornstein, *The New Congress* (Washington, D.C.: American Enterprise Institute, 1981), pp. 78–79.

THE SIX-YEAR TERM. The founding fathers provided the six-year term of office for senators to make them less dependent upon the people, and to give the upper body a deliberative character that the framers thought would be impossible to create in a body subject to frequent elections. The often irrational whims of the electorate would be felt more directly in the House than the Senate.

Ironically, the Senate has become a more direct barometer of voters' opinions than the House, in part due to the very six-year term that was initially designed to insulate the Senate from the changing and frequently capricious political moods of the electorate.

The two-year House term keeps congressmen close to the people in ways that help to ensure their reelection. And the two-year term, which the framers saw as a way to make representatives dependent upon the people, instead makes the people dependent upon their representatives. Congressmen, knowing they must enter the electoral arena every two years, strenuously strive to develop home styles that will ensure their reelection regardless of the positions they are forced to take on major issues of public policy. They have made their constituents depend on them for casework and the ever-important pork-barrel projects, upon which many districts depend for their economic well-being.

Senators, because of their six-year term, do not have the same incentive constantly to campaign for reelection that is present in the House. Nor do they have the time or staff resources to become effective and recognized ombudsmen for their statewide constituencies.

Senators close to election often behave differently than those who have recently been elected. When the controversial AWACS vote came up in the Senate in 1981, members knew that they faced a difficult choice. A vote for the sale to Saudia Arabia of reconnaissance planes and the arms package that went with them would alienate Jewish voters, who considered the sale to be a major threat to Israel. Many senators who had significant Jewish populations in their states knew that the safe position to take would be against the sale. The senators from New York and Florida, for example, registered "No" votes regardless of party pressures. Florida Republican Paula Hawkins and New York Republican Alfonse D'Amato, who had just been elected in 1980 by extremely close votes, took safe positions. It was not only senators from the states where the Jewish vote was important who voted against the sale, but those who were up for election in 1982. Fully twenty-two of the thirty-three senators whose terms expired in 1982 voted against the sale. Senators often feel freer to take controversial positions when they do not confront an immediate electoral challenge.

Electoral Politics and Washington Careers

At the same time as members of Congress diligently pursue reelection, they strive to increase their power and status within Congress and in the broader political world of Washington. Legislators retain their seats by campaigning successfully and paying proper attention to constituents' needs. But their constituency careers are in many ways entirely separate from the careers they pursue in Washington. A representative's reputation for power on Capitol Hill is not particularly enhanced by reelection activities.

Power within Congress, however, is not solely an internal matter. Members seek to cultivate power relationships beyond Capitol Hill in the world of Washington, with the political establishment of administrative agencies, Washington lawyers, interest groups, the press, and even the social elite; their goal is to create a reflective image of power on Capitol Hill. The president and his entourage, themselves outsiders and necessarily only a temporary component of the political establishment, nevertheless while they are in power are treated as ex officio members of the establishment and become vital to members of Congress who wish to enhance their reputations for holding power.

Dealings with the Washington political establishment are also important to members for reelection purposes, for the president, for example, may have the necessary clout to release funds for a member's favorite porkbarrel project. Administrative agencies, too, may indirectly help reelect incumbents by supporting their activities at home. The Army Corps of Engineers may support a member's proposal to build a dam in his or her district, and interest groups, a permanent fixture on the Washington political scene, not only engage in political machinations in the nation's capital, but also constantly seek to influence the electoral process.

Congress and the Washington Political Establishment

CHAPTER SEVEN

Congress:
Keystone of the Establishment

Ronald Reagan found, as presidents had before him and will after him, that many complex strands make up Washington political life. He knew that he would have to court powerful members of Congress, lobbyists, prominent oracles, pundits, members of the social elite, and at least a few top-echelon bureaucrats if he was to be a successful leader. The "establishment" contains not only prominent members of Congress, but also the social and economic elite of the city and powerful individuals outside of Washington as well. The political, economic, and social establishments of Washington are intertwined in networks of power that only sophisticated and experienced observers can comprehend. Members of Congress seek a place in the wider power establishments of Washington at the same time as they may be on the establishment roster themselves, provided they have achieved positions of prominence on Capitol Hill.

When President-elect Reagan barnstormed Washington before his inauguration, he touched base both with the congressional establishment and with prominent Washington figures who were considered to be the movers and shakers of the town. He lunched with Republican members from both sides of Capitol Hill, and dined with the new Senate GOP majority. He sipped wine with members of the Supreme Court, and had his picture taken with Chief Justice Warren Burger in front of the Supreme Court building. He called on Frank Fitzsimmons, president of the Teamsters Union, who had been a strong supporter of Reagan and represented part of the Washington interest group establishment.

The President-elect met with the political, economic, cultural, and sports establishments of Washington at an elaborate candle-lit dinner given at the exclusive F Street Club. The dinner reflected the eclecticism of power in Washington. Political deals are cut as frequently over caviar and champagne as during regular working hours. Social gatherings provide an opportunity for relaxed conversation, convivial give-and-take, which later may influence the course of government.

The guests at the Reagan "Hello Party" included the governors of Maryland and Virginia; Abe Pollin, the owner of the Bullets, a basketball team that takes second place in the hearts of Washingtonians only to the frequently beleaguered Redskins who nevertheless became National Football League and Super Bowl champions; John T. Walker, Bishop of the Episcopal Diocese of Washington; Gene Firstenberg, Director of the American Film Institute; James Cheek, President of Howard University; Melvin Payne, Chairman of the Board of the National Geographic Society; Vincent Burke, Chairman of the Board of the Riggs National Bank; Austin Kiplinger, publisher of the *Kiplinger Newsletter*; and John Hechinger, owner of a building and household supplies department store that is one of the most prosperous in the city.

Also attending the dinner were National Gallery director Jay Carter Brown, Mstislav Rostropovich, musical director of the National Symphony Orchestra, and Joe Hirshhorn, who had given his world-renowned art collection to the government to be displayed in the Hirshhorn Museum. Democrats, too, attended the events, such as Edward Bennett Williams, owner of the Baltimore Orioles, formerly president of the Washington Redskins, and a famous Washington lawyer known for his ability in representing unpopular figures before congressional investigating committees. Although a Democrat, Williams's well-known Washington connections caused Reagan to appoint him to his transition team. Washington Mayor Marion Barry was also in attendance.

Politics in Washington is often conducted in a social atmosphere. The "power lunch" takes place in restaurants throughout the town that have achieved a cachet identifying them as places where the rich and powerful gather to conduct their business. For several decades, beginning with the Kennedy administration, the elite used to meet to lunch at the Sans Souci Restaurant on 17th Street, a few blocks from the White House. Sans Souci was more a club at lunchtime than a restaurant. It was, like Bernard Baruch's bench in Lafayette Park, a gathering place for political conversation and discussion of strategies among the powerful. Humorist Art Buchwald and the maître d'hôtel Paul De Lisle were the mainstays. Buchwald could often be seen conducting court from his table that was strategically located on the side wall where he could observe every table in the small establishment, and always be seen by those entering and leaving. Buchwald wrote, perhaps only half facetiously, that when "people in the Johnson, Nixon, Ford and Carter administrations needed advice they knew where to find me." He continued, "When I held court at the Sans Souci, the inflation rate never rose above 5 percent, people could purchase a decent home for $40,000, banks were begging the public to borrow money at 6 percent, social security was safe, and the United States had twice the military might of the Soviet Union." [1]

During the Nixon and Ford administrations, while Buchwald hosted such members of the Washington political establishment as Executive Editor Benjamin Bradlee of the *Washington Post*, others including Secretary of State Henry Kissinger, columnists Robert Novak, Joe Alsop, and Jack Anderson frequently lunched at Sans Souci along with Walter Cronkite, Tom Brokaw, presidential Press Secretary Ron Nessen, and occasionally a senator or two. Sans Souci's cachet of power reached its peak during the Ford administration, when Betty Ford frequently lunched there and on one memorable occasion treated the president to a birthday party, much to the delight of the Secret Service, which enjoyed at adjacent tables the unusual treat of French cuisine.

The power lunch at Sans Souci ended with the 1970s, when the restaurant stopped serving to the public, in part because it had lost its power cachet during the Carter years; the president's Georgia aides were more frequently seen at the adjacent McDonald's than in the elegant atmosphere of Sans Souci. More important, Paul De Lisle had a fight with the owner and left for the nearby Maison Blanche, taking Art Buchwald with him.

The demise of Sans Souci, however, did not mean the end of the power lunch in Washington. Just as there will always be a Four Seasons Grillroom in New York, where the publishing, media, and eco-

[1] Art Buchwald, "Where the Elite Used to Meet," *Washington Post*, September 20, 1981, p. H1.

nomic elite meet, there will always be a Sans Souci in Washington.
During the Reagan administration the power lunch shifted to Maison
Blanche, The Palm, and the Jockey Club. Washington lawyer Joseph
Califano, whose career has alternated between holding Cabinet posts
and practicing Washington law, conducted business from his regular
corner table in The Palm during the Reagan years. Different Washington establishments lunch in different places, and the downtown
restaurants have always catered to White House aides (Maison
Blanche), lawyers (The Palm and Mel Krupin's), and to lobbyists,
who entertain and are entertained in all the power restaurants. On
Capitol Hill The Monocle is the home of the power lunch, hosting
senators and their aides, who can frequently be observed in deep
conversation about the politics of the day. Mel Elfin, *Newsweek*'s
Washington Bureau Chief, commented about the power lunch, "If
some food manages to slide in your mouth while you're talking, so
much the better, but in Washington, what comes out of your mouth
is much more important than what goes into it." [2]

The Washington power lunch, like its counterpart in New York,
takes place not only in restaurants open to the public but also in
private clubs and dining rooms, such as the Pentagon's Executive
Dining Room, the F Street Club, the Metropolitan Club, and the
Democratic and Republican Clubs of Capitol Hill.

After the sun sets, the power establishments of Washington meet
at elegant candle-lit dinners in the grand homes of the city's pundits,
oracles, and politicians emeriti in Kalorama, where Woodrow Wilson
once lived; Georgetown, where Averell Harriman's exquisite N Street
home entertains the rich and the prominent; and in suburbs such as
Chevy Chase.

Even the most sophisticated new political appointees are often dazzled, intrigued, and even exhausted by Washington's social scene and
the demands it makes upon people in power. Henry Kissinger wrote
that

> Everyone at the higher levels of government meets constantly
> in the interminable conferences by which government runs it-
> self; they then encounter the same people in the evening to-
> gether with a sprinkling of senior journalists, socially adept
> and powerful members of Congress, and the few members of
> the permanent Washington Establishment. To all practical
> purposes there is no topic of conversation except government,

2 *The New York Times*, July 24, 1981, p. A16.

and that generally in Washington means not the national purpose but the relationship to one another of the key personalities in the administration of the day: who, at any given point, is "up" and who is "down." [3]

Kissinger observed that, "The criteria of this social life are brutal. They are geared substantially to power, its exercise and its decline. A person is accepted as soon as he enters the charmed circles of the holders of power. With the rarest exceptions, he is dropped when his position ends, his column is discontinued, or he is retired from Congress." [4]

Social life, continued Kissinger, "provides a mechanism for measuring intangibles and understanding nuances. Moods can be gauged by newspapermen and ambassadors and senior civil servants that are not discernible at formal meetings. It is at their dinner parties and receptions that the relationships are created without which the machinery of government would soon stalemate itself." [5] Commenting upon the Nixon administration, Kissinger concluded that the "disdain of the Nixon entourage for this side of Washington complicated its actions and deprived it of the sensitivity to respond to brewing domestic anxieties." [6]

Congress, especially the more senior members of the House and most senators, is an important part not only of the upper-echelon political and social elite, but also is the keystone of a second-tier political establishment composed of the bureaucracy, Washington lobbyists and lawyers, and the press. The lower-level Washington power establishment makes many of the important decisions that affect the lives of citizens. Informal networks of power in the nation's capital buttress the political careers of congressmen, bureaucrats, Washington lawyers, lobbyists, and journalists. The Washington community is an important congressional constituency that in large measure determines how Congress works.

CONGRESS AND THE BUREAUCRACY

Congress and the bureaucracy are members of the same family, and like family members they often squabble and orally assault each other,

---

[3] Henry Kissinger, *White House Years* (Boston: Little, Brown, 1979), p. 20.
[4] Kissinger, *White House Years*, p. 20.
[5] Kissinger, p. 20.
[6] Kissinger, p. 20.

but in the end are mutually supportive. Administrative agencies receive their authority and money from the authorization and appropriations committees of Congress. The size of the bureaucracy itself is an indication of strong Capitol Hill support over the years. Congress creates and sustains administrative agencies and constantly seeks to make the bureaucracy an extension of Congress itself.

The role of the bureaucracy in the Washington political establishment and its relationship to Capitol Hill are shaped both formally, by the Constitution and statutory law, and informally, through off-the-record communications between legislators and bureaucrats.

Congress has made the bureaucracy an important part of the Washington political establishment, in many respects creating a powerful fourth branch of the government. Congress is responsible for the size of the bureaucracy, and for the extensive quasi-legislative (law-making), quasi-judicial, and executive powers the agencies exercise. Congress has created a bureaucracy in its own image, not only by giving agencies direct legislative responsibilities, but also by supporting and encouraging the administrative branch to check the president.

Rise of the Bureaucracy

Although Congress was created before the bureaucracy, administrative departments and agencies were established even before the seat of national power moved to Washington in 1800. The framers of the Constitution did not foresee that the bureaucracy would become a powerful, often dominant, and frequently independent fourth branch of the government that would take its rightful place in the Washington political establishment on an equal basis with Congress, the president, and the Supreme Court. But the authority to create departments and agencies clearly resided with the Congress, which, after forming the initial departments that were necessary to the fundamental running of the government, later responded to political demands for establishment of clientele departments and regulatory agencies.

The political affiliation between Congress and the bureaucracy was buttressed by the constitutional powers of Congress over administrative agencies. Most important, only Congress possesses the constitutional authority to create agencies, delineate their powers and responsibilities, and determine to whom the agencies are to be responsible. The president also has large constitutional powers over the executive branch. The president is to see that the laws are faithfully executed. Only he can appoint "public ministers" who are the heads of departments, ambassadors, and other top-level political officials. The president, too, is commander-in-chief of the armed forces.

Although the president is given extensive authority over the executive branch by the Constitution, the bureaucracy essentially remains an agent of Congress. Political demands dictate the establishment of agencies, their location within the bureaucratic structure, and their powers. The great clientele departments of the government, such as Agriculture, Commerce, Labor, and Health and Human Resources, came into being because farmers, business groups, labor unions, and social beneficiary groups such as the elderly under social security, demanded of Congress direct representation in government.

The same political demands that led to the creation of departments and agencies supported the organization and powers of congressional committees in the same policy areas. The Agriculture committees of the House and Senate, for example, established in 1820 and 1825, respectively, were greatly enhanced in power and prestige after the debut of the Department of Agriculture in 1862. Agency creation also boosts the power of appropriations subcommittees that are given responsibility for determining government outlays for programs administered by the bureaucracy. Mississippi Congressman Jamie Whitten, who has chaired the Agriculture Subcommittee of the Appropriations Committee since 1949 with only a two-year interruption when the Republicans controlled the House from 1953 to 1955, is commonly referred to in Washington as the Permanent Secretary of Agriculture. Whitten, like other powerful Hill chairmen, closely supervises and even administers in many important respects the Department of Agriculture.

The organization, procedures, powers, and politics of the bureaucracy reflect the world of Capitol Hill. Committees and subcommittees are organized to represent the same interests that led to creation of administrative agencies and continue to dominate administrative constituencies. The agencies themselves are main components of the constituencies of congressional committees. For example, the armed services committees and the defense appropriations subcommittees have virtually exclusive jurisdiction over the Defense Department, and their chairmen jealously guard their power against marauders from other congressional committees. The president too may find it difficult to break the strong linkage between committees and agencies.

Committee chairmen generally defend departments and agencies within their jurisdictions against outside attacks because a major ingredient of their own power is their ability to exercise exclusive control over the parts of the bureaucracy that "belong" to them. Congress has a great power incentive to protect and even expand the bureaucracy to enlarge its own influence in the broader world of Washington. Moreover, political scientist Morris Fiorina has concluded that electoral benefits accrue from a large bureaucracy that gives members of Congress expanded opportunities to ingratiate themselves with constituents through casework that effectively handles complaints against the agencies and cuts red tape.[7]

Presidents, both Democrats and Republicans, experience a common frustration in dealing with a bureaucracy many aspects of which are beyond comprehension and control mainly because Congress has carefully spun a protective web around the agencies. The formal organization of the bureaucracy appears to be haphazard, but in reality reflects the politics of Capitol Hill. The constitutional system of checks and balances provides Congress with a major incentive to resist presidential encroachments upon the administrative branch, and to keep a tight rein on the bureaucracy. Congress frequently provides by law for the administration of programs independently of White House supervision. Many regulatory agencies in particular, such as the Securities and Exchange Commission, the National Labor Relations Board, the Interstate Commerce Commission, and the Nuclear Regulatory Commission, have been made almost independent of presidential control. Even within executive departments, agencies are frequently given independent statutory authority to act without direct presidential supervision. Congress has often successfully battled the president to retain its control over administrative turf.

Congressional Resistance to Presidential Intrusion

Twentieth-century presidents from Theodore Roosevelt to Ronald Reagan have grappled with the problem of administrative efficiency and attempted to integrate and streamline the bureaucracy under

[7] Morris P. Fiorina, *Congress: Keystone of the Washington Establishment* (New Haven: Yale University Press, 1977).

presidential control. The best presidential efforts, though, have failed to stem the bureaucratic tide as the rolls of federal employees have swelled and more and more agencies have been established. Reagan's ambitious attempt to eliminate many types of federal programs caused the demise of the Federal Poverty Agency during the first year of his administration, but to the surprise of the White House the actual number of federal employees increased by more than 25,000 during the same period.

FORCES FAVORING THE STATUS QUO. Congress and the federal bureaucracy have established a highly effective relationship for preserving the status quo. Committee chairmen and powerful committee members join with Cabinet officers and career civil servants to preserve their mutual domains of power. Bureaucrats intent on resisting attempts to dismantle agencies and programs under their control readily find allies on Capitol Hill among the chairmen and members of committees and subcommittees that control their authorizations and appropriations. The civil servants obviously need the congressmen to keep their agencies and programs alive and funded. The congressmen, less obviously, need the civil servants whose expert knowledge of their areas helps to build the congressmen's legislative reputations. Moreover, jurisdiction over agencies and programs represents power on Capitol Hill.

President Reagan found congressional intransigence to his attempts to cut administrative programs not only among Democratic committee chairmen in the House but also among some members of his own party in the Senate. Overall, Reagan succeeded remarkably in swaying Congress to accept budget cuts and reductions in federal programs during the first session of the 97th Congress in 1981. Great congressional opposition smoldered, however, beneath the surface of the apparent tranquility between the two ends of Pennsylvania Avenue. Kentucky Democrat Carl Perkins, who had served in Congress for thirty-three years and as chairman of the House Education and Labor Committee since 1967, remarked, "We are meeting with a gun pointed at our heads. The majority of this committee does not want to make these drastic cutbacks." [8] Perkins had successfully guided many liberal programs through the committee, gaining him a reputa-

[8] *Congressional Quarterly Weekly Report*, vol. 39, no. 24 (June 13, 1981), p. 1031.

tion as a highly effective lawmaker. His power, legislative reputation, and ideological beliefs were directly challenged by the Reagan White House.

On the Senate side, though the new Republican committee chairmen were more than willing at first to cooperate with the Reagan administration, automatic approval of cutbacks in the federal bureaucracy were not given even by the most conservative chairmen, who did not have the kind of sway over their committees that exists in the House. The Senate and its committees operate far more on consensus than does the House. Utah Republican Orrin Hatch, chairman of the Labor and Human Resources Committee, was one of the conservatives who had to work out a compromise because committee Democrats and several Republicans opposed Reagan's proposals to dismantle social-service programs carried out by the agencies of the Health and Human Services Department. Hatch explained, "The administration understands that this is a difficult committee. The chairman can't just snap his fingers and expect things to happen." [9]

Powerful members of Congress back virtually every Cabinet department and administrative agency of any consequence. Even the beleaguered Energy Department, which the Reagan White House scheduled for elimination, had scattered Capitol Hill support, although its lack of backing from the petroleum industry seemed certain to doom it in the end. An important reason for congressional advocacy of administrative agencies is the strong support they generally receive from their private constituencies.

The Energy Department was an easy target, not only because it had no private constituency, but also because its demise would not affect the balance of power among congressional committees. The Energy Department, unlike other Cabinet departments, was more an embarrassment than a source of power to the committees, such as the Energy and Natural Resources Committee of the Senate, which had jurisdiction over it. Most committee hearings subjected the department and its representatives to ridicule, Republicans attacking the agency for promulgating poorly conceived and unnecessary regulations, and Democrats accusing the agency of not doing enough. The department was originally supported enthusiastically by Senator Henry Jackson (D, Wash.), whose Energy Committee had exclusive

9 Ibid., p. 1031.

Senate jurisdiction over it. Jackson lost his chairmanship, however, when the Senate turned Republican in 1981. Idaho Republican James McClure, the new chairman, had no interest in continuing the Energy Department, which, as a conservative, he opposed. More important, his power as committee chairman in no way depended upon continuation of the Energy Department, for the committee retained jurisdiction over the vast programs administered by the Interior Department controlling use of public lands. McClure was also chairman of the Interior Appropriations Subcommittee, which completed his domain of power over public lands and natural resources.

Powerful members of the House had even less reason to support the Energy Department than did their Senate counterparts. Jurisdiction over energy in the House is scattered among numerous committees. No chairman's power is augmented by exclusive jurisdiction over energy.

Congress supports the status quo of the bureaucracy because generally a change in the organization of the administrative branch is a threat to the status quo of power on Capitol Hill. Chairmen, committee members, and committee staffs as well may be threatened by changes in administrative organization and programs that reduce or shift committee jurisdiction. The tremendous growth in congressional staff, particularly committee aides, has created a congressional bureaucracy that often has a vested interest in supporting its counterparts in the federal bureaucracy. The jobs of committee staff may depend upon the continued existence of an administrative agency. Moreover, a great deal of circulation goes on between Capitol Hill and the agencies downtown, with Hill staffers frequently finding lucrative positions in the very agencies they oversee when they find it necessary to change jobs because of shifting political winds on Capitol Hill. Just as staffers fight to preserve their committees when they are threatened by plans for internal congressional reorganization, they generally come to the aid of threatened agencies. When the Federal Energy Administration (FEA) was due to expire in 1976, the eighteen staff members of the Energy and Power Subcommittee of the House Interstate and Foreign Commerce Committee automatically backed its extension, knowing that their jobs depended upon continuation of the agency.

The Reagan administration's success in budget cutting and reducing federal programs seemed to defy the power of the congressional-bureaucratic Washington establishment. That establishment has been mainly Democratic for decades, the Republicans having controlled only two Congresses (1947–1949; 1953–1955) since 1933. Nearly all the top-level bureaucrats for almost half a century had been hired under Democratic administrations, and the most significant increase in administrative agencies in history occurred during the same period. The Reagan administration and the Republican Senate clearly had different ideas about how government was to be conducted than did their Democratic predecessors. Reagan's successes, however, although considerable, did not break the power of the iron triangles of Washington politics — the committees, agencies, and interest groups that come together for their mutual advantage. Federal programs were reduced, agency budgets were severely pared, and disgruntled bureaucrats began to feel threatened for the first time since the New Deal. But the Reagan administration managed to abolish only the poverty agency, but not the targeted Energy Department and the Department of Education. The Reagan victories made some inroads on the powers and prerogatives of committees and agencies, but in no way destroyed the linkage between Congress and the bureaucracy that continued to be a bulwark against presidential power.

Reagan's budget cutter, the director of the Office of Management and Budget (OMB), David Stockman, recognized along with the president that in certain untouchable areas of policy the political iron triangles would inevitably prevail. For example, Stockman wanted to cut the defense budget, and succeeded in convincing many Cabinet members that such a course of action should be taken. Even if the president had been willing to go along with Stockman in making defense cutbacks, which he was not, it would have been difficult to make significant inroads on the power of the "military-industrial complex," as President Eisenhower called the defense establishment, which includes the powerful armed services committees of Capitol Hill, the defense appropriations subcommittees, the Pentagon, and the vast and profitable armaments industry.

The Defense Department and its congressional allies are a formidable force, as are other agencies such as the FBI and the Veterans' Administration, and agencies such as the Social Security Administration whose programs directly touch the growing elderly population. Stockman, discussing his budget-cutting strategy, pointed out, "Once you set aside Defense and Social Security, the Medicare complex, and a few other sacred cows of minor dimension, like the VA and the FBI, you have less than $200 billion worth of discretionary room [in the federal budget]." [10] Many of the Reagan budget cuts succeeded because they did not touch the most powerful components of the congressional-bureaucratic establishment. Programs that were severely cut or eliminated, such as the Job Corps, Head Start, Nutrition, CETA, and even General Revenue Sharing, all had backers on Capitol Hill and private constituencies, but they lacked the clout to prevent the budget axe from falling. The vulnerable social programs lacked the support of the most prestigious committees in Congress, and the agencies administering them were relatively small and insignificant, located within the vast Department of Health and Human Services. The constituencies for the targeted social programs were narrow and mostly poor, making it more difficult for their voice to be heard in Washington, which had turned in a conservative direction after the election of Ronald Reagan.

From the vantage point and perspective of Capitol Hill, presidents come and go, but administrative agencies, their programs, and corresponding congressional committees remain. Continuity is on the side of Congress and the bureaucracy, not the White House, which is so profoundly shaped by the personal styles of presidents. Congress deals with the agencies day by day, year after year, as individual members strive to use the agencies in their personal quests for power, reelection, and good public policy.

CONGRESSIONAL SUPERVISION OF THE BUREAUCRACY: FORMAL CONTROLS

The constitutional doctrine of separation of powers precludes Congress from directly administering federal programs. Congress cannot appoint or remove administrative officials. Members of Congress cannot act as administrators on a day-to-day basis, but Congress oversees the bureaucracy both formally and informally in a variety of ways. It is Congress, after all, which creates the agencies in the first place and determines their responsibilities. Congress specifies in statutory law the terms under which the agencies are to act, the *standards* that bureaucrats are to follow. The statutory delegation of authority to

---

[10] William Greider, "The Education of David Stockman," *The Atlantic* (December 1981), p. 40.

administrative agencies is the formal way in which Congress controls the bureaucracy, for the agencies are bound to adhere to the intent of Congress in carrying out their responsibilities.

Delegation of Powers

Congress delegates executive, quasi-legislative, and quasi-judicial powers to the bureaucracy. Our government, as the old adage states, is one of laws and not of men. The Constitution initially determines the powers and responsibilities of the three branches of the government. Congress is the principal law-making body, whose powers are delineated in Article I of the Constitution. Congress creates administrative agencies to help it carry out its constitutional responsibilities, but those agencies, like Congress itself, are bound by a higher law. The powers of the agencies cannot exceed the constitutional authority of Congress itself. The bureaucracy is bound by the Constitution, as are the other branches of the government. Moreover, agencies are additionally bound to adhere to the directives Congress gives them in legislation.

CLARIFYING LEGISLATIVE INTENT. Congress must be fairly specific in defining standards for the bureaucracy if it is effectively to supervise administrative agencies through statutory law. Administrators must be able to understand clearly the intent of Congress. Failure to follow legislative intent may subject an agency to sharp congressional criticism as administrators are called to testify before congressional committees, and may even result in curtailment of an agency's powers. Moreover, administrative decisions may be subject to judicial review, which generally results in overturning, or more commonly, remand of decisions that have not followed legislative intent. Both the statutes of the agencies and the broader Administrative Procedure Act of 1946 grant aggrieved parties to administrative decisions the right to appeal to the courts. Often such appeals are grounded on the charge that the agencies have not carried out the will of Congress.

When President Nixon's Secretary of Transportation, John Volpe, approved use of federal funds to construct a six-lane highway directly through Overton Park in Memphis, Tennessee, outraged citizens joined local and national conservation groups to sue him, in part on the ground that the action violated the intent of Congress expressed in the Federal-Aid Highway Act. The highway would have taken up 26 acres of the 342-acre city park, severing the city zoo from the rest of the park. The law provided that the secretary "shall not approve any program or project" requiring the use of public park land "unless (1) there is no feasible and prudent alternative to the use of such land, and (2) such program includes all possible planning to minimize harm to such park." [11] The secretary's action was upheld by the lower courts, but the Supreme Court reversed and remanded the case to the district court to determine whether or not the secretary had made adequate findings to support his decision.[12] The district court in turn found that the secretary had not adequately backed his decision with the factual determinations required by law, and remanded the case to him. A chastened Secretary of Transportation reversed his decision in January 1973, stating in part:

> On the basis of the record before me and in light of guidance provided by the Supreme Court, I find that an interstate highway as proposed by the state through Overton Park cannot be approved. On that record I cannot find, *as the statute requires*, and as interpreted by the courts, that there are no prudent and feasible alternatives to the use of park land nor that the broader environmental protection objectives of the NEPA [National Environmental Protection Act] and the Federal-Aid Highway Act have been met, nor that the existing proposal would comply with FHWA standards on noise.[13]

In the Overton Park case the courts were able to ascertain the standards of Congress without difficulty, and to determine that the Secretary of Transportation had failed to demonstrate that his action was in accordance with the law.

The intent of Congress, however, is not always clear. Congress has frequently found it both practically and politically necessary to delegate broad authority to the agencies to carry out the law. From the practical standpoint, Congress can go only so far in clearly expressing its intent. Federal programs are often broad and complex, requiring administrators to fill in the details of legislation as they implement the programs. It is almost impossible for legislators to devise statu-

[11] 23 U.S.C. Section 138; 49 U.S.C. Section 1653 (F).
[12] Citizens to Preserve Overton Park, Inc. *v.* Volpe, 401 U.S. 402 (1971).
[13] Walter Gellhorn et al., *Administrative Law* (Mineola, N.Y.: Foundation Press, 1979), p. 337, n. 2. Emphasis added.

tory language that will foresee all the varied circumstances that invariably arise in implementation. Nor can statutory language be precise enough to entirely eliminate administrative discretion.

POLITICS OF DELEGATION. Congressional intent is most clearly stated in tax legislation and entitlement programs, such as social security, food stamps, and veterans' benefits. It is relatively easy to write clear formulas for raising and disbursing government revenues. Even here, however, some administrative discretion is inevitable because agencies such as the Internal Revenue Service must promulgate extensive regulations to carry out the Internal Revenue Code passed by Congress. Even entitlement programs require administrative regulations governing methods of proof of entitlement. Disability claims under social security, for example, are defined more by the rules of the Social Security Administration than by Congress.

Congress finds it most difficult to define standards for administrative agencies in regulatory policy. Agencies such as the Food and Drug Administration (FDA), the Securities and Exchange Commission (SEC), the National Labor Relations Board (NLRB), the Interstate Commerce Commission (ICC), the Environmental Protection Agency (EPA), the Consumer Product Safety Commission (CPSC), carry out broad programs of economic regulation. The statutes of these and other regulatory agencies are necessarily vague, because substantive regulatory standards are elusive and difficult to define in advance of actual situations in the regulated sphere. Regulation is a continuous process requiring decisions based upon constantly changing facts. The purpose of most regulation is to balance the broad public interest against private interests in a variety of areas, including health and safety; rate making by common carriers such as airlines, railroads, truckers, and shippers; deceptive business practices; and restraints of trade. Congress can only set broad policies in these areas, and must leave the details to administrators.

Regulatory statutes typically charge agencies to carry out the "public interest, convenience, and necessity," and to establish "just and reasonable" rates. Such terminology delegates vast discretion to administrators, and it is well recognized on Capitol Hill that in most regulatory spheres public policy is made more by the agencies than by Congress. The superior power of the agencies over Congress is reflected in numerous statutory provisions granting Congress and its committees the authority to veto administrative regulations. The legislative veto of administrative rules is a recognition that the initiative in regulatory policy making lies with the agencies.

Political reasons are even more important than practical ones for many broad congressional delegations of authority to the bureaucracy, especially in the regulatory realm. Congressional policy, it has been argued, falls into three broad categories: redistributive, distributive, and regulatory.[14] Redistributive politics generally are those which undertake some redistribution of wealth, such as the progressive income tax, welfare programs, food stamps, and even social security where beneficiaries have not contributed in proportion to the benefits they receive. Redistributive policies also exist in noneconomic areas, such as civil rights, where the government has attempted to redress imbalances of the past through such programs as affirmative action. The politics of redistribution involves broad classes of people who make their demands known to Congress and the president, and where an apparent majority favors a particular redistributive course, Congress is bound to take concrete action. Mobilization of a vast civil rights movement in the early 1960s led directly to passage of the 1964 Civil Rights Act and the Voting Rights Act of 1965, major pieces of legislation attempting to equalize the rights of all Americans. Although the civil rights laws require administrative interpretation and implementation, the standards of the legislation are as clear as any legislative criteria can be.[15]

Redistributive politics in the economic sphere is illustrated first by the New Deal–Fair Deal–Great Society programs that aided the poor disproportionately to their financial contributions to the federal government. The New Deal and its progeny constituted *downward*

---

[14] Theodore Lowi, "American Business, Public Policy, Case-Studies, and Political Theory," *World Politics*, vol. XVI (July 1964), pp. 673–715. See also Randall B. Ripley and Grace A. Franklin, *Congress, the Bureaucracy, and Public Policy* (Homewood, Ill.: Dorsey Press, 1976).

[15] Even the clear standards of the civil rights laws have been subject to sharply contrasting interpretations, particularly in affirmative-action programs. President Lyndon Johnson by executive order implemented affirmative action in the federal government and required private institutions receiving federal funds to establish affirmative-action programs. In *Regents of the University of California v. Bakke*, 438 U.S. 265 (1978), the Court held in a split decision that affirmative-action programs establishing quotas for admission of minorities to a medical school constituted "discrimination" in violation of the 1964 Civil Rights Act. The majority opinion in the Bakke case limited the scope of affirmative-action programs that had been established administratively throughout the country.

redistribution. By contrast, the majority of middle- and upper middle-class America that elected Ronald Reagan supported *upward* redistribution, and Congress responded by cutting social programs of the past and revamping the tax structure to benefit in particular upper middle-class and wealthy American citizens. Congress responded to redistributive politics by enacting specific legislation that left little room for administrative manipulation during implementation.

The broad politics of redistributive policies may be contrasted with the micropolitics of "distributive" polices. Pork barrel and subsidies are major examples of distributive policies, which pass the largesse of government to narrow sectors of the community. Congress has little difficulty in defining precisely the content of distributive policies. Agricultural subsidies for tobacco and wheat, for example, are provided by Congress under precise guidelines that cannot be altered by the Department of Agriculture, which is the implementing agency. The incentive of Congress in distributive policies, as in redistribution, is to shoulder the responsibility of making concrete decisions that respond respectively to the demands of narrow interests and broad aggregated interests.

Regulatory politics contrasts sharply with the politics of distribution or redistribution. The regulatory sphere generally involves sharply conflicting *narrow* interests. The major incentive of Congress under such circumstances is to pass the burden of reconciling group conflict on to the bureaucracy, which is readily accomplished by passing laws that vaguely direct administrators to regulate in the public interest. If Congress wrote specific standards into regulatory legislation, assuming that it had the knowledge and foresight to do so, its members would be placed on the political hot seat. Regulatory policies "are distinguishable from distributive in that in the short run the regulatory decision involves a direct choice as to who will be indulged and who deprived." [16]

Political pressures force Congress to create the arena in which the zero-sum game of regulatory politics is played, but legislators seek to withdraw from playing the game itself, lest they be continuously blamed by the losing players. Congress cannot similarly withdraw from the broad political game of redistributive politics, which also has its losers. National attention focuses upon Congress where re-

[16] Ripley and Franklin, *Congress, the Bureaucracy, and Public Policy*, pp. 690–691.

distribution is involved, and demands passage of concrete policies. Groups demanding government regulation, however, are content with creation of an administrative agency under a broad legislative mandate to uphold the public interest. Both proponents and opponents of strong regulation continue to have a fighting chance to prevail.

The delegation of powers to the bureaucracy, then, differs sharply in the redistributive, distributive, and regulatory spheres, with the greatest administrative discretion given in regulation. The bureaucracy is a more faithful agent of Congress when its statutory intent is clear. The failure of Congress to clarify its intent creates a special constitutional problem when the delegation of *legislative* powers to the bureaucracy arises.

DELEGATION DOCTRINE. When Congress delegates legislative authority to administrative agencies, that is, the power to make rules and regulations that are in effect law, it is giving to the agencies power that under the Constitution is supposed to reside exclusively in Congress itself. Article I, Section 1 states that "All legislative powers herein granted shall be vested in a Congress of the United States, which shall consist of a Senate and a House of Representatives." The legislative powers granted to Congress are those enumerated in Article I, and all powers "necessary and proper" to implement them. The separation-of-powers system and the principles of representative government embodied in the Constitution require Congress to retain the lawmaking power. Congress, however, has made broad delegations of its legislative authority to the agencies, which in turn have promulgated rules and regulations that are greater in scope than the laws of Congress. Administrative agencies in a typical year fill more than 60,000 pages of the *Federal Register* with their regulations, which have the same effect as congressional laws. The bureaucracy has become an important legislative branch of the government.

Administrative agencies exercise more or less discretion in law making, depending upon the clarity of congressional intent. Statutory ambiguity gives administrators vast powers to fill in legislative details, which often amounts to writing the legislation itself.

Although Congress may be practically and politically motivated to delegate broad legislative authority to the bureaucracy, the Supreme Court has not always allowed what it considers to be law-making authority to reside in the hands of the agencies. In only two cases, however, has the Court declared congressional statutes to be unconstitutional on the ground that they delegated legislative authority to the executive branch. Both cases occurred during the New Deal, when Chief Justice Charles Evans Hughes and his brethren were highly antagonistic to President Franklin D. Roosevelt and his innovative programs for solving the problems of the Great Depression. Prior to the New Deal the Court had confronted many challenges to legislation that had been made on the grounds that Congress had unconstitutionally delegated legislative authority to the executive. In no case, however, were delegations declared to be unconstitutional.[17]

The two New Deal cases declaring congressional delegations unconstitutional affected only one piece of legislation, the National Industrial Recovery Act of 1933. The Court overturned a section of the law that it considered to be an overly broad delegation of legislative authority in *Panama Refining Company* v. *Ryan* in 1935.[18] The Court's most historically outstanding decision on delegation came in the same year in *Schechter Poultry Corp.* v. *United States*, in which it declared the entire National Industrial Recovery Act to be an unconstitutional delegation of legislative authority. The law granted the president the power to establish on his own initiative or after petitions from private businesses codes of fair competition for entire industries that set wage and price ceilings. The Court's unanimous opinion was that

> . . . [T]he Recovery Act is without precedent. It supplies no standards for any trade, industry or activity. It does not undertake to prescribe rules of conduct to be applied to particular states of fact determined by appropriate administrative procedure. Instead of prescribing rules of conduct, it authorizes the making of codes to prescribe them. For that legislative undertaking, [the Act] sets up no standards, aside from the statement of the general aims of rehabilitation, correction, and expansion described in Section 1 [of the Act]. In view of the scope of that broad declaration, and of the nature of the few restrictions that are imposed, the discretion of the President in approving or prescribing codes, and thus enacting

---

[17] See, for example, J. W. Hampton, Jr., and Co. v. United States, 276 U.S. 394 (1928), upholding the Tariff Act of 1922, which gave the president broad discretion to adjust tariffs whenever he found differences in production costs between the United States and competing foreign countries; and Field v. Clark, 144 U.S. 649 (1892), sustaining the Tariff Act of 1890, which also delegated broad discretion to the president to set tariffs.

[18] Panama Refining Company v. Ryan, 293 U.S. 388 (1935).

laws for the government of trade and industry throughout the country, is virtually unfettered. We think that the code-making authority thus conferred is an unconstitutional delegation of power. . . .[19]

The scope of the law was too broad even for Justice Cardozo, who was sympathetic to the purposes of the New Deal and had indicated his willingness to allow flexible congressional delegations in the Panama case.

The Schechter rule rigidly required Congress to clarify its intent in the delegation of legislative authority to administrative agencies. The rule, however, was not applied in cases that arose during World War II and thereafter. The stance of the Supreme Court changed dramatically as Roosevelt began to make his first appointments during his second term. The emergency of the Depression was replaced by an even greater national threat during World War II, requiring virtual congressional abdication to the bureaucracy to promote governmental efficiency. The Schechter rule became an anachronism as new agencies were spawned to deal with the wartime emergency. The Court no longer insisted upon congressional control over legislative standards in such areas as wage and price controls, and the determination of the "excess profits" of corporate contractors with the government. Administrative discretion in these and other spheres was recognized as a wartime necessity.[20]

The Court's leniency in allowing broad delegation of legislative authority continued after the end of the wartime emergency. In *Arizona* v. *California*, the majority of the Court upheld a grant of legislative authority to the Secretary of the Interior that was described by Justice Harlan in dissent as "a gift to the Secretary of almost 1,500,-000 acre feet of water a year, to allocate virtually as he pleases in the event of any shortage preventing the fulfillment of all of his delivery commitments." [21]

In *Zemel* v. *Rusk*, the Court again construed a very broad dele-

---

[19] Schechter Poultry Corp. *v.* United States, 295 U.S. 495, 541–542 (1935).

[20] See, for example, Yakus *v.* United States, 321 U.S. 414 (1944), upholding the Emergency Price Control Act of 1942, which granted broad discretion to the head of the Office of Price Administration to establish price ceilings; and Lichter *v.* United States, 334 U.S. 742 (1948), upholding a virtually uncontrolled delegation of legislative power to the executive branch to determine and retrieve excess corporate profits.

[21] Arizona *v.* California, 373 U.S. 546, 625 (1963).

gation of legislative authority to be constitutional. The plaintiff, whose request to have his passport validated to travel to Cuba as a tourist was rejected by the State Department, challenged the decision in part on the ground that it was undertaken under a statute that delegated excessive authority to the president and the Secretary of State. The law provided that "the Secretary of State may grant and issue passports, and cause passports to be granted, issued, and verified in foreign countries ... under such rules as the President shall designate and prescribe." [22] Chief Justice Earl Warren's opinion for the Court's majority of six acknowledged that the legislative delegation was broad, but dismissed the constitutional challenge on the ground that the executive must have more discretionary authority in foreign than in domestic affairs.[23] Justice Black strongly dissented, arguing that the Schechter rule should prevail in foreign as in domestic policy spheres, especially where power had been delegated to administrators that affected the civil liberties and rights of citizens. Black stated:

> quite obviously, the government does not exaggerate in saying that this act "does not provide any specific standards for the Secretary" and "delegates to the President and Secretary a general discretionary power over passports" — a power so broad, in fact, as to be marked by no bounds except an unlimited discretion. It is plain therefore that Congress had not itself passed a law regulating passports; it has merely referred the matter to the Secretary of State and the President in words that say in effect, "We delegate to you our constitutional power to make such laws regulating passports as you see fit."
> ... For Congress to attempt to delegate such an undefined law-making power to the Secretary, the President or both, makes applicable to this 1926 Act what Mr. Justice Cardozo said about the National Industrial Recovery Act: "This is delegation running riot. No such plenitude of power is susceptible of transfer." ... *Schechter Poultry Corp.* v. *United States,* ... *Panama Refining Co.* v. *Ryan.* ...
> Our Constitution has ordained that laws restricting the liberty of our people can be enacted by the Congress and by the Congress only. I do not think our Constitution intended that this vital legislative function could be farmed out in large

[22] 44 Stat. 887, 22 U.S.C. Section 211a (1958 ed.).
[23] Warren cited the classic case, United States v. Curtiss Wright Corp., 299 U.S. 304 (1936).

blocs to any governmental official, whoever he might be, or to any governmental department and/or bureau, whatever administrative expertise it might be thought to have.[24]

Congress's limited ability to control the bureaucracy formally by enacting clear statutory guidelines for policy making necessitates resort to other methods of supervision, both formal and informal. The authorization and appropriations processes involve both formal limitations and opportunities for legislators to communicate informally during hearings and outside the hearing rooms to make their wishes known.

Authorizations and Appropriations

Administrative programs require both authorizations and appropriations legislation. Authorization bills establish programs, specify general administrative procedures and goals, and generally place ceilings on the amount of money that may be spent. Authorization legislation usually precedes appropriations bills, which within the authorization limits grant the actual monies that may be spent by government agencies. The best way to look at the authorization and appropriation process is to view authorizations as creating the authority to open a checking account at the Treasury for a designated amount of money, and appropriations as putting money into the account. Once the appropriations legislation has deposited a specified sum with the Treasury, which generally is less than the authorization ceilings, the agencies may draw upon their accounts, making outlays, which is analogous to writing checks on their Treasury accounts.

The politics of authorizations and appropriations differ. The authorization committees, such as Agriculture, Armed Services, Commerce (Senate), and Interstate and Foreign Commerce (House), are often more sympathetic to the bureaucracy than are the appropriations committees. The authorization committees tend to support and vote for expansion of administrative programs, but the appropriations committees, along with the budget committees, tend to demonstrate their power within Congress by reducing the amount of money that may be spent for government programs from the levels approved by the authorization committees. The chairmen and staffs of powerful congressional committees that have overlapping jurisdictions, such as

[24] 381 U.S. 1, at 21–22 (1965).

the armed services committees and the defense appropriations sub-committees, constantly challenge each others' powers. The appropriations and budget committee on each side of Capitol Hill exercise overlapping jurisdiction with the entire spectrum of authorization committees and subcommittees in their respective bodies.

Administrative agencies are pawns in the power politics of Capitol Hill, which are moved differently depending upon the strategies of individual committee chairmen, members, and aides. The formal congressional intent of statutory law is continuously supplemented by nonstatutory techniques for the expression of congressional desires, particularly the views of individual legislators and staffers. Members and their aides want the bureaucracy to do their bidding. The authorization committees formally control the programs of their agencies, and the appropriations and budget committees have the final authority to determine spending.[25] Intricate informal relationships between Congress and the bureaucracy are often more important than formal legislation in shaping the balance of power between Capitol Hill and the downtown bureaucracy. Frequently during hearings members of Congress read the riot act to administrators who they feel have misinterpreted legislative intent, taken a wrong course of action, or generally have acted improperly. Though much of the Reagan legislative program sailed through Congress with only a few minor tacks, disgruntled Democrats continued to chair the committees of the House, positions from which they frequently launched attacks upon the administration. Eighty-one-year-old Florida Democrat Claude Pepper, spokesman for the twenty-five million Americans over age sixty-five, did not hesitate to use his position as chairman of the Select Committee on Aging to accuse Secretary Richard S. Schweiker of Health and Human Services of sabotaging congressional intent in the Social Security Program. Pepper's influence was all the more remarkable because his committee, unlike the authorization and appropriations panels, could only recommend but not report legislation. Pepper, however, who had served fourteen years in the Senate

---

25 For an analysis of the effects of the Congressional Budget Act of 1974 on the distribution of power in Congress, see Allen Schick, "The Three-Ring Budget Process: The Appropriations, Tax, and Budget Committees in Congress," in Thomas E. Mann and Norman J. Ornstein, eds., *The New Congress* (Washington, D.C.: American Enterprise Institute, 1981), pp. 288–328. In addition, see Robert W. Hartman, "Congress and Budget-making," *Political Science Quarterly*, vol. 97, no. 3 (Fall 1982), pp. 384–394.

and nineteen as a member of the House, a career that spanned administrations from Franklin D. Roosevelt to Ronald Reagan, made his committee the spokesman of the House for social security.

NONSTATUTORY TECHNIQUES FOR CONTROLLING THE BUREAUCRACY

Claude Pepper's effective use of a nonlegislative committee to become the spokesman for Congress in an important sphere of public policy illustrates well the importance of nonstatutory techniques to make the wishes of Congress known. Administrators are highly sensitive to the informal expressions of legislative intent by powerful legislators, particularly those on the committees that oversee their agencies.

Informal Communications

The informal expressions of legislative intent that are made by members during congressional hearings can often be conflicting, leaving administrators puzzled. Officials from Cabinet secretaries to bureau chiefs may be subjected to praise and damnation during their appearances before committees. Under such circumstances informal legislative intent may be as difficult to ascertain as formal statutory intent. Committees often find it as difficult to speak with one voice as Congress itself does.

Smart administrators recognize, however, that their fate and the destiny of the programs they administer depend greatly upon the views of committee chairmen and their aides, who do speak with one voice. Committee chairmen and staff have an attentive bureaucratic audience. Their views are conveyed to administrators orally during hearings, informally over the telephone or at social engagements, and in committee reports on legislation or particular policy problems. When Claude Pepper's Committee on Aging called Reagan's budget director, David A. Stockman, to testify about proposed budget cuts for fiscal year 1982, his attention focused upon the chairman, not upon the other fifty-three committee members. It was the chairman who closely quizzed Stockman. "Are you able to assure us, Mr. Stockman," said Pepper, "that [the proposed budget cuts] comply with the assurance the President gave to the people that his program for budget cutting would not adversely affect the truly needy of the country?" [26] Stockman replied, "I think, in the main, I can give you that assurance." [27]

On another front, John F. Seiberling (D, Ohio), chairman of the House Energy Committee's Public Lands and National Parks Subcommittee, called Interior Secretary James Watt on the carpet for refusing to let his department's employees testify before the committee on the state of the parks. Watt was not as cooperative as Stockman had been, commenting, "I do resist committees sending staff to ramble through our files and interrogate and question our staff." [28] Seiberling joined with other subcommittee chairmen having jurisdiction over the department to recommend that Watt be cited for contempt. Ultimately the Interior Secretary's failure to establish close ties with congressional committees, combined with a few extraordinary political gaffes, led to his involuntary resignation.

REPORT LANGUAGE. The verbal ripostes of committee chairmen to testimony by bureaucrats they consider to be unresponsive are supplemented by the language of official committee reports that may chastise administrators for not doing their jobs. Long before the graying of America and the recognition that problems of the elderly would become a major public-policy dilemma, the House Labor–Health, Education and Welfare Subcommittee informally urged the Department of Health, Education and Welfare to initiate new programs for the elderly. A 1956 committee report stated:

> The committee was likewise again disappointed this year that the Department made such a poor showing insofar as accomplishments are concerned with respect to the problems of the aging. Since it is well recognized that this is a growing problem with the steady increase in the number of older people in our population, it has been a source of considerable concern on the part of the committee that so little in the way of a program in this field could be presented by the Department or its many constituents whose activities naturally come in contact with this program. It is certainly to be hoped that

[26] John Egerton, "Courtly Champion of America's Elderly," *New York Times Magazine,* November 29, 1981, p. 127.
[27] Egerton, "Courtly Champion," p. 127.
[28] *New York Times,* February 23, 1982, p. A21.

in another year something substantial, in the way of a program, will be developed.[29]

Committee chairmen, and especially their staff who write reports, expect administrators to take their directions seriously. Because appropriations subcommittees have substantial influence on agency outlays, administrators pay particular heed to the requests of their chairmen.

Legislators and staffers never hesitate to involve themselves in the day-to-day operations of the bureaucracy, accomplishing informally what the constitutional doctrine of separation of powers proscribes. For example, the Indian Health Bureau was once rebuked by its House Appropriations Subcommittee for failing to build new hospitals for which funds had been appropriated. "Congress appropriated funds for construction of a new hospital ... over two and a half years ago," stated the committee report. It continued: "The details of the fumbling around on this project are set forth in the hearings. ... The committee is at a complete loss to understand why with this big increase [in appropriations], the Public Health Service has not been able to reopen the closed ward at the Fort Defiance Hospital. ... The committee will expect the Secretary to take a personal interest in correcting the administrative shortcomings." [30]

Other appropriations subcommittee reports have explicitly or implicitly ordered administrative action: "The committee *expects* the [State] Department to make every effort to reduce the number of [international] organizations to which we contribute to avoid duplication and waste and also to obtain reductions in the amounts we are requested to contribute"; "the [House Agriculture] Committee is disturbed by evidence of efforts to gradually eliminate this [Soil Conservation] program. ... It is requested that the Committee be notified by the Department as soon as official recommendations are received from the Commission"; "it seems quite apparent that ... the Joint Chiefs of Staff, as a corporate body, is not providing the kind of advice and leadership which this country requires. ... The Joint Chiefs of Staff should look at what is available for what purposes and

[29] *Congressional Record*, vol. 102, p. 3451 (1956), quoted in Michael W. Kirst, *Government Without Passing Laws* (Chapel Hill: University of North Carolina Press, 1969), pp. 89–90.
[30] Kirst, *Government Without Passing Laws*, p. 99.

attempt to match it with the needs. As an example, the Joint Chiefs should take a look at the combined forces of the Marine Corps and the Army." [31]

All committees order agencies about, but only the budget and appropriations committees can use their powers over the purse strings of the agency as a sword of Damocles. The appropriations subcommittees are particularly important because they are the specialized panels that deal with the agencies on a day-to-day basis. Before creation of the budget committees by the Budget and Impoundment Control Act of 1974, the appropriations committee in both the House and the Senate were the dominant panels as far as the bureaucracy was concerned. The House Appropriations Committee in particular, which reflected the broader constitutional role of the House as the originator of appropriations bills, was given virtually complete discretion by House members to represent the body to the outside world. Although the authority of the appropriations committees has been pared somewhat by creation of the budget committees, appropriations subcommittees remain critical links between Congress and the bureaucracy.

SUBCOMMITTEE CONTROL. Subcommittee hearings provide ample opportunities for chairmen and committee members to oversee the agencies. Sometimes direct orders are given, as when a House subcommittee chairman ordered the director of a bureau to fire employees who had used a subterfuge to circumvent the budgetary limits Congress had placed on personnel levels by hiring private consultants. The subcommittee chairmen called the bureau director on the carpet:

> Representative Jensen: It certainly is going to take a house-cleaning of all people who are responsible for this kind of business.
> Official: We are going to do it, Mr. Chairman.
> Representative Jensen: I do not mean maybe. That is the most disgraceful showing that I have seen of any department.
> Official: I am awfully sorry.[32]

[31] The quotations from committee reports are in Kirst, pp. 99–102.
[32] Quoted in Aaron Wildavsky, *The Politics of the Budgetary Process*, 3rd ed., (Boston: Little, Brown, 1979), p. 77.

Direct sarcasm may substitute for direct orders in congressional dealings with the bureaucracy. New York Congressman John Rooney (D), who represented his Brooklyn district from 1944 until he retired in 1974, reigned for years as chairman of the State, Justice, Commerce, and Judiciary Subcommittee of the House Appropriations Committee. From his chairman's perch he terrorized many State Department representatives and diplomats seeking increased appropriations. Rooney made the intent of Congress known by roasting State Department officials during the hearings. On one occasion he questioned the purpose of a Department Chinese language program at a time when the United States had no formal relationships with the People's Republic:

> Representative Rooney: I find a gentleman here, an FSO-6. He got an A in Chinese and you assigned him to London.
>
> Mr. X: Yes, sir. That officer will have opportunities in London — not as many as he would have in Hong Kong, for example —
>
> Representative Rooney: What will he do? Spend his time in Chinatown?
>
> Mr. X: No, sir. There will be opportunities in dealing with officers in the British Foreign Office who are concerned with Far Eastern affairs. . . .
>
> Representative Rooney: So instead of speaking English to one another, they will sit in the London office and talk Chinese?
>
> Mr. X: Yes, sir.
>
> Representative Rooney: Is that not fantastic?
>
> Mr. X: No, sir. They are anxious to keep up their practice. . . .
>
> Representative Rooney: They go out to Chinese restaurants and have chop suey together?
>
> Mr. X: Yes, sir.
>
> Representative Rooney: And that is all at the expense of the American taxpayer?[33]

Congressman Rooney, however, like other subcommittee chairmen, supported the agencies he liked. He consistently increased appropriations for the FBI above those requested by the administration. The budgetary cuts made by appropriations subcommittees, at least before the unusual actions of Congress in the first years of the Reagan

[33] Wildavsky, *Politics of the Budgetary Process*, pp. 96–97.

administration, rarely threatened administrative programs. Appropriations cuts were designed more to demonstrate the power of the appropriations committees *within* Congress by demonstrating both to the agency and to their authorization committees where the real power over programs resided.

Although the chairmen of appropriations subcommittees may seek to enhance their reputations for power by adopting short-term budget-cutting strategies, most committee chairmen remain supportive of the bureaucracy over the long run. Committee chairmen whose names are identified with important programs in the agencies, such as the Defense Department, the FBI, NASA (especially during the 1960s), and the National Institutes of Health, sometimes bask in the reflected glory of the programs they have sponsored. Power and status on Capitol Hill attach more to legislators who have taken a positive rather than a negative approach to government. Even administrative programs with low visibility and narrow constituencies may inspire the kind of congressional support reflected in the statement one congressman made to the administrator of the Soil Conservation Service during hearings on the agency's budget:

> You know every man serving in Congress hopes to leave his imprint in some small way upon work in which he is interested.
>
> The activities of our Government and the responsibilities are so vast that we are fortunate if we leave Congress even after twenty or thirty years and have our name attached even in a slight degree to something really worthwhile, and I am proud of the fact that sixteen years ago, gentlemen, I was fighting to increase in this very room the money set aside for soil conservation operations.[34]

Congress has regularly increased budget requests for popular and glamorous agencies such as the Defense Department and the FBI, causing even more administrative expansion than has always been supported by the White House and Office of Management and Budget (OMB). The phenomenal growth of the National Institutes of Health was spurred by key Capitol Hill chairmen, particularly Rhode Island Congressman John Fogarty, chairman of the appropriations subcommittee that urged expansion of the NIH from the very beginning. At the first hearing on NIH appropriations Fogarty or-

[34] Wildavsky, pp. 48–49.

chestrated testimony from the agency's director reflecting the congressman's view that more money should be appropriated than had been requested by the administration:

> Fogarty: What did you ask the Department [of Health, Education, and Welfare] for?
> Shannon: $885,314,000.
> Fogarty: What did you get from the Bureau of the Budget?
> Shannon: $780,000,000.
> Fogarty: Between the two, they only cut you $100 million. Did you ask for too much?
> Shannon: No, sir.
> Fogarty: Do you think you could use that $100 million if Congress voted it. . . ?
> Shannon: I think we could use the bulk of it; yes, sir.[35]

The budget requests of administrative agencies are formally channeled through the OMB (formerly the Bureau of the Budget), but as Fogarty's questioning of the director of NIH illustrates, informal exchanges between legislators and bureaucrats have encouraged appropriations over the limit set by the president's budget staff.

CONGRESSIONAL OVERSIGHT OF THE BUREAUCRACY

Congress indirectly oversees the bureaucracy through nearly all its legislative activities, and by acting as ombudsman for constituents' grievances, most of which affect the activities of agencies. In the generic sense, statutory law is a method of overseeing the bureaucracy, as are authorization and appropriations hearings.

Special Committee Responsibility

Aside from the pervasive oversight activities inherent in the legislative process, Congress has singled out oversight as a special responsibility of certain committees and of its watchdog agency, the General Accounting Office. The origin of the specific responsibility for legislative oversight is found in the Legislative Reorganization Act of 1946, which assigned to each standing committee of Congress the

---

[35] Wildavsky, p. 22, n. 13.

responsibility to "exercise continuous watchfulness of the execution by the administrative agencies concerned of any laws, the subject matter of which is within the jurisdiction of such committee." That charge was repeated in the Legislative Reorganization Act of 1970, which required standing committees to "review and study, on a continuing basis, the application, administration, and execution of those laws, or parts of laws, the subject of which is within the jurisdiction of that committee." The Government Operations and Governmental Affairs Committees in the House and Senate, respectively, are given especially broad mandates to oversee the bureaucracy. Each committee has jurisdiction over executive reorganization, works closely with the Comptroller General, who heads the General Accounting Office, and reviews the entire operations of government to promote economy and efficiency.

Oversight Hearings

Texas Congressman Jack Brooks (D), chairman of the House Government Operations Committee, has been particularly active in conducting oversight hearings on topics ranging from problems in the defense procurement system to computer problems threatening Social Security operations and the failure of the Paperwork Reduction Act to reduce federal paperwork. Brooks also took the opportunity of the appointment of a new Comptroller General by President Reagan to announce oversight hearings on the General Accounting Office (GAO) itself. "The GAO not only provides Congress with essential information about federal programs," stated Brooks, "but it, in effect, represents Congress in conducting oversight and evaluation of government programs and agencies." [36] Charles Bowsher, the new comptroller general, was the principal witness. The hearing, commented Brooks, "gives us a good chance to learn his views on how GAO intends to carry out its duties." [37]

Oversight hearings are listed separately from legislative, appropriations, and investigative hearings. A quick glance at the congressional calendar published daily by the *Washington Post*, or the Daily Digest

[36] U.S. Congress, House, Committee on Government Operations, news release, November 13, 1981.
[37] Ibid.

of Congress printed each day in the *Congressional Record*, will reveal which hearings are oversight. In a typical day the Subcommittee on Energy and the Environment of the Committee on Interior and Insular Affairs held an oversight hearing on nuclear safety, taking testimony by the chairman and commissioners of the Nuclear Regulatory Commission. The Subcommittee on Civil and Constitutional Rights of Judiciary called Department witnesses to testify on school desegregation to determine what progress was being made under the civil rights laws. Oil and gas leasing was the subject of oversight hearings conducted by the Subcommittee on Public and National Parks of the Committee on Interior and Insular Affairs. The Subcommittee on Fisheries, Wildlife Conservation and the Environment of the Merchant Marine and Fisheries Committee held an oversight hearing on wetland deterioration in the Mississippi Flyway. Interior and Commerce Department officials testified. On the Senate side, the Judiciary Committee held extensive oversight hearings on government policies on merger enforcement, which were focused especially on the antitrust enforcement procedures of the Federal Trade Commission. The Subcommittee on Intergovernmental Relations held oversight hearings on state implementation of federal standards for hazardous waste management.

The oversight mandate of congressional committees gives their chairmen almost carte blanche to call administrators to testify. Although oversight hearings are an important aspect of congressional-bureaucratic relations, providing Congress with information and giving administrators the gist of congressional intent in the enforcement of legislation, oversight has been at best a sporadic activity that has not greatly affected agency activities. Oversight committees are less important than appropriations subcommittees in the life of the bureaucracy. Nevertheless, administrators called to testify before oversight committees are once again reminded that their principal responsibility is to a Congress that intends to see its wishes carried out.

ADMINISTRATIVE SUPERVISION OF CONGRESS

Almost every department and agency employs a congressional liaison staff, mostly drawn from former Capitol Hill aides, to promote their interests and those of the administration. An OMB survey taken during the Carter administration found that twenty-nine major agencies employed 1,013 congressional liaison staffers at an annual cost of more than $24 million.[38] The OMB study found that most of the liaison aides were career civil servants who suffered from agency provincialism, subordinating presidential to agency interests. By contrast, the heads of agency liaison terms are political appointees who have had congressional and other Washington experience outside of the agencies they represent.

Congressional Clans in the Bureaucracy

Members of Congress are particularly interested in extending their congressional clan, loyal staffers who have been with them for many years, downtown to the bureaucracy. They push hard for choice appointments for aides, and the assistant secretary posts for congressional liaison are choice strategic positions that, when filled by former congressional aides, help key members of Congress to keep their influence in the bureaucracy at the same time as the agencies gain expertise in dealing with Congress.

President Reagan's congressional liaison team reflected extensive Capitol Hill experience. The Departments of Agriculture, Commerce, Defense, Education, Interior, Justice, Labor, Transportation, and Treasury hired former Hill staffers to head their congressional lobbying teams. Not only Hill staffers, but former lobbyists for the private sector joined the congressional liaison staffs of the agencies. Experience in any of the political sectors of Washington is interchangeable, creating a politically incestuous relationship among the players of the Washington power game. New presidents strive valiantly to bring in fresh talent, but inevitably find that they must draw upon experienced Washington hands to fill the thousands of patronage posts in the bureaucracy. New presidents adjusting to their environment are at first highly dependent upon advice from those wise in the ways of Washington. In the first year of his administration, President Reagan was embarrassed by an *Atlantic* article by his budget director, former Michigan Congressman David Stockman. Stockman "told all," admitting that he had doubts about Reagan's economic program and moreover that in his dealings with Capitol Hill he often had to guess at budget estimates. Reagan kept Stockman on, however, not out of a gracious spirit, but because he and other White

---

[38] "The Cabinet's Ambassadors to Capitol Hill," *National Journal*, vol. 10, no. 30 (July 29, 1978), p. 1196.

House aides knew that they could not duplicate Stockman's knowledge of federal programs and his understanding of how to deal with Congress.

White House and Administrative Lobbying

The White House has its own Office of Legislative Affairs, which is in charge of formally supervising the congressional liaison teams throughout the executive branch.[39] Although the White House appoints the chiefs of all agency liaison staffs, however, the White House often cannot practically or politically direct all agency relations with Capitol Hill.[40] Agencies have their own political interests, which they often informally push on Congress outside of the formal White House channel, which confines them in their relationships with Capitol Hill. Agencies are supposed to coordinate their legislative activities with OMB and with the White House staff. Bureaucrats and even Cabinet secretaries cannot give testimony before congressional committees without prior approval by OMB. Agencies do not rely upon formal testimony, however, to present their views.

The independence of administrative agencies in dealing with Congress, as in other areas, depends mainly upon the vigor and skill with which the White House pursues its interests with the bureaucracy and Congress. William Gribben, a deputy to Max Friedersdorf, who headed Reagan's legislative staff, described the congressional relations staffers of the agencies as "the President's shock troops." [41] The Reagan White House clearly wanted to keep a tight rein on the bureaucracy, ensuring that it would represent the president's viewpoints on Capitol Hill. Deputy Undersecretary of Labor for Congressional Relations Donald Shasteen commented, "One of the first

---

[39] See Eric L. Davis, "Congressional Liaison: The People and the Institutions," in Anthony King, ed., *Both Ends of the Avenue: The Presidency, the Executive Branch, and the Congress in the 1980s* (Washington, D.C.: American Enterprise Institute, 1983), pp. 59–95, at pp. 78–83.

[40] In fact, as Eric L. Davis points out, President Carter stressed, "the importance of reducing the influence of the White House within the executive branch and of evolving authority and responsibility to the departmental level. The practice during his administration was, therefore, for the Secretary to appoint his or her own liaison officers without White House involvement." Davis, "Congressional Liaison," p. 80.

[41] *Congressional Quarterly Weekly Report*, vol. 39, no. 49 (December 5, 1981), p. 2387.

things Max Friedersdorf said to me is, 'There is no such thing as a departmental position. There is an administration position.' " [42]

PRESIDENTIAL VS. AGENCY LOBBYING. Modern presidents have always sought to control the relationship between the bureaucracy and Congress, but with varying success. Republican Presidents Nixon and Reagan, Washington outsiders, viewed the mostly Democratic career bureaucracy with suspicion and sought to curtail the flow of information from career civil servants to Capitol Hill. Nixon went so far as to have his political appointees in the bureaucracy accompany career bureaucrats who had been called to testify before congressional committees. The Reagan administration sought to curtail pockets of "covert partisanship" in the bureaucracy by having its political appointees in departments such as Labor, Health and Human Services, and the Environmental Protection Agency issue memos that required all Capitol Hill contacts of lower bureaucrats to be cleared. The memos were, of course, leaked, and cries of "gag order" were heard from the civil servants. "We haven't really tried to put the muzzle on people," said Reagan's labor spokesman Shasteen. "If the Hill wants information, this place is like a sieve, but when they want a policy decision, we want to be the spokesman for that position." [43]

White House and agency styles of congressional liaison vary widely, depending on the personal style of the president, the personalities of agency heads, differing agency constituencies that give them more or less clout on Capitol Hill, and the character of committee chairmen and other powerful congressional leaders. The Carter administration liaison teams often seemed to go their own way, representing department interests as much as those of the White House.[44] Carter's liaison chief, Frank Moore, was a novice in dealing with Congress. Other Carter lieutenants, such as Hamilton Jordan, paid scant attention to Capitol Hill.[45]

Terry Bracy, Carter's assistant secretary of transportation for leg-

[42] Ibid., p. 2392.
[43] Ibid., p. 2391.
[44] Eric L. Davis, "A Legislative Liaison in the Carter Administration," *Political Science Quarterly*, vol. 95 (Summer 1979), pp. 287–302.
[45] Eric Davis points out that "Carter did not consider it necessary to keep in operation a legislative liaison system that emphasized cultivating members of Congress on a personal basis and establishing cooperative lobbying relationships with a wide range of participants in the legislative process." See Davis, "Congressional Liaison: The People and the Institutions," p. 65.

islative relations, blamed the failures of the White House on the dispersion of power in Congress. "Ten years ago," he said, "if you wanted a highway bill, you went to see [former House Public Works Committee Chairman John A.] Blatnik [D, Minn.], the Speaker and Chairman of the Rules Committee. There would be a small collegial discussion — and all the political decisions would be made. Now, there's no one person to see.... You have to deal with everybody." [46]

Lobbying Congress is entrepreneurial politics, reflecting the contrasting goals, resources, and techniques of both the agencies and their Capitol Hill targets. President Carter's transportation lobbyist Bracy, who was a staffer in Arizona Congressman Morris Udall's 1976 presidential primary campaign, commented, "You have to manage congressional liaison the way you'd manage a political campaign. It's just like precinct politics. We set up a direct mail operation, a telephone operation, a door-to-door operation, a thank-you operation. You have to deal with everybody." [47]

Bracy, like many departmental liaison chiefs during the Carter administration, dealt with Congress mainly in his own way, representing departmental interests and using the White House for support when necessary. Under Carter, liaison staffers from different agencies would frequently meet to negotiate common positions to give them more clout on the Hill. For example, the liaison chiefs of Treasury, and Health, Education and Welfare (HEW, now Health and Human Services), conducted a joint strategy session on the issue of tuition tax credits. Gene Godley, Assistant Treasury Secretary for Congressional Relations, met with Richard Warden, who ran congressional relations at HEW using what he had learned as a former lobbyist for the United Auto Workers. "Dick and I would sit down," said Godley, "split up the list of Members [of Congress], exchange information and decide who would do what." [48]

Under the Reagan administration both the White House and the agencies adopted a far more aggressive stance toward Congress than had prevailed during the Carter years. The entrepreneurial spirit was evident both in the techniques of the White House liaison team and in the agencies themselves. Department of Transportation (DOT)

[46] Shirley Elder, "The Cabinet's Ambassadors to Capitol Hill," *National Journal*, vol. 10, no. 30 (July 29, 1978), p. 1196.
[47] Elder, "The Cabinet's Ambassadors," p. 1199.
[48] Elder, p. 1199.

Secretary Drew Lewis, who had gained fame for singlehandedly "breaking" the strike of the air controllers, joined former Senate aide Lee Verstandig in making frequent appearances at campaign fund-raising and social events for congressmen. All legislators were given free passes to the department's parking garage to encourage visits. When Idaho freshman Senator Steven Symms (R) introduced the department-backed highway authorization bill, which was passed unanimously, DOT lobbyist Verstandig waited off the Senate floor to congratulate the junior senator.

The congressional liaison activities of DOT during the first years of the Reagan administration reflected understanding by the White House and the bureaucracy that Congress was indeed the keystone of the Washington political establishment. The beleaguered Interior Department Secretary, James Watt, had his liaison staffer invite lawmakers to fairly regular breakfast and luncheon meetings to discuss Interior Department business. Watt's cultivation of Congress seemed particularly urgent after the Sierra Club and other conservationist groups presented a petition to Congress with more than one million signatures, attacking the Interior secretary. More than one legislator too had been unhappy with Watt's performance, not only because they disagreed with his policies but because he did not always keep Congress informed. For example, departments commonly apprise members of Congress of grants and other forms of federal largesse in their districts and states. When the Interior Department's Bureau of Land Management announced a controversial oil and gas lease in a wilderness area of New Mexico it failed to inform the area's congressman, Manuel Lujan, Jr. (R), the ranking Republican on the House Interior Committee. The congressman was surprised one morning to read about the lease in the *New York Times*. He moved immediately to cancel it.

DEFENSE DEPARTMENT LOBBYING. The Defense Department occupies a unique place in the galaxy of agencies that lobby Congress. Reagan's Assistant Secretary of Defense for Congressional Liaison, Russell Rourke, commented on the Department's role on Capitol Hill. "We're kind of orchestrators." [49] The Pentagon, however, not only orchestrates the legislative process, but often writes the script.

[49] *Congressional Quarterly Weekly Report*, vol. 39, no. 49 (December 5, 1981), p. 2388.

It alone among administrative agencies has a full-time staff of more than 200 high-ranking officers engaged full time in legislative liaison. Only the military services have been allocated space in the Senate and House office buildings to facilitate their communications with legislators. The chairmen of the armed services committees and the defense appropriations subcommittees are in constant contact with Pentagon representatives, working closely with them to develop legislation and provide appropriations for the vast military establishment.

The military services take care of Congress not only by providing expert advice on matters that few congressmen fully comprehend, but also by making the life of legislators on the committees that supervise the Pentagon more comfortable and glamorous than they would otherwise be. Committee chairmen traveling abroad are given military escorts, from the time they leave Washington until their return. Members of the armed services committees and defense appropriations subcommittees are always given special attention by the military, and their foreign travel is paid for as much by the Pentagon as by Congress.

The military is solicitous of Congress as a whole, however, when an appropriate occasion arises. When Congress voted during the bicentennial celebrations to send a delegation to London to accompany the return of the Magna Carta, which had been on loan to the United States, fifty-one persons went on the trip. The delegation included nineteen members of Congress, fifteen congressional wives, the son of Congressman Peter Rodino, Jr., of New Jersey, ten congressional aides, the chairman of the American Revolution Bicentennial Administration, and five escorts from the State and Defense Departments. An Air Force plane was used, stocked with liquor and food by the department for a sumptuous inflight meal. The Pentagon made certain that the delegation would be both content and happy, supplying the plane with 8 quarts of vodka, 4 quarts of Beefeater gin, 4 quarts of Jack Daniel whiskey, 2 fifths of Wild Turkey, 2 quarts of Canadian Club, 6 fifths of Chivas Regal, and a quart of Bacardi rum. Chesapeake Bay oysters, live lobsters from Maine, filet mignon, and caviar were included, along with an expensive list of wines.

The Air Force, too, rose to the occasion, when in 1981 the air controllers' strike prevented senators from returning to Washington for a special one-day Saturday session when a crucial vote was to be taken. Most of the Senate had left town on the eve of what they thought would be a recess, only to find that parliamentary maneuvering by Massachusetts Senator Edward Kennedy required their further presence. The Pentagon cooperated by dispatching planes around the country to return the senators from their vacations for the vote.

The chairmen and often the members of the armed services and defense appropriations subcommittees are given special treatment by the Pentagon, not only in facilitating foreign travel, but in invitations to review military maneuvers that can, for the moment, make an ordinary legislator feel like a general. Congressmen are flown to aircraft carriers to review naval operations, and to the Sudan to review the maneuvers of the Rapid Deployment Force. The National Aeronautics and Space Administration (NASA) is the only other agency that can begin to match the glamor of the Pentagon when dealing with congressmen. Chairmen and many members of the space committees of Congress always attend the exciting launchings and returns of NASA spacecraft.

CONTROL OF ADMINISTRATIVE LOBBYING

Administrative agencies act in their relations with Congress very much like freewheeling interest groups. Often the only major difference between agency and private interest-group activities is that the bureaucracy finances its lobbying of Congress from public funds. Agencies spend tens of millions of dollars to support their liaison or lobbying staffs, and expend even more in propaganda activities that are tantamount to grass-roots lobbying. Former Arkansas Senator J. William Fulbright estimated that the executive branch spends more than half a billion dollars a year on public relations and public information programs.[50]

Agencies, like private pressure groups, hope that their careful cultivation of grass-roots support will ultimately be reflected in strong congressional backing. The Pentagon is at the forefront of the advertising world of the bureaucracy, producing motion pictures, extolling the virtues of particular weapons systems and military operations of units such as the Special Forces. The Department has admitted to the Senate Appropriations Committee that it spends

[50] J. William Fulbright, *The Pentagon Propaganda Machine* (New York: Vintage, 1971), p. 17.

more than $40 million a year for public-relations activities, and employs more than 4,000 people in a public-relations capacity.[51] The Pentagon gives advertising advice to private contractors seeking in their own interest to advocate adoption of particular weapons systems. The Pentagon will forge political alliances wherever it can find them, as in its support for the National Rifle Association sharpshooting programs throughout the nation that teach children how to handle rifles and at the same time encourage a strong defense posture.

Reagan's cost-cutting efforts touched the programs of most departments, but did not undermine the public-relations and liaison staffs of the agencies. Agriculture Secretary John Block, for example, strongly backed publication of the Department's annual yearbook, which cost a considerable sum. Thousands of copies of the book are distributed annually to members of Congress, who in turn frank them to constituents. The book is one of scores of Department publications that bolster its image on Capitol Hill and in the agricultural community. "Should the Department continue to publish the yearbook," asked one journalist of Secretary Block, "when budget reductions were being made in such critical social programs as food stamps?" The secretary cryptically replied, "We have cut many programs, but the publication of the yearbook is not one of them."[52]

Statutory Controls

Although administrative lobbying is pervasive, accepted in the bureaucracy as well as on Capitol Hill, ironically the practice is technically illegal. "Lobbying? We don't lobby," said Assistant Secretary of State for Congressional Relations Richard Fairbanks III. He continued, "You know it's illegal to lobby with appropriated funds."[53]

The secretary was correct, for as long ago as 1919 Congress, in response to charges that agencies were using public funds to telegraph citizens to support increased appropriations, passed a strict antilobbying law covering the bureaucracy. Agencies are proscribed from using appropriated funds "directly or indirectly to pay for any per-

[51] Fulbright, *Pentagon Propaganda Machine*, pp. 25–27.
[52] Block's comments were made during a public launching of the yearbook on December 15, 1981.
[53] *Congressional Quarterly Weekly Report*, vol. 39, no. 49 (December 5, 1981), p. 2391.

sonal service, advertisement, telegram, telephone, letter, printed or written matter, or other device, intended or designed to influence in any manner a member of Congress to favor or oppose, by vote or otherwise, any legislation or appropriation by Congress...." [54] The poor administrator who violates the law is subject to a fine of $500 or a year in prison. In addition to the blanket proscription upon lobbying by the executive branch, Congress for more than thirty years has routinely attached amendments to White House appropriations bills providing that: "No part of any appropriation contained in this or any other act ... shall be used for publicity or propaganda purposes designed to support or defeat legislation pending before Congress."

The antilobbying legislation would seem to bar absolutely most of the "lobbying" or the euphemistically named "legislative liaison" activities of the agencies that are conducted daily. The law does contain an escape clause, which provides that it does not bar communications between the bureaucracy and Congress through "proper official channels" about legislation or appropriations that administrators "deem necessary for the efficient conduct of the public business." "Proper official channels" would not include much of the informal contacts between administrators and legislators. While allowing certain formal communications between agencies and Congress, the law absolutely bars the kind of grass-roots lobbying and propaganda activities such as Defense uses.

The legal bar on executive-branch lobbying has never been enforced. Occasionally members of Congress use the law to embarrass administrators by crying foul, accusing an official of trying to undermine the integrity of Congress. Usually such episodes are treated as a joke both on the Hill and in the Justice Department, which must interpret the law. Glenard Lipscomb, a conservative California congressman, accused John F. Kennedy's Peace Corps Director, Sargent Shriver, of violating the antilobbying law when he sent letters on official government stationery to all members of Congress in an effort to bolster the agency's request for a substantial increase in appropriations. Lipscomb's charge was relayed to Attorney General Robert Kennedy to determine whether or not his brother-in-law had broken the law. Robert Kennedy concluded, surprising no one, that the law does not apply to the heads of agencies who, as deputies of the presi-

[54] 18 U.S.C. 1913.

dent, have a responsibility for recommending legislative proposals to Congress and cannot be restricted in their congressional relations.

In another incident, Michigan Congressman John Dingell, chairman of the powerful House Subcommittee on Energy and Power, joined other members on both sides of the Hill to criticize what they considered to be the excessive public-relations activities of Frank Zarb, director of the Federal Energy Agency. The agency, created on a temporary basis in 1973, rapidly formed an extensive congressional liaison staff with a view to ensuring its continuation. By 1976 an FEA public-relations and liaison staff of more than 120 persons looked after the interests of the agency on Capitol Hill, and cultivated grass-roots support for policies it and the president supported, including deregulation of natural gas. Congressional criticism caused the agency to back down, cutting its public-affairs staff in half and formally agreeing to cease and desist from excessive lobbying on Capitol Hill.

Administrative agencies continue to lobby Congress regardless of statutory restrictions and occasional congressional outbursts against administrative propaganda and attempts to influence legislation. Congress informally permits what it formally forbids, recognizing its inevitable political linkage with the bureaucracy. While Congress looks aside, the agencies easily circumvent formal restrictions upon "lobbying" by proclaiming their innocence. Officials do not lobby, they conduct congressional liaison. They do not hire "publicity experts" in violation of the law, but do employ large numbers of persons necessary for public information and the efficient conduct of public business. For the most part, there is a gentleman's understanding between the executive branch and Congress that the law permits direct agency pressure but, as one agency liaison chief said, "You can't go out and stir up private lobbyists to lean on people for you, with appropriated funds." [55]

Conclusion

Relations between Congress and the bureaucracy are particularly close, not only because the two branches often find it in their interest to forge alliances, but also because Congress recognizes the bureaucracy as a legitimate branch of the government that in many ways is an

[55] Ibid., p. 2391.

extension of itself. The bureaucracy occupies a unique position between the White House and Capitol Hill, sometimes bridging the gap between the president and Congress, but often siding with Congress and sometimes acting independently. Members of Congress recognize that the executive branch is not unified under the direction of the president. Dealing with the executive branch means confronting both the president and the agencies, negotiating with each, often on a separate basis.

CHAPTER EIGHT

Congress and the President

Presidents always attempt to bring unity to the seeming chaos of Washington politics. The White House tries to control the far-flung activities of administrative agencies in their dealing with Capitol Hill. The presidential bureaucracy, the Executive Office of the President, has developed over the years to give the White House the necessary resources for effective leadership. Political professionals and the public both judge presidents by how effectively they lead Congress, the bureaucracy, the private sector, and indeed the free world to achieve national goals.

WHITE HOUSE VIEW OF CONGRESS

President Andrew Jackson, it is rumored, was so mad at Congress that he ordered the Treasury Department Building to be constructed in the middle of Pennsylvania Avenue so that he would no longer have to see the Capitol Dome and be reminded of what it represented.[1] Jackson's apparent frustration with the first branch of the government has been repeated at one time or another by every president.

Support of Executive Prerogatives

All but the weakest presidents have more or less accepted the Hamiltonian perspective that energy in the executive is the primary charac-

---

[1] The Treasury Department does stand in the direct line of vision from the White House to the Capitol, occupying a position that would have intruded onto a direct and straight Pennsylvania Avenue between the two branches. A more plausible explanation than Jackson's ire is that the surveyors made an error at a time when the distance between the Capitol and the White House was not easily traversed in a city that was just growing from the wilderness.

teristic of good government, and by implication that executive energy
should not be undermined by Congress.

Hamilton's support of executive prerogative was familiar to early
presidents, and generally was accepted if not practiced by Federalists
and Republicans alike. Thomas Jefferson, who warned that the Constitution did not contain sufficient limits upon the presidency, later
as Washington's Secretary of State and as president himself supported
and undertook independent executive action.

The framers of the Constitution were all well acquainted with John
Locke's *Second Treatise of Government.*[2] Locke, of course, is one of
the most famous advocates in English political philosophy of government by the people. However, there is a caveat to Locke's principle
of government by consent when the very foundations of the state are
threatened. Legislatures are generally too unwieldy always to be able
"to foresee, and so by laws to provide for, all accidents and necessi-
ties." Occasionally, continued Locke, "a strict and rigid observation
of the laws may do harm." In times of national crisis there would be
times when "the laws themselves *should* . . . give way to executive
power, or rather to this fundamental law of nature and government,
namely, that, as much as may be, all the members of society are to
be preserved."

SEPARATION OF POWERS. The Constitution provides for executive
prerogatives at the same time as it establishes a separation-of-powers
system that pits Congress against the president. From the vantage
of the White House, however, the separation of powers is often
viewed as a cumbersome and inappropriate mechanism to be overcome even in "normal" times by vigorous and often independent
presidential action. The "imperial presidency," an executive that intrudes excessively upon what backers of Congress consider to be its
proper domain, has characterized the twentieth century. Nineteenth-
century presidents until the end of the Civil War often independently exercised war and diplomatic powers that caused observers,
such as Justice Story in 1834, to charge that under the Jacksonian

[2] Locke's *Second Treatise* was published in 1690 to support the English Revolution of 1688. He attacked the divine right of Kings, supported government by
the consent of the people, but recognized the need for strong executive power
to preserve the state in times of crisis.

presidency, "Though we live under the form of a Republic we are in fact under the absolute rule of a single man." [3]

The presidency of Abraham Lincoln followed the Lockean and Hamiltonian precepts of the proper exercise of executive power in a time of national crisis. For eleven weeks in 1861 the president essentially ruled the nation on his own under his Article II powers of commander-in-chief and chief executive. No president was more responsive to or supportive of the need to maintain "government by the people, for the people, and of the people." But Lincoln was not about to let the Union fail because vigorous exercise of executive power was lacking. Even if Congress had not delegated the authority the executive needed to meet the national emergency, it was the president's responsibility to use his prerogative powers under Article II to deal with the crisis. "It became necessary for me to choose," stated Lincoln, "whether, using only the existing means, agencies, and processes which Congress had provided, I should let the government fall at once into ruin, or, whether, availing myself of the broader powers conferred by the Constitution in cases of insurrection, I would make an effort to save it, with all its blessings, for the present age and for posterity." [4]

Modern presidents followed precedents of the Lincoln wartime presidency. Woodrow Wilson, Franklin D. Roosevelt, Harry S Truman, Lyndon B. Johnson, and Richard M. Nixon did not hesitate to take unilateral presidential action to meet foreign crises. The support of Congress was solicited, if at all, in a rhetorical way to back the president. The Gulf of Tonkin Resolution, for example, giving President Johnson carte blanche to deal with the rising emergency in Vietnam, was earnestly solicited by the president and passed almost unanimously by Congress. It was the president, however, who controlled the information given to congressional leaders about the impending crisis, information that seemed to require the broad delegation of authority to the White House to meet the crisis.

Congress finally reacted to the imperial presidency in foreign affairs by passing the War Powers Resolution of 1973, which requires

---

[3] Arthur M. Schlesinger, Jr., *The Imperial Presidency* (Boston: Houghton Mifflin, 1973), p. 35.
[4] Quoted in Clinton Rossiter, *Constitutional Dictatorship* (New York: Harcourt, Brace and World, 1963), p. 225.

congressional assent to presidential orders for deployment of the armed forces beyond a ninety-day period. The War Powers Resolution was an unusual congressional attempt to curb presidential prerogatives in foreign and military affairs. Congress has generally supported far greater presidential authority in foreign than in domestic affairs, although there are always voices to be heard on Capitol Hill opposing unilateral foreign-policy decision making by the White House.

EXERCISE OF PRESIDENTIAL PREROGATIVES IN FOREIGN AFFAIRS

Traditionally in foreign affairs presidents act, and Congress reacts.[5] The power of committee chairmen and their key role in the iron triangles of Washington politics means little when strong presidents make important foreign and military policy decisions. Even the War Powers Resolution of 1973, ostensibly a congressional limit upon the authority of the president to declare war, was viewed by Senator Thomas Eagleton (D, Mo.) and a minority of legislators as "a blank check to be used as legal tender for claims of inherent executive power." The resolution recognized, in Eagleton's view, an inherent executive authority to declare war. It was "an unconstitutional delegation of congressional war powers."[6]

President Johnson's and, more important, President Nixon's unilateral actions in pursuit of the Vietnam War led to passage of the War Powers Resolution, which most legislators viewed as limiting a power that by constitutional custom had become a presidential pre-

---

[5] Even the resurgent Congress of the 1970s and the 1980s continued to be dominated by the president in foreign affairs. See Lance T. Leloup and Steven A. Shull, "Congress versus the President: The 'Two Presidencies' Reconsidered," *Social Science Quarterly*, vol. 59, no. 4 (March 1979), pp. 704–719. The authors reassess Aaron Wildavsky's 1966 thesis that the president is weak in the domestic arena, but strong in the international realm. They conclude, "There remains a part of the foreign policy presidency in which the president is clearly dominant over the Congress." In foreign affairs "there are still strong pressures for presidential dominance, both from international actors and from the American public. . . . In the sphere of defense and foreign policy, Congress has increased its checks, but there will never be a balance with the executive. There are still fundamental differences in presidential power between foreign and domestic policy." Quoted at p. 717.

[6] Thomas F. Eagleton, *War and Presidential Power* (New York: Liveright, 1974), p. 221.

rogative to make war. Alexander Hamilton explained that the president was to be the "first general and admiral of the Confederacy." [7] Although Hamilton stressed that the authority to declare war would reside in Congress, as early as 1795 Congress began to relinquish its war-making power. The Militia Act of 1795 empowered the president to call up the militia "whenever the United States shall be invaded, or be in imminent danger of invasion." [8] President John Tyler, on his own initiative and over congressional criticism, dispatched troops to the Texas Territory and the Gulf of Mexico before he finally maneuvered Congress into annexing Texas by a joint resolution. President James Polk in 1846 sent American troops to seize disputed land between Texas and Mexico, involving the country in a Mexican war without a formal congressional declaration of war.

The presidencies of Lincoln, Wilson, Roosevelt, and Truman established what occupants of the White House came to believe was almost their divine right to lead the nation to war regardless of popular or congressional opposition. President Lyndon B. Johnson wrote that in making life-and-death decisions for the nation, "I was sustained by the memory of my predecessors who had also borne the most painful duty of a President — to lead our country in a time of war. I recalled often the words of one of these men, Woodrow Wilson, who in the dark days of 1917 said, 'It is a fearful thing to lead this great peaceful people into war ... but the right is more precious than peace.' " [9]

Presidents typically, especially in foreign affairs, exalt their own position and derogate the responsibility of Congress. Lyndon B. Johnson recalled in his memoirs, "I saw my primary task as building the consensus throughout the country, so that we could stop bickering and quarreling and get on with the job at hand. Unfortunately, the word consensus came to be profoundly misunderstood." [10] To Lyndon Johnson, consensus meant "deciding what needed to be done regardless of the political implications, and second, convincing a majority of the Congress and the American people of the necessity of doing those things. I was President of the United States at a crucial

[7] *Federalist* 69.
[8] Schlesinger, *Imperial Presidency*, p. 36.
[9] Lyndon B. Johnson, *The Vantage Point* (New York: Holt, Rinehart and Winston, 1971), p. 531.
[10] Johnson, *Vantage Point*, p. 31.

point in its history, and if a President does not lead he is abandoning the prime and indispensable obligation of the presidency." [11]

Vietnam Example

The history of the Gulf of Tonkin Resolution, passed by Congress in August 1964, reveals the true relationship between president and Congress in the foreign-policy area. At 11 A.M. on August 4, 1964, a message was received by the Pentagon that two United States destroyers were being attacked by North Vietnamese torpedo boats. Immediately the Joint Chiefs selected target options for reprisal air strikes, drawn from a list that had been prepared as a contingency plan in May 1964. A National Security Council meeting had been previously scheduled for 12 o'clock on August 4. The Tonkin Gulf crisis was discussed briefly at that meeting, and according to Johnson's memoirs, after the meeting his principal advisers unanimously recommended retaliation for what had been a second strike against the United States naval vessels off the coast of Vietnam. President Johnson agreed with his advisers, and "we decided on air strikes against North Vietnamese P.T. boats and their bases plus a strike on one oil depot." [12] According to *The Pentagon Papers*, while President Johnson was at lunch with his advisers (Rusk, McNamara, Vance, McCone, and Bundy) the director of the Joint Chiefs of Staff telephoned McNamara reporting that the Joint Chiefs had unanimously agreed on the nature of the retaliatory action that should be taken. The recommendation of the Joint Chiefs was in fact the decision that was unanimously endorsed by the president's advisers and supported by the president himself. [13]

President Johnson officially ordered the reprisals at a second National Security Council meeting early in the afternoon. After a short delay, due to uncertainties about whether or not an attack on the destroyers had actually occurred, the formal execution orders for retaliation were sent to Honolulu at 4:49 P.M., specifying that within approximately two and one-half hours United States aircraft carriers were to launch their planes for the attack. [14] At the second National

[11] Johnson, p. 27.
[12] Johnson, p. 114.
[13] See Neil Sheehan, "The Covert War in Tonkin Gulf: February–August, 1964," in *The Pentagon Papers* (New York: Bantam Books, 1971), p. 262.
[14] Sheehan, "Covert War in Tonkin Gulf," pp. 262–263.

Security Council meeting on August 4, it was decided that a congressional resolution of support should be sought immediately, and with this in mind the president met with sixteen congressional leaders from both parties at approximately 6:45 P.M. By this time, of course, the decision to launch a retaliatory strike had already been made on the basis of plans drawn up months earlier. According to Johnson's memoirs, at this meeting with congressional leaders:

> I told them that I believed a congressional resolution of support for our entire position in Southeast Asia was necessary and would strengthen our hand. I said that we might be forced into further action, and that I did not "want to go in unless Congress goes in with me." At this meeting "McNamara described in detail what had happened in the Gulf of Tonkin and what we proposed to do." I then read a statement that I planned to deliver to the American people later in the evening.[15]

Whether or not the congressmen present were fully aware that the formal order had been issued for the attack, and that the planes were in fact to be airborne while the meeting was taking place, is not fully clear, although it can be inferred that they were apprised that the decision had been made. This inference is confirmed by *The Pentagon Papers*, which reported that the president "told them that because of the second unprovoked attack on the American destroyers, he had decided to launch reprisal air strikes against the North and to ask for a congressional resolution...."[16] Presented with this *fait accompli*, the congressional leaders had no alternative but to support the president. As President Johnson remarked at the conclusion of the meeting:

> I went around the table asking each Senator and Representative for his frank opinion. Each expressed his whole-hearted endorsement of our course of action and of the proposed resolution.
> "I think it will be passed overwhelmingly," said Congressman Charles Halleck.
> "I will support it," said Senator Fulbright.
> At the close of the meeting I felt encouraged by the show

[15] Johnson, *Vantage Point*, pp. 115–116.
[16] Sheehan, p. 263.

of solidarity and support. As Speaker McCormack said near the end of our discussion, we were presenting a "united front to the world." [17]

Cuban Missile Precedent

During the Cuban Missile Crisis, President Kennedy also consulted with congressional leaders after the internal executive decision-making processes had come to the conclusion that a blockade of Cuba was the suitable response to the Soviet Union's installation of missiles on the island. At no time during the deliberations leading to this decision did President Kennedy or his staff feel that it was appropriate to extend the discussions to include congressional leaders. The decision was made on the basis of inputs from presidential advisers, the Joint Chiefs of Staff, several members of the Cabinet, and a few other selected individuals from the executive branch, and Vice President Johnson.[18] This group reflected the spectrum of views on what action should be taken, from those few who felt no action was required to those who wanted to take the most drastic military reprisals against Cuba.

After settling upon the decision to carry out the blockade, President Kennedy informed those members of the Cabinet not present during the deliberations of the crisis and the decision that had been made. After this, and shortly before he was to announce his decision in a nationwide address, the president called in congressional leaders and informed them for the first time of the crisis and the action he was going to take. They reacted sharply, as Robert Kennedy describes:

> Many congressional leaders were sharp in their criticism. They felt that the president should take more forceful action, a military attack or an invasion, and that the blockade was far too weak a response. Senator Richard B. Russell of Georgia said that he could not live with himself if he did not say in the strongest possible terms how important it was that we act with greater strength than the president was contemplating.
>
> Senator J. William Fulbright of Arkansas also strongly advised military action rather than such a weak step as a block-

---

[17] Johnson, *Vantage Point*, p. 117.
[18] Robert F. Kennedy, *Thirteen Days* (New York: W. W. Norton, 1969), p. 8.

ade. Others said that they were skeptical but would remain
publicly silent, only because it was such a dangerous hour for
the country.[19]

The president carefully explained to the congressional leaders that
military action might produce devastating consequences, and therefore he was not willing to take such a gamble until he had exhausted
all other possible courses of action. The initially militant reaction of
most of the congressional leaders was, according to Robert Kennedy,
similar to the first reactions of the executive group upon hearing of
the missiles. It is quite possible that if the congressmen had been
consulted longer, and put into a position where they would have
had to bear part of the collective responsibility for the decision that
was ultimately made, they would have taken a more judicious approach and weighed the alternatives carefully. Nevertheless, it is interesting that at the time the response of the congressional leadership, including Senator Fulbright (who was later to lead the doves
in an attack on President Johnson's Vietnam policies), was in favor
of direct military intervention. Consultation with the leaders of Congress inevitably means consultation with the most conservative parts
of the legislature, and at the time of the Cuban Missile Crisis these
key legislative leaders leaned toward strong military intervention
where they felt United States interests were at stake. Many of these
same individuals by the latter stages of the Vietnam War were far
more cautious in their attitudes toward military involvement, and led
congressional efforts to curb the discretionary authority of the president to make war.[20]

CONTINUING PRESIDENTIAL DOMINANCE. Although Congress has made
efforts to put itself on a more nearly equal footing with the presidency
in foreign affairs, from the vantage point of the White House it remains more a force to be dealt with than one to be seriously consulted. Presidents and their advisers have openly stated that they
do not consider the War Powers Resolution of 1973 an important
limitation upon presidential war-making prerogatives. Shortly after
the Resolution was passed over President Nixon's veto, Secretary of

[19] Kennedy, *Thirteen Days*, pp. 31–32.
[20] See James L. Sundquist, *The Decline and Resurgence of Congress* (Washington, D.C.: Brookings Institution, 1981), pp. 238–314, for a discussion of congressional resurgence in the defense and foreign-policy arenas.

Defense James Schlesinger held a press conference at which he said the Resolution would "make it possible for President Nixon to order new bombing in Indochina in the event of a new major North Vietnamese offensive in South Vietnam." [21] In response to a request by Missouri Senator Thomas Eagleton for a legal interpretation of the Resolution, the State Department replied: "It is the Department's opinion that [the Resolution] does not constitute a legally binding definition of the president's constitutional power as Commander-in-Chief. It does not contain language which requires or prohibits any particular action." [22]

President Reagan's victory over Congress in the highly controversial Airborne Warning and Control System (AWACS) and arms package sale to Saudi Arabia in 1981 illustrates continued domination by the White House in foreign affairs. Congress can block major arms sales by adopting a concurrent resolution of disapproval within thirty calendar days after it has received formal notice of the proposed sale from the executive branch. The law holds an important escape clause, however, granting the president the authority to waive the right of Congress to veto a sale if he certifies to Congress that "an emergency exists which requires such sale in the national security interests of the United States." Moreover, the Foreign Aid Bill of 1981 has an additional provision allowing presidents to waive legal restrictions on arms sales if Congress is notified by the White House that the sale "is vital to the national security interests of the United States." Before acting unilaterally, the president must consult with and provide a written justification to the Foreign Policy and Appropriations Committees.

Presidents have not had to use their waiver power over congressional vetoes of arms sales because Congress has never nullified a presidential request. Congress is clearly unwilling to limit presidential initiatives in foreign affairs. During a Senate debate over the AWACS sale, Senate Foreign Relations Committee Chairman Charles Percy (R, Ill.), went so far as to say that the president should act unilaterally under the waiver provisions of the law and not force a Senate vote.

Although President Reagan won an important victory over Congress on the AWACS issue, and held the integrity and power of the

---

[21] Thomas F. Eagleton, *War and Presidential Power*, p. 221.
[22] Eagleton, p. 222.

presidency in foreign affairs intact, the 48 to 52 senate vote rejecting a resolution to disapprove of the sale came only after the most strenuous White House lobbying of senators that had been seen in decades.[23] The White House wooed marginal senators to its side by skillful horse trading. Iowa Republican Charles Grassley was promised acceleration of appointment to United States attorney for his favored candidate; Washington Republican Slade Gorton was given the Public Health Service hospital in his state that he wanted. The president promised not to campaign against Arizona Senator Dennis DeConcini (D) in 1982, and approved money for a power plant desired by Montana Democrat John Melcher.

The narrow Reagan victory margin on the AWACS issue seems to have been due more to the failure of the White House to consult legislators in advance than to a resurgent Congress. Representative Jonathan Bingham (D, NY), one of the authors of the vetoed legislation, remarked, "The administration doesn't want to go through a battle like this [again]. Consultation will improve." [24] Senator Claiborne Pell (D, RI), an AWACS opponent, concluded, "This whole exercise could have been prevented had there been proper consultation with the Congress." [25]

In the mid-twentieth century, from the era of Franklin D. Roosevelt that began in 1933 and until the Vietnam War, custom and tradition gave the president a dominant role in foreign affairs that was generally accepted at both ends of Pennsylvania Avenue. Congress began efforts to curb presidential power over foreign policy because of widespread dissatisfaction over unilateral White House actions in Vietnam. Ronald Reagan found that a resurgent Congress in foreign affairs was a legacy of Vietnam that weakened his power to pursue the national interest as he saw it in Central America and other parts of the world. (See Chapter 10.)

Although the Hamiltonian presidency has often prevailed in foreign policy, in domestic affairs the Madisonian system of checks and balances supports congressional opposition to the president. Presi-

[23] The president, recognizing that he needed a victory in only one branch of Congress to sustain the sale, never lobbied the House, which voted to disapprove of the sale by a lopsided 301 to 111.

[24] *Congressional Quarterly Weekly Report*, vol. 39, no. 44 (Oct. 31, 1981), p. 2096.

[25] Ibid., p. 2098.

dents, however, often feel strongly that they should dominate Congress in the domestic as in the international arena.

PRESIDENT, CONGRESS, AND DOMESTIC AFFAIRS

Modern presidents often consider themselves to be engaged in crisis management in domestic as well as in foreign affairs. Sometimes the two spheres are connected in the minds of the occupants of the Oval Office, a foreign emergency necessitating prerogative action at home. During the Korean War, President Harry S Truman cited his constitutional authority as chief executive and commander-in-chief to seize the nation's steel mills to prevent a strike. Congress, in the Taft-Hartley Act of 1947, had provided explicitly for strikes against the national interest. Under the law, the president could obtain a court order enjoining for eighty days a strike that threatened the national health and safety. During the "cooling-off" period, a board of inquiry would seek an amicable settlement. Truman, however, who had attacked the Taft-Hartley legislation and made it a major issue in his 1948 presidential campaign, decided to use his prerogative powers. "A wise president," wrote Truman in his memoirs, "will always work with Congress, but when Congress fails to act or is unable to act in a crisis, the president, under the Constitution, must use his powers to safeguard the nation." [26] The Supreme Court declared Truman's quest for domestic prerogative powers to be excessive, and concluded that he should have adhered to the intent of Congress by invoking the machinery of the Taft-Hartley Act. [27]

Search for Prerogative Powers

Truman, a former senator himself, respected Congress and the constitutional separation of powers. But as president he felt it was his responsibility to take unilateral action in the domestic as well as the foreign-policy spheres when necessary. Strong presidents like Truman seek domestic prerogative powers to deal with economic and social problems. President Franklin D. Roosevelt, in the dark days of the Depression, persuaded Congress to grant him wide powers to cope

---

[26] Harry S Truman, *Memoirs*, vol. 2, *Years of Trial and Hope* (Garden City, N.Y.: Doubleday, 1956), p. 478.
[27] Youngstown Sheet and Tube Company *v.* Sawyer, 343 U.S. 579 (1952).

with the emergency. President Nixon was granted emergency authority to establish wage and price controls under the Economic Stabilization Act of 1970.

President Lyndon Johnson, who probably understood Congress better than most presidents had before or would after him, expressed a view with which most presidents would agree: Congress is an unfortunate obstacle to the effective exercise of executive power at home. "Under our system of government," wrote Johnson, "with its clearly defined separation of powers, the greatest threat to the Chief Executive's right to 'govern' comes traditionally from the Congress. Congress is jealous of its prerogatives. All too often jealousy turns into a stubborn refusal to cooperate in any way with the Chief Executive." [28] For example, he continued, an "entire program of social legislation proposed by President Kennedy — from aid to education to food stamps to civil rights — remained bottled up in committee while the Congress defiantly refused to budge or act in any way." [29]

In words which could be repeated in any presidency, and which undoubtedly have been thought by all presidents, Johnson stated,

> We were, in my opinion, facing a real crisis, and it was more than a crisis of unfulfilled needs throughout the nation. There was also a crisis of confidence in our system of government. There was a clear reason for moving forward, and moving with dispatch and energy; for acting while the sobering influence of national tragedy [Kennedy's assassination] caused men in all walks of life to think of the country's interest rather than their own.[30]

Johnson was not referring to the Vietnam War, which was to come later, but to the need for leadership in civil rights and the war on poverty.

Presidents find domestic crises in many areas. President Carter, for example, compared the domestic energy crisis to a state of war, calling upon Congress to rise to the occasion by passing his energy program intact. President Reagan referred in his inaugural address to the "crisis we are facing today," which included "an economic affliction of great proportions," including "the longest and one of the

[28] Johnson, *Vantage Point*, pp. 33–34.
[29] Johnson, pp. 33–34.
[30] Johnson, pp. 33–34.

worst sustained inflations in our national history," and idle industries that "have cast workers into unemployment, human misery, and
personal indignity." Reagan's "crisis" also resulted from excessive tax
burdens, and particularly from unwarranted government spending.
The Reagan administration let it be known that though Congress
would be properly courted, it should not be allowed to stand in the
way of the president's sweeping program for tax and spending cuts.
Like many presidents before him, Reagan appealed directly to the people when confronted with the possibility of adverse congressional
action.

Even though most presidents have viewed Congress as a necessary
evil, and on occasion as an unnecessary evil, Congress remains in its
own view the first branch of the government.

CONGRESSIONAL VIEW OF THE PRESIDENCY

The constitutional separation of powers creates an adversary relationship between Congress and the presidency that dictates how each
branch views the other. Each of the three branches of the government, wrote Harry S Truman,

> must jealously guard its position. This jealous concern is a
> good thing. When I was a senator, I was always anxious to
> see the rights and the prerogatives of the Congress preserved.
> If I had ever held judicial office, I would have considered it
> my duty to keep alert to any possible interferences with the
> independence of the judiciary. As president, it was my duty
> to safeguard the constitutional position of the office I held —
> the presidency of the United States.[31]

In the political world of Washington, Congress, and especially the
Senate, is an exclusive club whose members enjoy the powers, privileges, and emoluments of their offices independently of the presidency. Members are elected through their own efforts, for presidents
rarely have the power or inclination to sway voters in congressional
districts or states in favor of candidates of their choice. Within Congress, power does not depend upon the backing of the White House.
Legislators steer their own course in pursuing their committee and
legislative interests. Representatives taking stands in opposition to
the White House are frequently admired by their colleagues.

[31] Truman, *Memoirs,* vol. 2, p. 453.

Legislators, from the most junior and unknown to the most senior and prestigious, enjoy attending White House events, from state dinners to breakfasts with the president. Representatives respect the power and symbolic importance of the White House in the broader political world of Washington and the nation. When the president chooses to take a firm stand his voice is heard on Capitol Hill, and his interests often prevail. But there is no automatic acceptance of presidential interests either by members of the president's own party on Capitol Hill or by the opposition. Members follow the lead of the president only when they find his interests coincide with their own for reelection or power and influence within Congress. Understandably, members of the president's party are more subject to his influence than is the opposition.

Response to Presidential Intrusions

Congress protects its turf from what it considers to be unwarranted presidential invasions. Smart presidents understand and respect the integrity of Congress.

President Jimmy Carter, for example, failed during much of his administration to understand Capitol Hill. His staff even failed to see how important it was to give House Speaker Tip O'Neill an adequate supply of tickets to the inaugural parade. On more important fronts, the Carter White House often ignored congressional protocol and custom. *Washington Post* reporter T. R. Reid wrote that

> During his first month in the White House, Carter had shocked Congress by compiling a "hit list" of proposed waterway projects that he considered "wasteful and unjustified." He had threatened, at least implicitly, to veto authorization bills for projects on the hit list. This kind of interference in an area that had always been Congress' special preserve was unprecedented, and though Carter did have the support of many junior members of Congress who were not yet accustomed to the pork-barrel ethic, the hit list was attacked by the leadership in both Houses — even by Tip O'Neill.[32]

EXECUTIVE PRIVILEGE. Congress not only guards the pork barrel against White House intrusions, but also jealously protects its pre-

[32] T. R. Reid, *Congressional Odyssey: A Saga of a Senate Bill* (San Francisco: W. H. Freeman, 1980), pp. 90–91.

rogatives in other areas. Congress considers the bureaucracy to be
its own. Committee powers are sacrosanct, and White House claims,
for example, of executive privilege to withhold information from
Congress are not accepted by powerful committee chairmen.

Congress typically takes issue with assertions such as that made by
Richard Nixon's attorney general Richard Kleindienst, who told a
committee, "Your power to get what the president knows is in the
president's hands." [33] The Senate Government Operations Committee responded by reporting out a bill, later passed by the Senate, requiring the executive branch to provide information to Congress unless the president, in writing, ordered the information to be withheld. The report on the Senate bill stated, "The power of the executive branch to screen the conduct of its officials from inquiry would
overwhelm and invalidate the power of Congress to make those inquiries." [34] The executive-privilege legislation was not passed by the
House, primarily because Government Operations Committee Chairman Jack Brooks (D, Texas) and other powerful members felt the
legislation would recognize for the first time in statutory law an inherent presidential prerogative to withhold information.

Congress can do little when the White House refuses to cooperate
with its committees. Most presidential claims of executive privilege
have been based on the undesirability of disclosing national-security
information or on the grounds that disclosure would be against the
public interest. President Truman stood behind his Secretary of Commerce, Averell Harriman, who had refused to release a loyalty file on
a department employee that had been subpoenaed by a subcommittee
of the House Un-American Activities Committee. President Nixon
in particular raised the ire of Congress by refusing not only to dis-
close Watergate information, but also by declining to give Congress
defense and foreign-policy information on more than fifteen occasions. During the Ford administration the House Intelligence Committee voted to cite Secretary of State Henry Kissinger for contempt
because he had refused, on the orders of the president, to turn over
State Department documents involving "highly sensitive military and
foreign affairs assessments and evaluations." [35]

The controversy over executive privilege continued during the

---

[33] *Guide to Congress*, 2nd ed. (Washington, D.C.: Congressional Quarterly, Inc.,
1976), p. 152.
[34] *Guide to Congress*, p. 152.
[35] *Guide to Congress*, p. 158.

Carter administration. The president's National Security Adviser, Zbigniew Brzezinski, according to tradition, could not be required even to appear before a congressional panel. Members of the Senate Foreign Relations committee were often frustrated and sometimes infuriated because they felt the committee's role in foreign policy making was being ignored by Brzezinski, who could not be held accountable for his actions. When the president nominated Senator Edmund Muskie to be Secretary of State, the Foreign Relations Committee took the opportunity to express a strong viewpoint that foreign policy should be conducted by the State Department and not by the National Security Adviser. "I don't think this country can speak with two voices," said committee Chairman Frank Church (D, Idaho). "That has become a common pattern," he continued, "one that erodes away the authority of the Secretary of State, one that leads to confusion abroad about what American foreign policy really is. I strongly believe we should have only one spokesman." [36]

From the perspective of Congress, the problem of executive privilege is part of the larger dilemma of the imperial presidency, characterized by executive action beyond the control of Congress. The growth of presidential power has occurred not only because of unilateral presidential action, but also because Congress itself has acquiesced in the growth of presidential power. Congress has made wide delegations of authority to the president, and supported the establishment and growth of the Executive Office of the President, which constitutes an independent presidential bureaucracy. When the growth of the executive seems to threaten the separation of powers, however, "resurgent" Congresses take action to put their house in order and counterbalance the executive threat to their independence.

EBB AND FLOW OF CONGRESSIONAL STRENGTH OVER THE EXECUTIVE

Congress acts against imperial presidents to redress what it considers to be the imbalance of power between the two branches. Executive usurpations of congressional power and intrusions into the legislative sphere give many legislators an incentive to strengthen the collective

[36] *Congressional Quarterly Weekly Report*, vol. 38, no. 19 (May 10, 1980), p. 1231.

capacity of Congress to deal with the executive branch. It is not easy for Congress to act collectively, because it is intrinsically pluralistic. Both the reelection incentive and the constant quest for personal power on Capitol Hill encourage dispersion rather than concentration of power. The long-term trend on Capitol Hill is toward decentralization, but when legislators widely perceive that the executive has gone too far in asserting power, centripetal forces momentarily overcome centrifugal momentum. Confronted with an imperial executive, members of Congress momentarily subordinate their own interests to the collective will of Congress to maintain itself as an equal partner with the executive in the constitutional system.

Congress strengthens itself through what is generally referred to as a process of "reform." The rhetoric of reform, however, often obscures the underlying reasons for congressional action. When members support "reforms" they do so for a variety of reasons; therefore it is inaccurate to speak of Congress as a whole voting for reform for a single purpose. Some members advocate reform because a committee reorganization will enhance their personal power. When the House voted in 1973 to enact a "Subcommittee Bill of Rights," reducing the power of committee chairmen to control the budgets, staffs, and even legislative jurisdictions of subcommittees, the "reform" was strongly supported by subcommittee chairmen. Many of those chairmen, predictably, opposed the Subcommittee Bill of Rights. The word "reform" in the English language connotes improvement by altering existing practices; in politics, though, improvement is usually thought of as added power. And reforms that improve one person's power invariably detract from the power of another. Entrenched power interests, such as committee chairmen, generally favor the status quo on Capitol Hill.

Because reform in Congress alters balances of power among members, important reforms occur only under compelling circumstances. The threat of a significant diminution of legislative power because of executive action is one occurrence that may provide the impetus for change. Over the years Congress has reacted to the threat of executive power in several ways.

Budget and Accounting Act of 1921

The power of the purse, the authority to determine government expenditures and revenues, has always been considered the most important legislative prerogative in the Anglo-American political tradition. James Madison stressed, in *The Federalist*, that the "legislative department derives a superiority in our governments . . . [because it] alone has access to the pockets of the people, and has in some constitutions full discretion, and in all a prevailing influence, over the pecuniary rewards of those who fill the other departments, [creating] a dependence . . . in the latter, which gives still greater facility to encroachments of the former." [37] Madison pointed out that under the Constitution the House of Representatives

> cannot only refuse, but they alone can propose the supplies requisite for the support of government. They, in a word, hold the purse — that powerful instrument by which we behold, in the history of the British constitution, an infant and humble representation of the people gradually enlarging the sphere of its activity and importance, and finally reducing, as far as it seems to have wished, all the overgrown prerogatives of the other branches of the government. [38]

Hamilton concluded that the power of the purse may "be regarded as the most complete and effectual weapon with which any constitution can arm the immediate representatives of the people, for obtaining a redress of every grievance, and for carrying into effect every just and salutary measure." [39]

Congress has seen its power of the purse gradually eroded as the president has increasingly seized the initiative both in setting budget allocations for the executive branch and in shaping tax measures. [40] Ironically, Congress has often unintentionally increased the power of the president over the budget at the same time as it has sought to tighten its control over the purse.

For example, Congress integrated and strengthened the power of its appropriations committees under the Budget and Accounting Act of 1921. At the same time, the law directed the president to prepare and transmit to Congress each year a budget for the federal government, showing proposed expenditures and revenues. To assist the president, the Bureau of the Budget was created, and to aid Congress,

[37] *Federalist* 48.
[38] *Federalist* 58.
[39] *Federalist* 58.
[40] For an excellent historical and analytic account of presidential budgeting, see Lewis Fisher, *Presidential Spending Power* (Princeton: Princeton University Press, 1975).

the General Accounting Office was established to oversee administration of federal expenditures. The new budget process was to replace the former haphazard system in both the executive and legislative branches under which the Secretary of the Treasury transmitted directly to Congress the budgetary requests of departments and agencies. Within Congress eight separate committees controlled appropriations.

The Bureau of the Budget was first located in the Treasury Department, but President Roosevelt transferred it to the newly created Executive Office of the President in 1939. The Bureau of the Budget (BOB) soon became the right hand of the president in dominating both the bureaucracy and the Congress in the budgetary process. After 1939, BOB was to put the president's stamp on all budget recommendations, and the White House initiative was difficult for Congress to overcome, although it did succeed informally in changing executive recommendations when it could muster enough political backing within Congress and the bureaucracy for such a course of action.

Bureau of the Budget Becomes Office of Management and Budget (OMB)

At the time the Budget and Accounting Act of 1921 was passed, the Bureau of the Budget was clearly perceived on Capitol Hill as an agent of Congress. Many members of Congress retained that viewpoint even after President Roosevelt made BOB the key component in his newly created Executive Office in 1939. Fifty-eight statutory provisions delegated specific functions to BOB that Congress wished to see performed. President Roosevelt's placement of BOB in the Executive Office began a power struggle between the president and Congress over the role the agency should perform.

The Bureau of the Budget, in the meantime, buttressed by congressional support and independent statutory mandates and claiming at the same time to speak for the president, became independently powerful. While the president was preoccupied elsewhere, particularly in foreign affairs, BOB often struck out on its own to control both the budgetary and legislative flow of information from the bureaucracy to Capitol Hill. The growing independence of the agency caused President Nixon to propose its abolition as a *statutory* agency to be replaced by a new Office of Management and Budget created by executive order in 1970. Under Nixon's plan, the new agency (OMB) would serve only the president, not Congress. The president alone would determine its functions and responsibilities.

Since 1939 Congress had delegated to the president, with only a few lapses, the authority to reorganize the executive branch at will, provided a majority of either branch of Congress did not veto a president's proposal. Congress made only feeble objection to the Nixon plan to create OMB. Representative Chet Holifield (D, Calif.), expressed the viewpoint of the opposition in charging that the president was attempting to act unilaterally without heeding the intent of Congress. The OMB reorganization plan, stated Holifield,

> by the simple action of transferring all statutory authorities of the Bureau of the Budget and its director to the president, in one fell swoop, changes numerous congressional enactments made throughout the years, not in the quantitative sense of repealing or diminishing the statutory wording, but in the qualitative sense of placing the authority personally in the hands of the president, to be withheld, redelegated, or assigned elsewhere, according to his decision, within such interpretations as he gives to the statutory boundaries of his permissible action.[41]

Nixon finally got his way, however, not because Congress wished to enhance the power of the White House, but because many powerful members viewed the Bureau of the Budget as an entrenched bureaucracy that needed to be changed. "The happiest group in the government today," declared Senator Abraham Ribicoff (D, Conn.), "will be the Bureau of the Budget by the rejection of this plan, because this gives the Bureau of the Budget a chance to keep playing one element of the government against the other to keep their power. The Bureau of the Budget has become power hungry and power crazy." [42]

The willingness of Congress to cooperate with Nixon soon evaporated. The president began to push his conservative philosophy hard, and attempted to make a series of end runs around the Democratic

[41] U.S. Congress, Senate, Committee on Government Operations, Hearing Before the Subcommittee on Executive Reorganization and Government Research of the Committee on Government Operations, "Reorganization Plan No. 2 of 1970," 91st Cong., 2nd Sess. (May 8, 1970), p. 61.
[42] Ibid., p. 35.

Congress by impounding funds that had been appropriated by Congress for thirty-nine social programs. Congress, seeing its wishes blatantly ignored by the White House, took immediate action to curtail the impoundment authority of the president and at the same time strengthen its own budgetary procedures to counterbalance what had become executive domination of the budget process. To make OMB more accountable to Congress, Senate confirmation of OMB directors was required by a 1974 amendment to the Budget and Accounting Act of 1921. In the same year Congress passed major legislation to strengthen its own budgetary procedures.

Budget and Impoundment Control Act of 1974

President Nixon's impoundment of congressionally appropriated funds was in the best tradition of strong presidential leadership. Presidents from Thomas Jefferson to Nixon had withheld appropriated funds on numerous occasions, basing their actions on the president's Article II mandate to see that the laws are faithfully executed. Moreover, as early as 1870 Congress itself passed an Anti-Deficiency Act, granting the president broad discretionary authority to apportion funds in an effective and economical way, withholding appropriations where necessary.[43]

Congressional response to what the Democratic majority on Capitol Hill considered presidential "excesses" during the Nixon administration was politically motivated. The Republican president had simply gone too far in making domestic and foreign-policy decisions that ignored the wishes of Capitol Hill.

IMPOUNDMENT PRECEDENTS AND CONTROVERSIES. In historical perspective, however, Nixon's impoundment decisions and tight White House control over the budget were not unusual. President Franklin D. Roosevelt used the newly strengthened Bureau of the Budget to ignore the wishes of Congress on a number of occasions by impounding appropriated funds. Roosevelt frequently used pressing war needs as an excuse for impounding funds for domestic programs. By 1943 the patience of Congress had worn thin, and Roosevelt's Budget Director Harold Smith was called on the carpet before the Senate

---

[43] 31 U.S.C. 665, 16 Stat. 251 (1870). In the budgetary sphere, as in so many other areas of public policy, Congress had not only acquiesced in but affirmatively supported wide presidential discretion to act unilaterally.

Appropriations Committee and closely questioned about impoundment practices. Later in that year the Senate passed a rider to the Defense Appropriations bill proscribing impoundment of any appropriated funds under the legislation.[44]

Congress continued to challenge the president's impoundment authority during the Truman administration. President Truman had ordered the largest impoundment in history up to that time when he directed his Secretary of Defense to withhold $735 million that Congress had appropriated for the Air Force in 1949. Congress was as unhappy with Truman's impoundments as it had been when President Roosevelt withheld appropriated funds. A House report charged that the president's actions circumvented the will of Congress, and concluded that "there is no warrant or justification for the thwarting of a major policy of Congress by the impounding of funds." [45] Although the House was displeased, the funds remained impounded.

Congressional displeasure continued over presidential impoundments. President John F. Kennedy in particular raised the ire of Congress when he ordered his Defense Secretary, Robert McNamara, to withhold funds that had been appropriated for development of the RS70 bomber, the precursor of the controversial B1 bomber supported by the Reagan administration. Powerful legislators opposed the president, particularly the legendary chairman of the House Armed Services Committee, Carl Vinson of Georgia. Vinson, first elected from the 2nd district in rural southern Georgia in 1914, had served in Congress for forty-seven years when the impoundment controversy erupted in 1962. He had been chairman of the Armed Services Committee for all but two years since 1949, and was a strong supporter of the military. Vinson, like powerful chairmen before him, considered his prerogatives to determine policy within his committee's jurisdiction to be superior to those of the president. Vinson represented a congressional era when seniority reflected virtually lifetime tenure on Capitol Hill. He began his long chairmanship of the Naval Affairs Committee in 1931, when John F. Kennedy was in grammar school.

[44] The anti-impoundment provision failed to become law when the House rejected the amendment.
[45] U.S. Congress, Senate, Committee on the Judiciary, Subcommittee on Separation of Powers, "Executive Impoundment of Appropriated Funds," *Hearings*, 92nd Cong., 1st Sess. (March 1971), p. 300.

The Kennedy administration threat to impound funds for the
RS70 bomber program that went beyond the prototype stage was
countered by a vote of the House Armed Services Committee that
"directed, ordered, mandated, and required [the Secretary of De-
fense] to utilize the full amount of the $491 million authority granted
... for an RS70 weapons system." [46] The report continued, "If this
language constitutes a test as to whether Congress has the power to
so mandate, let the test be made." [47]

A direct confrontation between the White House and Congress
over the RS70 bomber issue was avoided when President Kennedy
called Vinson to the White House and persuaded him not to take
his fight to the House floor. It was not simply Kennedy's charm and
the aura of the presidency that made Vinson back down, but also
recognition that a victory on the floor for the Armed Services Committee point of view was by no means certain. The fragmented politics of Congress that inevitably caused power struggles among its
committees, and between powerful committee chairmen and party
leaders, had worked to the president's advantage in the RS70 bomber
dispute. Most important, Texas Democrat George Mahon, chairman
of the powerful Appropriations Committee on Defense, supported
the president, as did the House leadership. Although Congress finally
appropriated $362 million for development of the bomber, the House
members of the conference committee that made the appropriation
had a tacit agreement with Defense Secretary Robert McNamara that
he would impound most of the appropriated funds.

Impoundment controversies continued during the Johnson and
Nixon administrations. The chairman of the House Armed Services
Committee, Mendel Rivers, challenged an administration impoundment of defense funds in 1967. By a vote of 356 to 2 the House
supported a Rivers amendment to the authorization bill providing:
"Notwithstanding the provision of any other law, the Secretary of
Defense and the Secretary of the Navy shall proceed with the design,
engineering, and construction of the two nuclear powered guided
missile frigates as soon as practicable." [48] The wording was essentially
dropped in a Senate-House conference committee, but Rivers con-

[46] U.S. Congress, House, Armed Services Committee, H. Rept. 1406, 87th Cong.,
    2nd Sess., 1962, p. 9.
[47] Ibid., p. 9.
[48] U.S. Congress, House, Armed Services Committee, 89th Cong., 2nd Sess.,
    1966, H. Rept. 1536, p. 2.

tinued to put pressure on the Secretary of Defense to abide by the intent of Congress by spending all the appropriated funds for the Navy.

Congress finally acted to curb the president's impoundment authority because of what it considered to be the excesses and unprecedented impoundments of the Nixon administration. Nixon's impoundments for domestic and defense programs far exceeded those of any previous administration. The president in some cases ignored congressional mandates to spend money. He impounded more than half of the $4.5 billion appropriation for federal aid to highways, although Congress had provided in the 1968 Federal Highway Act that no part of the appropriated funds under the legislation "shall be impounded or withheld from obligation." [49]

NIXON IMPOUNDMENTS. By 1973 President Nixon had impounded funds for more than a hundred programs, in some cases eliminating entire programs, many of which originated during the New Deal. Nixon's budget knife fell on the low-interest loan program under the Rural Electrification Act of 1936, and on urban grant-in-aid programs that had been vastly expanded in the previous administration of Lyndon B. Johnson.

Nixon's impoundments not only stirred up Congress, but resulted in thirty-eight successful court challenges to the president's impoundment authority. In one case after another the federal courts declared that the president had acted unlawfully in failing to follow the intent of Congress to spend appropriated funds. The courts rejected Nixon's unprecedented argument that the president had a *constitutional* right not to spend money, "when the spending of money would mean either increasing prices or increasing taxes for all the people." [50] Previous presidents had used impoundment more to balance the budget and economize under the terms of the Anti-Deficiency Act than to redirect and ignore the goals of Congress. Before Nixon, presidents agreed with Roosevelt that impoundment "should not be used to set aside or nullify the expressed will of Congress." [51]

[49] 23 U.S.C. Sec. 101(c), 1973.
[50] *Weekly Compilation of Presidential Documents* 9, No. 5: 109–110. Cited in James P. Pfiffner, *The President, the Budget, and Congress: Impoundment and the 1974 Budget Act* (Boulder, Colo.: Westview Press, 1979), p. 43.
[51] The Roosevelt quotation is cited in Pfiffner, *President, Budget, and Congress*, pp. 43–44.

THE RESOLUTION. One of the excuses Nixon used for his impoundments was the profligacy of congressional spending. Until Congress could get its house in order, said the president, he had the responsibility for putting a cap on excessive expenditures. Congress responded to the president's linkage of impoundment with its budget process by passing legislation addressing both issues. The Budget and Impoundment Control Act of 1974 ended the president's statutory authority to impound permanently funds appropriated by Congress. At the same time, the law established new budgetary procedures to end the admitted excesses in spending, most of which resulted from lack of integration and coordination among congressional committees, each of which went its own way in authorizing and appropriating money for a seemingly endless array of federal programs.[52]

To bring about better coordination of the budget process, the 1974 law created budget committees in the House and the Senate, and a new Congressional Budget Office to give Congress expert advice on budgetary matters.[53]

The Budget Act of 1974 was a major congressional attempt to meet the threat of growing presidential power by strengthening the capacity of Congress to cope with the budget, which the White House had used for many years as its principal means of leverage over the legislature. Although Congress seemed to be winning the budgetary battle in the 1970s, the forceful presidency of Ronald Reagan once again seemed at first to make Capitol Hill subordinate to the White House and OMB. Ironically, the president, with the cooperation of Capitol Hill Republicans, used the newly centralized congressional budget process to facilitate achievement of his goals. Without the existence and cooperation of the budget committees the president would have been unable to achieve the wide-ranging budget reductions proposed by the White House and backed by Congress in 1981. During the Reagan honeymoon the budgetary machinery that Congress had created to withstand presidential assaults was neatly turned on its head by a clever president and an astute Budget Director, former Representative David Stockman, who knew the ways of Capi-

---

[52] See Allen Schick, *Congress and Money: Budgeting, Spending, and Taxing* (Washington, D.C.: Urban Institute, 1980), for an excellent background analysis of congressional budgeting.

[53] For further discussion of the congressional budget process, see Chapters 4 and 11.

tol Hill. The president relied upon the powers of the budget committees to facilitate passage of his program.

Conclusion

The ebb and flow of power between Congress and the president is
constant. Through much of the twentieth century Congress broadly
supported a strong presidency by delegating wide discretionary authority to the White House to make both foreign and domestic
policy. Beginning in the 1970s, Congress increasingly challenged
presidential authority and took measures to buttress its collective
strength against the executive. Congress has always been careful, especially through its committees, to keep tight reins on the bureaucracy to buttress its power in Washington politics. Washington
lobbyists are also part of the permanent political establishment of
the city who use and are used by legislators playing the game of
power politics on Capitol Hill.

CHAPTER NINE

Washington Lobbyists

Lobbyists are part of the closely knit political establishment of Washington. They are not born there, but they are always nurtured in the political world of the city, which includes Congress. Lobbyists sell their political expertise to clients, skill that is gained by both members and their aides in the chambers, committee rooms, offices, corridors, and hidden recesses of Capitol Hill. The most effective lobbyists on Capitol Hill are not outsiders, but individuals who have long experience in congressional politics.

The common view of lobbyists as outsiders who pressure and often dominate Congress is false. Lobbyists play the game of Capitol Hill politics in the same way as it is played by members and staffers. Essential to a lobbyist's success is a reputation for power on Capitol Hill, and even more important, with clients. Lobbyists continually engage in the self-serving exercise of publicizing at every opportunity their experience and power, which generally impresses clients far more than it does savvy legislators and their staffs.

The political landscape of Washington is populated by lobbyists representing every conceivable cause, often drawing large salaries to support a life-style that is far better monetarily than they had when they were in Congress or the bureaucracy.

Washington is the superbowl of politics. Having arrived, the players neither want nor have to return to their hometowns.

"You can't go back to Pocatello," is a truism of Washington politics. The origin of the saying is Jonathan Daniels's description of the city in his personal account of Washington during the waning days of Franklin D. Roosevelt.

Daniels wrote about a lunch he had with an old writer friend, Captain Richard Neuberger of Portland, Oregon:

> Neuberger had just come back from Alaska and was telling me about the cold up there and the state of his kidneys.
>
> "There's [former Idaho Senator] Worth Clark," he said suddenly. . . .
>
> The ex-senator joined a party at a table.
>
> "Is he living here now since he was defeated?" I asked. "He probably doesn't know it, but he's a distant cousin of mine."
>
> "Yes," said Dick. "I think he is practicing with Tommy Corcoran. . . ."
>
> "You know," he said suddenly, "somebody ought to write an article, 'You Can't Go Back to Pocatello.'"
>
> "Pocatello?"
>
> "That's his home town. It's a big town for Idaho. Oh, I guess 20,000 people."
>
> "Why can't he go back?"
>
> "It isn't Clark. They just can't. They come down here to the Senate or something. Then they get beat. It isn't easy to go back and practice local law and live local lives."
>
> "It is not only the little towns it's hard to go back to," I said.
>
> And while we watched, Big Jim Watson, of Indiana, walked across the room. Nobody noticed him. He had been Republican Majority Leader of the Senate under Hoover. He was an old man, 80, I guessed. He had been defeated, too, but he was in Washington still.
>
> "You can't go back to Pocatello," I said.[1]

Many who enter Washington politics catch Potomac fever. Elected politicians may be defeated at the polls, but often they stay on as lobbyists, using their knowledge of Capitol Hill and their access to the House and the Senate floors, which is given to former members, to benefit their clients.[2]

Capitol Hill aides, too, frequently join the ranks of the lobbyists

---

[1] Jonathan Daniels, *Frontier on the Potomac* (New York: Macmillan, 1946), pp. 142–143.

[2] See "Class of '74," *Congressional Quarterly Weekly Report*, vol. 42, no. 9 (March 3, 1984), pp. 498–503 for an analysis of how the ex-members of one class fared.

when they suddenly find themselves out of work because their bosses are defeated, or when they decide to leave for the greener pastures of lobbying so that they can send their children to college or afford that special town house or condominium in Georgetown.

FORMER CONGRESSMEN AND STAFFERS AS LOBBYISTS

Democrat Carter Manasco faithfully served his Alabama district from his first election in 1940 until he was defeated in his bid for a fifth term in 1948. His Washington experience, however, did not end in 1948, for he became a lobbyist for the National Coal Association, a position that he held into the 1980s. Manasco's tenure for more than thirty-two years as a lobbyist after he left Congress is unusual but not unprecedented. "They say I'm the senior member of the lobbying racket," he boasts.[3] And indeed he is "kind of part of the wallpaper around here," remarks a Senate Energy Committee aide.

Norman J. Ornstein and Shirley Elder have observed, "To maximize access and to enhance their 'inside' contacts, interest groups frequently will employ former members of Congress, former staff aides, or old 'Washington hands' — that is, people who already have close ties with Congress." [4]

The demand for ex-members of Congress has grown with government, as more and more corporations, trade associations, professional groups, and labor and farm organizations expand their Washington-based operations. Private groups more than ever want to employ lobbyists who know the ins and outs of Washington politics. Lobbying Congress and attempting to influence the bureaucracy is not a simple matter. The politics of Congress is not easily understood. Nor is the role of the bureaucracy in policymaking comprehensible to those who have not been directly involved in overseeing or administering the agencies.

"A former U.S. congressman, no matter how capable, is worth more in Washington than any place else — considerably more," commented former Tennessee Republican Representative Dan Kuykendall. He

---

[3] *Congressional Quarterly Weekly Report*, vol. 38, no. 52 (December 27, 1980), p. 3644.
[4] Norman J. Ornstein and Shirley Elder, *Interest Groups, Lobbying and Policymaking* (Washington, D.C.: Congressional Quarterly Press, 1978), pp. 83–88 at p. 83.

pointed out, "Even those members who go to law firms back home end up getting sent back to Washington." [5]

Advantages of Being a Former Member or Staffer

Ex-members and staffers sell their knowledge of the legislative process. Groups seeking lobbyists assume that former members and their aides understand better than outsiders the intricacies of Capitol Hill. The decentralization and individualism of Capitol Hill politics places a premium upon the insider. Lobbyists must understand the intricacies of the committee system, the often dominant role of staff, the limits upon congressional leadership, and the way in which parliamentary procedure affects how decisions are made.

KNOWING HOW THE SYSTEM WORKS. Former Representative James O'Hara (D, Mich., 1959–1977), who joined a lobbying law firm after he left office, emphasized the importance in his work of an insider's knowledge of Congress: "The secret is knowing how the system works," he commented, "how to get your issue to one committee instead of another, how to see that it gets acted on first instead of second, how to see that the amendments you don't want are nongermane, and the amendments you do want are germane." [6]

EXPERTISE. Ex-members sell not only their skill in legislative procedures, but also their specialized knowledge in areas of public policy they concentrated on while they were in Congress. Former Congressman Fred Rooney (D, Pa., 1963–1979), was a consumer and labor-oriented representative of the industrial Lehigh valley for many years. His seniority on the Commerce Committee made him chairman of the key Transportation Subcommittee, which has jurisdiction over railroads and trucking. He developed expertise in railroad matters over the years, and generally supported strict regulation of the private roads and centralization of the Conrail system. Rooney's long tenure in Congress gave him a false sense of security, for his Democratic district returned him year after year by large margins. He won in 1976 by 65 percent of the vote, but lost in 1978, 47 to 53 percent.

---

[5] *Congressional Quarterly Weekly Report*, vol. 38, no. 52 (December 27, 1980), p. 3643.
[6] Ibid., p. 3646.

There were several ironies in Rooney's defeat. First, his Republican opponent, Don Ritter, a Lehigh University administrator and engineer, attacked his views on railroad regulation, arguing that the railroads should be deregulated. Unknown to the novice Ritter, however, many railroads preferred protective regulation over deregulation. After Rooney's defeat he set himself up as a Washington "political consultant," commonly referred to as a lobbyist, and his first client was the Association of American Railroads. The railroads bought Rooney's knowledge of Congress and of their special problems. He would become an invaluable link with the new chairman of the Transportation Subcommittee, New Jersey Democrat James Florio, a member of the "Watergate Class" of 1974.[7]

The railroad industry also employed former Congressman and Cabinet Secretary Brock Adams (D, Wash., 1965–1977). Adams had risen to the position of Budget Committee chairman in his last term, and was the ranking Democrat on the Transportation Subcommittee behind Rooney. He had helped to fashion the Conrail legislation, and had been deeply involved in other aspects of railroad regulation before he resigned to become Jimmy Carter's Secretary of Transportation in 1977. Before he left Congress, Adams had helped to write legislation on railroad and trucking deregulation, which he eventually helped to pass, not as a congressman but as a lobbyist.

Ex-Staffers as Insiders

The stories of Rooney and Adams are representative of the lobbying activities of former members. Less visible, at least to the general public, are ex-staffers who have become lobbyists. Like former members, staffers move to Washington law firms and lobbying organizations, selling their specialized knowledge of Congress and public policy. Staff, particularly in the Senate, has a generally more intimate knowledge of the intricacies of congressional procedures and often better understanding of substantive policy issues than do members. Legislators constantly have to scurry about to touch base with constituents, and keep up Washington appearances at endless social functions, but

---

[7] Florio represents the 1st district of New Jersey, which includes Camden. He was reelected in 1978 and 1980 by overwhelming margins, 79 and 77 percent of the vote, respectively. He lost a bid for the New Jersey governorship in 1981 by a razon-thin margin and on Capitol Hill continues to be an effective and active chairman of his subcommittee.

their aides can quietly concentrate upon the business at hand on Capitol Hill.

Lobbyists admit that they often deal more with staff than with members, an aspect of lobbying that gives ex-staffers particular advantages. Former Senator and Congressman Robert Taft, Jr., of Ohio (House, 1963–1965; Senate, 1971–1976), who became a successful Washington representative for a number of private interests, remarked, "A very, very small percentage of your work [as a lobbyist] is really dealing with members. You deal mostly with staff, and most of them I did not know [while in Congress]; many of them were not there." [8]

Ex-aides, particularly those who were staff directors or general counsels of important committees, are often considered by law firms and lobbying groups to be better positioned to influence Congress than ex-members. One Washington lawyer commented, "A lot of former members of Congress don't understand the mechanics of the procedure well enough to get very far. A lot of them just like to float around seeing their old buddies, hanging out in the Speaker's lobby." [9] Another attorney stated, "The last thing a small law firm needs is a former member of Congress who thinks he's still running the show." [10] Even former representative John McCollister (R, Neb., 1971–1976), concurred with the view that ex-members might not be the best lobbyists, "I believe a lot of companies find the employment of a former member of Congress is a handicap rather than a benefit." [11] Former Senate aide Kenneth Davis, who represents Rohm and Haas Company in Washington, concluded, "I tend to find a former member doesn't make all that good a lobbyist. A lobbyist has to do the grunt work. Members of Congress have staff to do the grunt work." [12]

Lobbying Techniques of Ex-Members and Staffers

Former members and staffers continue to be part of the congressional club. They maintain their connections on Capitol Hill and constantly

[8] Ibid., p. 3646.
[9] Ibid., p. 3648.
[10] Ibid.
[11] Ibid.
[12] Ibid.

develop new ones. Sitting members often have greater respect for their former colleagues than for "outside" lobbyists.

Even when former members do not understand the positions they are supposed to represent particularly well, they can use their connections to introduce their clients to powerful members and staff. Former congressman Wilbur Mills (D, Ark., 1939–1977), for example, who had been chairman of the powerful House Ways and Means Committee, represented the Encyclopedia Brittanica Company by setting up appointments for its lawyers with friendly legislators. Senate Commerce Committee Chairman Howard W. Cannon (D, Nev.), even let Mills sit with the committee's staff and consult informally during the proceedings while the committee conducted hearings on legislation that would affect his clients.[13]

Former members use their access to the floor, the members' gymnasium and dining rooms, and the hidden rooms of the Capitol where private conversations among members often take place, in their lobbying pursuits. Ex-members cannot lobby on the floor of the House, but former Senators are permitted to circulate in the chamber while legislation is being debated.

William "Fishbait" Miller, who spent forty-two years working on Capitol Hill, and for twenty-eight years was the Democratic Doorkeeper of the House, commented, "My job was to keep out the cleverist of the lobbyists, the ex-congressmen. According to the House rule which was passed in the last century, former congressmen cannot come on the floor of the House during debate if they have a financial interest in a bill." [14] Miller continued, "It had gotten so bad with past congressmen coming on the floor and making deals and standing like watchdogs to see that 'the man' continued to vote 'right,' meaning 'as bought,' that a rule was necessary." [15]

Whether in or outside of the chambers of Congress, a congressional fraternity facilitates the access of former members to Capitol Hill. Former congressman Roger Zion (R, Ind., 1967–1975), who continued to attend House prayer breakfasts after he left Congress, pointed out, "When you're talking to somebody you've played paddle ball with or played in the Republican-Democratic golf tournament with, or seen regularly in the Capitol Hill Club, there's no question

13 Ibid., p. 3646.
14 William "Fishbait" Miller, *Fishbait: The Memoirs of the Congressional Doorkeeper* (Englewood Cliffs, N.J.: Prentice-Hall, 1977), Warner Books Edition, p. 237.
15 Ibid.

that helps. I think most sitting members go out of their way to be helpful to former members." [16]

Members and former congressmen socialize together in many ways, attending Redskins games, sailing on the Chesapeake, going to dinner parties, and working out together in the House and Senate gymnasiums. Although ex-aides do not have continued access to the chambers and facilities of Capitol Hill that they had when they were employed there, they too are members of a congressional fraternity that continues to buttress their access to Capitol Hill.

Former members and staffers must register as lobbyists if they are attempting to influence legislation, but there are no other restrictions on their activities. Top-level officials in the bureaucracy, by contrast, are prohibited under a 1978 Ethics in Government Act from lobbying their former agencies for a period of one year on matters they had handled while in government.

The congressional community understandably does not want to limit the opportunity of its members on the outside. Congressman Bob Carr (D, Mich.) expressed the views of most of his colleagues, "Look, everybody in this life essentially sells their knowledge and experience. I don't see why members of Congress ought to be excluded from that club." [17]

CAUSES AND CLIENTS OF FORMER MEMBERS AND STAFFERS

Ex-members and staffers represent many types of clients, many of whom seek to employ former members who have specialized on Capitol Hill in policy areas that directly affect them. The causes that congressmen have backed on Capitol Hill are not necessarily those they espouse as lobbyists. Private interests generally care more about the influence of ex-congressmen and staffers than about their ideological viewpoints.

Corporate Emphasis

The Reagan electoral sweep in 1980 helped to increase the ranks of Democratic congressmen, who turned to lobbying in order to stay in

---

[16] *Congressional Quarterly Weekly Report*, vol. 38, no. 52 (December 27, 1980), p. 3646.
[17] Ibid., p. 3647.

Washington. Bob Eckhardt (D, Texas, 1967–1981), was one of many Democrats who did not want to go back to his Pocatello — Houston. Eckhardt had risen to prominence on Capitol Hill as a powerful consumer advocate, a role that was strengthened by his chairmanship of the Consumer Protection Subcommittee and, at the end of his career, of the Oversight and Investigation Subcommittee. In the 1970s Eckhardt's district was not considered to be marginal, because the incumbent generally won easily with more than 60 percent of the vote. Eckhardt's liberal record, and more important, his opposition to the oil companies, encouraged conservative Texans to mount an all-out effort to defeat him in 1980. The successful Republican candidate, Jack Fields, spent almost $800,000, almost twice as much as Eckhardt, in his campaign. Eckhardt became the Washington representative of the Investment Company Institute, which was primarily interested in legislation affecting money-market funds, which benefited small consumers by giving them high interest rates they could not obtain in their banks and savings institutions.

Bob Eckhardt had a great deal of company from former colleagues who joined the Washington lobbying brigade. Former representative Al Ullman (D, Ore., 1957–1981), who had risen to one of the highest positions in the House, chairman of the Ways and Means Committee, decided that he too did not want to go home. After all, he had lived nearly his entire adult life in the heady atmosphere of Capitol Hill. He had been involuntarily retired from Congress, but he did not want to leave the congressional fraternity. He started out in Congress as a fiery liberal, but gradually became more conservative to reflect his constituents' views. His voting record was erratic. In 1978 the Americans for Democratic Action (ADA) gave him a 30 percent approval rating, but in each of the next two years he received a 65 and 75 percent ADA approval score. He was a strong advocate of the interests of the lumber industry, which were important to his district, and suspicious of environmental causes. His district, like that of so many defeated Democrats in 1980, was considered safe, for Ullman had had little opposition, generally winning by 70 percent of the vote. But 1980 was different; a young Republican challenger, Denny Smith, who had substantial financial backing and was more than able to equal the $663,000 Ullman spent on his campaign, defeated the incumbent with the help of Reagan's coattails, by 49 to 47 percent of the vote.

When ex-Congressman Ullman sought clients in order to continue living in Washington as a lobbyist, he found his prior contacts, made when he was chairman of the Ways and Means Committee, to be extremely helpful. The committee's jurisdiction over revenue legislation affected the entire spectrum of corporate America. Ullman's expertise and influence on tax legislation helped to launch his new lobbying firm, Ullman Consultants, Inc. The largest pharmaceutical firm, Merck and Co., hired Ullman to look after tax legislation affecting its interests. The American Guaranty Financial Corporation employed the former Oregon representative to keep in touch with legislation affecting the insurance industry, and the Western Forest Industries Association employed Ullman Consultants to protect the interests of the lumber industry.

The Western Forest Industries Association also hired ex-Oregon Congressman Robert Duncan (D, 1975–1981; 1963–1967), who had won the general elections in 1976 and 1978 by 85 percent of the vote but lost to youthful Ron Wyden by 40 to 60 percent of the vote in the 1980 Democratic primary. Duncan, like Ullman, was accused by his opponent of being out of touch with his district. Both had become distant figures to their constituents. The dynamic and somewhat eccentric Wyden, who at age thirty had become director of the older citizens' Gray Panthers lobby in Portland, appealed not only to the city's elderly population but to many of its other citizens who considered themselves part of the avant-garde. With the help of a large force of elderly volunteers, Wyden simply outcampaigned his primary opponent and, in the mostly Democratic district, easily won over his Republican challenger, 72 to 28 percent.

Ex-Congressman Duncan had more than the Western Lumber Industry as his client. His congressional seniority had made him chairman of the important Transportation Subcommittee of the Appropriations Committee in the 96th Congress (1979–1980). Although he had decided that "You can't go back to Portland," the city did not hesitate to employ him as its Washington lobbyist, for a reported retainer of $100,000, to help channel federal mass transit and highway funds into the city.[18]

Congressmen can easily make the transition to lobbying for the same or similar interests outside that they once represented within Congress. The lobbying careers of Eckhardt, Ullman, and Duncan

---

[18] *Congressional Quarterly Weekly Report*, vol. 39, no. 24 (June 13, 1981), p. 1052.

nicely complemented their congressional interests. State and local governmental groups and private interests are delighted to employ former members who represented them in Congress. Ex-representative Jerome Ambro (D, N.Y., 1975–1981), stayed in Washington as a lobbyist for Suffolk County, which comprised half of his district. He was also hired by the New York State Department of Transportation, and by the Associated Universities of New York. Although Ambro was defeated in 1980, he continued to think of himself as a permanent member of Congress. He still regularly attended the caucuses of the New York congressional delegation.

Lobbying Firms

Many congressmen strike out on their own as Washington lobbyists, but they sometimes join to form lobbying firms. An interesting example is the Industrial Team, established by former representatives Richard Ichord (D, Mo., 1961–1981) and Bob Wilson (R, Calif., 1953–1981).

Both congressmen when they retired in 1980 were important members of the Armed Services Committee. Ichord was the fourth-ranking Democrat on the full committee, and chairman of the Research and Development Subcommittee. Wilson was the ranking Republican member of the full committee, and of the Procurement and Military Nuclear Systems Subcommittee. Ichord was a controversial member of the House, having chaired the Internal Security Committee, which was the successor to the House Un-American Activities Committee. Ichord's committee conducted investigations, mostly of left-wing groups, and also of such right-wing organizations as the Ku Klux Klan, but produced no legislation. House liberals attacked the Internal Security Committee as they had the Un-American Activities Committee, and it was abolished in the mid-1970s.

Ichord's district was a safe one, in which he was regularly reelected by margins of more than 60 percent, although he was a Democrat in a mostly Republican district. He faced significant Republican opposition, however, in 1980, and that was one of the reasons for his retirement. Another was that although he normally could have looked forward to becoming chairman of the Armed Services Committee, if he had stayed in Congress, there was a distinct possibility that the Democratic Caucus, which has to approve of all committee chairmanships after they are recommended by the Steering and Policy Committee, might have turned Ichord down. The Caucus had previously abolished his Internal Security Committee, an almost unprecedented action, because the Caucus's liberal majority not only felt the committee was unnecessary but was distinctly unhappy with the way Ichord conducted investigations; they sometimes seemed similar to the witch hunts of the early 1950s that were carried out by the Un-American Activities Committee and Wisconsin Senator Joe McCarthy's Government Operations Committee on the Senate side.

The long congressional tenure of Ichord and Wilson, and the contacts they had established through their positions on the Armed Services Committee, helped their new lobbying group to unusual success in attracting clients. They were retained to follow "defense issues" by such companies as General Dynamics, McDonnell Douglas, United Technologies, Boeing, Hughes Aircraft, Raytheon, Grumman, Westinghouse, and TRW, which collectively held $18.6 billion in military contracts in fiscal year 1980.[19] The defense firms added the services of Ichord and Wilson to supplement the lobbying activities of their permanent Washington offices.

Hired Guns

The close linkage between the interests congressmen sponsor while they are on Capitol Hill and those they advocate when they become lobbyists is not always apparent. Sometimes members seem to reverse their policy orientations completely after they leave Congress. Seattle Democrat Brock Adams, who had sponsored environmental legislation while he was in Congress, and had generally been a strong supporter of environmental causes, was hired by the Japanese government to protect their interests within the 200-mile fishing zone of the United States. Save-the-Whales activists accused the congressman of a sell-out.[20]

Former Congressman James Symington (D, Mo., 1969–1977), who was a strong civil-rights advocate while on Capitol Hill, became a lobbyist for the government of South Africa. Symington, who opposed apartheid, said his job was simply to "open lines of communica-

[19] *Congressional Quarterly Weekly Report*, vol. 39, no. 24 (June 13, 1981), p. 1052.
[20] *Congressional Quarterly Weekly Report*, vol. 38, no. 52 (December 27, 1980), p. 3647.

tion" with the South African government, and facilitate its commerce with the United States. "There's nothing that I have done or would agree to do on that particular account that I don't deem to be in the interest of the United States and of peace in the world," stated Symington.[21]

Ex-Representative Lloyd Meeds (D, Wash., 1964–1977), whose 2nd congressional district in the far northwest corner of Washington state contained many environmental activists, had a strong record in support of environmental causes as a member of the Interior and Insular Affairs Committee, and a member of its subcommittees dealing with Alaskan Lands, Indian Affairs, and as chairman of the Water and Power Resources Subcommittee. Meeds had one of the most liberal records in Congress on foreign and domestic policy issues. Meeds failed to solve the most pressing problem confronting his district, which was Indian fishing rights. He leaned toward granting more rights to the Indians than to whites, a distinctly unpopular stand in his district, which reduced his 61 percent vote margin in 1974 to 542 votes in 1976. Sensing defeat, Meeds decided to retire in 1978. During his last term the congressman made a complete about-face on the Alaskan Lands issue, sponsoring legislation that would allow oil and mineral development in the state. After his retirement he was hired by the Alaskan government to represent its viewpoint on Capitol Hill.[22] As a lawyer, stated Meeds, "You represent clients. It may not in all instances be a position which you would have philosophically had as a member." [23]

Another former congressional liberal, Michigan Democrat James O'Hara (1959–1977), commented, "God knows, I didn't feel strongly about 90 percent of the stuff I voted on [in Congress]. It was just a matter of going along with what the district wanted or what the party wanted." [24] As a Washington lawyer, stated O'Hara, he was willing to represent timber interests attempting to gain a foothold on Alaskan lands, but as a member he would have opposed them. There are limits, however, concluded O'Hara, to what he would do as a lobbyist. "If somebody asked me to repeal [the Occupational Safety and Health Act], I'd say 'I think you need some other firm.' " [25]

21 Ibid., p. 3648.
22 Ibid.
23 Ibid.
24 Ibid.
25 Ibid.

HOW EX-MEMBERS VIEW THEIR ROLE
AS LOBBYISTS

Politics is contagious, and so too is Potomac fever. Many former congressmen who become lobbyists find that their new life helps them to deal with Potomac fever, but does not match the world of politics they experienced on Capitol Hill. No lobbying activity, for example, can substitute for the contact sport of elections. Every time an election approaches, stated one ex-member-turned-lobbyist, he feels "like a firehouse Dalmatian when the alarm bell goes off." [26] Former Utah Senator Frank Moss reminisced about the politics of Capitol Hill, "You never get over missing it. Time just sort of hangs heavy." [27]

Some former members are not entirely comfortable with their new role as lobbyists. Frank Moss was "slightly uncomfortable" when the law firm he joined helped corporate clients in their fight against government regulation. Moss had been a leading consumer advocate during his Senate career, and an active chairman of the Consumer Subcommittee of Commerce. Although Moss may have been a little uncomfortable representing corporate clients, he recognized that the largesse of the Washington lobbyist comes mainly from corporate interests. Rarely do ex-members give up lobbying because they have to represent corporate interests that may not be entirely in line with their own views.

Remaining in the Capitol Hill Community

Although many former members of Congress who turn to lobbying miss the political excitement of Capitol Hill, they are happy to be in the second-best world of lobbying, which enables them to continue to be indirectly part of the congressional community. Happiest are those who continue to espouse the causes they advocated while they were members. Roger Zion (R, Ind., 1967–1975), cheerfully evaluated his role as a lobbyist, saying, "I'm still working the same beat in a sense [as I worked on Capitol Hill]. I'm still trying to save the world for democracy, further the free market system and reduce government interference in the private sector." [28] After his defeat, Zion handed

[26] Ibid.
[27] Ibid., p. 3645.
[28] Ibid.

out engraved cards advertising himself as a "Resource Development Consultant to People, Industry, and Government." [29] Independent oil producers in Indiana, Illinois, and Kentucky signed him on as their Washington lobbyist.

HIGHER SALARIES, LESS PRESSURE. Although many members suffer separation pangs when they leave Capitol Hill, they enjoy the higher salaries and relatively calmer life that lobbyists live in comparison to members of Congress. A minimum salary for ex-members and aides alike is $75,000 a year, and those who join prestigious Washington law firms earn upward of $200,000 per annum. A Colorado Republican, Mike McKevitt, who represented his Denver district for only two years (1971–1973), turned his defeat by Patricia Schroeder into a career as a Washington lobbyist. McKevitt found his new job more satisfactory. "It's a much saner life," he said, "you're not barreling to National Airport every Friday night to catch the last flight to Denver. Your weekends are your own. You can spend time with your family. You don't have to keep saying goodby to your friends." [30]

Other ex-members too settled comfortably into their new careers as lobbyists. Congress, once an exclusive club on both sides of Capitol Hill, began to change in the late 1960s. Ralph Nader, Common Cause, and other public-interest pressure groups began to penetrate the inner sanctums of Congress, making life uncomfortable for its members. Congressmen began to feel that they were under greater pressure than ever before, even though reelection became increasingly easy as marginal or competitive districts declined. [31] Donald Riegle, who held the congressional seat that included Flint, Michigan, from 1956 until he was elected to the Senate in 1976, recalled in his memoirs of the House:

> Some of the members in the cloakroom were talking about the recent flock of retirement announcements by our senior colleagues. It's without precedent for nine ranking minority members to call it quits voluntarily over the span of several months. . . . Included in this group are the ranking Republicans on the Appropriations, Ways and Means, and Judiciary

[29] Ibid.
[30] Ibid., p. 3648.
[31] Congressmen's increased perceptions of electoral uncertainty may have increased their reelection efforts, helping to cause a decline in marginal districts.

Committees as well as the Senior Republicans on Rules, Interstate and Foreign Commerce, and Merchant Marine and Fisheries. This exodus surely reflects a collective belief that the party has no chance to capture control of the Congress in the foreseeable future. Otherwise, these men would be determined to hang on until they received a chance to serve as chairmen of their respective committees. It reflects other factors as well: the pressures of redistricting, the higher pension benefits available for retiring members — it's possible now for some of them to draw as much as $34,000 per year; the frequency with which senior members are being stricken fatally while in office here; the longer sessions of Congress, and the growing assertiveness of the newer members.

In recent years a congressman's job has changed dramatically, and this has imposed a new set of pressures on the old soldiers of both parties. Fifteen years ago the House was largely an island unto itself. Few Americans knew or seemed to care very much about what happened here. That's not true any longer. Today the country is peering directly over our shoulder. It's Ralph Nader who is watching over us, and Common Cause, and the League of Women Voters. It's newly politicized groups of blacks, women, young people and Chicanos. It's groups such as SOS, NAG, and Vietnam Veterans Against the War. They've learned that Congress determines our national priorities; that we provide the men and money to fight undeclared wars; that we have the power to clean up the environment, restore the cities, and help old people. They're letting us know their demands and lobbying aggressively to make sure we act. The pressures on members, already intense, are multiplying rapidly. As [Congressman] Cederberg said to me, "It's just not as much fun to be here anymore." [32]

The sentiments recorded by Riegle reflected a turning point on Capitol Hill, when many long-term members who faced uncertain electoral battles at least did not view leaving Congress as the end of the world. Those who began new careers as Washington lobbyists found that their exodus from Congress was not a political death sentence. They continued to be part of the Washington political scene, but often without the pressures that impinge upon Capitol Hill. Former members-turned-lobbyists admit there are aspects of congres-

---

[32] Donald Riegle, with Trevor Armbrister, *O! Congress* (New York: Doubleday, 1972), pp. 284–285.

sional life they do not miss — not only the physical pressures but the constant demands from special-interest groups, and attacks from the press.

MEMBERS AS LOBBYISTS

Many former members of Congress become successful Washington lobbyists because they effectively sponsored special interests while they were on Capitol Hill. Members of Congress are not lobbyists in the strict sense of the term, but their representative role often goes beyond reflecting the views of their constituencies to the consistent advocacy of policies that benefit special interests. Congressional advocacy is generally but not exclusively tied to interests within the legislator's district or state.

Advocates of Special Interests

Cynics proclaim that legislators often become advocates of special interests in order to obtain high-paying jobs as lobbyists once they leave Congress. A report of Ralph Nader's Congress Project commented, "A more subtle form of compensation to the legislator for his labors on behalf of a corporation or lobby organization is the potential of a high-paying job when he retires from Congress. What has been called the 'deferred bribe,' not that Congressmen *expect* to be out of office in the near future, but the unhappy possibility can never be entirely out of their minds." [33]

Individual legislators are often the best representatives of private interests regardless of whether or not they are looking forward to lucrative lobbying jobs. Democrat Edward Kennedy of Massachusetts, for example, has sponsored the National Institutes of Health and medical research for years. In the House, Congressmen John Fogarty (D, RI, 1941–1967) and Paul Rogers (D, Fla., 1955–1979) almost singlehandedly established and nurtured the National Institutes of Health, Public Health Service hospitals, and a vast array of medical programs that both created and benefited specialized medical interests. Groups favoring increased funds for medical research would go to their "spokesmen" on Capitol Hill for support. Neither Kennedy nor the congressmen were "bribed" in any way, for they supported

---

[33] Mark J. Green et al., *Who Runs Congress?* (New York: Bantam, 1972), p. 43.

health legislation because they believed in it and could use it to make their mark on Capitol Hill.

OIL. Capitol Hill spokesmen have a wide array of special interests. Senator Russell Long (D, La.), who since 1948 has held a seat that is virtually a sinecure, is considered one of the strongest and most powerful supporters of oil interests on Capitol Hill. Ironically, the son of Huey Long holds substantial family investments in oil, mostly due to the efforts of his father, "The Kingfish," who made a name for himself in Louisiana politics by attacking the big oil companies. Long became chairman of the key Senate Finance Committee in 1965, a position he held until the election of the Republican Senate in 1980. The top executive officers of Exxon, Atlantic Richfield, Shell, and a host of other large and small oil companies alike, commonly testified before Long's committee, which controlled most of the tax legislation that substantially affected oil profits. Long and other "oil senators" were considered to be such important representatives of oil interests that they had little difficulty in raising substantial sums to swamp their electoral opponents. Long spent more than $2 million in the 1980 Louisiana primary to defeat state legislator Lewis (Woody) Jenkins, who, to the amusement of many, accused Long of being a left-winger. Other senators who effectively represented oil interests on Capitol Hill raised extraordinary sums, much of it from oil PACs and wealthy oil supporters. Senator Lloyd Bentsen (D, Tex.), for example, entered the 1982 election year with $2.4 million in his campaign chest, more than any other incumbent senator up for reelection in 1982.

ARMAMENTS. Although the oil industry has powerful representatives in Congress, the armaments industry, part of what President Eisenhower called the "military-industrial complex," has even more powerful emissaries on Capitol Hill. In his final address to the nation, President Eisenhower warned, "In the councils of government, we must guard against the acquisition of unwarranted influence, whether sought or unsought, by the military-industrial complex. The potential for the disastrous rise of misplaced power exists and will persist. We must never let the weight of this combination endanger our liberties or our democratic processes." [34] At the time of Eisenhower's warning, Congress was appropriating $40 billion each year for defense, in con-

[34] *Congressional Record*, March 26, 1961, p. 4557.

trast to the Reagan defense budget, which was in excess of $200 billion. Generally Congress has strongly supported increased defense expenditures. The armed services committees and the defense appropriations subcommittees have consistently been chaired by hawks who represented Defense Department views on Capitol Hill. Powerful members of the armed services committees, such as Nevada Democrat Howard Cannon and South Carolina Republican Strom Thurmond, have held high positions in the military reserves at the same time as they have served on the armed services committees. Cannon was a brigadier general in the Air Force reserves, and Thurmond held the position of major general in the Army reserves. The past military careers of most members of the armed services committees have buttressed their hawkish support of the Defense Department in its constant quest for increased armaments.

IRON TRIANGLES. The linkage among congressional committees, administrative agencies, and private interests become "iron triangles" representing special causes. Committee chairmen often adopt the strategy of protecting and expanding their administrative bailiwicks, not to strengthen their electoral positions but to buttress their power and status within Congress. Legislators often gain prestige by effectively representing special interests, and becoming known, for example, as "Mr. Health" of the Hill, which were the attributions of Senator Edward Kennedy and Paul Rogers. Utah Congressman Morris Udall, chairman of the Interior and Insular Affairs Committee, elevated his status by becoming known as the principal House spokesman for environmental interests. The "Permanent Secretary of Agriculture," Mississippi Congressman Jamie Whitten, who was elected from his district, which contains the home of novelist William Faulkner, a month before Pearl Harbor in 1941, jealously guarded his jurisdiction over agricultural programs as chairman of the Agricultural Appropriations Subcommittee, and as chairman of the full committee. In 1982, he had chaired his subcommittee for all but two years since 1949. No outside lobbyist could even begin to approach Whitten's power over agricultural policy and his effective representation of varied agricultural interests, including crop subsidies and, somewhat of a surprise for a legislator known to be conservative, of the food stamp program.

The list of congressional spokesmen for special interests could be greatly extended to include representatives of minority groups, women, veterans, the scientific community, education, labor, small business, and many others. Powerful legislators represent views far beyond those of their constituents. The reelection incentive as well as the quest for personal power and recognition on Capitol Hill, however, supports special-interest representation, because interest groups give substantial financial backing to their congressional advocates. Money, perhaps more than any other factor, determines the outcome of elections.

STYLES OF WASHINGTON LOBBYISTS

Individual and group lobbying styles vary widely. Outside of Washington, groups engage in grass-roots lobbying, attempting to influence the electoral choices of voters. Within the city, lobbyists attempt to mobilize support for their positions among the power brokers on Capitol Hill, the bureaucracy, the presidency, the press, Washington lawyers, and other lobbyists, all comprising the Washington political establishment.

Understanding Politics

The politics of lobbying on Capitol Hill reflects the politics of Congress itself. Lobbyists must understand the complex interconnections and subtleties of Washington politics to be successful. Congress is not always moved by electoral demands, which rarely exist in concrete form. Congress acts only when its entangled political machinery is put in gear, which can be accomplished only when intricate and diversified power interests among party leaders, committee chairmen, staff, and members themselves mesh.

Lobbyists can succeed with few if any concrete legislative accomplishments. The game of lobbying, like the game of politics, is one of appearances as much as substance. A lobbyist with a reputation for power is by definition a success. And a reputation for power is gained more by style than by substantive results.

Paradigm of a Successful Lobbyist — Charls E. Walker

Charls E. Walker, whose firm Charls E. Walker and Associates represents a long list of corporate clients, is one of Washington's best-known lobbyists because of his *reputation* for power. Clients ranging from the American Iron and Steel Institute to the Bank of New York and the Cigar Association of America have been eager to retain Walker's firm because of his reputed inside knowledge of Washington and wide acquaintance in its political establishment. Walker comes from an unlikely background for a successful lobbyist. A Ph.D. in economics, he taught at the University of Texas and the Wharton School of the University of Pennsylvania. He was an assistant to the Secretary of the Treasury during the Eisenhower administration when he caught Potomac fever and decided to make a career of Washington politics as a lobbyist.

Charls Walker, writes Elizabeth Drew, "while he works very hard, is a buoyant figure who clearly has a good time at what he does. There is definitely an element of fun in the sport of influence: it is enjoyable to have people call you up to ask you what you think; it is satisfying to be, or to think you are, up on what's going on. Walker is steadily securing his position as someone whom a lot of people call." [35]

Walker's success depends in large part upon his keen understanding of the political world of Washington. He comments that in order to be a good lobbyist,

> The basic thing you got to understand is what makes a good politician. In the simplest terms, it is an understanding of people: what motivates people, what they fear, their hopes and aspirations. So in working with elected officials, as contrasted with appointed officials or the bureaucracy, you have to have some of the same qualifications as the successful politician. You got to understand what motivates the politician. [36]

Walker knows that even though politicians of course strive for reelection, they do so primarily to play the power and status game on Capitol Hill. Ohio Democrat Thomas Ashley was one of the many representatives who wanted to make his mark on legislation. Elected in 1954, he rose to chairman of a banking subcommittee and, in the 95th Congress (1977–1978), was appointed by House Speaker Tip O'Neill to be chairman of the new Ad Hoc Energy Committee. Ashley worked closely with the leadership and powerful chairmen to salvage President Carter's energy program. Though Ashley's House career elevated his status on Capitol Hill, his hard legislative work

---

[35] Elizabeth Drew, "A Reporter at Large: Charlie," *The New Yorker* (January 9, 1978), p. 33.
[36] Drew, "A Reporter at Large," pp. 56–57.

did not prevent his defeat in 1980 at the hands of Republican Ed Weber, who ran a skillful and well-financed campaign.

Ashley's Washington career was separated from electoral politics. Toward the end of his career his principal incentive was to gain influence in the House. Effective Washington lobbyists understand the gap that so often separates the pursuit of power within Congress from the quest for reelection that takes place in distant constituencies. "Dummies, even in this town, think that politicians just want to be reelected," declared lobbyist Walker, who had worked closely with Ashley on the energy program during the Carter years. He continued, "But what is the purpose of getting reelected? A handful will use it to try to become President of the United States. But what motivates a Lud Ashley? He doesn't want to run for President of the United States, or for Senator or for governor. He's a House man. He takes extreme pride in doing a good legislative job. So if I'm talking to Lud I'm talking merits." [37]

Walker's style with Ashley was characteristic of lobbyists attempting to influence the careerists of Capitol Hill. Lobbyists strive to make themselves and their organizations staff adjuncts of legislators, supplying them with expert information and viewpoints that will be useful in their quest for personal power. Effective legislators know their subjects, and understand the contrasting positions of powerful interest groups. Ambiguous constituent attitudes often play a very small part in shaping what has become a highly expert and politically specialized legislative process. Helping members to become good legislators in the eyes of their colleagues is as important as boosting their electoral prospects.

Other Heavy Hitters

Like Charls Walker, other Washington lobbyists seek to build their reputations for power. They want their clients to know that they can open the right doors. Craig Spence, who represents multinational companies and Japanese business interests, is another lobbyist who has convinced his clients that he has vast influence. *New York Times* Washington correspondent Phil Gailey writes of Spence, "What most impresses, if not benefits, his clients is his ability to master the social and political chemistry of this city, to make and use important con-

[37] Drew, p. 57.

nections and to bring together policy makers, power brokers and opinion shapers at parties and seminars." [38] Moreover, "Knowing Mr. Spence can be good business for government officials, members of Congress and their staffs, and even some journalists, who cash in on it by accepting speaking and writing fees." [39]

Not all lobbyists can successfully conduct their business in Washton's fashionable restaurants and at candle-lit dinners in their Kalorama or Georgetown homes. Some, like Evelyn Dubrow, a lobbyist for the International Ladies Garment Workers Union, wear out "twenty-four pairs of shoes each year trudging the corridors of congressional power." [40] "Evvie" Dubrow "is nearly as much a part of the congressional scene as the lawmakers themselves." Although very few members of Congress in 1985 were representatives when Dubrow beban her lobbying career in 1958, most agreed with House Speaker Tip O'Neill, who said simply, "I love her." [41]

THE WASHINGTON LAWYERS

The legal profession in Washington, from superlawyers to lowly associates, is an important part of the lobbying establishment. John Adams described American government as one of laws and not of men. Perhaps a more apt description would be that our government is one of laws and lawyers. From the early days of the Republic lawyers have dominated the political process at all levels of government. The quintessential symbol of the lawyer-politician was Abraham Lincoln, Honest Abe, who studied law by candlelight.

Law as the Route to Success in Politics

The self-taught and individually tutored lawyers of the nineteenth century have been replaced by highly trained and commonly socialized law school graduates. Lawyers speak a language that binds them at the same time as they are trained to be adversaries in the courtroom and in pursuit of their clients' interests. An understanding of

---

38 Phil Gailey, "Have Names, Will Open Right Doors," *New York Times*, January 18, 1982, p. A14.
39 Gailey, "Have Names, Will Open Right Doors," p. A14.
40 Marjorie Hunter, "Lobbying Is Her Life," *New York Times*, December 9, 1981, p. A26.
41 Hunter, "Lobbying Is Her Life," p. A26.

the language of the law is an invaluable asset in political discourse in and out of Congress. The masters of the art, such as former New York Senator Jacob Javits, who had an unusually acute understanding of legal intricacies and constitutional law, are accorded an elevated status by their colleagues, many of whom are lawyers themselves. Typically, a majority of legislators are drawn from the legal profession.[42] An even higher percentage of top congressional staffers are lawyers, including all the chief counsels and most of the staff directors of the multitude of committees that control the legislative process.

Lawyers as Advocates

Prestigious law firms, such as Arnold, Porter, and Fortas; Covington and Burling; and the firms of Clark Clifford, Joseph Califano, and many other illustrious Washington figures, dot the landscape of the city. Reflecting more emphasis on the executive than on the legislative branch, the firms are clustered in the downtown area, particularly around Lafayette Square across from the White House. Corporate America hires Washington lawyers primarily to fight their causes before administrative agencies, whose procedures have become highly judicialized over the years. Legal expertise is essential to effective representation before such regulatory agencies as the Securities and Exchange Commission (SEC), the National Labor Relations Board (NLRB), the Federal Communications Commission (FCC), the Environmental Protection Agency (EPA), and a host of other regulatory agencies.

The technical skills of lawyers are indispensable to effective advocacy before administrative agencies, but the political influence, knowledge, and skills of old-time Washington lawyers, many of whom have served in Congress or the executive branch, are invaluable to those seeking access to Capitol Hill.

CONGRESSIONAL ENVIRONMENT. Although Congress is, of course, a legislative body, many of its procedures have been molded and continue to be practiced by its lawyer-members and staffers. The atmosphere of congressional hearings often resembles court proceedings, as witnesses are called to testify, often accompanied by counsel, and

[42] In the 98th Congress (1982–1984), 200 members of the House and 61 senators were lawyers.

are cross-examined from the "bench" or dais by members and their counsel. As in a court, a stenographic record is kept of the proceedings. Witnesses are accorded many of the same rights they would have in court proceedings, such as protection against self-incrimination where the hearing is investigative or quasi-criminal, and the right to counsel. The physical presence of congressional hearings also resembles the courts, for the hearing rooms generally have the same dark paneling, and are arranged so that the witnesses, with spectators to their backs, face a raised podium upon which there is a circular bench behind which the members and their aides sit. It is no surprise that witnesses before committees often want to be accompanied by counsel, for the atmosphere that is intimidating to the layman is one in which a practiced attorney is comfortable.

The Superlawyers

The influence of Washington's "superlawyers," such as Clark Clifford was for many years, is often so great that their mere presence in a hearing room gives their witness-client a protective shield against hostile committee action.

THE SELF-MADE ARISTOCRAT: CLARK CLIFFORD. Clifford, a Washington University Law School graduate, was a successful St. Louis trial attorney before he became White House Counsel during the Truman administration. He became a close adviser to the president, representing the White House in its dealings with the Congress, the bureaucracy, and the power brokers of the Washington political establishment. In these positions Clifford began a career that made him a Washington legend with a reputation for power almost unparalleled in the city. Presidents John F. Kennedy and Lyndon B. Johnson called upon Clifford when they needed advice on particularly difficult political problems. Clifford, like all the city's superlawyers, knew not only the technical intricacies of the law, but even more important, the avenues of influence in the capital. Even before the Kennedy administration he had become the prototypical Washington establishment lawyer which, ipso facto, gave him directly and his clients indirectly deep respect in Congress and throughout the government.

On one occasion, when President Jimmy Carter's Budget Director, Bert Lance, found himself under congressional attack because of questionable financial dealings, he retained Clifford to advise him when he was called before the Senate Governmental Affairs Committee. Clifford, impeccably tailored in a custom three-piece suit, with a precisely folded three-point silk handkerchief protruding from his jacket pocket, mostly sat silently beside Lance, as a symbol of the political establishment. Clifford's presence did not prevent close questioning of the budget director, but it did help to prevent any direct committee action against him. It was one of the few times the Carter administration called upon Clifford, the consummate Washington insider. Had the Georgians sought and heeded his advice earlier, their understanding of and access to power would have been greatly enhanced.

THE LAWYER-POL: TOMMY THE CORK. Clark Clifford's Washington style, although entirely his own, was a smoother version of the style practiced by one of the capital's most famous lawyers, Thomas Corcoran, in the 1940s and 1950s. "Tommy the Cork," President Franklin D. Roosevelt's nickname for him, became a Washington legend. A member of FDR's inner circle, he cultivated a reputation for power that launched a successful career ending only with his death in 1980. Thomas Corcoran, wrote Joseph Goulden,

> is the prototype of a legend most Washington lawyers wish they could expunge from the public's conception of government. He is a lawyer who does not practice law — although of course his firm is equipped to do conventional legal work. He is an insider who has said publicly that his utility to a client derives from his ability to find out things a few hours earlier than other people. He is a man who has dealt with the federal government for more than thirty years on public policy issues, yet has left a minimal public trace. The back room, not the courtroom or hearing room, is Tommy Corcoran's haunt.[43]

Corcoran's style was apparently as effective in convincing clients of his power on Capitol Hill as in other quarters of the government. A former staffer who worked for three United States senators "remembers occasions when Corcoran came around to talk to his boss about campaign contributions. That is what he *thinks*, at least, and was told by at least one of the senators. Anything Corcoran had to say on the

[43] Joseph C. Goulden, *The Superlawyers* (New York: Weybright and Talley, 1972), p. 145.

subject was for the senator's ears only." [44] Another aide commented, "Tommy doesn't like to mess around with staff people. He'll wait an extra day or two, if it's necessary, to go directly to the senator. It's part of his mystique, and I used to get the idea he wasn't keen about letting too many people know exactly what he was doing." [45]

The Cliffords and Corcorans of the legal profession, the superlawyers, are rare and unusually effective in guiding their clients through the maze of Washington politics. In the city of power, clients seek those with a reputation for power to represent them.

THE MODERN PRACTITIONER: THOMAS HALE BOGGS, JR. The world of the Washington superlawyer continues, combining behind-the-scenes influence, in which personal relationships and skillful manipulations of the incentives of politicians often determine outcomes, with new strategies for dealing with the broader and more complex system of power relationships on Capitol Hill. Thomas Hale Boggs, Jr., whose elegantly furnished office overlooks fashionable Georgetown with a view of the National Cathedral in the background, is one of Washington's new superlawyers. Starting his career, Boggs had a great deal of credibility because of his family. His father, the late Hale Boggs of Louisiana, had served twenty-eight years in the House and became Majority Leader a year before he died in a plane crash in Alaska along with freshman Democrat Nick Begich, for whom Boggs was campaigning. Corinne Clayborne Boggs, widow of the Majority Leader, won a special election for his seat in 1973 with 81 percent of the vote. Thomas Boggs, Jr., was unable to transfer the family's electoral appeal to Maryland, where he ran unsuccessfully for Congress in 1970.

Boggs embarked upon his successful legal career in the capital soon after his defeat for Congress. Within a decade he had become more powerful in the broader political world of Washington, and perhaps as influential in Congress, as he would have been had he won the 1970 election. Boggs feels that the Washington law firms of the 1980s have to adopt new approaches to the exercise of influence in Congress because of the increasing dispersion and even bureaucratization of the legislative process.

> Not only has government grown, but power has been dispersed. Instead of ten committee chairmen, you now have

[44] Goulden, *Superlawyers*, p. 147.
[45] Goulden, p. 148.

seventy people running the House and a hundred people running the Senate. In the past, a lobbyist needed to know only about ten people on the House side. He could call the Speaker of the House or Sherman Adams [President Eisenhower's Special Assistant] at the White House and say, "Help me." All that has changed as power has dispersed. Now you need a law firm to act as quarterback because the firm knows how to use the whole system. With our computers, our firm has access to more information more quickly than people working in Congress.[46]

ORGANIZATIONAL LOBBYING

Organizations as well as individual lobbyists influence Congress differently. Business groups, trade associations, think tanks, labor unions, farm organizations, professional groups, the elderly, and the persistent advocates of special causes, such as the National Rifle Association, are a permanent part of the lobbying establishment. In addition, a host of ad hoc lobbying groups that represent special but more transitory demands periodically arise to press their views upon legislators.

Permanent Lobbying Establishment

Only the permanent lobbying organizations are part of the political establishment. Unlike the ad hoc groups, who visit Washington once a year to march up Pennsylvania Avenue to present their demands to legislators, the permanent lobbying organizations operate out of permanent headquarters with large staffs that supply expert advice and constant opinion to committee chairmen, staffs, and party leaders on Capitol Hill. The occasional and often dramatic marches on Washington, conducted mostly by the ad hoc groups but occasionally by the permanent interests as well, may get on the evening news, but in the end legislators are more influenced by the continuing and generally behind-the-scenes lobbying efforts of the interests of long standing that have made their home in the capital.

GROUP LOBBYING STYLES. The lobbying groups that reside in Washington attempt to cement relationships with Congress that will give

---

[46] Philip Shabecoff, "Big Business on the Offensive," *New York Times Magazine,* December 9, 1979, p. 146.

them enduring influence over public policy. They seek to become critical links in the iron triangles that are formed when congressional committees, administrative agencies, and private interests work together for their mutual benefit. The AFL-CIO and the Farm Bureau Federation, for example, have worked closely with the labor and agriculture committees on Capitol Hill, as well as with the Departments of Labor and Agriculture. A permanent Washington agricultural establishment consisting of committees, the Department of Agriculture, and agricultural pressure groups, dates to the late nineteenth century, when the Department of Agriculture was established. A labor iron triangle began early in the twentieth century with creation of the Department of Labor, which paralleled the establishment of labor committees in Congress.

TIES TO CONGRESSIONAL COMMITTEES. Committee representation is essential to effective interest-group power. Committees are the lifeblood of the legislative process, and groups whose interests are under the jurisdiction of special committees often find that they are under a protective legislative cloak. Many of the committees of Congress were created in the first place because of pressure from interests for Washington representation. The early importance of agricultural interests, for example, led to establishment of a House Agriculture Committee in 1820, followed by a corresponding committee in the Senate in 1825. The education and labor interests surfacing in the 1860s led to establishment of the House and Senate education and labor committees in 1867. Committee representation expanded as private groups focused more and more upon Washington. In the House, Merchant Marine and Fisheries (1887), Select Small Business (1942), and Science and Astronautics (1958) Committees responded to the needs of special interests. The establishment of committees often paralleled congressional creation of departments and agencies in the executive branch. The political linkage between committees and agencies provided the basis for the iron triangles of Washington.

Private groups fight to preserve "their" committees on Capitol Hill against occasional efforts to eliminate or reorganize them. Committee chairmen and their staffs, who also have strongly vested interests in preserving the status quo, know that they can count on the groups under their jurisdiction to battle against any efforts to diminish committee power.

For example, in the 1970s the House leadership and Missouri Congressman Richard Bolling (D), who aspired to be part of that leadership, pushed for the reform and reorganization of a committee structure that they considered to be an impediment to its power. Committee chairmen, however, some of whom would lose their posts under the Bolling plan, fought hard to retain the status quo, mobilizing groups outside of Congress to support them.[47]

The Merchant Marine and Fisheries Committee was one of Bolling's targets. The committee was one of the most notorious in the House for being captive of the industry under its jurisdiction, which for years had given large campaign contributions to committee members. The combative chairwoman of the committee, Lenore Sullivan of Missouri, who had just taken over the chairmanship post, joined with twenty-one staffers to work diligently for the committee's preservation. The staff contacted industry lobbyists and the Federal Maritime Commission to marshal support. The Bolling Committee received 175 letters and telegrams in support of the Merchant Marine and Fisheries Committee, along with a unanimous resolution passed by the Federal Maritime Commission advocating continuation of the panel. Congresswoman Sullivan and her staff won the battle, not only against their committee's extinction, but also against reduction of its jurisdiction over wildlife, fisheries, and marine affairs. Other committees, too, such as Small Business, successfully fought attempts to eliminate them or reduce their power.

Proposals for committee reorganization in the Senate, spearheaded by Adlai Stevenson (D) of Illinois and Charles Mathias (R) of Maryland and culminating in 1977, met a fate similar to that of the Bolling plan in the House.[48] Again, not only were powerful chairmen opposed to invasions of their turf, but outside interests were mobilized to support the existing committees. The original Stevenson plan called for eliminating several panels that had powerful interest-group support, such as the Indian Affairs and Veterans' Affairs Committees, the Small Business Committee, the Committee on Aging, and the Joint Economic Committee. As the Senate was about to take up the re-

---

[47] Roger H. Davidson and Walter J. Oleszek tell the story of the Bolling committee reforms and their fate in *Congress Against Itself* (Bloomington: Indiana University Press, 1977).

[48] See Roger H. Davidson, "Two Avenues of Change: House and Senate Committee Reorganization," in Lawrence C. Dodd and Bruce I. Oppenheimer, eds., *Congress Reconsidered*, 2nd ed. (Washington, D.C.: Congressional Quarterly Press, 1981), pp. 116–117.

organization resolution (Senate Resolution 4) in January 1977, it was deluged with complaints from the American Legion protesting against the proposed elimination of the Veterans' Affairs Committee, and from the National Small Business Association advocating continuation of the Senate Small Business Committee. Joint Economic Committee Chairman Hubert Humphrey (D, Minn.) introduced letters from labor and business interests alike in support of his committee when he testified before the Senate Rules Committee on the reorganization proposals. Special-interest groups also appeared before the Rules Committee to support "their" committees.

An interest group of growing importance in Washington is the elderly, represented by a variety of groups. Both the House and the Senate have Special Committees on Aging. When confronted with the Stevenson proposal to abolish the Senate Committee on Aging, its staff immediately mobilized the support of many interest groups that represented senior citizens. The staff solicited "seniorgrams" and letters from senior-citizens' groups, state agencies on aging, and gerontological experts on behalf of their research and oversight efforts. Hundreds of telegrams and letters bombarded senators supporting continuation of the Committee on Aging. The campaign worked, for the staff secured fifty Senate cosponsors for an amendment to reinstate the committee. Idaho Democrat Frank Church, the committee's chairman, commented on the Stevenson proposal, "I do question the denial of 23 million senior citizens the same consideration which we are extending to veterans, native Americans, and small business." The committee, said Church, was a "home for the elderly in the Senate." Not surprisingly, the Senate restored the committee by the overwhelming vote of 90 to 4. The vote guaranteed continuation of direct representation for the elderly in the Senate.

Just as the Committee on Aging was saved by politically skillful staff work in marshaling the support of its outside constituency, and by the strong opposition of its chairman, the Veterans', Small Business, and Indian Affairs Committees were reinstated for the same reasons. When the extension on the life of the Indian Affairs Committee again came before the Rules Committee in 1978, Indian groups testified that abolition of their committee would deny them the same representation in Congress that was accorded to other interests. Rules Committee Chairman Howard Cannon (D, Nev.) threatened to filibuster the proposal to extend the committee, but even his delaying tactics failed to prevent its continuation. Maine Republican William Cohen chaired the Select Indian Affairs Committee in the 97th Congress, and Barry Goldwater, who had defended the panel, was the second-ranking majority member.

All but a few private interests in Washington have direct representation in one or more of the hundreds of committees on Capitol Hill. Special committees represent interests in energy, defense, labor, agriculture, health, science, the environment, consumer affairs, transportation, the elderly, minorities, women, and veterans. At one time, fifty-six committees had jurisdiction over energy. Committee reorganization reduced the number of committees representing energy interests to a handful, including the House interior and Senate energy committees.

Boosting credibility. Organizational lobbying does not stop after the infrastructure of committee representation has been created. Organizations, like individuals, seek to boost their power and credibility. Groups that have committees and agencies to represent them are considered to be members of the political establishment, with legitimate interests that may be pressed upon legislators and administrators.

New lobbying organizations, seeking a foothold on the ladder of power, establish credibility by respecting the norms and rules of the Washington political game. They must, above all, know how the game is played. The Ralph Nader organizations, for example, although strongly disliked in many quarters of Congress, were able to capitalize on the consumer movement of the 1960s to move Congress in the direction of tightening consumer-protection laws. Nader, a lawyer, hired fresh law school graduates and trained them in the often arcane ways of Washington politics. A Ralph Nader Congress project report highlighted some of the ways in which consumer-oriented groups and individuals might exert influence.[49] The report stressed that although congressmen are, of course, interested in votes, and nationwide organizations can be effective in grass-roots lobbying, Congress is frequently moved by considerations that go far beyond the electoral connection. Above all, the personal and individualistic character of Congress, the fact that personal and not electoral incentives often determine outcomes, was emphasized. Citizens' groups were advised to establish Washington offices, and to staff them with persons

[49] See Mark J. Green et al., *Who Runs Congress?* (New York: Bantam, 1972), pp. 246–286.

who understood the distribution of committee power and knew the personal motives of members. The Nader group concluded, "A serious lobbying organization working on a legislative effort begins with an analysis of the legislative forum in which it must do combat. Who are the key players? What role will they play? What committee or subcommittee will consider the legislation? Who chairs it? Who are the important staff members? Are there legislative assistants on the staffs of congressmen who have shown an interest in similar issues in the past?" [50]

Private Individuals as Lobbyists

The Nader team pointed out that understanding not only the infrastructure but also the personalities of Capitol Hill is a key to successful lobbying, which may be carried out by individuals as well as organizations. The report told the story of Abe Bergman, a young Seattle pediatrician, who became outraged when he saw case after case of severely burned and scarred children, the victims of inflammable fabrics, household poisons, and other unsafe products. He set out, some would say naively, on a journey to Washington to influence Congress to tighten its regulations over potentially dangerous consumer products. Fortunately for Dr. Bergman, he found that his senator, Warren Magnuson, had developed a Capitol Hill reputation as a strong advocate of consumer interests. Not only was Magnuson personally sympathetic to the cause, but in his position as chairman of the powerful Commerce Committee, he could do something about it. With the help of an astute committee staff, Magnuson skillfully maneuvered amendments to the Flammable Fabrics Act through his committee and to passage on the floor. The efforts of a powerful senator and his aides, helped by poignant testimony by Bergman, overcame the opposition of the Textile Manufacturers' Trade Association, which had promised that if the "punitive legislation" passed, "blood would run in the halls of Congress." [51]

Bergman continued his close relationship with Magnuson, and became the senator's unofficial adviser on the safety of consumer products, ranging from hazardous lawnmowers to poisonous drain cleaners. Eric Redman, a Magnuson staffer who described Bergman's role

[50] Green, *Who Runs Congress?*, p. 263.
[51] Green, p. 247.

in planning a National Health Service Corps, wrote that when Magnuson became chairman of the Senate Appropriations Subcommittee for the Health, Education, and Welfare Department,

> Bergman had visionary (some would say unrealistic) dreams about what Magnuson could accomplish through his new hold on the pursestrings of HEW. He organized for Magnuson a loose-end unofficial consortium of "health advisors," floating legislative proposals to them by mail and occasionally convening the group in Washington, D.C., for special "skull sessions." To the amusement and sometimes the ire of the Subcommittee staff, Bergman flew to Washington repeatedly to "help" in preparing the HEW appropriation bill, to lobby for worthwhile programs, and to "carve out a role" (as he put it) for Magnuson in health affairs. When asked why Dr. Bergman spent so much time in Washington instead of at his hospital back home, the Senator's staff had a standard reply: "It's simple — he can't stand the sight of blood." [52]

Ingredients of Success

Whether lobbying is carried out by organizations or individuals, Congress respects expertise, dedication, persistence, and, above all, an appreciation of legislative norms and the goals of members beyond reelection, for power and recognition within Congress, and for good public policy. For their part, lobbyists want to be considered as adjuncts, not as outsiders, in the legislative process.

BUSINESS ROUNDTABLE. An example of a relatively new and highly effective part of the capital's lobbying establishment is the Business Roundtable. Created in 1974, it rapidly became the leading spokesman for the business elite, approximately 200 of the most powerful corporations, including General Motors, IBM, AT&T, General Electric, DuPont, and Exxon. The Business Roundtable's credibility is greatly enhanced because, instead of relying upon hired hands to influence Congress, it is composed of the chief executive officers (CEOs) and sometimes the chairmen of the boards of the corporations, who quietly make their views known to key legislators. The Roundtable does not influence Congress by raising campaign funds,

[52] Eric Redman, *The Dance of Legislation* (New York: Simon and Schuster, 1973), pp. 28–29.

although the corporations represented by the group have their individual PACs. The CEOs of the Roundtable may occasionally mobilize stockholders, suppliers, and employees to pressure government decision makers, but usually the mere presence of the highest-ranking corporate officers in America is sufficient to impress those who count in government.

Philip Shabecoff of the *New York Times*, in a study of the Roundtable's lobbying, wrote that the group's most effective resources in influencing policy

> are the chief executives themselves. They are able to command respectful attention when they testify in Congress; they are invited to the White House (among those who have been to see the President [Reagan] are [Thomas] Murphy [Chairman of General Motors Corporation], Irving S. Shapiro, Chairman of E. I. DuPont de Nemours and Co.; Reginald H. Jones, Chairman of the General Electric Co., and Clifton C. Garvin, Jr., Chairman of the Exxon Corp.); they attract media attention. Moreover, the chief executive officers are in a position to arouse armies of suppliers, stockholders, and even customers to put pressure on government policy-makers.[53]

The Business Roundtable has been quietly effective on Capitol Hill. Mark Green, director of the Nader-sponsored Public Citizen Congress Watch, refers to the Roundtable as "The most powerful secret lobby in Washington." [54] Although unknown to the general public, the Roundtable is anything but secret in Washington. Its credibility is such that members of Congress often feel it is a distinct honor to be asked to address the group. The Business Roundtable does not have its captive committees that represent the more traditional pressure groups of long standing in the lobbying establishment. But the Roundtable knows which of the powerful members of Congress are sympathetic to its cause, and has carefully cultivated their support.

GRASS-ROOTS LOBBYING

Interest groups attempt to influence Congress in a major way by lobbying at the grass roots, striving to mold public opinion and encour-

---

[53] Philip Shabecoff, "Big Business on the Offensive," *New York Times Magazine*, December 9, 1979, p. 141.
[54] Shabecoff, "Big Business on the Offensive," p. 138.

aging voters to write to their congressmen in support of the positions advocated by the lobbying groups. A survey of 123 congressional staffers in 1981 by the public-relations firm of Burson-Marsteller revealed that legislators are influenced more by communications from their constituents than from other sources. Interest-group leaders recognize the importance of letters, telegrams, and telephone calls from constituents to their Capitol Hill representatives and have increasingly emphasized the importance of cultivating grass-roots opinion in their favor.

An independent Washington lobbyist emphasized the importance of cultivating grass-roots opinion: "If you bring fifty people to Washington, or generate 500 letters or 400 phone calls on an issue, even though the member has half a million people in his district and not very many of them care about the issue, the member responds as if it's the end of the world." [55]

Political scientist Norman J. Ornstein has found that most congressmen do not want to take chances on alienating even a small segment of their constituencies on the assumption that even small groups of voters may make a difference in close elections. Viewing the outside world from Capitol Hill, comments Ornstein, "Even if you know a lobbying campaign is manipulating public opinion and the public opinion really isn't there, you may be inclined to go along anyway." [56] Freshmen members of Congress are particularly prone to be overly sensitive to constituents' communications.

There are varying techniques of grass-roots lobbying. When the Reagan administration and Congress contemplated placing restrictions on interest payments by the rapidly expanding money funds, the financial institutions running the funds embarked upon a nationwide grass-roots lobbying campaign to encourage depositors to contact their congressmen to oppose government regulation. Suddenly hundreds of letters weekly began to pour into congressional offices, taking members and aides by surprise; many of them were unaware of the Reagan proposals or the restrictive legislation before the banking committees. The recommendations to curb money-market funds were buried within weeks after the start of the grass-roots lobbying campaign. As Richard Viguerie, the Falls Church, Virginia conservative who is the mastermind of many mass-mailing campaigns stated, "If

[55] *Congressional Quarterly Weekly Report*, vol. 39, no. 37 (September 12, 1981), p. 1740.
[56] Ibid.

an official tells you he got 40,000 pieces of mail from his district on a particular issue and he's going to ignore them, you know one of two things. He's lying to you, or he's not going to be around very long." [57]

The passage of President Reagan's budget proposals at the outset of his first term was not only the consequence of the president's extraordinary skills as a communicator and politician, talents that helped him to win over congressmen and constituents alike, but also the result of grass-roots lobbying by many interest groups in favor of the Reagan economic package. The securities industry, for example, encouraged investors throughout the nation to contact their representatives to support the president's tax plan, which they expected to be highly beneficial to stockholders and traders. Many businesses joined the Republican Party in mounting phone and letter campaigns on behalf of the president's economic proposals. In some cases employers encouraged their workers to use company telephones on company time to call members of Congress. House Speaker Tip O'Neill, Jr., referred in a floor speech before a vote on the president's tax program to "Phillip Morris, Paine Webber, Monsanto Chemical, Exxon, McDonnell Douglas, who were so kind as to allow the use of their staffs to the President of the United States in flooding the switchboards of America." [58] O'Neill's press aide told reporters about a call the Speaker received from a woman stockbroker who complained that her employer had told the firm's employees to phone their congressmen. "She said she didn't believe in it," said the aide, "but she felt she had to do it for her job. She felt there was a measure of coercion." [59]

Firms specializing in grass-roots lobbying have expanded to meet the growing market for their services. The North American Précis Service, for example, tells clients that it can "generate tons of letters to legislators" by placing ads and editorials expressing clients' views in newspapers, and on radio and television programs. The firm writes editorial features subtly expressing the views of its clients that are broadcast under such titles as, "Washington Wants to Know," and "Capitol Ideas." [60] "Our IBM 5120 computer," states a North American brochure, "will address your material to the editors who are most likely to print it." [61] The clients of the North American Grass Roots

[57] Ibid.
[58] Ibid., p. 1741.
[59] Ibid.
[60] Ibid.
[61] Ibid.

Service include 600 corporations, 90 trade associations, and the ten largest public-relations firms.

Harley Dirks, a former Senate aide and hero to aficionados of staff power, turned his talents to grass-roots lobbying when he resigned his Senate position, after fabricating committee hearings, including a list of witnesses and their testimony. Apparently Dirks felt that he knew congressional politics so well he could make his fiction a reality! Dirks had been a top staffer on the Senate Appropriations Committee, a perch that at once used and challenged his highly honed political skills and increased his already considerable knowledge of the way in which power was exercised behind the scenes. Many former members of Congress and staffers become lobbyists, and Dirks was no exception. His firm trained clients, particularly medical groups, to keep open the lines of communication with Congress. Letter writing, arranging congressional visits to medical facilities, using media to exert political pressure, and teaching doctors how to encourage clients to take their side in writing letters to lawmakers, are all part of Dirks's activities as a political consultant. Using his insider's knowledge of Capitol Hill, Dirks also coaches clients on how to testify effectively before congressional committees to present themselves in the best possible light not only before committee members, but to state their position concisely and persuasively for the public record.[62]

Although grass-roots lobbying usually focuses upon Capitol Hill, sometimes political consultants advise their clients to pressure the district offices of their representatives. The district office is an integral part of the members' campaign organization and he or she pays close attention to apparent groundswells of sentiment that may be channeled to district staffers. Congressmen periodically visit their district offices and are available to meet constituents who find it far easier to travel the short distance to the office than to go to Washington.

The increasing sophistication of techniques used in cultivating and transmitting back-home sentiment to members of Congress has strengthened the electoral connection between legislators and constituents. Perhaps more important, interest-group power, particularly the influence of groups with large memberships or constituencies themselves, has been strengthened.

The flow of communications between constituents and their representatives is not all one-way. Just as interest groups gear up their com-

62 Ibid., pp. 1741–1742.

puters to direct letter-writing and phone campaigns to Capitol Hill, members of Congress use their own computer system to record the names and addresses of those who contact them so that they may be placed on the mailing list for congressional newsletters and other electoral propaganda in favor of incumbent legislators.

Imperfect Mobilization of Political Interests

The law of the imperfect mobilization of political interests, devised by political scientist E. E. Schattschneider, affects the ability of interest groups to influence voters at the grass-roots level of politics. Simply stated, the "law" is that each individual voter is a member of more than one group, often having identifications with widely varied interests.[63] The multiple group membership of voters makes it impossible for any one interest group to mobilize completely the votes of its members behind all the stands supported by the group leaders. For example, the American Medical Association's persistent attack upon socialized medicine and an expanded government role in health insurance might not appeal to doctors working in veterans' hospitals or in medical clinics. Veterans' organizations, led by the Veterans' Administration, have taken a strong stand in support of veterans' hospitals, but the AMA's position against government medicine supports the closing of as many "unnecessary" government medical facilities as is feasible. While the veterans' organizations mobilize their members and employees to support the type of socialized medicine practiced by veterans' hospitals, the AMA attempts to persuade its members that private medicine is the keystone of our constitutional freedoms.

There are many examples of overlapping group memberships that dilute the ability of any one group to sway voters. Catholic or fundamentalist Christian doctors, for example, find themselves torn between the political stands taken by their churches and the leaders of such groups as the Moral Majority, and their orientation as doctors to use their specialized knowledge in the interest of patients. Labor-union members may identify with many interests that advocate political positions contrary to those of union leaders. In the 1984 elections a majority of blue-collar workers voted for Reagan, and did not follow the lead of the AFL-CIO by supporting Mondale.

---

[63] Schattschneider's law was stated in his now out-of-print work, *Party Government* (New York: Holt, Rinehart and Winston, 1942).

SINGLE-ISSUE POLITICS. Interest groups are increasingly attempting to influence congressional campaigns by focusing upon single issues, such as abortion, gun control, the Equal Rights Amendment, and particular economic and tax policies. Contributions are given only to candidates who take a clear position on the one issue, and the group's members are exhorted to vote only for legislators supporting the issue. In the 1980 congressional elections, anti-abortion groups were able to mobilize at least a strong minority of voters against targeted candidates, such as Iowa Senator John C. Culver. Anti-abortion votes were a factor, although probably not a deciding one, in former Republican Representative Charles E. Grassley's defeat of Culver by an 8 percent margin. In the 1978 Iowa senatorial election, however, the anti-abortion campaign against Democrat Dick Clark could very well have been the reason for his defeat at the hands of Republican Roger W. Jepsen by only 2 percent of the vote.

Single-issue groups, such as the National Rifle Association, tend to attract singleminded voters who are less subject to conflicting identifications with other interests when it comes to supporting congresssonal candidates. The leaders of single-issue groups know that their followers are zealots. There is little doubt that single-issue politics is becoming more important in congressional elections. The growing significance of single-issue politics reflects a change toward greater fragmentation of the political process. As single-issue groups increase in power, political compromise becomes more difficult, and counterbalancing power among groups is less likely to act as a check.

CONCLUSION: DOES LOBBYING MAKE A DIFFERENCE?

A humorous but biting indictment that has become part of American folklore is Will Rogers's well-known adage, "The United States Congress is the best that money can buy." That the well-financed interest groups control Congress, not only with effective lobbying in Washington, but even more important, by trading campaign contributions for political support, is the common assumption. "Hired guns without principles or values," is the public image of most lobbyists.[64] Corporate lobbyists have formed the American League of Lobbyists (ALL)

[64] Gregg Esterbrook, "They don't get no respect," *Common Cause* (December 1981), p. 22.

to improve their image. Though many lobbyists and interest groups are respected members of Washington's political establishment, in which politics is recognized as a contact sport involving compromises and trade-offs of all kinds, beyond the limits of what President Reagan refers to as the Emerald City, the public applauds Will Rogers's description of Congress and remains suspicious of the secret deals it believes are constantly consummated between politicians and pressure groups.

Sensational media coverage of lobbying activities buttresses the depiction of lobbyists as behind-the-scenes operators who control puppet legislators. Moreover, the self-annointed public-interest groups, such as Common Cause, continually draw sharp contrasts between the selfish interests of corporate America and their own noble endeavors. They assume that the public interest is somehow separate from the goals of individual groups. Congress, too, from time to time, enhances the public image of the all-powerful lobbyists when its members call for stricter lobbying disclosure laws. "Day after day armies of lobbyists patrol the corridors of Congress and every federal agency," testified Massachusetts Senator Edward Kennedy before a committee considering lobbying-reform legislation.[65] He continued, "Vast amounts of influence and money are spent in secret ways for secret purposes, and many private interests are rich and powerful, and their secret operations corrupt the public interest." [66] Kennedy concluded, "The time has come to end that undue influence over the executive branch and really over the Congress. And too often we have allowed the voice of the people to be silenced by a special interest group clamoring for favored treatment." [67]

Lobbying does, of course, make a difference. But the difference is very hard to assess, and is probably nowhere near as great as is commonly assumed. Members of Congress do not passively transmit the views of pressure groups into law. First, in many areas of public policy, pressure-group politics is a zero-sum game; that is, for every group that wins there is one that loses. Labor-union lobbyists, for example, are frequently pitted against the Business Roundtable and other corporate interests. Labor has traditionally been one of the strongest

---

[65] U.S. Congress, Senate, Committee on Government Operations, "Lobby Reform Legislation," Hearings, April 22, 1975, p. 8.
[66] Ibid.
[67] Ibid.

lobbies in Washington, especially effective during Democratic administrations. In the long term, however, Congress is no more a pawn of labor than it is of business. Congressional votes may favor contrasting labor and business interests at different times, but votes cannot be simply explained as reflex reactions to outside pressures.

Political scientist John Kingdon concludes, from an extensive study of group pressures upon Congress, that even where legislators know the positions of groups, "the probability that a congressman will vote with that position is . . . only somewhat higher than chance." [68] Members are far more likely to cue their votes to fellow congressmen, or to follow their general perceptions of constituency interests. Where interest groups have some connection with the constituencies of congressmen, they understandably have greater influence upon the member's vote. Congressmen, *when asked*, "tend to dismiss the efforts of Washington-based lobbyists." [69] It is hardly likely, of course, that legislators would admit that they pay close attention to the demands of the capital's lobbyists. But congressional votes are a matter of public record, and the fact that they are not meaningfully connected with *unopposed* interest-group positions suggests that lobbying, although vital to clients and advocates alike, does not have the substantial effect upon public policy that is commonly assumed.

Norman J. Ornstein and Shirley Elder conclude, "Members of Congress . . . rely on groups to provide valuable constituency, technical, or political information, to give reelection support, and to assist strategically in passing or blocking legislation that the members support or oppose. Groups need Congress, and the Congress needs groups." [70] They conclude, "Regardless of the causes, legitimate concerns are being expressed about the fragmenting effects of the contemporary explosion in groups and lobbying." [71] A healthy democratic process, however, cannot deny interest groups their rightful place. As James Madison pointed out long ago in *Federalist* 10, the only alternative to interest-group freedom is intolerable suppression of political expression.

The lobbying game will continue to be played, both in electoral politics and in Washington, regardless of whether or not there are

[68] John W. Kingdon, *Congressmen's Voting Decisions*, 2nd ed. (New York: Harper and Row, 1981), p. 147.
[69] Kingdon, *Congressmen's Voting Decisions*, p. 151.
[70] Ornstein and Elder, *Interest Groups, Lobbying, and Policymaking*, p. 224.
[71] Ornstein and Elder, p. 229.

measurable and provable effects upon public policy. The Washington offices of interest groups keep the channels of information open to Capitol Hill, and although their views may not dictate policy outcomes, it is clearly important for the advancement of their interests that pressure groups take stands on issues that concern them. Through their lobbyists, interest groups are a vital component of the political establishment of Washington, a club whose members exchange ideas and advance positions that indirectly if not directly determine the course of government.

CHAPTER TEN

Congress and Public Policy

Congress is first and foremost a *legislative* body, making laws for the nation and overseeing their implementation. Congressional organization and procedures affect the content and implementation of public policy in many ways. The committee system fragments policy making on Capitol Hill, buttressing congressional responsiveness to special interests that focus their demands upon committees and agencies to form iron triangles of politics in different policy arenas. Many committees represent special interests in areas such as agriculture, small business, banking, education, and labor. Congressional laws specifically respond to interests that are well represented by separate committees.

The way in which committees, political parties, and other Capitol Hill forces come into play in making public policy may depend upon the characteristics of the policy arena. A simple diagram of how a bill becomes a law (see Figure 10.1), is useful as a procedural guide, but does not reveal the contrasting dynamics of policy making in different areas. Committees may be far more important in determining subsidy policies that affect relatively narrow interests than in shaping national policies in areas such as taxation that affect many interests. The chairman of an agricultural subcommittee may almost singlehandedly set subsidies for tobacco, peanuts, or whichever commodity is under his or her committee's jurisdiction; however, income tax policy touches all legislators and their constituents, as well as the president and the political parties. The characteristics of taxation policy affect the way in which Congress deals with it. Party leaders, special caucuses, regional coalitions, and other internal influences join with committees to shape public policies that have far-reaching political and economic consequences.

Figure 10.1

How a Bill Becomes a Law. Committees Play a Dominant Role in the Legislative Process

This graphic shows the most typical way in which proposed legislation is enacted into law. There are more complicated, as well as simpler, routes and most bills fall by the wayside and never become law. The process is illustrated with two hypothetical bills, House bill No. 1 (HR 1) and Senate bill No. 2 (S 2).

Each bill must be passed by both houses of Congress in identical form before it can become law. The path of HR 1 is traced by a solid line, that of S 2 by a broken line. However, in practice most legislation begins as similar proposals in both houses.

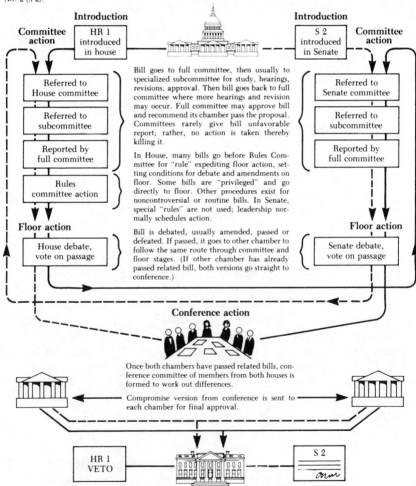

Introduction · HR 1 introduced in house · **Committee action** · Referred to House committee · Referred to subcommittee · Reported by full committee · Rules committee action · **Floor action** · House debate, vote on passage

Bill goes to full committee, then usually to specialized subcommittee for study, hearings, revisions, approval. Then bill goes back to full committee where more hearings and revision may occur. Full committee may approve bill and recommend its chamber pass the proposal. Committees rarely give bill unfavorable report; rather, no action is taken thereby killing it.

In House, many bills go before Rules Committee for "rule" expediting floor action, setting conditions for debate and amendments on floor. Some bills are "privileged" and go directly to floor. Other procedures exist for noncontroversial or routine bills. In Senate, special "rules" are not used; leadership normally schedules action.

Bill is debated, usually amended, passed or defeated. If passed, it goes to other chamber to follow the same route through committee and floor stages. (If other chamber has already passed related bill, both versions go straight to conference.)

Introduction · S 2 introduced in Senate · **Committee action** · Referred to Senate committee · Referred to subcommittee · Reported by full committee · **Floor action** · Senate debate, vote on passage

Conference action

Once both chambers have passed related bills, conference committee of members from both houses is formed to work out differences.

Compromise version from conference is sent to each chamber for final approval.

HR 1 VETO · S 2

Compromise version approved by both houses is sent to President who can either sign it into law or veto it and return it to Congress. Congress may override veto by a two-thirds majority vote in both houses; bill then becomes law without President's signature.

Source: Guide to Congress, November 1976 (Washington, D.C.: Congressional Quarterly, Inc.) p. 345. By permission.

NATURE OF PUBLIC POLICY

Law making, an exclusive congressional function under the Constitution, is the first step but not the last in the formulation of public policy. Laws set standards that bind the community as a whole or a class of persons within it. For example, tax laws apply to the community as a whole, but also to separate classes of persons for different treatment depending upon their income and other circumstances.

Although congressional laws broadly or specifically set public policy, the executive branch and the courts too are involved in the policy process. Administrative departments and agencies, acting under statutory authority, often fill in the details of legislation through rule making and through administrative adjudication as well.[1] The courts, too, may affect congressional policy making, not only through their power to overturn congressional laws that are not in accordance with the Constitution, but more often through their continuous involvement in statutory interpretation when cases involving the legal rights of individuals and groups come before them.

Types of Policies and Arenas of Politics

The politics of congressional policy making is not the same for all types of policies. We have discussed the broad characteristics of redistributive, distributive, and regulatory policies.[2] Additional categories are foreign, defense, and crisis policies.[3]

Even a brief, impressionistic look at Congress highlights the different ways in which institutional and political forces come into play in these contrasting policy spheres. The president more than Congress sets the foreign-policy agenda, makes treaties, and manages crises. On Capitol Hill the Senate Foreign Relations Committee is principally involved in reviewing foreign policy, but its role is more that of a consultant than an initiator of policy. Congress tends to be more passive in foreign policy making than in other policy spheres, but it does from time to time attempt to assert its authority. An example is the War Powers Resolution of 1973, requiring that Congress approve of a presidential commitment of troops in foreign hostilities after sixty

[1] See pages 303–305.
[2] See pages 306–309.
[3] See Randall B. Ripley, *Congress: Process and Policy*, 3rd ed. (New York: W. W. Norton, 1983), pp. 397–400.

days. Congress has also passed many laws that give it veto power over presidential decisions to sell arms abroad. The Supreme Court, however, declared the legislative veto unconstitutional in 1983, which will presumably void many of these congressional restrictions upon presidential power.

In contrast to foreign policy and crisis management, Congress is active in domestic policy making. Redistributive policies, such as progressive taxation, because of their wide political effects, engage all members. Congressional parties take positions on redistributive issues, and though the relevant committees may exercise an important leadership role in shaping the outcomes, they must actively forge a consensus of members before legislation can be passed. Redistributive policies also activate broad political forces outside of Congress, and engage the president as well, who may take the lead in attempting to shape what Congress does.

The politics of public policy narrows in the *distributive* sphere, where individual committees and members, acting in consultation with special interests and administrative agencies, often unilaterally determine what policies will be enacted. Traditionally the iron triangles of politics have controlled the content of distributive policies. Periodically presidents have attempted to break the control these triangles have over distributive policies, but over the long run the White House has had to retreat before fierce Capitol Hill opposition to cuts in pet subsidy programs.

Finally, *regulatory* policies produce yet another breed of Capitol Hill politics. Fairly broad political forces are initially involved in the passage of regulatory statutes, making this sphere somewhat akin to the redistributive arena. Regulatory policies, like redistributive policies, take away benefits from some groups and give them to others. *Conflicting* groups fight with each other for favorable government treatment, pressuring the president and political parties to take a stand. Macropolitical forces, then, shape regulatory statutes, which may be quite specific, as with the Interstate Commerce Act of 1887 regulating railroads, or quite vague, like many New Deal laws regulating labor relations, communications, securities transactions and exchanges, airlines, and truckers.

Once the initial impetus behind regulatory statutes wanes, usually because the groups that wanted regulation are satisfied with the result of government action, regulatory politics narrows as congressional committees and regulatory agencies take center stage along with the *regulated* groups. The macropolitics that produced passage of the regulatory legislation in the first place becomes micropolitics as the regulated groups seek protection for their interests, which no longer particularly concern the president, party leaders, and beneficiary groups such as consumers or farmers, who have long since departed from the political battleground, feeling that they have won the war. Political iron triangles come into play at this stage, making regulatory politics similar to distributive politics as congressional committees and administrative agencies act together for the benefit of special interests and for their own political support.[4]

EXAMPLES OF CONGRESSIONAL POLICY MAKING

Beginning with the domestic sphere, a few examples readily illustrate the different congressional approaches to redistributive, distributive, and regulatory policies.

Redistributive Policy: Taxes, Taxes, Taxes

Not only are all citizens profoundly affected by the tax policies of the federal government, but they *know* it. They are painfully aware of their tax burdens. Even more sensitive to taxes are special interests. They crowd the offices, lobbies, and corridors of Capitol Hill to plead their causes, to preserve special benefits for themselves.

The president, the departments and agencies of government, congressional leaders, and committee chairmen all become deeply involved in shaping and reshaping tax policies. Political-party platforms address tax issues, reflecting a wide range of intraparty interests. Sometimes, as in the 1980 Republican platform, tax policy takes center stage. Ronald Reagan ran on a platform promising tax cuts for all, both for individuals and businesses. Also promised were sharp cuts in spending for federal programs.

The macropolitical character of tax policies, the *broad* forces involved, affect the way in which Congress treats tax programs.[5] The president more than Congress may set the agenda. Congressional

---

[4] A classic depiction of the way in which an administrative agency became the captive of the groups it regulated is Samuel P. Huntington, "The Marasmus of the ICC," *Yale Law Journal*, vol. 61, no. 4 (1952), pp. 467–509.

[5] Not all tax policy is macropolitical. Tax relief that in effect subsidizes narrow interests does not always raise broad political conflict. Under such circumstances, the political character of tax policy becomes distributive. Even narrow tax subsidies, however, such as the oil depletion allowance that encouraged oil exploration, may become general political issues.

party leaders take a stand, encouraging their troops to vote along party lines. Institutional committees, such as the Ways and Means and Budget Committees in the House, work closely with the leadership to forge a majority consensus. The administration carefully prepares its position in testimony before Congress, as the more parochial interests of the executive departments and agencies are pushed to the background. The tax-writing committees hear and must take into account many rather than a few interests.

Redistributive Policy: A Case Study

A highly instructive example of the way in which Congress develops and responds to tax policies is the passage of the Economic Recovery Tax Act of 1981, keystone of Reagan's tax program.

THE PRESIDENT'S ROLE. The Reagan tax program was based upon "supply-side" economics. The supply-siders theorized that increasing consumer demand for products and services by lowering the tax rate would lead to economic prosperity. The theory differed from Keynesian economics in its insistence that the consumer was the key to prosperity, rather than increased government spending, which the Keynesians believed was necessary to prevent recessions.

Two Capitol Hill Republicans, Delaware's Senator William Roth, Jr., and New York Representative Jack Kemp, originally proposed massive tax cuts in legislation they introduced in 1977. Their bills languished until Ronald Reagan and the Republican Party adopted supply-side economics and a revised version of the Kemp-Roth legislation. Congressional Republicans gathered on the Capitol steps June 25, 1980, to pledge their support for an across-the-board tax cut along the lines of Kemp-Roth. The proposal had now moved from the presidential candidate and the national party to the congressional party, reflecting the broad rather than the narrow politics involved.

CONGRESSIONAL ROLE. President Reagan submitted his tax bill to Congress on February 18, 1981, calling for a $53.9 billion tax cut, to begin with a 10 percent reduction in individual taxes by July 1, 1981. His plan had other features, including accelerated business depreciation. Many political forces began to be felt on Capitol Hill as Congress grappled with the president's plan. Clearly, macropolitics, not micropolitics, was involved.

TRADITIONAL CONGRESSIONAL TAX POLITICS. Bipartisanship, the striving for a broad consensus, usually is part of the politics of congressional tax legislation. Party discipline is inadequate for passage of highly partisan measures. Reflected in tax policies are political ideologies, which fit, although not always tidily, into liberal and conservative categories that cross party lines. The House coalition of conservative Democrats and Republicans often holds the balance of power in tax matters, as it did on the Reagan bill.

ROLE OF THE TAX-WRITING COMMITTEES. The first to recognize the inclusive political nature of their task are the chairmen of the House Ways and Means and Senate Finance Committees, which have jurisdiction over tax legislation. House and Senate members respect the expertise of the staffs and usually of the chairmen and key members of the tax-writing committees; however, the congressional rank and file want to have a say in the final product, which always is perceived as profoundly touching their constituents' interests.

One of the most politically skillful chairmen of the Ways and Means Committee was Arkansas Democrat Wilbur Mills, who served in Congress from 1909 to 1977, and as chairman for the last seventeen years of his tenure. An expert in all tax matters, Mills was also politically astute. He invariably built a consensus for his revenue bills, after taking into account the views of the White House, congressional leaders, and his own committee. He was successful because he recognized the broad effects of tax legislation, and the need to build supportive coalitions behind his measures.

Most successful in shepherding tax legislation to final passage are chairmen who can build a bipartisan consensus within Congress, which depends in large part on building a supportive coalition of outside interests as well. Presidential tax proposals may be entirely partisan when they come to Capitol Hill, but presidents who understand congressional politics know that many compromises must be made before their programs can become law.

REAGAN PROPOSALS IN CONGRESS. Broad and often heated political debate, congressional party confrontations, and at the same time a striving for bipartisanship and compromises all characterize the Capitol Hill politics of the Reagan tax bill.

On the Senate side, Finance Committee Chairman Robert Dole joined majority leader Howard Baker in directing political maneuvers that they hoped would lead to acceptance of the Reagan plan. Dole had taken over the committee's chairmanship from the venerable Louisiana Senator Russell Long when the Republicans gained a majority after the 1980 election. Long and Dole had a cordial relationship, and both had personal leadership styles that encouraged committee decision making by consensus. They knew that on controversial tax measures committee agreement was essential to floor success, and, perhaps even more important, to victory in the conference with their House counterparts from the Ways and Means Committee.[6]

Although the House, under the Constitution, originates revenue legislation, which gives a special aura to its Ways and Means Committee, the Senate Finance Committee has more and more become an equal partner in writing tax bills. Finance Committee chairmen who do not want to wait for House action before they proceed have adopted the technique of attaching tax bills as riders to House-passed bills, which in the view of some constitutional scholars meets the prescription for House origination of revenue legislation. Under Dole's astute guidance, the Finance Committee, by a vote of 19 to 1, adopted almost all of Reagan's tax program, and attached it to a House-passed debt-limit bill. Dole wanted to meet the president's August 1 deadline, and his preemptive legislative strike upstaged the House Ways and Means Committee, which was dragging its feet. Although the Reagan proposals were highly partisan, Dole's skillful political maneuvering, compromises, and consensus politics helped to achieve overwhelming passage of the bill by a vote of 89 to 11 on July 29. The almost unanimous Senate approval of the measure resulted from acceptance of numerous amendments to the bill during floor debate.[7]

HOUSE ACTION. On center stage as the House grappled with the Reagan plan were the congressional party leaders, House Speaker Tip O'Neill and Majority Leader Jim Wright on the Democratic side, and Robert Michel, the Minority Leader; the chairman and the ranking minority member of the House Ways and Means Committee, Dan Rostenkowski, and New York Congressman Barber Conable,

---

[6] Major House and Senate tax bills always go to a conference committee, which works out differences. The chairmen of the tax committees lead their respective delegations into the political battle of the conference, and each strives to come out victorious by yielding the fewest concessions.

[7] See *Congressional Quarterly Weekly Report*, vol. 39, no. 30 (July 25, 1981) pp. 1323–1326.

Jr., respectively; members of the Conservative Coalition of Republicans and Democrats, who had been instrumental in the passage of Reagan's budget cut; outside of Congress, a broad array of interest groups, and perhaps most important, the president and his aides, who constantly pressured Congress and mobilized public opinion.

Congressional responses to outside forces, especially the president, distinguished the politics of the tax bill. Ways and Means Chairman Rostenkowski found himself in a political juggernaut engineered by the White House. Although tax issues generally activate wide political action and involvement, key figures in developing tax legislation have usually been the chairmen of the Ways and Means Committee. Rostenkowski set out to follow the example of the powerful chairmen of the past, but was unable to seize the initiative and control the outcome. He wanted to draft a bill which would gain bipartisan support, but which would also have his individual stamp on it. He had taken over the chairmanship as the 97th Congress opened, with the goal of making his mark on Capitol Hill. Speaker Tip O'Neill had persuaded a reluctant Rostenkowski, who had the choice either of becoming Ways and Means Chairman or Majority Whip, to take the committee post that over the years had been one of the most prestigious chairmanships. More a party tactician than a tax expert, Rostenkowski soon found himself in a tenuous position. He proposed his own bill, calling for a lesser tax cut than Reagan supported, and although it was supported by the Speaker and a number of prominent House Democrats, Rostenkowski was unable to marshal the necessary political support on his committee or in the House to overcome the Reagan onslaught. "Danny couldn't understand why the President's proposal was good and his own was bad," commented a business lobbyist. "He wants to be in control of the process, but he feels he can't get into the game." [8]

The frustrated Ways and Means chairman apparently could not even control his committee, or even the members of his own party who were on it. After Rostenkowski had met with administration officials and tentatively agreed to a multi-year tax cut, the Ways and Means Democrats caucused and voted to reject the proposal.

As the tax-cut issue became increasingly partisan, Rostenkowski tried once again to seize the initiative by persuading the Democrats on his committee to draft a bill that would reflect the views of mod-

[8] *National Journal,* vol. 13, no. 24 (June 13, 1981), p. 1059.

erate House Democrats. Provisions of the bill were announced at a
press conference on June 25. Essentially it targeted for tax cuts groups
with lower incomes than had been proposed under Reagan's proposal,
but the cuts were nowhere near as large as those the president wanted.

WHITE HOUSE PRESSURE. President Reagan dominated and shaped
congressional tax politics, making the issue highly partisan by refusing
to compromise and by drawing upon the support of his party on Capitol Hill. He also marshaled public opinion and many business lobbyists behind his cause. The Republican National Committee and the
National Republican Congressional Committee joined in the president's media blitz, spending more than half a million dollars for radio
and television advertising for the tax cut.

But President Reagan himself was the best advertisement. On the
day after he addressed the nation on the eve of the vote, the Capitol
Hill switchboard lit up like a Christmas tree, as thousands of calls in
support of the president were received. The office of a Kansas Democrat reported 1,500 calls, and other members, particularly Democrats, acknowledged that they, too, were buried under calls and Western Union Mailgrams. White House Chief of Staff James A. Baker,
3rd, summed up the result: "The bottom line is, the President blew
them away." [9]

The president's television address was the capstone to the most intensive White House lobbying ever seen on a tax measure. "They've
been giving us the works," remarked veteran Congressman Claude
Pepper (D, Fla.), adding that he had experienced nothing like it
during his thirty-three years of service in the Senate and the House.[10]
Mississippi Congressman Trent Lott, the Republican Whip, admitted,
"I've got the best whip organization because Ronald Reagan is in it." [11]

Invited to Camp David to meet with the president on a sultry July
weekend were fifteen fence-sitting members, of whom twelve re-

[9] *Congressional Quarterly Weekly Report*, vol. 39, no. 31 (August 1, 1981), p.
1372.
[10] Ibid. Pepper served in the Senate from 1937 to 1951. In 1950, George Smathers defeated Pepper in the Democratic primary, scurrilously and falsely attacking him for being a communist sympathizer because of his strong support for
Franklin Roosevelt's New Deal. Pepper returned to Congress as a representative in 1960, becoming at age eighty-three chairman of the Rules Committee
in 1983.
[11] Ibid.

turned to vote with Reagan. Strong supporters of the president also received the prize White House invitations to breakfast with the president, and to have their photos taken with the Chief for the folks back home. The president even took the unusual step of going to Capitol Hill to meet with the House Republican Conference. Throughout, the president and his staff demonstrated keen knowledge of the district politics of important members, often promising White House intervention to help congressmen in their districts. In Georgia Democrat Charles Hatcher's district, peanuts were a major crop, and subsidies for peanuts were vital to the prosperity of the district's farmers. Hatcher's predecessor, Dawson Mathis, had been chairman of the Tobacco and Peanut Subcommittee when he left to run for the Senate in 1980. After Hatcher's election, he continued the tradition and secured a post on the subcommittee. Unhappily, he immediately confronted David Stockman's budget axe, which was about to fall on peanut subsidies along with many other sacred cows among federal subsidy programs. The White House wanted Hatcher's vote, and apparently told him that OMB opposition to the subsidy would be dropped, after which the congressman found it easy to vote with the White House.[12] To gain other votes, many White House deals were reportedly struck with congressmen.

The president also mobilized the business community, causing House Speaker Tip O'Neill to remark angrily, "Phillip Morris, Paine Webber, Monsanto Chemical, Exxon, McDonnel Douglas ... were so kind as to allow the use of their staffs to the President of the United States in flooding the switchboards of America." [13]

A frustrated Rostenkowski summed up the outcome of the tax battle: "Make no mistake about it. This is the President's bill. It outlines a bold — and risky — economic strategy. Only time will tell whether the risks involved ... were worth taking." [14]

Throughout the struggle over taxes the macropolitical nature of the process was evident. The tax-writing committees had less than their usual power, for the president skillfully took matters out of their hands by widening the political arena.

[12] In the end, Hatcher and his district lost the subsidy program.
[13] *Congressional Quarterly Weekly Report*, vol. 39, no. 31 (August 1, 1981), p. 1372.
[14] *Congressional Quarterly Weekly Report*, vol. 39, no. 32 (August 8, 1981), p. 1431.

Distributive Policy: Government Subsidies and Services

Iron triangles are the focus of distributive politics. Congressional committees, linked with administrative departments and agencies and private interests, are the political actors that mainly determine government payouts to farmers, veterans, porkbarrel programs, tariffs, defense procurement, and government services to special interests. Micropolitics shapes distributive policies because they are not *perceived* to affect broad interests and classes of persons. Only when government action is thought to significantly affect groups and individuals will they become engaged in the political process. The micropolitical nature of distributive politics ends when policies once considered to be distributive are viewed as redistributive. Theodore Lowi points out that in the long run "all governmental policies may be considered redistributive, because in the long run some people pay in taxes more than they receive in services." [15] Normally, however, most government subsidies and many services are not of broad political interest, especially in the short run.

A fascinating example of how the normally limited political arena of distributive policies can become one of redistributive politics occurred during the Reagan push for expected budget cuts as his administration took over in 1981. The president and his Budget Director, David Stockman, were simply unwilling to accept "politics as is" in the budgetary sphere involving extensive government subsidies and services. They sought to mobilize broad political forces to change the micropolitical world of distributive politics into one where these policies were perceived to be redistributive. Congressional committees attempted to preserve their prerogatives, and took a stand against cuts in programs under their jurisdiction.

The Reagan strategy was to undercut conventional budgetary politics, which was mostly distributive and parochial, by linking all aspects of the budget in one package. Broad redistributive politics would replace the piecemeal approach of the past. The task was formidable.

David Stockman was the president's point man. He confronted head-on the traditional distributive, porkbarrel politics of Capitol Hill in an attempt to break the political iron triangles that for so long had dominated legislative decision making. He began by appealing to Re

[15] Theodore J. Lowi, "American Business, Public Policy, Case Studies, and Political Theory," *World Politics*, vol. 16 (July 1964), pp. 673–715, at p. 690.

publican congressional leaders to take charge. It was a radical approach. Normally subcommittee chairmen and special-interest lobbyists are the principal players in the distributive political game.

Journalist William Greider described Stockman's strategy and his ordeal: "In the early skirmishing on Capitol Hill, Stockman actually proposed a tight control system: Senator Baker and the House Republican Leader, Robert Michel of Illinois, would be empowered to clear all budget trades on particular programs — and no one else, not even the highest White House advisers, could negotiate any deals."[16]

Making deals is the core of distributive politics. Stockman knew that unless he was in control of the process the iron triangles would prevail: "If you have multiple channels for deals to be cut and retreats to be made," he observed, "then it will be possible for everybody to start side-dooring me, going in to see Meese, who doesn't understand the policy background, and making the case, or [James] Baker [Reagan's domestic policy adviser] making a deal with a subcommittee chairman."[17]

Stockman's strategy of presenting the diverse budgetary proposals as a package, making them collectively a national and party issue, succeeded quite well. He "could see the status quo yielding to the shock of the Reagan agenda. In dozens of meetings and hearings, public and private, Stockman perceived that it was now inappropriate for a senator or a congressman to plead for his special interests, at least in front of other members with other interests."[18]

Special-interest lobbyists and their allies did try to "side-door" Stockman by going directly to the White House, but Reagan stood behind his proposals and his budget director. Stockman "began to believe that the Reagan budget package, despite its scale, perhaps *because of its scale*, could survive in Congress. With skillful tactics by political managers, with appropriate public drama provided by the President, the relentless growth rate of the federal budget, a perma-

---

[16] William Greider, "The Education of David Stockman," *The Atlantic* (December 1981), p. 37. Greider's article embarrassed both Stockman and the president by reporting the disingenuousness of much information that the administration gave to Congress on the effect of budget cuts. After the article appeared, President Reagan took Stockman to the "woodshed," chastising him for his frankness in revealing the administration's deliberations and for criticizing the comprehensiveness and validity of its approach.

[17] Greider, "Education of David Stockman," p. 37.

[18] Greider, p. 37.

nent reality of Washington for twenty years, could actually be contained." [19]

USE OF THE CONGRESSIONAL BUDGET PROCESS. Raising budgetary politics on Capitol Hill to a macropolitical level was the principal purpose of the 1974 Budget Act. The budget committees were to take the lead, setting goals for expenditures and revenues as well. The law did not easily change the parochial politics of Congress, however; that continued to be dominated by powerful committee chairmen and special interests. Budget-committee chairmen on both sides of the Hill found that they did not have the broad support required to change the customary way of doing business.

The Reagan administration at least temporarily resurrected the congressional budgetary process, helping it become what its sponsors intended it to be. The president's linkage of the disparate components of the budget into one package facilitated the work of the budget committees and the reconciliation process under which committees could be instructed to bring their authorizations, appropriations, and revenue goals into line with the budget resolutions. The Budget Act had authorized reconciliation, but Congress had been reluctant to use it in the past. The committee fiefdoms perceive reconciliation to be an intrusion into their once-protected power preserves.

Reconciliation was clearly a macropolitical technique, permitting Congress, under the guidance of its budget committees, to rein in its often prodigal committees. First used at the tail end of the Carter administration in 1980, reconciliation came into its own in 1981. Now under Republican control, the Senate for the first time used reconciliation in its first budget resolution to order committees to make retroactive cuts. Greider observes that the package voted by the Senate was "close enough to the administration's proposals to convince Stockman of the vulnerability of 'constituency-based' politics." [20] Stockman commented on the Senate action, "That could well be a turning point in this whole process [of traditional distributive politics]." [21]

The unified Republican majority in the Senate was the key to changing the micropolitics of government subsidies and services into a new macropolitical procedure. One incident described by Greider illustrates the change:

[19] Greider, p. 37. Emphasis supplied.
[20] Greider, p. 38.
[21] Greider, p. 38.

After a week of voting down amendments to restore funds for various programs — "voting against every motherhood title," as Stockman put it — moderate Republicans from the Northeast and Midwest needed some sort of political solace. Led by Senator John Chaffee of Rhode Island, the moderates proposed an amendment spreading about one billion dollars over an array of social programs, from education to home-heating assistance for the poor. Stockman had no objection. The amendment wouldn't cost much overall, and it would "take care of those people who have been good soldiers." Senator Pete Domenici of New Mexico, the Senate budget chairman, decided, however, that the accommodation wasn't necessary, and he was right. The Chaffee amendment lost.[22]

Stockman reflected on the change, remarking, "It was the kind of amendment that should have passed. The fact that it didn't win tells me that the political logic has changed." [23]

PUTTING TOGETHER A HOUSE MAJORITY. The budget process did not work as well in advancing Reaganomics in the House as it had in the Senate, simply because the Democratic leadership and the chairman of the Budget Committee, Oklahoma Congressman Jim Jones, backed an alternative plan. That the politics of the budget would be macro-politics was clear from the beginning, because the Reagan linkage of the multiplicity of budget issues into one package forced the congressional parties to take stands.

Budget Chairman Jones crafted a resolution that he hoped would command a majority. Jones "was drawing up a resolution that would restore some funds to social programs, to keep the liberals happy; that projected a smaller deficit than Stockman's, to appear more responsible in fiscal terms; and that did not touch the defense budget, which would offend the Southerners." [24]

In the end, however, Jones lost to the conservative coalition of Republicans and Democrats who supported Reagan.

SUBSURFACE DISTRIBUTIVE POLITICS. The Regan administration's inroads into what normally would be special interests and narrow politics, controlled by subcommittees and their client groups, was im-

22 Greider, p. 38.
23 Greider, p. 38.
24 Greider, p. 38.

pressive but not complete. Perhaps more important, it was probably a short-term phenomenon.

Special interests and political iron triangles had their say on more than one occasion during the 1981 budget and tax debates over government subsidies and services. The Export-Import Bank and its client corporate constituency succeeded in restoring trade subsidies in the Senate, and veterans' groups joined with the chairman of the House Veterans' Affairs Committee to retain important subsidies for staffing veterans' hospitals.

Tax as well as budget legislation contains subsidies in the form of tax expenditures, the various forms of tax relief given to special interests. Although the Reagan administration was able to deal with broad tax cuts at the macropolitical level, tax expenditures were another matter. Lobbyists descended upon Washington after introduction of the Reagan tax plan, seeking special favors. Stockman stated

> I think we're in trouble on the tax bill, because we started with the position that this was a policy-based bill . . . that we weren't going to get involved in the tax-bill brokering of special-interest claims. But then we made the compromise [allowing business more lenient depreciation schedules]. . . . My fear now is that if we do that too many times, it becomes clear to the whole tax lobby constituency in Washington that we will deal with them one at a time, and then you'll find their champions on the tax writing committees, especially Finance, swinging into action, and we are going to end up back-pedalling so fast that we will have the "Christmas tree" bill before we know it.[25]

Reagan won an overall victory on the budget, but special interests prevailed in a number of areas. Sugar subsidies were revived, real-estate tax shelters preserved, and a variety of tax loopholes maintained or even expanded. As the battle was winding down, Stockman observed, "Do you realize the greed that came to the forefront? The hogs were really feeding. The greed level, the level of opportunism, just got out of control." [26]

Stockman solved the inevitable mixture of macro- and micropolitics in the budgetary and tax arenas. "I now understand," he observed, "that you probably can't put together a majority coalition unless you

25 Greider, p. 47.
26 Greider, p. 47.

are willing to deal with those marginal interests that will give you the votes needed to win. That's where it is fought — on the margin — and unless you deal with those marginal votes, you can't win." [27]

In the final analysis, concluded Stockman, "power is contingent. The power of these client groups turned out to be stronger than I realized. The client groups know how to make themselves heard. The problem is, unorganized groups can't play in this game." [28]

Turning distributive into redistributive politics, by linking the diverse political arenas that normally control government subsidies and services, is difficult at best. "I can't move the system any faster," said Stockman. "I can't have an emergency session of Congress to say, Here's a resolution to cut the permanent size of government by 18 percent, vote it up or down. If we did that, it would be all over. But the system works much more slowly. But what can I do about it? Okay? Nothing. So I'm not going to navel-gaze about it too long." [29]

Omnibus Bills and Redistributive Politics

The Reagan administration's strategy to reduce government subsidies and services stressed *omnibus* legislation, which packages a multiplicity of items, many of which would normally fall into separate legislative spheres, into one massive bill. The omnibus approach, which is macropolitical, undermines conventional distributive politics. Subcommittee chairmen cannot easily control the omnibus process, and they find their proposals discarded or substantially changed after broad congressional review and debate.

Extraordinary times brought about increased use of omnibus legislation in the 1980s. But the Reagan administration never failed to remind Congress periodically that it could not afford the luxury of dealing with pressing if not emergency problems of runaway government spending and ever-mounting deficits in the customary piecemeal action of the past. President Reagan was determined to keep the issues of spending and taxes at the macropolitical level, to prevent subcommittee chairmen, special interests, and administrative departments and agencies from having their way.

Whether or not government by omnibus will continue depends

---

[27] Greider, p. 52.
[28] Greider, p. 52.
[29] Greider, p. 54.

upon the ability of future presidents to keep budget issues at the top of the legislative agenda and always in the public eye. On Capitol Hill centrifugal forces, particularly the normally overriding incentive to keep power fragmented among committees, support fragmentation rather than centralization.

Committee chairmen understandably express misgivings about the omnibus approach that diminishes their power. Chairman Mark O. Hatfield (R, Ore.), chairman of the Senate Appropriations Committee, commented on the 1983 budget resolution, an example of omnibus legislation, that he would "hold my nose and do certain things here for the purpose of getting the job done, but certainly not with enthusiasm or anything other than recognizing . . . that we are doing things under emergency conditions." [30] House Appropriations Chairman Jamie Whitten (D, Miss.) echoed the views of his Senate counterpart about the centralized and omnibus budget process: "It's a sad way to do business. We've been forced to do it. It's not because we want it that way." [31]

PORKBARRELING THROUGH OMNIBUS LEGISLATION. Government by omnibus does not always increase the power of the president in the legislative process, or the influence of congressional party leaders. Only if omnibus legislation is perceived to be macropolitical does it become so, and is raised to the level of general debate and involvement that overcome the power of the political iron triangles.

A congressional technique frequently used to distribute benefits and services to special interests has been to put them into a broad legislative package that will guarantee congressional support and even a two-thirds majority to override a presidential veto. For example, in 1982 Congress passed a $14.2-billion supplemental appropriations bill, an omnibus piece of legislation that funded a wide range of government subsidy and service programs. The $6 billion was given for salary increases for employees of the federal government. Farm price-support and loan programs received $5 billion, the second largest item in the legislation. Money was also provided for, among other things, loans to economically depressed communities; the Fisherman's Protective Fund; minority business loans; student loans; mili-

---

[30] *Congressional Quarterly Weekly Report*, vol. 40, no. 39 (September 25, 1982), p. 2379.
[31] Ibid., p. 2381.

tary housing and foreign-duty pay; foreign economic and military aid; acquisition of land for federal parks in Oregon, Florida, Texas, Massachusetts, and Georgia; Indian programs; health programs; urban mass transportation; education for the disadvantaged; retired railroad workers; and community-service jobs for the elderly.

Reagan vetoed the bill on August 28, 1982, stating in his veto message that "This bill would bust the budget by nearly a billion dollars." [32] Congressional reaction was swift, overriding the veto shortly after the president's address. Congressional leaders of both parties appealed to institutional patriotism. Democratic Majority Leader Jim Wright stated that the override vote would reveal "how many [members] are going to let the White House lead them around with a ring in their nose like a prize bull at the county fair." [33] Massachusetts Congressman Silvio Conte, ranking Republican on the Appropriations Committee, had tried to get Reagan to sign the bill. After the override vote he commented, "You just don't have 435 robots up here in Congress that are going to vote in lock step." [34] The veto was, he said, "an affront to Congress. I hope [Reagan] learned a lesson." [35]

The bill's linkage of benefits to special interests and inclusion of porkbarrel projects clearly helped the override of the veto. The president would have liked Congress to accept House Minority Leader Robert Michel's statement on the floor during the debate over the override: "I will have to admit that in this bill is a $3 million item to replace an antiquated railroad bridge in my district. But I cannot allow that project to sway my judgment on a $14 billion bill that our President says is too much to spend at this time." [36] More than two-thirds of the Congress, however, considered the distributive benefits in the bill to be too important to allow the president's veto to be sustained.

Senator Mark Hatfield of Oregon, whose state received special benefits under the legislation, supported the override, telling his colleagues during the debate that he had not opposed the president

[32] *Congresional Quarterly Weekly Report*, vol. 40, no. 36 (September 4, 1982), p. 2220.
[33] *Congressional Quarterly Weekly Report*, vol. 40, no. 37 (September 11, 1982), p. 2237.
[34] Ibid.
[35] Ibid.
[36] *Congressional Quarterly Weekly Report*, vol. 40, no. 39 (September 25, 1982), p. 2383.

before but, "there comes a time when conscience and principle transcend loyalty to party and president." [37] On the House side, eighty-one Republicans voted to override, including many who had previously supported the president when he had vetoed another supplemental appropriations bill. Republican Congresswoman Marge Roukema of New Jersey expressed the views of many of her colleagues who supported the override: "I just wasn't going to make a trade-off between defense and these service programs that have already undergone severe cuts." [38]

FUTURE OF OMNIBUS LEGISLATION. Congress overrode the president's veto of the Supplemental Appropriations Bill in 1982, but it was not an easy victory. The House vote to override, 301 to 117, required an almost totally united Democratic Party and defection of eighty-one Republicans. The Senate vote to override, 60 to 30, garnered the two-thirds majority to prevail without a vote to spare. Omnibus legislation invariably draws presidential attention and a presidential veto if the White House and Capitol Hill are not in agreement.

A majority of congressmen are generally skeptical about omnibus legislation. The omnibus approach reduces the power of the individual member and the ability of committee chairmen to maneuver. It enhances the role and influence of the budget committees, reflecting a centralization of the legislative process that over the long run has been antithetical to the way things are done on Capitol Hill. House Budget Chairman Jim Jones, who would have had his power enhanced by the omnibus method but instead saw it reduced because of presidential domination, observed, "In the future I think we will settle down and get back to the normal way of legislating." [39] He added, however, that "Until we straighten the economy out, we're going to be doing a lot of things differently. Congress operated differently for eight or nine years during the New Deal. We are living through the most important times since then." [40]

Missouri Congressman Richard Bolling, chairman of the Rules Committee before he retired from Congress in 1982, echoed Jones's views. "I think we're going to have to come up with a much different

[37] *Congressional Quarterly Weekly Report*, vol. 40, no. 37 (September 11, 1982), p. 2238.
[38] Ibid.
[39] *Congressional Quarterly Weekly Report*, vol. 40, no. 39 (September 25, 1982), p. 2383.
[40] Ibid.

kind of approach," he said, "A budgetary cycle that's longer than a year, a legislative process that's longer than a year, and a return to the old divisions of power." [41]

The drive of the Reagan administration against customary distributive politics continued into the mid-1980s. The focus of White House attention became the growing federal deficit, which the president used in his efforts to maintain budgetary and tax issues at the macro-political level. Temporarily in the ascendancy on Capitol Hill were the forces of centralization, the party leaders, and the budget committees that work together to reduce the deficit. But the committee chairmen and special interests that comprise iron triangles persisted in their own efforts to dominate the legislative process. They were down but far from out; the congressional override of the president's Supplemental Appropriations Bill veto, referred to above, reflected their power.

SUBCOMMITTEE POWER REASSERTED. Even while Congress was struggling to make the packaging of traditional distributive proposals into omnibus bills work, subcommittees persisted in attempting to control funding for programs under their jurisdiction. The reconciliation process imposed retroactive cuts and ordered committees to conform to them; however, reconciliation bills began to include spending *increases* by 1984, reflecting special interests and subcommittee pressure upon the reconciliation process itself. House Minority Leader Robert Michel called the 1984 reconciliation bill a hoax because it contained spending increases. Minority Whip Trent Lott (R, Miss.), agreed with Michel, stating that the "budget process has gone from sham to shambles." [42]

Congressional party leaders began to squabble with their budget committees as they sought control of the budget process. Although that process intrudes upon the prerogatives of committees, it also respects final committee authority to determine where the cuts that are mandated shall be made. Party leaders on both sides of the Hill were rebuked when they attempted to shortcut the budget process by proposing a budget resolution which had not been reported out of the budget committees, and which would not have required committees to give their stamp of approval on the final product. Power

---

[41] Ibid.
[42] *Congressional Quarterly Weekly Report*, vol. 42, no. 15 (April 14, 1984), p. 827.

was the bottom line, and Congress was not about to scuttle completely its normal procedures that would have significantly reduced the role of committees in the budget process.

SUBCOMMITTEE PRESSURE FOR INCREASED SPENDING. While the macropolitical debate over budget deficits and the need to control spending whirled around them, subcommittees did not abandon their customary advocate's role in funding and protecting programs under their jurisdiction. Subcommittees typically increased their budgetary authorizations beyond presidential requests, and often added programs of their own that were not even in the federal budget. The agriculture committees, for example, continued to support farm subsidies that did not meet the president's guidelines. The Senate Labor and Human Resources Subcommittee on Education added $40 million to the president's fiscal 1985 request for adult-education programs. The House Science and Technology Committee authorized $40 million more than President Reagan wanted for research and development on the manned space station, causing one Republican commitee member to ask, "When will this all stop?" [43] California Democrat George E. Brown, Jr., responded, "We cannot balance the federal budget in this committee." [44]

Only the future will determine how the character of distributive policy making in Congress has changed, if at all. A true challenge has been mounted against the conventional micropolitics of distribution. Over the long run Congress has been dominated by the forces of decentralization, reflected in weak political parties and dominant committees on Capitol Hill, which serve members' incentives for personal power and reelection. The exception rather than the rule has been an active and centralized budget process, including reconciliation, and presidential domination of political iron triangles. The struggle between the forces of centralization and decentralization will continue, but a good bet is that in the future Congress will return to its conventional way of making distributive policy.

REGULATORY POLICIES

Regulatory policy making generally takes place in stages, involving first macropolitical forces that act upon Congress to provide for regu-

[43] *Congressional Quarterly Weekly Report*, vol. 42, no. 12 (March 24, 1984), p. 670.
[44] Ibid.

lating a sphere of private, usually economic, activity. Once Congress meets the demand for action, the second regulatory stage is at hand, characterized by a withdrawal of Congress, which has delegated regulatory authority to an administrative agency or department to determine by rule making or adjudication the rights and obligations of the regulated parties. Micropolitics distinguishes stage two, as the broad political interests featured in stage one retreat to the background, satisfied that their political demands for regulation were met by congressional passage of a regulatory statute. Stage three begins when the original or new macropolitical forces activate themselves to change the *statute* because they are dissatisfied with the way in which it has been administered. Involvement of the president, political parties, coalitions of interest groups, and congressional parties and their leaders accounts for macropolitics in the regulatory as in other policy arenas.

Regulatory policies and processes reflect alternating macro- and micropolitical cycles. A broad historical perspective now suggests that the first macropolitical cycle creates regulation, the second brings regulatory policy under the control of regulated interests, and a broad push for *deregulation* takes place in the third cycle.

Congressional Policy Making in Stage One

Macropolitical demands are made upon Congress to make regulatory policy in stage one. Extensive political movements helped to create railroad regulation and antitrust laws late in the nineteenth century, regulation of banking and deceptive business practices in the first decades of the twentieth. Under President Franklin D. Roosevelt's leadership, the New Deal coalition spurred passage of a host of statutes in the 1930s regulating the securities, trucking, public utilities, airline, and communications industries, as well as labor relations.

National political parties and the president were involved in early regulation, forcing Congress to act. As early as 1880, the Greenback Party, a coalition of labor and farm groups, forged a platform at its second party convention calling for regulation of monopolies:

> It is the duty of Congress to regulate inter-state commerce. All lines of communication and transportation should be brought under such legislative control as shall secure moderate, fair and uniform rates for passenger and freight traffic.[45]

[45] *Guide to U.S. Elections* (Washington, D.C.: Congressional Quarterly, 1976), p. 48.

By 1884 the Republicans adopted the Greenback platform, calling for government regulation of the railroads. Congress passed the Interstate Commerce Act two years later, a detailed law creating the Interstate Commerce Commission (ICC) to regulate railroad rates and other aspects of the industry.

Congress responded to the public clamor, especially from Populist agrarian interests, for railroad regulation. Though the law was more detailed than most future regulatory statutes in specifying what the ICC could and could not do, the burden of future policy making inevitably passed to the agency, and, even more significantly, in the early stages of railroad regulation, to the courts that had the authority to review ICC orders *before* they could go into effect.

Congress tends to act in a *symbolic* way in the first stage of regulatory policy making. Both practical and political considerations dictate broad congressional delegations of authority to regulatory agencies.[46] Even highly detailed statutes require that agencies interpret and judge facts in individual cases, giving administrators the final say, often subject to judicial review, on how the law will be implemented.

Congress, in stage one, broadly responds to macropolitical pressures upon it. Relevant committees consider the legislation but cannot ignore the macropolitical arena. They cannot control policy substance when faced with constant pressures from party leaders, the White House, wide interest coalitions, and sometimes the public.

President Jimmy Carter activated the public and many interests when, under the banner of "the moral equivalent of war," he called in 1977 for comprehensive energy regulation. Energy politics had already passed through several macro- and micropolitical cycles when the Carter plan was announced. The Carter initiative began yet another stage one macropolitical cycle.

House Speaker Tip O'Neill placed the president's energy proposals at the top of the legislative agenda. Trying to avoid the customary committee control and often delay of the legislative process, he appointed an ad hoc energy committee of forty members, representing both parties and the chairmen of the standing committees that had energy jurisdiction. On the Senate side, Majority Leader Robert Byrd (D, W.Va.), joined with Henry (Scoop) Jackson (D, Wash.), chairman of the Committee on Energy and Natural Resources, to secure passage of an energy bill. On both sides of the Hill committees were

[46] See pages 306–307.

important in developing energy legislation, but Congress adopted a comprehensive rather than a fragmented approach to solving the problem.

Role of Congress in Stage Two

The resurgence of committee and subcommittee power marks the beginning of stage two, as macropolitics recedes and micropolitics becomes ascendant. Political iron triangles are forged as committees, agencies, and special interests join for their mutual political benefit. The broad political demands of the past, having been satisfied by congressional and agency actions, fade. The agencies are now left without the political support of the constituencies that led to their creation in the first place and sustained them fully during their early years. Politics dictates that all administrative agencies maintain a balance of political support over opposition, and after stage one they turn to the very groups they regulate for support while strengthening their ties to the congressional committees that have jurisdiction over them.

The example of the ICC and the railroads readily illustrates the transformation from macro- to micropolitics that can take place in the regulatory arena, and the development of an iron triangle that has effectively warded off numerous attempts to reorganize the agency, which continued in existence even after Congress, in 1980, broadly deregulated the railroads. Railroad regulation was a macropolitical issue until the end of World War I. In response to agrarian-shipper interests, Congress had not only passed the original 1887 law, but, with the strong backing of President Theodore Roosevelt, widened the ICC's powers in the Hepburn Act of 1906. By 1920 the commission had completed the job for which it was created, effectively eliminating the railroad rate discrimination that had so angered shippers. The railroads themselves suffered an economic decline, and were briefly nationalized during World War I.

By 1920 the principal participants in the politics of railroad regulation became the railroads themselves, as they sought government protection to allow them to charge rates and engage in other practices that would ensure their economic health. The Transportation Act of 1920 responded to the demands of the railroads, charging the ICC to fix rates at a level that would guarantee a fair return to the railroads, and to permit certain quasi-monopolistic practices if necessary for the economic survival of the industry. The commission became an outpost of railroad interests, and on Capitol Hill those interests were linked to committees and subcommittees that took control of the congressional side of regulatory policy making. The committees, like the ICC, became the captives of railroad interests, because those interests were the only ones to be heard. Presidents Franklin D. Roosevelt and Harry S Truman, among others, attempted to make an issue of ICC independence, but could not singlehandedly break the iron triangle that sustained the status quo.[47] It was not until the forces of deregulation began to gain momentum in the White House and on Capitol Hill that the ICC's authority to regulate and protect the railroads was reduced.

Although Congress, in stage one, reacts to wide political input by passing broad regulatory legislation, in stage two its committees affect policy with specialized legislation reflecting the interests of regulated groups more than those of the general public. Specialization and expert knowledge as well as ties to special interests increase committee power after Congress has provided for government regulation. A vital ingredient of influence in regulatory policy making is expertise. Senior committee members and their staffs develop it through long acquaintance with the subject matter under their jurisdiction. Once Congress has acted at a macropolitical level, it is willing to allow its committees to shape future policy independently with specialized legislation, oversight hearings, and informal expressions of legislative intent.

A top staffer at the Federal Communications Commission (FCC) recalled that when the chairman of the Senate Commerce Committee, which has jurisdiction over the agency, calls the commissioners, "they bow and scrape for him. He doesn't have to ask for anything. The commission does what it thinks he wants it to do." [48] At the same time, the House chairman of the Interstate and Foreign Commerce Committee, which supervised the FCC, "cracked the whip lots of times down here." [49] Congress as a whole, prodded by President Franklin D. Roosevelt and widespread dissatisfaction with the regulatory scheme then in effect, had disposed of the issue of broadcast regulation by passing the Communications Act of 1934, directing the

[47] Samuel P. Huntington, "The Marasmus of the ICC: The Commission, the Railroads, and the Public Interest," Yale Law Journal, vol. 61, no. 4 (1952), pp. 467–509, at pp. 469–471.
[48] Erwin G. Krasnow and Lawrence D. Longley, The Politics of Broadcast Regulation, 2nd ed. (New York: St. Martin's, 1978), p. 70.
[49] Krasnow and Longley, Politics of Broadcast Regulation, p. 70.

FCC to regulate the industry in the "public interest, convenience, and necessity." Having acted, Congress willingly let its committees represent it in determination of broadcast policies in the future.

Congress in Stage Three

Macropolitics resurfaces in stage three. Widening interest in regulatory policy threatens the iron triangles, congressional committees, agencies, and special interests that for years have controlled most of the policy process.

Many reasons account for the new macropolitical shift. Ralph Nader's consumer movement that began in the 1960s focused on the need to change many regulatory policies. He toured college campuses and organized citizens' groups, which he spearheaded to pressure Congress to strengthen regulatory statutes dealing with food and drugs, unsanitary meat, and safety of gas pipelines. At the same time as he was introducing macropolitics into existing regulatory programs, he activated stage one regulatory politics by initiating macropolitical appeals for new regulatory laws dealing with automobile safety, air pollution, control of chemicals, and occupational safety and health. Other consumer groups, such as the conservationist Sierra Club, mobilized wide support both for changing statutes and introducing new environmental laws.

An important change in emphasis occurred in stage three regulatory politics in the mid-1970s, as *deregulation* was pushed to the top of the political agenda. For the most part, regulated groups, feeling comfortable under the protective cloak of the federal government, wanted to maintain the political iron triangles that increased their influence over regulatory policies. Prominent economists, however, such as Alfred Kahn of Cornell University, who chaired the Civil Aeronautics Board during the Carter administration, effectively argued that government regulation was usually contrary to the public interest. Although not all academics agreed, the *idea* of deregulation was growing in the academic community and elsewhere. That idea was attractive to hard-line Republicans, who had always espoused laissez-faire, at least rhetorically. But rhetoric became reality in the Ford administration when the president himself became a chief sponsor of deregulation, soon to be joined by *both* Republicans and Democrats on Capitol Hill. The issue had appeal for political entrepreneurs in Congress who wanted to make a name for themselves, both staffers and members. When President Ford seized the issue, and when prominent legislators in both parties, such as Charles Percy (R, Ill.) and Edward Kennedy (D, Mass.) endorsed it, the micropolitics of stage two was transformed into the macropolitics of stage three in many regulatory arenas. The mostly autonomous committee power of stage two was reduced.

For years, the Senate Commerce Committee under the leadership of Chairman Warren Magnuson (D, Wash.), was the congressional link with administrative agencies and special interests in the transportation field, shaping regulatory policies. In the 1960s, Magnuson, with the help of an astute staff, had gained a reputation as a leading consumer advocate on Capitol Hill, sponsoring truth-in-packaging bills and a traffic-safety law, among others. These laws were no threat to the regulated transportation industry, though, the large firms of which prospered in a regulated environment that discouraged competition.

Howard Cannon (D, Nev.) became chairman of the Senate Finance Committee in 1977, fully intending to play his political cards close to the vest and retain his prerogative to control regulation of transportation. He immediately confronted a rising political tide for deregulation. As early as November 1974, Massachusetts Senator Edward Kennedy, prodded by his staff, used his position as chairman of the Subcommittee on Administrative Practice and Procedure to forge a political constituency for deregulation of airlines. Kennedy's subcommittee did not have formal jurisdiction, which resided in Cannon's Subcommittee on Aviation under the Commerce Committee. But Kennedy and his staff agreed that deregulation was an idea whose time was coming, and they knew that by helping it to arrive they would gain, with the help of good press relations, the political credit for it. Kennedy's actions helped to create the macropolitical environment that eventually led to passage of airline deregulation, later followed by deregulation of the trucking and railroad industries.

Kennedy and his staff helped to mobilize the broad political constituency necessary for deregulation. One of his key staffers pointed out,

> There was no consituency for [deregulation] in the beginning. Kennedy did not act because of outside pressures. None of the members of the Senate and staff who have been leaders in pushing for the legislation have acted on the basis of con-

stituent pressures. Most constituent pressures, in fact, have
been against it. The constituencies were generated by the congressional supporters of the legislation — Kennedy and others
going out and convincing people of the necessity for the bill.[50]

In the early stages of airline deregulation the Civil Aeronautics
Board (CAB) and most of its constituency of large carriers understandably opposed change. The Commerce committees on both sides
of Capitol Hill also favored the status quo; the iron triangle was intact. Kennedy and his allies mobilized charter and other small carriers
dissatisfied with the CAB, travel agencies, Ralph Nader's consumer-
action project, and the Justice Department to form a broadening
political constituency in support of deregulation.

As the deregulation movement grew, Cannon saw the handwriting
on the wall. Above all, he wanted to protect his committee's turf,
and become the leader of change if it was inevitable. Careful staff
negotiations helped pave the way for a Kennedy-Cannon alliance that
led to passage of the airline deregulation bill in the Senate, and in the
House the new constituency for deregulation, which included the
president, led to committee and floor action supporting deregulation.

The revival of macropolitics in the regulatory sphere also brought
about degrees of deregulation in banking and broadcasting, and pressures for decontrol of natural gas. Industry forces were arrayed in
various ways, some segments of the broadcasting industry and banking groups opposing decontrol, and gas producers favoring it. Intensive lobbying by a wide range of interests focused upon Congress as
a whole, as well as on the committee that had the legislative jurisdiction. The continuing pressures for deregulation on a broad front
supported continuation of stage three macropolitics in Congress, involving congressional leaders, parties, and conflicting interests, forcing
the issue of change upon committees that in the past usually supported the status quo.

FOREIGN POLICY MAKING

Both under the Constitution and by political custom the president
and Congress share policy-making responsibilities in the foreign and
defense arenas more than in other policy spheres. Although in the

---

[50] Rochelle Jones and Peter Woll, *The Private World of Congress* (New York:
Free Press), p. 64.

original constitutional scheme the White House and Capitol Hill were to be equal partners in foreign policy, with the Senate the key actor for Congress, presidents from the very beginning have struggled to assert their supremacy. Congress as an *institution* has repeatedly confronted the president in the continual struggle for power over foreign and defense policy, acting through the Foreign Relations Committee in the Senate and, because of the less important role of the House, the weaker Foreign Affairs Committee of the lower body.

Constitutional Context

Congressmen and their committees always operate under the shadow of the presidency in foreign policy making.[51] The president's constitutional authority cannot be denied. He alone, with the State Department as his adjunct, conducts foreign relations. He appoints ambassadors and receives foreign ambassadors and heads of state. He makes treaties, requiring Senate approval, but can negotiate executive agreements without acquiescence by Congress. He is commander-in-chief of the armed forces, the First General and Admiral of the Confederacy, which was Hamilton's apt description.

The Supreme Court has recognized that the conduct of foreign relations is exclusively executive in character, and has strengthened the president's prerogative powers to make and carry out foreign policy. Justice George Sutherland, a member of the New Deal Court who had voted against extensions of executive authority in the domestic sphere, nevertheless supported along with his brethren executive prerogatives in foreign affairs. In rendering the Court's opinion in the historic case, *United States* v. *Curtiss-Wright*, in 1936, he emphasized that "The president alone has the power to speak or listen as a representative of the nation. He *makes* treaties with the advice and consent of the Senate; but he alone negotiates. Into the field of negotiation the Senate cannot intrude; and Congress itself is powerless to invade it." [52] Sutherland recognized "the very delicate, plenary and exclusive power of the president as the sole organ of the federal government in the field of international relations — a power which does not require as a basis for its exercise an act of Congress." [53]

---

[51] Presidential-congressional relations in foreign policy are discussed on pages 338–346 above.

[52] United States *v.* Curtiss-Wright, 299 U.S. 304, 306 (1936).

[53] Ibid.

Presidents have asserted their prerogative power to make foreign policy from the time that George Washington unilaterally proclaimed American neutrality in 1793 in the war between Britain and France, to the present. Members of Congress who supported France argued that Washington's action was beyond his constitutional authority. The debate was heated, and a precursor of future controversies between the president and Congress.

All presidents want maximum flexibility to conduct foreign affairs. They all cite constitutional scripture to support their position. Ronald Reagan spoke for presidents past and future when, replying to a news-conference question about congressional meddling in foreign policy, he said: "In the last ten years the Congress has imposed about 150 restrictions on the president's power in international diplomacy, and I think that the Constitution made it pretty plain way back in the beginning as to how diplomacy was to be conducted and I just don't think that a committee of 535 individuals, no matter how well intentioned, can offer what is needed in actions of this kind or where there is a necessity." [54] The president added, "Do you know that prior to the Vietnamese War, while this country had only had four declared wars, presidents of this country had found it necessary to use military forces 125 times in our history?" [55]

Politics of Foreign Policy

The foreign-policy spectrum is broad and highly complex, ranging from issues of war and peace to narrow economic subsidies and protective tariffs. Different foreign-policy categories feature distinctive politics, shaping congressional processes and responses.

TYPES OF FOREIGN POLICIES. The redistributive, distributive, and regulatory categories have usefully been applied to domestic policies to illustrate the contrasting political forces in each sphere, and the way in which they affect Congress. The categories are associated with macro- or micropolitics, predicting whether Congress as a whole deals with an issue or allows its committee freely to make decisions for it.

Foreign policy, as it affects both the international and domestic

---

[54] Text of presidential news conference, April 4, 1984, *Congressional Quarterly Weekly Report*, vol. 42, no. 14 (April 7, 1984), p. 795.
[55] Ibid.

spheres, can be thought of at least partially in similar terms. For example, foreign aid is clearly redistributive, export subsidies and protective tariffs distributive, and controls over the export of strategic materials are regulatory. Particularly in the redistributive area, however, these foreign-policy categories do not necessarily invoke the same kinds of politics that are associated with them in the domestic arena. The president is, to a greater or lesser degree, a constant and insistent force in all foreign-policy areas. The public, even when its tax dollars are being redistributed abroad, is rarely involved. Both domestic and foreign special interests lobby Congress intensely, particularly in the distributive area, focusing not only upon committees but also on the wider membership. The congressional decision-making process tends to be a broad one in foreign policy, involving both leaders and the rank and file.

Influences on Congress

THE PRESIDENT. President Reagan's news-conference remarks cited above, lamenting the multiple congressional restrictions upon his authority to conduct foreign affairs, illustrates that presidential dominance of Congress is more a myth than a reality. The extent of presidential supremacy over Congress depends upon the political environment of the time, which determines in a general way the willingness of Congress to accede to dominance by the White House. Whether or not Congress is willing to go along with the president also hinges upon the category of foreign policy involved. Historically, presidents have had more discretion to decide issues of war and peace than whether or not there shall be protective tariffs, export subsidies, and other economic protections for domestic industries. When President Lyndon B. Johnson first committed troops to Vietnam, there was no political constituency to oppose him. At the time his action was considered to be a presidential prerogative, and Congress supported his decision as it had similar unilateral presidential actions in the past. If, however, President Johnson had attempted unilaterally to end protective tariffs and subsidies his authority would immediately have been challenged and Congress would have been in an uproar. Even on matters of the highest national interest, though, presidents ignore Congress at their peril and can usually do so only for brief periods.

The balance of power between the president and Congress is cyclical, with periods of presidential supremacy always followed by an assertive if not ascendant Congress. As the framers of the Constitution intended, Congress jealously guards its powers over the long run, although in the short run it may willingly acquiesce to executive domination.

The prolonged crisis of World War II, followed by the cold war, supported an unusually long stretch of presidential supremacy in foreign affairs. Presidents from Roosevelt through Kennedy enjoyed more than the customary congressional deference when they made major foreign-policy decisions. The period before controversy over the Vietnam War began to heat up was a time of bipartisanship in foreign policy that was reflected in cooperation between the president and Congress. Presidents in the mid-twentieth century always had their congressional critics, and they often had to be politically astute in foreign-policy dealings with Congress to gain its backing, but in the end the White House mainly controlled the course of foreign policy.

The period of presidential ascendancy in foreign affairs came to an abrupt end during the turbulent Vietnam War years in the late 1960s and early 1970s. The Senate Foreign Relations Committee, under the chairmanship of J. William Fulbright (D, Ark.), led an unprecedented attack on the Johnson administration, even though Fulbright himself, along with most of his Senate colleagues, had fully supported the president in the early stages of the war. The growing strength of the antiwar movement stiffened the backbone of Congress, spurring it on to oppose the president. During the Nixon administration, the Democrat-controlled Congress, speaking through its House Judiciary Committee, even went so far as to cite the president's secret escalation of the war by bombing Cambodia as one of the reasons he should be impeached!

Congress has reasserted its role in all aspects of foreign policy since the Vietnam era. President Reagan commented on the aggressive congressional stance as his first term was coming to a close: "The most far-reaching consequence of the past decade's congressional activism is this: bipartisan consensus building has become a central responsibility of congressional leadership as well as of executive leadership. If we're to have a sustainable foreign policy, the Congress must support the practical details of policy, not just the general goal." [56]

---

[56] From text of speech made before Georgetown University Center for International and Strategic Studies, April 6, 1984, *Congressional Quarterly Weekly Report*, vol. 42, no. 15 (April 14, 1984), p. 870.

But, continued Reagan, that responsibility has not been met by congressional leaders. "Unfortunately," he said, "many in the Congress seem to believe they are still in the troubled Vietnam era, with their only task to be vocal critics, and not responsible partners in developing positive, practical programs to solve real problems." [57]

Reagan concluded, "Presidents must recognize Congress as a more significant partner in foreign policymaking, and, as we tried to do, seek new means to reach bipartisan executive, legislative consensus. But legislators must realize that they, too, are partners. They have a responsibility to go beyond mere criticism to consensus-building that will produce positive, practical and effective action." [58]

POLITICAL PARTIES. The national parties always take stands on issues of foreign policy, but they are usually stated in such vague generalities that they have little meaning as a guide for either presidential or congressional action. Presidents tend to have more than the usual influence over members of their own party on Capitol Hill on *major* foreign-policy issues, on which the White House takes a strong stand. Political scientist Robert Dahl found that from 1933 to 1948 a high degree of cohesion existed among House and Senate Democrats in voting on foreign-policy issues where the president's position was known. He concluded, "A significant degree of party unity exists on *important* issues of foreign policy." [59] Although the positions of party leaders may sway rank-and-file members on major foreign-policy issues, however, where the economic interests of congressional constituencies are touched, or special concerns such as those of ethnic minorities are involved, members place their constituents' views above party loyalty.

INTEREST GROUPS. Robert Dahl points out, from a historical perspective, that "When the pressures run wild, it is every man for himself and the party take the hindmost." He observes, "Neutrality, the Spanish Civil War, repeal of cash and carry, lend-lease, United Nations, the British loan, Greek-Turkish aid, European recovery, Palestine — such basic issues of foreign policy as these were automatically

[57] Ibid.
[58] Ibid.
[59] Robert A. Dahl, *Congress and Foreign Policy* (New York: Norton, 1964), p. 46.

at the center of a field of forces of which the private pressure groups were among the most important." [60]

Pressure groups, both foreign and domestic, have always strongly influenced foreign policy. In the 1980s, while domestic automobile producers fought for protection from Japanese imports, the Japanese automakers, taking a leaf from the American political notebook, organized their own lobbying effort on Capitol Hill. Hideaki Otaka, the lobbyist for Toyota Motor Sales, USA, observed, "Lobbying should not be a bad word. In America, especially in Washington, everybody has a right to speak." [61] Although the "Japan lobby" is loosely organized, it has targeted domestic content legislation, under which automobiles sold in America would have to have a percentage of domestic labor and parts, as well as potential restrictions upon other Japanese imports — such as video-cassette recorders.

Foreign lobbies are clearly at a disadvantage, for they are not directly part of the political constituencies of members of Congress. Washington lawyer Karl J. Green commented, "The reality in Washington is that to lobby, in the usual sense of the word, you have to have votes or money for political contributions. Neither of those things are present in the case of representing foreign interests that cannot vote and are barred by law from making political contributions." [62]

House passage of the Domestic Content bill on the eve of adjournment in 1982 illustrated the power of domestic interest groups in foreign-policy making. One hundred and seventy-one Democrats were joined by forty-four Republicans to pass a bill that was strongly opposed by the Reagan administration, called by U.S. Trade representative William E. Brock III, "The worst piece of economic legislation since the 1930s." [63] The United Auto Workers (UAW) lobbied vigorously for the legislation, which was supported by the Energy and Commerce Committee, chaired by Michigan Congressman John Dingell. Although the UAW was initially successful, strong counterpressures succeeded first in weakening the effect the bill would have,

[60] Dahl, *Congress and Foreign Policy*, p. 55.
[61] *Congressional Quarterly Weekly Report*, vol. 41, no. 27 (July 9, 1983), p. 1395.
[62] Ibid.
[63] Ibid., p. 1399. The vote is in *Congressional Quarterly Weekly Report*, vol. 40, no. 51 (December 18, 1982), p. 3070.

and later became organized in a powerful coalition that neutralized the bill's proponents. Among the opposing interests were the Automobile Importers of America, the International Longshoremen's Association, many of whose members depended upon unloading imports for their jobs, and agricultural groups that wanted to maintain the more than $5 billion in yearly exports to Japan.

Foreign-trade issues are generally macropolitical, which means that they are seldom relegated to committees to decide. Political iron triangles find it difficult, if not impossible, to operate independently in matters of international economic policy. Congressmen consider the issues of protectionism and free trade far too important to delegate to any one committee. The Energy and Commerce Committee not only found wide opposition within and outside of the House to its Domestic Content bill, but also confronted a hostile Ways and Means Committee, whose free-trade chairman considered trade policy to be under his jurisdiction.[64] The Ways and Means chairman was carrying out the traditional *institutional* role of the committee, which is to "put a damper on particularism in tax and tariff matters. . . ."[65]

CONSTITUENTS. Robert J. Dahl observed what is undoubtedly a continuing truth about constituent influence on foreign policy, "On balance, so far as their constituents are concerned, most congressmen probably have much more discretion on foreign policy (at least within a very wide range of alternatives) than is often supposed. This is not to say that constituents *cannot* be influential. It is merely to register the fact that in many situations, particularly in the short run, they *are not*."[66]

The power of public opinion always suffers from the difficulty of translating general views into specific demands. Members want to be able to explain their votes and actions to the voters back home. In most foreign-policy arenas, though, it is difficult for the voters themselves to assess exactly how they are affected. From the standpoint of the congressman, rarely can he assess accurately what a majority of his constituency wants. He may know, for example, that if his constituency has a large proportion of Jewish voters he should sup-

---

[64] *Congressional Quarterly Weekly Report*, vol. 41, no. 38 (September 24, 1983), pp. 1987–1989.

[65] David R. Mayhew, *Congress: The Electoral Connection* (New Haven: Yale University Press, 1974), p. 154.

[66] Dahl, *Congress and Foreign Policy*, p. 44.

port Israel, but what position and action should he take on aid to Latin America? In the latter category he can readily explain his vote either way in the unlikely event that he is asked.

Legislators primarily deal with their constituents in foreign policy through position taking, which is often mostly rhetorical. They have wide latitude to phrase their positions in ways that will not antagonize constituents. Even in tariff and trade, the foreign-policy arena that most directly affects local interests, position taking has replaced credit claiming in communications with constituents.[67]

Congress conveniently created the Tariff Commission in 1934, giving it responsibility for determining tariff levels and protectionist policies. Even before creating the commission, Congress had delegated substantial authority to the president to set tariffs. Other executive agencies also deal with tariff policy. The result, according to one comprehensive study, is that

> Congress has freed itself from much local pressure by yielding up to the executive branch the power of setting specific rates. The individual Representative can placate a local industry by writing to the Tariff Commission about an escape-clause proceeding, or to the Committee on Reciprocity Information when a trade agreement is about to be negotiated. But letters are cheap. He can also make a speech on the floor of Congress or before a trade association. Having done his bit for local industry in this way, he is not necessarily called upon to try to translate local interests into the law of the land.[68]

Congressional Decision-Making Process

Broad rather than narrow politics distinguishes the congressional approach to foreign policy. Primary jurisdiction over most aspects of foreign policy resides in the Foreign Affairs Committee in the House and the Foreign Relations Committee in the Senate. The strategic premises, the game plans of these committees, reflect the broader political environment. During periods when the executive dominates foreign policy, the committees become the president's representatives in Congress, advocates for his programs. During times of congres-

---

[67] Mayhew, *Congress: The Electoral Connection*, p. 172.
[68] Raymond A. Bauer, Ithiel de Sola Pool, and Lewis Anthony Dexter, *American Business and Public Policy* (New York: Atherton, 1967), p. 247.

sional resurgence, when legislators are more likely to question presidential authority, the committees shift their strategic premises, becoming more independent and willing to question presidential initiatives.

FOREIGN AFFAIRS COMMITTEE. In Richard Fenno's study of congressional committees he concluded that the Foreign Affairs Committee of the 1950s and the 1960s was strongly influenced by the reality and acceptance of executive control over foreign policy.[69] Having the president and other parts of the executive foreign-policy establishment as its principal constituent distinguishes Foreign Affairs from other committees that are tied to special interests or, like the institutional committees, serve the House. Another distinctive feature of Foreign Affairs is that its members' goals are primarily good public policy. Membership on the committee is not a route to power in the House, nor, for most of its members, does it appreciably boost their prospects for reelection.

During periods of executive domination, Foreign Affairs Committee members agree that their principal task is "To approve and help pass the annual foreign aid program." "Really, we are sort of a Committee on foreign aid," said one member, "We have other bills . . . [but] they aren't the kinds of bills you spend six months on." [70]

When the cycle of executive control changes and Congress seeks to become at least an equal partner in foreign-policy making, the committee reflects congressional pressures for reassertion of power. Both within the committee and on the floor increased attempts to control foreign policy are made by attaching amendments to foreign-aid legislation. In 1981, when Congress continued its flexing of muscles that began after Watergate, an amendment was added to the Foreign Aid Authorization bill requiring the president to report twice yearly on human-rights violations in El Salvador. President Reagan vetoed the bill, causing an uproar on Capitol Hill.

A resurgent Congress breeds an active Foreign Affairs Committee, which challenges administration policies rather than blindly supporting them. The mission of the committee continues to be passage of foreign-aid legislation, but with conditions attached that reflect

---

[69] Richard F. Fenno, Jr., *Congressmen in Committees* (Boston: Little, Brown, 1973), pp. 69–73.
[70] Fenno, p. 69.

an independent congressional stance. The committee chairman's job becomes far more difficult as he seeks to compromise the often clashing positions of the president and Congress. His task is particularly arduous when the president and the House are of different parties.

Florida Democrat Dante Fascell, who became chairman of Foreign Affairs in 1984, confronted highly partisan conflict over foreign policy at every level — on his committee, between the president and Congress, and between House Democrats and Republicans. The ranking Republican on the committee charged that the Democrats "will do anything to embarrass the president." He added, however, "Dante's not leading this movement; he's just as disturbed about it as I am. But it's made his job and our job very difficult." [71]

Fascell had to deal with subcommittees that had become independent and powerful under the previous chairmanship of Clement Zablocki (D, Wis.). The subcommittees, said Fascell, are "sovereign independent states, and they kind of like to fly their own flags." [72] While the eight subcommittees busily pursue their own goals, the chairman continues to seek the bipartisan compromises that are necessary for enacting foreign-aid legislation.

Members of the Foreign Affairs Committee were embarrassed by its failure to secure passage of foreign-aid bills in 1981 and 1983, when partisan disputes and Reagan opposition to some provisions in the legislation prevented the bills from reaching the floor. Fascell was determined to make the committee a more effective sponsor of foreign-aid legislation. "There's nothing more important . . . than the foreign aid bill," he remarked, "because it's the only vehicle, really, that you have to have some major input on the shaping of foreign policy." [73]

The new chairman recognized how important it was to maintain the traditional role of the committee in cooperating with the executive, but also stressed congressional oversight of foreign policy. Replying to a State Department charge that Congress is too involved in the "micro-management" of foreign affairs, he said:

> Yes, Congress can get too involved in the daily managing of foreign policy, and we should be very careful not to unneces-

[71] *Congressional Quarterly Weekly Report*, vol. 42, no. 17 (April 28, 1984), p. 967.
[72] Ibid., p. 968.
[73] Ibid.

sarily restrict, tie, inhibit, prohibit, or otherwise make the president sensitive, nervous, or upset. On the other hand, we certainly don't want to have a [foreign-aid] program that spends $11, $12, $13, $14, $15 billion worth of money through various institutions, with a president having total flexibility, absolutely no restrictions, no limitations, no conditions of any kind. I think that would be simply denying the role of the Congress.[74]

SENATE FOREIGN RELATIONS COMMITTEE. Because of the Senate's exalted constitutional role in foreign-policy making, the Foreign Relations Committee is both more prestigious and more important than its House counterpart. It initially carries out the Senate's constitutional responsibilities to advise and consent on treaties and ambassadorial appointments.

The power of the Senate committee, like that of the House committee, fluctuates with the political environment. Before the Vietnam War, it too operated in an environment of executive domination and bipartisanship. Its subcommittees, which had jurisdiction over different geographic areas, could not develop legislation, but had to bring their recommendations to the full committee.

Whether in times of executive supremacy or congressional resurgence, the chairman puts his stamp on the way in which Foreign Relations operates. Under Arkansas Democrat J. William Fulbright during the later stages of the Vietnam War, the committee actively challenged the executive by holding hearings that mainly aired antiwar sentiment. Under Alabaman John Sparkman, who succeeded Fulbright in 1975, the committee became lethargic, to be revived only when Idaho Senator Frank Church took the reins in 1979. Church had acted as an informal leader of the committee in securing approval of the controversial Panama Canal Treaty in 1978, continuing the committee's most common strategy, which has been to cooperate with the executive. The committee, however, cannot help but mirror the politics of the Senate, which, in foreign policy, became highly partisan as the 1970s ended.

Treaties and confirmations can involve the Foreign Relations Committee in high political drama, but its principal policy focus is foreign aid, an area usually dominated by the executive. As Congress sought

[74] Ibid., p. 970.

a more active role in foreign-policy making in the 1980s, the Foreign Relations Committee became more assertive in dealing with the executive. Over the objections of its Chairman Charles Percy (R, Ill.) and conservative committee Republicans, a majority of members supported a move to assert the panel's authority over the reprogramming of foreign-aid funds by the executive. Although foreign-aid authorizations budget funds for specific countries, Congress has passively supported the president's authority to reprogram money from one country to another if he considers it to be in the national interest. President Reagan had redirected $60 million to El Salvador that had been budgeted for other countries. The committee wanted him to reduce the El Salvador aid to $30 million. Even its liberal members, however, acknowledged that the committee's position was tenuous at best. "The fact of the matter is," said Joseph Biden, Jr. (D, Del.), "constitutionally, the president can . . . ignore the committee." [75] Chairman Percy said that about the only thing the committee could do to strengthen its position with the executive was to threaten to turn down future presidential requests for aid. "They want a lot from this committee in the future," he stated, "and so I would hope that they would give it due weight." [76]

APPROPRIATIONS COMMITTEES. The reprogramming dispute in 1983 was not simply between the Foreign Relations Committee and the president, but, perhaps more important, between Foreign Relations on the one hand and the appropriations subcommittees on both sides of the Hill that had jurisdiction over foreign aid. For years the Appropriations Subcommittees on Foreign Operations in the House and the Senate have overseen reprogrammings, informally asserting a power that was rarely used to veto them. A senior member of the House committee, David Obey (D, Wis.), said that "It is awfully difficult for [the Senate Foreign Relations Committee] to establish a legal precedent for a claim to oversee [reprogrammings, which are] an Appropriations Committee mechanism." [77]

Of overriding importance in the foreign-policy process is the dominance of the appropriations committees. As a "third branch" of Congress, they scrutinize carefully not only the executive but the actions

[75] *Congressional Quarterly Weekly Report*, vol. 41, no. 13 (April 2, 1983), p. 668.
[76] Ibid.
[77] Ibid.

of legislative committees. Tension between the appropriations and other committees of Congress comes up in all areas of public policy.

The power of the appropriations subcommittees dealing with foreign operations and the State Department can be devastating to the Foreign Affairs and the Foreign Relations Committees. Executive agencies know that they can safely ignore the Foreign Affairs Committee because the "real" power lies with appropriations. A senior AID official recalled that when Otto Passman (D, La.) chaired the House Foreign Operations Subcommittee, "He used to be on the telephone to [the administrator] almost daily." [78] Whether by phone or by letter, the appropriations subcommittees keep in almost daily contact with the executive branch as their chairmen and expert staff attempt to influence foreign policy, primarily by closely supervising foreign aid. Though the Foreign Affairs and Foreign Relations Committees customarily see the passage of foreign-aid legislation as their primary mission, the appropriations subcommittees' principal goal is cutting back or even eliminating foreign aid outright.[79]

OTHER COMMITTEES. Foreign policy is not entirely under the jurisdiction of the foreign affairs and appropriations committees, although they are clearly the most important. The commerce and taxation committees are involved in many economic matters that directly or indirectly affect international trade. The judiciary committees have jurisdiction over immigration, which is an aspect of foreign policy.

LEADERSHIP AND MEMBER INITIATIVES. Rare is the foreign-policy issue that does not involve party leaders in taking positions, and rank-and-file members in participation. A broad cross-section of congressmen and senators, even without constituency pressures, which are usually lacking, take stands on issues of war and peace, free trade or protective tariffs, trade subsidies, and other economic matters. Foreign policy is often cast in ideological terms, with liberals confronting conservatives over such issues as aid to El Salvador and arms control. Macropolitics is a feature of foreign-policy making within Congress, activated by presidential pressures, conflicting ideological

[78] Thomas M. Franck and Edward Weisband, *Foreign Policy by Congress* (New York: Oxford University Press, 1979), p. 252.
[79] Franck and Weisband, *Foreign Policy by Congress*, pp. 249–253.

viewpoints, and sometimes by broad external forces as in the anti-Vietnam War movement.

A resurgent Congress encourages rank-and-file members to participate actively in the foreign-policy process. Many members do not hesitate to express their opinions by attaching amendments to appropriations bills and other foreign-policy legislation. But when Congress is in an environment of executive dominance in foreign policy, characterized by bipartisanship and close White House relations with Capitol Hill, the committees are ascendant while the members are quiescent. The Foreign Affairs Committee's major constituent is the president, and when he exercises strong leadership its power within Congress is correspondingly augmented.

Contrasting the 1950s and the 1960s, when the president was ascendant in foreign policy and it was conducted on a bipartisan basis, with the post-Vietnam era, when Congress challenged the White House, reveals the changing relationships between committees and the membership. In the mid-1950s, the chairman of the House Foreign Affairs Committee, James P. Richards (D, SC), who first came to the House in 1933, was able to say, "The committees of the two houses have a rather unique function in the foreign policymaking process. They are the links between the executive with its specialized knowledge, and the House or Senate as a body with generalized knowledge or lack of knowledge." [80]

The period of committee dominance lasted until approximately the end of the 91st Congress in 1971. But in that Congress members were becoming more active in expressing their own foreign-policy views and attempting to change committee legislation. The Foreign Affairs Committee reported 30 bills in the 91st Congress, and 39 floor amendments to these were offered, 14 of which were adopted. But 69 percent of the amendments came from dissenting Foreign Affairs Committee members. By the 94th Congress (1975–1976), the Foreign Affairs Committee was beginning to lose its grip, and faced 112 floor amendments to 42 committee bills and resolutions, 51 of which were adopted (49.9 percent). This time, most of the amendments (74 percent) came from the House rank and file who were not on the committee.

[80] Quoted in Franck and Weisman, *Foreign Policy by Congress,* from James P. Richards, "The House of Representatives in Foreign Affairs," *Annals of the American Academy of Political and Social Science* vol. 289 (September 1953), p. 69.

Thomas Franck and Edward Weisband concluded in their study of the congressional process in foreign policy, after reviewing the 1970s, that Congress as a whole had enormously increased its role in foreign affairs. Moreover, they found "a widespread inclination on the part of the members to perceive themselves as Chiefs, not Indians." [81] As more and more members involve themselves in foreign policy, the influence of party leaders is decreased along with the power of committees that relied so much upon effective White House liaison.

VOTING PATTERNS IN FOREIGN POLICY. Although the congressional process in making foreign policy seems disparate, defying any but the broadest generalizations, political scientists Barry Bozeman and Thomas James were able to conclude, after a thorough study of foreign-policy voting in the Senate, that the three most important determinants of senators' foreign-policy positions were party, support for the administration, and ideology. [82] The same factors appear to be important in the House as well. During the Reagan administration, for example, these factors largely determined divisions over aid to El Salvador, withdrawal of Marines from Lebanon, and arms control.

CONCLUSION. The executive is a dominant force in the congressional decision-making process on broad issues of war, peace, and national security. Moreover, the executive is involved in all areas of foreign policy, taking a stand that affects congressional decision making. The constantly active role of the executive distinguishes, over a period of time, the foreign-policy arena from many domestic policy areas. The congressional process is not as readily committee-dominated in foreign as in domestic policy making. Struggles between the legislative and appropriations committees characterizes both arenas, but the committees must operate in an environment not only of executive dominance but also of wide involvement by congressional party leaders and rank-and-file members. The traditional constituency and pressure-group influences, so frequently important in domestic policy making, exist but are less powerful factors in the foreign-policy sphere, where

[81] Franck and Weisman, p. 213.
[82] Barry Bozeman and Thomas E. James, "Toward a Comprehensive Model of Foreign Policy Voting in the U.S. Senate," *Western Political Quarterly*, vol. 28, no. 3 (September 1975), pp. 477–495.

ideology, party affiliation, and support for the president are often the controlling factors.

DEFENSE POLICY MAKING

Defense, like foreign policy, cannot readily be separated into the three categories we have used in analyzing the congressional process in the domestic sphere. Defense policy involves broad issues of national security and weapons systems, but also specialized and expert issues of weapons procurement, deployment, and manpower. At the broad level, defense policy is macropolitical in the sense that the president is always involved, as are political parties (which take positions in their platforms), congressional party leaders, and often broad coalitions of interest groups. As in foreign policy, the Vietnam War was the impetus for changing what had in the past been mostly a micropolitical sphere into macropolitics, reflected in greater public awareness and feelings about defense issues along with less congressional deference to its military committees and their Defense Department (DOD) allies.

Military-Industrial Complex

Ever since President Dwight D. Eisenhower's dire warning about it in his final address to the nation on January 17, 1960, the existence of a "military-industrial complex" has been widely accepted, and the characterization of the linkage between defense department, the armaments industry, and their congressional supporters has become part of our political language. The policy arena being described is a *distributive* one, in which the armed services committees and the appropriations subcommittees that deal with defense determine most weapons-procurement policies in response to the requests of DOD and the armaments industry.

Except for certain broad issues of weapons systems and procurement, such as the B-1 (RS70) bomber that was broadly debated on Capitol Hill in the 1960s, and the MX missile that engaged the entire Congress in 1984, the overriding reality of procurement policy is that it is controlled by the Defense Department. Although Congress attempted to become more assertive in defense-procurement policy after Vietnam, committee fragmentation, staff rivalries, the disinterest of most members in the technical aspects of weapons, and the tendency

to vote for weapons programs because they will have economic benefits to congressional districts have prevented Congress from exerting
strong influence.[83]

Congressional committees dealing with defense may disagree on
specific procurement policies, but most of their members side with
the Defense Department's overall goals for increased expenditures.
The alliance between the committees and DOD was particularly
strong until the Vietnam backlash in the 1970s. Although the committees continued to recruit members with "hawkish" and pro-DOD
points of view, new blood on both the House and Senate Armed Services Committees began to present a more balanced point of view
after Vietnam, adopting in some cases a skeptical view of DOD and
its never-ending quest for new weapons programs.[84]

As President Reagan and the Defense Department pushed for the
MX and other arms programs, a small but influential group of House
Democrats, drawn mostly from the Armed Services Committee itself,
took a stand against expansion of nuclear weapons programs and successfully guided the House in voting to slow them down. Les Aspin
(D, Wis.), chairman of the Military Personnel and Compensation
Subcommittee of Armed Services, was the leader of the group, which
also included two members of the Defense Appropriations Subcommittee, Norman D. Dicks (D, Wash.), and Les Au Coin (D, Ore.).
Aspin, however, surprised some of his colleagues when he became a
leading proponent in 1984 of limited MX production.

Although in the period of Vietnam backlash and congressional resurgence that has lasted into the 1980s some military committee
members have broken ranks with tradition by challenging DOD requests, even when supported by the president, the committees continue to represent "constituencies with disproportionately large involvement in DOD activities. This is especially true for more visible
and easily relocatable items such as direct employment. For private
sector defense contracts, however, there is no such 'overrepresenta-
tion.' " [85] The military committees recruit members whose districts

[83] G. Philip Hughes, "Congressional Influence in Weapons Procurement: The
Case of Lightweight Fighter Commonality," *Public Policy*, vol. 28, no. 4 (Fall
1980), pp. 416–449. See especially pp. 447–449.

[84] Edward J. Laurance, "The Changing Role of Congress in Defense Policy-
Making," *Journal of Conflict Resolution*, vol. 20, no. 2 (June 1976), pp. 213–
253.

[85] Bruce A. Ray, "Military Committee Membership in the House of Representatives and the Allocation of Defense Department Outlays," *Western Political
Quarterly*, vol. 34, no. 2 (June 1981), pp. 222–234, at p. 234.

have greater than average economic dependence upon defense projects. Committee members "tend to be more supportive of Defense Department desires than their colleagues," and committee decisions are important in determining the geographic distribution of DOD spending increments." [86]

Broadening Congressional Involvement in Decision Making

The wide congressional involvement in debates over the MX missile and many other aspects of the Pentagon budget illustrate that issues of weapons procurement and defense policy are of broad interest on Capitol Hill. The military committees cannot by themselves determine the allocation of defense contracts and military installations. A former secretary of defense pointed out, "If the Defense Department suggested cancelling the Air Force's Thor program, a congressional delegation from California would be down our necks. And elimination of the Army's Jupiter program would have half of the Alabama delegation plus a couple of representatives from the Detroit area fighting us." [87] Although members fight against termination of defense projects in their districts and states, constituency influence is notably absent when members consider new defense programs and policies.

The ideological predispositions of congressmen, reflected in part in their party affiliations, greatly influence their voting on general defense matters. "Doves" and "hawks" debate their respective positions, but congressional voting has a clear hawkish tilt that favors the DOD goal of armaments expansion. The majority in favor of incremental spending for arms is composed not only of those whose districts benefit, but also of members whose districts do not depend upon defense-related activities.

Apart from defense procurement, congressmen see national security policy, unlike most domestic programs, as an issue set apart from constituency interests. "Congressmen will still fight — and fight hard for a defense project with direct implications for their districts, but may allow their 'world' view, as opposed to their 'constituency' view,

---

[86] Ray, "Military Committee Membership," p. 234.
[87] Craig Liske and Barry Rundquist, *The Politics of Weapons Procurement: The Role of Congress* (Denver, Colo.: University of Denver Press, 1974), p. 5. I am indebted to Bruce A. Ray, "Defense Department Spending and 'Hawkish' Voting in the House of Representatives," *Western Political Quarterly*, vol. 34, no. 3 (September 1981), pp. 438–446, at p. 445, for bringing this quotation to my attention.

to determine their positions on more general national security measures." [88]

CONGRESS AND POLICY MAKING
IN THE FUTURE

Easy generalizations cannot be made about the congressional policy-making process. Common depictions of Congess make it the captive of pressure groups, the president's puppet, controlled by the bureaucracy, slave of constituent demands and public opinion. Congress itself is portrayed as fragmented and centralized, dominated by its committees and under the sway of its staff. An element of truth lies in each of these descriptions, but examining different policy arenas reveals distinctive and contrasting congressional decision-making processes.

The contrasting political forces in separate spheres of public policy will continue to affect the congressional policy process. The cyclical character of congressional and presidential power will also be important, especially in foreign policy and defense policy. Congress may once again yield, as it has in the past, to an imperial presidency during times of crisis. That deference, however, will never relegate Congress to a secondary role in most policy spheres. Political pluralism and the constitutional separation of powers guarantee that Congress will continue to be the first branch of government, determining through its legislative process the direction of national government.

[88] Ray, "Defense Department Spending," p. 444.

Index